This is a book for understanding, not just for doing, environmental management. It is a book for executives and practitioners, and everyone between.

— David Brooks, Director of Research,
Friends of the Earth, Canada

A powerful resource and a needed addition to the rapidly expanding literature on the topic. The book provides a comprehensive toolkit for those engaged in corporate environmental management, and those simply interested in understanding this growing force in business.

— Dr. Monika Winn, Associate Professor, Faculty of Business,
University of Victoria

Every profession has a need for a compendium and for professionals involved in environmentalism, Thompson's *Tools for Environmental Management* serves that purpose extremely well. It is a very comprehensive collection of environmental tools presented in a format and language that is accessible and easy to read.

— Jacques R. Giard, Professor and Director, School of Design,
College of Architecture and Environmental Design,
Arizona State University

Forget time consuming searches through myriad journals, books, articles and web sites to track down environmental management tools. Dixon Thompson has combined his vast experience and wisdom with the skills of his collaborators to capture it all in a comprehensive, handy reference book. Profound practicality and easy readability suggest that this book is destined to become a standard resource in the boardroom, cabinet room, office and field. — A timely reminder to all of us that we can make a difference, as well as an all-encompassing set of tools to get the job done.

— Dr Maxine Cooper, Executive Director, Environment,
Australian Capital Territory, Canberra, Australia.

TOOLS FOR ENVIRONMENTAL MANAGEMENT

TOOLS FOR ENVIRONMENTAL MANAGEMENT

A Practical Introduction and Guide

Dixon Thompson

New Society Publishers

Cataloguing in Publication Data:
A catalog record for this publication is available from the National Library of Canada.

Cover design by Diane McIntosh. Leaf image ©PhotoDisc.

Printed in Canada by Friesens Inc.

New Society Publishers acknowledges the support of the Government of Canada through the Book Publishing Industry Development Program (BPIDP) for our publishing activities.

Hardcover ISBN: 0-86571-458-4

Inquiries regarding requests to reprint all or part of *Tools for Environmental Management* should be addressed to New Society Publishers at the address below. To order directly from the publishers, please add $4.50 shipping to the price of the first copy, and $1.00 for each additional copy (plus GST in Canada). Send check or money order to:

New Society Publishers
P.O. Box 189, Gabriola Island, BC V0R 1X0, Canada
1-800-567-6772

New Society Publishers' mission is to publish books that contribute in fundamental ways to building an ecologically sustainable and just society, and to do so with the least possible impact on the environment, in a manner that models this vision. We are committed to doing this not just through education, but through action. We are acting on our commitment to the world's remaining ancient forests by phasing out our paper supply from ancient forests worldwide. This book is one step towards ending global deforestation and climate change. It is printed on acid-free paper that is 100 percent old growth forest-free (100 percent post-consumer recycled), processed chlorine-free, and printed with vegetable-based, low-VOC inks. For further information, or to browse our full list of books and purchase securely, visit our website at: www.newsociety.com

NEW SOCIETY PUBLISHERS   www.newsociety.com

DEDICATION

*To all those in their many different
capacities who are working to protect the environment
and improving our ability to do so.*

TABLE OF CONTENTS

LIST OF FIGURES

LIST OF TABLES

ACKNOWLEDGMENTS

MY HEARTFELT THANKS to my co-authors who made this book possible, especially Lisa-Henri Kirkland who was the catalyst for the project. Special thanks to Nick Pearce for his enthusiastic work on the graphics and Judith Brand for her detailed editing skills.

I must thank the many graduate students who I have supervised over the past 29 years for the learning processes we've gone through in doing the research and writing about environmental problems, Environmental Management Systems, and environmental management tools. I've also had to learn a great deal through feedback from students about the ideas and how to express them clearly by teaching graduate courses in environmental management in the Faculty of Environmental Design over the past 25 years and more recently in Quito, Moscow, and Trinidad. A real test of ideas is to teach them at the graduate level in different cultural, political, and economic settings.

The Faculty of Environmental Design at the University of Calgary, my academic home for 29 years, has been where I developed courses, supervised graduate students, and worked with colleagues to develop the basis for this book; it would have been difficult, if not impossible, in any other setting. I am grateful for the opportunity the Faculty provided.

My family played an important role by raising me in a small town in southwest Alberta where the outdoors was my playground that started my life-long relationship to the environment.

This book is based upon more than 30 years of work on environmental issues in academia, government, and industry and is the culmination of a long process to which many people contributed. I want to thank those who have helped my career and led me to try to bring environmental science and management together. The driving force for the book is the hope that it will help those who have contributed to the development and application of the skills and knowledge summarized here.

FOREWORD

PROFESSIONALS IN ENVIRONMENTAL MANAGEMENT must focus, and continually refocus, on results and, at the same time, ensure they obtain the necessary feedback to achieve their goals and objectives. Continually asking *why* helps in this process. Answering the question *why* also helps to clarify where you are going.

So, *why this book?* It is a result of a desire to share the knowledge and experience gained by a group of environmental management practitioners. This group represents professionals working in a wide variety of organizations, disciplines, and geographical areas who are connected by a common approach to environmental management, developed by Dixon Thompson. This approach, which we use on a daily basis, runs through each chapter in this book: recognizing the relationships between ideas and techniques in seemingly different technical and theoretical areas and synthesizing these into a workable whole. Over many years of teaching and supervising research in environmental management at the University of Calgary and working with national and international organizations as an environmental management consultant, Dixon has developed a cohesive framework for environmental management and a method of using environmental management tools that many of us have found invaluable in the field. This book allows us to share with you what we have learned.

We are all still learning and experimenting, so this book is a snapshot in time capturing what we know to this point. It is also a summary of a complex subject. Sources of further information are provided so you can continue to explore and update specific areas.

We hope that this distillation of our collective experience and knowledge will provide you with some insight, ideas, and tools you may not have previously encountered. We also hope this book will help to encourage a unified approach to environmental management.

Lisa-Henri Kirkland
Calgary
June 2002

PREFACE

IN THE MID-1970S I QUESTIONED ALBERTA GAS TRUNKLINE (now part of TransCanada Pipeline and Nova Chemicals in Pittsburgh) about their approach to energy conservation and protection of the environment. As a result, President and CEO Bob Blair invited me to work on environmental issues with the company's Research and Development subsidiary Noval Technologies. I discovered that my scientific knowledge of environmental problems alone was not sufficient to convince executives that the company would benefit from assessing its environmental opportunities and risks and taking appropriate action. I didn't understand corporate management systems. In order to influence corporate decisions I realized I needed to gain an understanding of how they operated. Scientific facts, in and of themselves, were not sufficient. I became convinced that, to be effective in the corporate world, environmental scientists had to develop skills in environmental management. With environmental management still in the very early stages of development, there was not much information available to me, but by 1979 I had developed a course on environmental management for my students. The course has evolved significantly over 20 years and influenced the careers of many of my graduate students. In 1998, a group of alumni who were now practicing professionals, particularly Lisa-Henri Kirkland, convinced me to work with them to put the course content into a book.

Goals and Objectives

The primary goals of the book are to describe Environmental Management Systems, present a set of 22 environmental management tools (the environmental manager's toolbox and depict practical means of applying them.

One objective of this book is to provide a resource for education and training and professional development for

- instructors and students in environmental science and environmental management at senior undergraduate and graduate levels;
- professionals in industry, government, and other sectors concerned with career development and continuing professional education;
- environmental managers wanting to improve their capabilities to carry out professional responsibilities; and
- senior students and practising professionals wishing to gain appropriate certification as certification processes are established.

A second objective is to improve the practice of environmental science and management by

- synthesizing information on environmental management tools and their applications;
- improving analysis and diagnosis of problems and selection of best options for effective intervention;
- improving abilities to anticipate and avoid problems;
- increasing the understanding of practical means of responding to environmental principles and concepts such as sustainable development, green design, and product stewardship;
- improving the effectiveness and efficiency of science and technology through better implementation and operations;
- promoting the harmonization, standardization, and, where appropriate, certification and accreditation of Environmental Management Systems, tools, and their applications; and
- providing regulators and policy makers with an understanding of the Environmental Management Systems and tools available to help obtain compliance with regulations and conformance with policies.

What Readers Cannot Expect (What this book is not about)

Because we wrote this book for readers of varying backgrounds and expectations, some readers may be disappointed by the content or level of detail, which had to be constrained due to space limitations. Further, because some of the definitions of terms are fuzzy and/or inconsistent, some readers may disagree with what the content should be. Readers will not find the following:

- a book about management of the environment. In fact, this book is based upon an understanding that the desire to manage (manipulate) the environment, at least on a large scale, to meet societies' needs is often the source of problems rather than the solution to those problems. Environmental management is understanding and controlling the activities of people, organizations, governments, and corporations in order to protect the environment.
- a book about the nature of environmental problems. Many other sources deal with that set of issues and describe the problems and controversies in great detail. The contributions of applied, natural, and social sciences to the definition and understanding of environmental problems are essential contributions to solving the problems. But those facts alone do not lead to effective implementation of solutions. That is where effective use of Environmental Management Systems and environmental management tools become essential.
- a book that describes the extremely wide range and complex nature of the scientific and technical options proposed for solving environmental problems.

- a detailed, technical description of Environmental Management Systems and individual environmental management tools. This book is not written the way specialists would write for other specialists in a particular field. Readers are referred to more detailed sources (books, journals, newsletters, and websites) for more information on each of the tools.

- a detailed, academic research paper which presents new research results, although efforts have been made to lead readers to such sources for more information.

Audiences

This book is written for five related, often overlapping, audiences: students and those wanting continuing professional education, practicing professionals, policy-makers and regulators, stakeholders affected by environmental management decisions, and environmental management team members.

- Students and those wanting continuing professional education

This is a basic textbook on environmental management that introduces Environmental Management Systems and tools, and provides a springboard to more detailed information. Very often people considering a career in environmental science and environmental management do not have a clear understanding of the wide range of options available to them, because that information has not yet become part of common knowledge and has not yet been synthesized for use in secondary schools and undergraduate curricula. We hope to give those in the education system a better understanding of their options and what they have to understand to become competent professionals.

- Practicing professionals

Many practicing professionals will not be fully knowledgeable about the complete set of tools available to the environmental science and management profession. It is impossible to become proficient at any more than a few of the tools. However, it is important to know about the complete set, what the tools can do for you, when to call in the needed specialist, and what to do with the results. Practicing professionals can become better informed about those tools that they do not use on a regular basis and understand the links to other tools and the context (within the tool box) for those with which they are familiar. Because we have tried to use simple language wherever possible, our definitions and descriptions may help practitioners explain what they do more clearly.

- Policy-makers and regulators

Policy-makers and regulators will have a much better opportunity to formulate effective and efficient policies and regulations if they have a clearer understanding of the systems and tools that managers could use to comply with regulations and conform with policies. Just as environmental management tools can be used in combination to mutually enhance their effectiveness, so policies and regulations can be combined to produce greater benefits. Trade policies can incorporate more effective environmental management to enhance the benefits of trade and reduce the adverse impacts. Voluntary compliance (self-regulation) can achieve improved credibility if auditing, indicators, and reporting meet strict management criteria. Environmental regulation can be more efficiently applied when combined with credible self-regulation and appropriate economic instruments.

Regulations designed with a clear understanding of the environmental management options available for compliance are likely to achieve improved performance for those operating under the regulations. There will likely be less need for regulation and for enforcement. Further, the resources available for enforcement can be focused on those not using effective environmental management practices. The same applies to policies: better policies can be developed if they are based upon an understanding of the environmental management options available to those who have to conform to the policies. The ability of those operating under such policies to achieve good environmental management would also be improved.

• Stakeholders affected by environmental management decisions.

There is a wide range of stakeholders inside and outside corporations and institutions who are affected by the decisions and actions of environmental managers. These include senior decision-makers, other managers, and employees inside the organization and customers, shareholders and investors, communities, and ENGOs (Environmental Non-Governmental Organizations), and politicians on the outside. These groups can understand better how they could affect environmental management decisions, and vice versa, when they gain knowledge about the environmental management options.

• Environmental management team members

Environmental managers must interact effectively with senior decision-makers above them (managing up) and with technicians, researchers, and others under their supervision or direction (managing down). Senior decision-makers do not want too much detail. However, if senior decision-makers have a basic understanding of the tools and the systems that provide them with information, they will have a better basis for their decisions. Technicians doing soil or water sampling or monitoring of environmental impacts often deal only with details. They do not have to know much about the larger system of which they are part, but again, some knowledge of the tools to which they contribute and the system within which they operate can lead to improved performance.

Dixon Thompson
Victoria
June 2002

CHAPTER 1

INTRODUCTION:
THE ENVIRONMENTAL MANAGER'S TOOLBOX

Dixon Thompson

> *Beware of the teachings of those theorists*
> *whose ideas are not corroborated by experience.*
> — Leonardo da Vinci

> *When your life is on the line,*
> *you want to make use of all your tools.*[1]

> *In distinguishing the advantages of the tools of warriors,*
> *we find that whatever the weapon, there is a time and situation*
> *in which it is appropriate.*[2]

ENVIRONMENTAL MANAGEMENT SYSTEMS (EMSs) and a set of 22 environmental management tools are available to those people in corporations, institutions, and governments who are responsible for meeting their organization's environmental obligations, goals, and objectives. A great deal has been written on Environmental Management Systems and individual tools, but it is scattered throughout the literature on environmental science and engineering, environmental management, and related disciplines, so a coherent description of the set of tools is not readily available. This book describes Environmental Management Systems and presents the environmental management tools as a coherent set. It is a practical and systematic approach to define and describe the systems and tools and to refine the definition of the profession of environmental management.

It is essential to state right from the start that environmental management is a misnomer, because environmental management is not about managing the environment, it is about managing the activities of corporations, institutions, and individuals that affect the environment.

1

The lack of a systematic approach to environmental management until the early 1990s is understandable. The field is characterized by rapid change and evolution. The systems and tools evolved from a wide range of sources: law and regulations, different professions, and disciplines (environmental science, engineering, management and accounting, economics, toxicology, human factors, etc.). Through borrowing and adapting, hybrid tools have evolved that bridge disciplines and professions. Some of the systems and tools have moved through national and international processes of standardization, or are themselves the products of private sector or non-profit organizations, as is the case with The Natural Step[3] (chapter 24).

The tools and systems have also been developed for different purposes, in response to different driving forces. Some were developed as a response to, or in anticipation of, government regulations. Others were developed in an effort to reduce direct costs, risks, and anticipated liabilities (contingency costs) or to meet expectations of corporate social responsibility — the triple bottom line.[4] Many are the direct result of efforts to conserve resources and to reduce adverse impacts on the environment.

Terms and Definitions

Because we are preparing a summary and synthesis of work from many disciplines and professions, there may not be complete agreement on the use of different terms and definitions. If an established standard exists, that has been used as the basis for our definition. If no standard has been set, we have tried to develop a definition that is complete, practical, and effective and which reflects our perceptions of the emerging trends in the field.

Environmental Management Systems and the Tool Set

The set of 22 environmental management tools is listed in Table 1.1. Each tool is described in more detail in the subsequent chapters. Because it is important initially to recognize the set of tools, readers are encouraged to review the list to identify those tools they already are familiar with and those they need to study. There is no specific order to the list, although it tends to go from those that have broader, general applications to more specific or newer tools. Environmental Management Systems such as ISO 14001 and Ecosystem Management Auditing Scheme and our approach to designing, implementing, and operating an EMS are discussed in chapter 2. Chapters 3 through 24 are devoted to the individual tools. Chapter 25 is the conclusion — Where Do We Go from Here?

Table 1.1. The Basic Toolbox: 22 Environmental Management Tools

- Analysis of Driving Forces
- Analysis of Barriers
- Strategic Environmental Management and Planning
- Environmental Policies
- Environmental Management Structures
- Environmental Auditing
- Education and Training
- Risk Management
- Environmental Site Assessment
- Environmental Indicators
- Environmental Reporting
- Environmental Impact Assessment (EIA)
- Environmental Accounting
- Economic Instruments
- Product and Technology Assessment
- Life Cycle Assessment (LCA)
- Purchasing Guidelines
- Environmental Communications Auditing
- Human Factors
- Clean Development Mechanism and Joint Implementation (CDM/JI)
- Ecosystem-Based Management
- The Natural Step (TNS)

At least nine more environmental management tools could be included in this set: modeling, cybernetics, geographical information systems, ecological footprints, information management systems, benefit cost analysis, monitoring, forecasting and backcasting. Public participation, public involvement, and stakeholder consultation are discussed in chapter 20, Environmental Communications.

A tool is something specifically designed to help accomplish a particular task: any instrument used in doing work (a shovel, computer, or accounting system, for example). An environmental management tool is a method or technique which managers can use to help complete a specific task. Just as different sets of tools are used to build a house or repair a car, so must environmental management tools be used as an appropriate set. Often, the results obtained from using one tool are required for another environmental management tool. Thus, the effectiveness of the tools often increases when they are used in combination rather than in a stand-alone operation. The particular combination of tools that may be needed for solving a problem depends upon the specific circumstances. The appropriate set of tools to get the job done in one instance may not be the same in another.

Environmental management tools generally have the following characteristics:
- They are applied the same way, having been standardized or being in the process of becoming standardized.
- They have specific instructions or guidelines to be followed — specific steps or methods.

- They should produce essentially the same results when applied by competent professionals in similar circumstances.

Two tools, the analysis of driving forces and analysis of barriers, are included on the list although they are not widely recognized as tools. However, all effective managers will understand both driving forces and barriers, even if they only do so implicitly. We believe that their importance as analytical tools in understanding the factors affecting environmental management is paramount. They are included in an effort to make their use more explicit and systematic.

The tools are at different stages of development and maturity. For example, Environmental Impact Assessment has been legislated and practiced for 30 years or more. Other tools are just emerging from the development stage. All of them continue to evolve and improve.

This book is a solid introduction and a handy desk reference. Readers must recognize that while it assists with professional development it is not sufficient to produce well-qualified professionals who should have three qualifications: education, experience, and ethics. To become competent practitioners, candidates require education by qualified instructors in well-recognized institutions. Courses on individual tools often take 40 hours, although some tools such as Life Cycle Assessment or environmental accounting require extensive training and professional development. Experience must be gained in the application of the tools under the supervision of a qualified professional, often for a specified period of time. Practitioners must learn and abide by the ethics of consulting and professional practice.

EXPANDING SET OF TOOLS

Because there is no conclusive definition of an environmental management tool, different practitioners will define the set of tools differently. Several tools, including ecological footprint and eco-efficiency, are developing rapidly and soon should be at the point where standard practice by organizations will become routine.

Ecological footprint uses estimates of imports and exports for a political jurisdiction (city or country) to determine the area of productive land and water required on a continuous basis to supply all energy and material resources and to absorb all wastes. It is an estimate of the natural capital requirements of the population in the jurisdiction. It estimates overshoot and ecological deficit and therefore is an effective tool in raising the emergent reality of unsustainable levels of consumption to consciousness.[5]

Ecological footprint has been used for political jurisdictions but could be adapted as a tool for corporations to show progress, or lack thereof, in improving their environmental performance.

Eco-efficiency is also evolving to the point where it can be used by corporations to demonstrate improved environmental performance. The World Business Council for Sustainable Development has published a guide to reporting company performance using the eco-efficiency concept. The guide recommends five generally applicable indicators related to energy, material and water consumption, and emissions of greenhouse gases and ozone depleting substances.[6]

Other authors have defined sets of environmental management tools. Welford describes a set of seven: Environmental Management Systems, environmental policies, environmental guidelines and charters, environmental auditing, Life Cycle Assessment, measuring environmental performance, and environmental reporting. He also makes explicit or implicit references to other tools on our list (driving forces, accounting, site assessments, etc.).[7] Dale and English describe three very different sets of "tools to aid environmental decision making": information or data, tools to gather data, and tools to organize and analyze data.[8] Greenbiz.com has a toolbox on their website, which includes a long list of reports on a wide range of environmental topics.[9]

Definition of Environmental Management

Much of the environmental science literature, especially from the applied biophysical sciences, defines environmental management as the manipulation of the resource, as in forest management, water management, pest management, waste management, etc.

We define environmental management as the system that anticipates and avoids or solves environmental and resource conservation problems by

- setting goals and objectives through a strategic planning process;
- identifying and organizing the people with skills and knowledge, technologies, finances, and other resources needed;
- identifying and assessing various options for reaching the goals;
- assessing risks and setting priorities;
- implementing the selected set of options;
- auditing and monitoring performance for necessary adjustments through feedback; and
- using the set of tools as needed.

This definition has the advantage of being explicit about the setting of goals and objectives and the need for feedback in the system.

ISO 14001 defines an Environmental Management System as "that part of the overall management system which includes organizational structure, planning, activities, responsibilities, procedures, processes, and resources for developing, implementing, achieving, reviewing, and maintaining the environmental policy."[10]

An important part of this definition is the explicit statement that the EMS must be part of the overall management system — integrated with the business activities, not separate. An important element in the system is the environmental policy, which appears at the end of the definition. Unfortunately, there is generally little advice on designing and implementing environmental policy, an issue we address in chapter 6.

The Canadian Standards Association states that: "the design of an Environmental Management System is an ongoing, interactive planning process that consists of defining, documenting, and continuously improving the required capabilities, namely: resources, training, information systems, operational processes and procedures, documentation, measurement, and monitoring criteria."[11]

The strengths of this definition are the references to ongoing process and continual improvement. Like the ISO 14001 definition, there is no explicit reference to auditing, although it can be assumed that reviewing, measurement, and monitoring imply the use of audits.

Clearly, the tools listed in Table 1.1 would be helpful, if not essential, in operating Environmental Management Systems as defined by ISO 14001 or the CSA. See chapter 2 for discussion of EMSs.

Figure 1.1 shows the Environmental Management Program (technical systems for reducing environmental impacts and improving efficiency) as the technical operations component of the Environmental Management System, which is fully integrated with the corporation's overall management system.

Figure 1.2 shows the roles for senior managers, environmental managers, technicians, researchers, and specialists.

Tools, Concepts, and Principles

It is important to distinguish the environmental management tools from concepts and principles, or very broad goals. Concepts and principles, or broad goals such as sustainable development, greening, green product design, eco-efficiency, and product stewardship, state what we want to do and/or provide important guidelines for activities. Some of them (eco-efficiency or design for the environment) could be considered as tools, or are closer to tools than others (greening, sustainable development). However, they do not specify the steps needed to achieve goals and objectives. There is not enough detail provided so that professional practitioners would understand what steps had to be followed. Like other concepts and

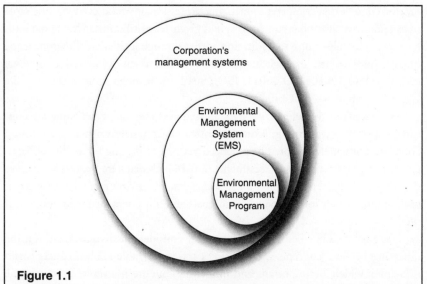

Figure 1.1
The EMS is an Integral Part of the Corporation's Management System. The Environmental Management Program is the part of the Environmental Management System (EMS) that is designed and operated to achieve the objectives and targets set by the EMS.

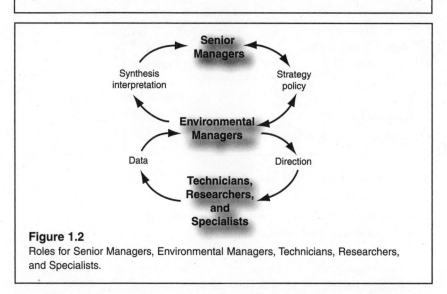

Figure 1.2
Roles for Senior Managers, Environmental Managers, Technicians, Researchers, and Specialists.

principles such as democracy, justice, and free trade, there is wide acceptance of their importance, but often disagreement on the details of their application.

Tools include goals, objectives, and principles but they must also provide specific instructions for successfully applying each tool. Those instructions should be specific enough that competent practicing professionals would carry out the same steps and arrive at similar conclusions in a given set of circumstances. Some tools have a very high level of standardization, either through legislation (Environmental Impact Assessment), through standardization and certification (environmental audits — ISO 19010, ISO 19011, ISO 19012), or through standardization (Life Cycle Assessment — ISO 14040).

Other tools in the set are not standardized and may never be. Some are controversial (strategic planning, economic instruments, environmental accounting). Some are not widely accepted or practiced yet (list of driving forces, list of barriers, product and technology assessment) but are included here because we believe that they are critical to environmental management. Environmental management tools are important for achieving broad goals and objectives, or for finding out if they are being achieved.

There will be some confusion and possibly considerable disagreement over the difference between concepts and principles and tools. Table 1.2 lists concepts and principles, which are important and influential, but are not tools, at least in the sense we are using here.

Table 1.2 Concepts and Principles

• Industrial Ecology[12]	• Sustainable Development
• Product Stewardship	• Appropriate Technology
• Pollution Prevention[13]	• Precautionary Principle
• Eco-efficiency[14]	• Triple Bottom Line[19]
• Steady-state Economics[15]	• Factor 4[20]
• Greening[16]	• Factor 10[21]
• Green Design[17]	• Zero Population Growth[22]
• Design for the Environment[18]	• Limits to Growth[23]

What Do the Tools Help Managers Do?

Tools help managers to

- conserve resources and reduce environmental impacts;
- anticipate and avoid problems;
- establish policies, goals, and objectives;
- analyze problems;
- develop, define, and select options for solutions;
- set priorities and allocate scarce resources;
- provide feedback on performance and meet the goal of continual improvement; and
- communicate effectively with stakeholders.

If the tools are used effectively to accomplish these objectives, then they will also help managers

- conform to policies and meet goals and objectives,
- improve efficiency,
- comply with laws and regulations and meet the needs of due diligence,
- reduce costs and increase revenues,
- keep up with rapid change, and
- satisfy internal and external stakeholders.

Tools help managers gain credibility because they

- use consistent, accepted methodology;
- produce reproducible, comparable results;
- reduce disagreement about information;
- support certification and/or registration;
- provide independent third party verification; and
- provide support and/or validation from recognized national or international organizations.

Why is the Toolbox Important?

The toolbox is important for the following reasons:

- Proficient professionals have to know the complete range of tools that can be applied to the tasks assigned to them.
- Stakeholders inside and outside the corporation will expect environmental managers to know about the set of tools.

Teamwork

Many aspects of environmental management require interdisciplinary teamwork. The scale and complexity of issues and the wide range of required skills dictate that several professionals, if not many, with different education, training, and skill sets, must be brought together in a team in order to be effective. So it is with the development and writing of this book, which involved 16 authors and an editorial assistant working as an interdisciplinary team. Only small-scale, relatively simple problems can be successfully attacked by individuals working on their own. Teamwork skills, interdisciplinary skills, and communication skills are of paramount importance in good environmental management.

Teamwork also requires specialists to have some understanding of other team members' specialties. This book will help those with particular skills and knowledge of one tool integrate their knowledge with those applying other tools in the set.

Professional Practice: Objectivity, Subjectivity, and Professional Judgement

One might argue that the level of standardization and uniform application is deceptive, because there are value judgments involved, and hence, some of the inputs are subjective. Personal likes and dislikes ("I like red but I don't like tomatoes"), subjectivity, should not be part of environmental management. However, professional opinion, which is not subjective in the sense of personal likes and dislikes, is a very important part of professional activity. Professional opinion or professional judgment involves three factors which clearly distinguish it from personal preferences and whims:

- Professional judgment involves specific education and training, in some cases leading to examination and certification.
- Professional judgment is often guided by a code or set of professional ethics, which generally forbids the inclusion of personal opinions.
- Professional judgment is informed by experience, so that, in some cases, professionals are not considered qualified to practice on their own until they have worked under the supervision of a senior practitioner for a specified period of time.

Keeping Up with Rapid Change

Rapid change in the field of environmental management is a major problem and challenge for educators, students, and practicing professionals. For example, it was less than four years between the decision to try to develop an environmental parallel to the ISO 9000 product quality standard and the publication of the official ISO 14001 international Environmental Management System specification document in September 1996.

The introduction of Buzz Holling's pivotal book *Adaptive Environmental Assessment and Management*[24] in 1978 was significant. In 1980, there was very little literature which could be clearly identified as environmental management; much of it only described environmental problems and dealt with the science and engineering. It was difficult for an instructor to find material suitable for teaching environmental management. There was a great deal of literature on management; however, translating that material for the emerging field of environmental management was not easy.

The field has now advanced to the point where it is very difficult to keep up with the literature that covers Environmental Management Systems, the 22 environmental management tools discussed here, and the other tools, principles, and concepts. The definitions, general principles, and processes described in the following chapters are not likely to change much, however, the details will. To help practitioners and students acquire current information, we have identified newsletters and websites for each tool.

One of the problems with rapid change and expansion in the field of environmental management is that many people are jumping into the field and starting to practice without taking the time to become familiar with existing standards and terminology. Therefore, you can expect to come across newly coined terms such as Environmental Management System Framework or Environmental Management System Program, which may or may not be an EMS. Such novel terms must be avoided if the level of confusion and frustration is to be kept to a minimum.

Continual Improvement

Continual improvement is often recommended or required as part of an EMS (see Figure 1.3). It is a system of implementation, assessment of performance, and improvement in light of experience. Continual improvement is required by ISO 14001. Without continual improvement, it is difficult or impossible to use due diligence as a successful defense in case of a prosecution for infractions. ISO standards, reviewed and updated every five years, are established on a continual improvement basis. ISO 14001 was set in 1996 and reviewed in 2001.

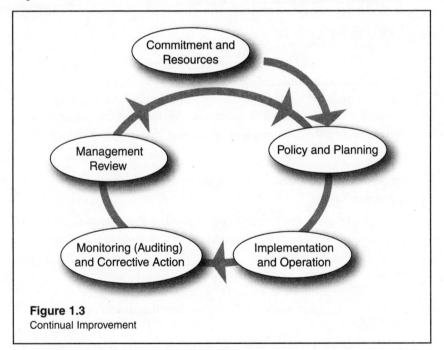

Figure 1.3
Continual Improvement

Because ISO 14001 EMS registration is relatively easy, the expectation is that continual improvement will result in steadily improved performance of the EMS. ISO 14001 has been criticized as being too easy. However, that is the nature of a standard set by international negotiations and initiated by market demand (ISO does not set a standard until there is a wide perception of a need for one) — ISO standards follow rather than lead issues. If the EMS standard were more demanding in the requirements for registration, it would present barriers to entry which would impede its adoption. Therefore, continual improvement is accepted as the means of allowing *easy entry*, with the expectation that performance will improve.

Organizations with goals and objectives require feedback to assure success and to continually improve performance. Continual improvement is irrelevant for organizations that have no goals or objectives.

Although not all tools are fully developed and standardized, we recommend that EMSs and tools still be used for four reasons:

1. The requirements for due diligence are continually changing because each new judgment establishes precedent, with the expectation that the precedent becomes part of basic knowledge so that the mistake should not be repeated.

2. The internal and external environments are continually changing, and so the nature and design of the tools and their applications will necessarily have to change.

3. It would take too long to develop an EMS or environmental management tool that was theoretically nearly perfect, if that were ever possible. Users can obtain benefits from the early application of an imperfect tool.

4. The refinement of the tools through continual improvement in the real world is recommended, if not required, by some EMSs, hence early introduction and refinement is preferred to a long period of refinement and a late introduction.

Designing, Implementing, and Operating an Environmental Management System

By 1997, we had identified eight components (nine if you include the practitioner) that must be taken into consideration in designing, implementing, and operating an EMS. See Figure 1.4.

This book deals with four of the eight components:

- the **Driving Forces** (chapter 3) which tend to improve the chances of acceptance and success of an EMS or the use of a particular environmental management tool,
- the **Barriers** (chapter 4) which may impede or prevent the development of an EMS or the application of a particular tool,
- the theoretical or formal Environmental Management Systems (chapter 2) and standards, and
- a set of Environmental Management Tools.

However, as can be seen in Figure 1.4, there are four other important elements: scientific facts; current practices; stakeholders, actors, and participants; and corporate culture.

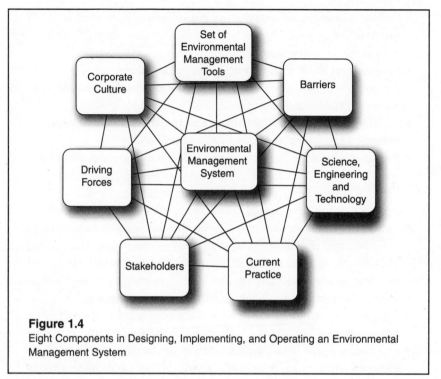

Figure 1.4

Eight Components in Designing, Implementing, and Operating an Environmental Management System

Scientific Facts

This approach is based on the understanding that successful professional practice in environmental management requires skills and knowledge in science, engineering, and technology on the one hand and management on the other. Sound, objective science which defines the problems, opportunities, and solutions in an integrated fashion is essential. This is generally achieved through an interdisciplinary approach that requires a specific set of teamwork, communication, and interdisciplinary skills. It is essential to *get the right sciences,* not just use those skills and facts which happen to be available. That is, what professionals are needed on the team in order to get a complete picture at an appropriate level of detail? And it is essential to *get the science right.* The science must be sound — based firmly on theory and the existing evidence — and must deliver high quality information through the careful application of established (standard) methodologies.

Need for Both Sound Science and Good Management

Scientific facts and analysis are essential; however, alone, they are never sufficient for the design and implementation of effective interventions to prevent or solve problems, for the following reasons:

- Reductionist science is necessary but not sufficient — synthesis is required.
- Facts alone do not produce action.
- Systems don't think or learn using scientific facts alone.
- Environmental management requires integration into political, social, economic, and cultural context.
- Environmental management requires effective communication with different audiences at appropriate levels of detail.
- Politics and ideology frequently become dominant factors in decisions.

Get the Right Sciences

Problems arise with getting the right sciences for at least five reasons:
- Individuals or groups work only at what they know and tend not to seek out other experts who should be included.
- There is centrism and egoism in disciplines and professions, which tend to downplay the importance of others.
- Tunnel vision can lead to a very restricted problem definition.
- Agencies and institutions can have biases, generally as the result of history, corporate culture, and the background of the decision makers.
- The basic research model, with the focus on new data, creates problems because too little attention is paid to timely decisions and effective implementation.

Get the Science Right

The following factors can lead to failure to get the science right:
- data is too narrow, detailed, or fragmented;
- failure of teamwork;
- failure of interdisciplinary work;
- failure to communicate with other scientists, engineers and with non-scientists;
- wrong, weak, or flawed models;
- complexity;
- no baseline data;
- intervention of politics, ideology, or myths; and
- distortion, misrepresentation, or selective use of facts.

Current Practice

Current practice refers to existing activities within an organization that are related to protection of the environment or management (or mismanagement) of resources. All organizations will generate waste and consume water, energy, and other resources. Understanding what those activities are is an important step in assessing the situation when starting an EMS. Where new activities or systems are being started, or when tools are applied to anticipate or avoid problems, no actions will have been initiated, so there will be no *current practice*. However, where operations are already active, the understanding of current practice, largely through specific audits, is very important. This will help identify the greatest risks and the opportunities for the largest savings. Careful definition of current practices offers the option of building on accomplishments to date and gives credit to those who have already taken initiatives.

Current practices and related opportunities and problems are identified through environmental audits (chapter 8), risk management (chapter 10), product and technology assessments (chapter 17), and Life Cycle Assessments (chapter 18). Specialty audits (energy, water, and waste, etc.) provide details on each of these topics.

Identifying Stakeholders, Actors, and Participants

Stakeholders, actors, and participants are interchangeable terms used to describe the people directly and indirectly involved in environmental management, or who affect, or are affected by, environmental management activities (or lack thereof). Identifying and characterizing stakeholders, actors, and participants is important for designing, implementing, and operating an EMS because the EMS must respond to their needs; take advantage of their information, skills, and knowledge; and/or identify the opportunities they can provide. Identifying these people and the organizations they are involved in also helps to clarify and further define the driving forces and barriers. They must be known in order to describe and understand the environmental management structure (chapter 7).

There is a wide range of people and organizations to be considered, not just the most obvious. Participants can be inside (internal) or outside (external) the EMS. They can be directly or indirectly involved. The relationship can be formal (regulated, official in some respect, or contractual) or informal. Involvement can be passive or active. Participants will be affected positively, negatively, or both.

It is particularly important to identify stakeholders, actors, and participants for environmental communication (chapter 20). The roles or relationships of participants can be changed positively or negatively by factors outside the control of the corporation or by an effective communications strategy. The perceptions and perspectives of stakeholders will determine whether they see particular elements or activities as positive or negative, as driving forces or barriers.

Table 1.3 Examples Of Stakeholders, Actors, and Participants

Internal	External
Board of Directors	Regulators
Executives	Local Community
Employees	Contractors
Union (could be external)	Suppliers
Business Units	Customers
Other Departments	Public
Legal	ENGOs
Accounting	Professional Associations
Finance	Industry Associations
Human Resources	Families of Employees
Health and Safety	Certification Agencies and Institutions
Purchasing	International Organizations
Marketing and Sales	Voluntary, Self-Regulation Programs
	Investors
	Banks
	Insurers

Corporate Culture

Corporate or institutional culture is formed by the values, attitudes, perceptions, politics, educational background, and personalities of employers and employees, which determine that organization's behavior and reaction to stress or to opportunities.[25]

It is often difficult to describe or define. It is "the way things are done here" and the willingness to change and innovate. However, difficult as it is to characterize corporate culture, it is often a determining factor in the design, implementation, and operation of an EMS. Therefore, understanding corporate culture is a key element in the success or failure of environmental management. The cultural context within which a corporation operates is also very important.

Four of the tools have a strong cultural component: strategic environmental management (how do you set goals and objectives and obtain feedback?), environmental policy (how do you formulate and implement policy?), driving forces, and barriers. If you are operating outside the North American or European context, we recommend workshops on these topics to gain an understanding of these four critical tools.

Elephants in the Living Room

Carl Frankel uses the provocative image of elephants in the living room studiously ignored by those present to illustrate the problem of focusing on the details and trying to pretend that everything is normal, while ignoring larger problems.[26]

Frankel's scene is one of elephants sitting quietly at a cocktail party but being unseen and/or ignored by technical environmental specialists at the gathering. While we know about the elephants, this book is not about them. Indeed, we would argue that before, or perhaps as, we come to grips with the elephants, so to speak, we also have to be able to understand, apply, and improve the environmental management systems and tools, in order to deal with these larger issues.

We have to acknowledge that the EMSs and tools described in this book are necessary conditions for improving resource conservation and environmental protection, but they are not sufficient for achieving the goals of sustainable development. There are larger, very important problems which these tools cannot affect: population growth, the growing gap between rich and poor, and the very short time frames for planning imposed by stock markets and speculators. Without changes to these factors, there is little likelihood of effective long-term control of environmental problems and conservation of resources necessary for sustainable development. Some of these issues are addressed in the concluding chapter.

Nonetheless, as the EMSs are improved and applied widely, effectively, and efficiently, we will have made considerable progress toward sustainable development. It would seem obvious that without the wide use of an improved tool set, sustainable development cannot be achieved.

Clearly there can be conflicts between environmental goals and other corporate and government priorities. In some cases, these are more apparent than real. For the developing world, there should be no conflict between fighting poverty and achieving environmental goals for the simple reason that it is easier to fight poverty in a clean environment where resources are being used efficiently. Environmental Management Systems and the tools will help developing countries achieve the goals of economic growth and alleviation of poverty without the expenses of damage to the environment and health and the cleanup costs that follow a policy of promoting economic growth at the expense of the environment.

We must note that allowing pollution, by not requiring that polluters make the necessary investment to eliminate the pollution or cease operations, is a mechanism for transferring money from those affected by pollution to the polluters. It is a form of subsidy to the polluting industry. Therefore, stopping pollution is an important element in resolving problems of fair and efficient distribution of benefits from resource exploitation. Allowing industry to increase short-term profits through inefficient or destructive use of resources is a mechanism to increase profits in the present at a cost to future generations. EMSs and use of environmental management tools is one way of reducing the pollution subsidy.

At the level of the national economy and corporate operations, there are two questions that are very important for the context within which the EMSs and tools are applied:

1. What will a national economy that is based upon sustainable development look like and how will it operate? At the very least, national well-being would be measured by an adjusted Gross Domestic Product (GDP), and systems that rewarded closed cycles rather than throughput would be in place (e.g., take-back legislation). Because a sustainable development economy would have to give due consideration to long-term goals and objectives and plans to meet them, it would be necessary to remove short-term exigencies and reward long-term planning and management.

2. How would a corporation operate within an economy based upon sustainable development principles? At the very least, there would be widespread, effective, and efficient use of the Environmental Management Systems and tools described here.

Recommended Further Reading

Business And The Environment (BATE), Aspen Publishing, 1185 Avenue of the Americas, New York, NY 10036

Business Strategy and the Environment

EM (AWMA magazine)

Enviroline

The Gallon Environment Letter: <www.gallon.elogik.com>

Greener Management International: The Journal of Corporate Environmental Strategy and Practice

Hazardous Materials Management

Websites

Academy of Management, ONE (Organizations and the Natural Environment): <www.aom.pace.edu>

Air and Waste Management Association: <www.awma.org>

Hazardous Materials Management: <www.hazmatmag.com>

Institute of Management: <www.iem.org.uk>

<www.greenbiz.com>

<www.greenleaf-publishing.com>

ENVIRONMENTAL MANAGEMENT SYSTEMS

Lisa-Henri Kirkland, Wolfwillow Environmental, and Dixon Thompson

ENVIRONMENTAL MANAGEMENT SYSTEMS (EMSs) help organizations manage environmental issues systematically, efficiently, and effectively. Almost 40,000 organizations around the world have an EMS that has been registered under international standards, and there are many more with effective EMSs that have not received registration.

ISO 14001, an international standard for Environmental Management Systems, defines an EMS in Section 3.5 as: "the part of the overall management system which includes organizational structure, planning, activities, responsibilities, procedures, processes, and resources for developing, implementing, achieving, reviewing, and maintaining the environmental policy."[1]

The Canadian Standards Association (CSA) states that: "the design of an environmental management system is an ongoing, interactive planning process that consists of defining, documenting, and continuously improving the required capabilities, namely: resources, training, information systems, operational processes and procedures, documentation, measurement and monitoring criteria."[2]

The ISO 14001 and CSA definitions lack explicit references to the processes of setting goals and objectives (policy) and auditing for feedback on success (or failure) of the EMS. *Policy* appears as the last word of the ISO definition, which seems to understate the importance of policy (goals and objectives) in the EMS. In the CSA definition, the setting of goals and objectives is buried in the term *planning*.

Our definition uses elements of the CSA and ISO definitions but includes explicit references to the processes of setting goals and objectives, providing feedback through auditing, and using the set of environmental management tools as required.

An Environmental Management System is an integral part of an organization's overall management system that is designed to improve environmental performance by

- setting goals and objectives (policy);
- identifying, obtaining, and organizing the people, skills, and knowledge, technology, finances, and other resources necessary to achieve the goals and objectives;
- identifying and assessing options for reaching the goals;
- assessing risks and priorities;
- implementing the selected set of options;
- auditing performance for necessary adjustments by providing feedback to the system; and
- applying the environmental management tools as required.

The design, implementation, and operation of an EMS can be a complicated and detailed exercise, especially for a large, complex organization. In preparing for design, implementation, and operation of an EMS, environmental managers must be familiar with eight other tools, all of which are mentioned explicitly or inferred in the definitions of EMSs.

- Driving Forces (chapter 3) — What is encouraging you or forcing you to implement an EMS?
- Barriers (chapter 4) — What might hinder design and implementation?
- Environmental Management Strategy (chapter 5) — How do you set goals and objectives? What do you hope to achieve?
- Environmental Policy (chapter 6) — How do you formulate one?
- Environmental Management Structures (chapter 7) — Who are the internal and external stakeholders and how should the EMS accommodate their interests? How does information flow? What are formal roles and responsibilities?
- Education and Training (chapter 9).
- Risk Management (chapter 10).

Other tools in the set will be useful, but the above tools are essential. Some of the processes are not covered in this chapter, because they involve the use of tools described in other chapters.

An Integrated System

An EMS cannot be isolated. It must be an integral part of the overall management system for an organization, as shown in Figure 2.1. Figure 2.2 shows the integrated relationships between the Environmental Management System, the Environmental Management Program, the internal stakeholders, and the external stakeholders. In theory, an EMS brings the components together, provides

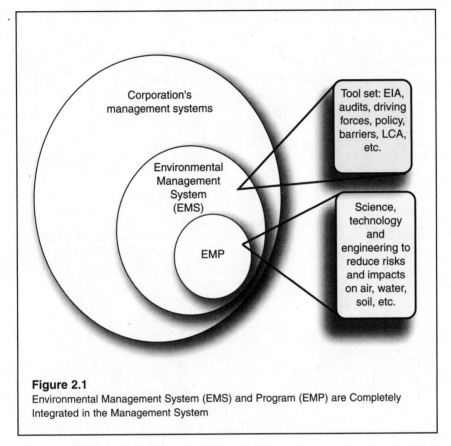

Figure 2.1
Environmental Management System (EMS) and Program (EMP) are Completely
Integrated in the Management System

information, and implements decisions in a smooth, integrated fashion. In practice, implementation, integration and operations are not always easy, especially when people are struggling up a learning curve in a new system and changing circumstances.

An EMS is more than pollution treatment, pollution prevention, and conservation of resources and energy. The technical details necessary for meeting the objectives of the environmental policy are called the Environmental Management Program (EMP). As stated in Section 4.2.6 of ISO 14004, the Environmental Management Program should

- address schedules, resources, and responsibilities for achieving the organization's objectives and targets;
- identify specific actions in order of their priority;
- deal with individual processes, projects, products, services, sites, or facilities within a site; and
- be dynamic and revised regularly to reflect changes.

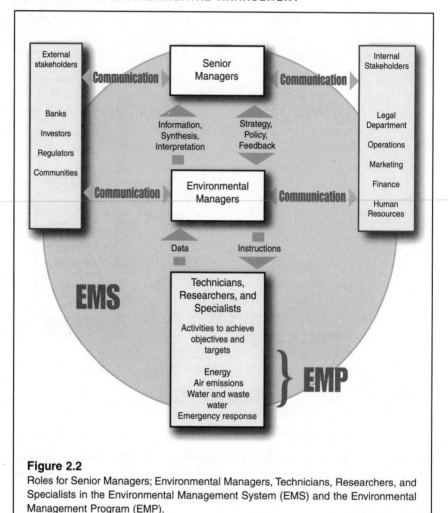

Figure 2.2
Roles for Senior Managers; Environmental Managers, Technicians, Researchers, and Specialists in the Environmental Management System (EMS) and the Environmental Management Program (EMP).

Problems arise when there is confusion about the differences between the EMS and the EMP. This is prevalent in organizations dominated by scientists and engineers who focus on the technical details and with managers who ignore the technical details and focus on the management aspects. If education, training, and teamwork are used effectively, then this confusion can be avoided.

The factors that make an EMS system successful are
- commitment at senior levels,
- integration with the business plan,
- goals and objectives set (or at least approved) at senior levels,

- feedback on success with appropriate adjustments, and
- continual improvement.

The characteristics of an Environmental Management System (EMS) and an Environmental Management Program (EMP):

EMS	EMP
Systematic and comprehensive	Relatively independent subsystems
Proactive	Applied sciences and engineering
Corporate level commitment	Focus on error-free operations
Feedback and continual improvement	Data on day-to-day operations
Teamwork	

If an EMS is properly designed, implemented, and operated and is integrated with the business plan, executives can meet corporate goals and objectives using it to

- identify and control risks,
- achieve a high level of regulatory compliance,
- protect corporate assets,
- increase profitability through improved eco-efficiency,
- gain easier access to banks and financing,
- increase investor confidence, and
- meet requirements of partners, markets and customers.

An EMS can also assist environmental managers to

- follow trends in management so they can make changes when appropriate,
- meet the requirements of existing regulations and anticipate new ones,
- identify and communicate effectively with important stakeholders, and
- meet the requirements of international codes of conduct (International Chamber of Commerce [ICC], World Business Council for Sustainable Development [WBCSD], or Coalition for Environmentally Responsible Economies [CERES]), and industry codes.

History

Environmental management was carried out in an informal, ad hoc fashion until the late 1960s, when it was recognized as an issue separate from resource management. As public concern about the environment increased and was reflected in legislation that created government departments responsible for protection of the environment, the response of corporations became more systematic and Environmental Management Systems began to evolve. While some began to use the term *Environmental Management System* at this time, the term did not take on a more recognized and formal meaning until standards were developed in the early 1990s.

Responsible Care, started by the Canadian Chemical Producers Association in 1984 in an effort to improve its image, has since been adopted in 44 other countries. It has many of the elements of an Environmental Management System. Responsible Care is now considering using ISO 14001 as its formal EMS. Development of standards for Environmental Management Systems took place about the same time in several locations. Test-piloted in 1993, and formally introduced in 1994, the British Standards Institute's BS 7750 was the first national environmental management standard to be established. A Canadian standard, Z750, was published by the Canadian Standards Council in 1994. Both the British and Canadian standards organizations now use ISO 14001. Legislated in 1993, the European Community's Eco-Management and Audit Scheme (EMAS) was also published in 1994.

No one national Environmental Management System standard developed in the United States during the early 1990s. However, groups of companies and individual industries established a variety of standards including the Global Environmental Management Initiative (GEMI).[3] GEMI now uses ISO 14001.

The first international environmental management standard to be developed was ISO 14001 by the International Organization for Standardization.[4] The success of the ISO 9000 product quality control standard and increasing international concern about environmental management led to a proposal for an international environmental management standard. As part of the preparation for the UN Conference on Environment and Development (Brazil '92), the International Organization for Standardization was asked to form an international group to make recommendations on standards for the environmental quality. The resulting group, the Strategic Advisory Group on the Environment (SAGE), created ISO Technical Committee 207 to develop a uniform international environmental management standard and other documents on environmental management tools. The new standard, ISO 14001 Environmental Management System, was published in 1996.

Normally agreements on new international standards take a long time to draft, negotiate, and establish. However, in the case of ISO 14001, development progressed quickly — only five years elapsed from the request to the International Organization for Standardization to the first version of ISO 14001. This rapid success was due to the experience gained with the product quality standard ISO 9000 and the use of a prototype EMS (BS 7750) rather than a process starting from step one and reinventing the wheel.

EMAS

The European Eco-Management and Audit Scheme (EMAS) was designed as an industry-specific and site-specific standard for companies operating in Europe.[5]

The EMAS standard is somewhat more stringent than ISO 14001, particularly in the area of reporting to the public. Under EMAS, organizations must disclose specific information on their environmental issues and environmental management initiatives to the public.

Requirements in EMAS, but not in ISO 14001, include

- an initial review,
- an auditing process that must be carried out at least every three years,
- external reports,
- an external verification of the audit and review,
- replies to external stakeholders when there are questions from the public,
- no self-declaration of systems, and
- the promotion of EMAS by member countries, especially for small and medium-sized enterprises.

ISO 14001

ISO 14001, an international EMS standard, is designed to be applicable for organizations worldwide, regardless of their size or particular business sector. ISO 14001 must be appropriate to the scope, scale, and the nature of the activities of the organization.

ISO 14000 is a series of documents, prepared under the supervision of Technical Committee (TC) 207 of the International Organization for Standardization. It consists of one specification document (14001) and a growing number of guidance documents. (See Table 2.1) The specification document captures requirements for an EMS that meet ISO standards and is the standard that can be audited. The guidance documents explain requirements more fully, contain additional information that EMSs need not meet to conform to the standard but which are generally desirable, and describe some environmental management tools.

It is important to note that the formal EMSs tend to be minimum requirements. ISO 14001 especially is user-driven and so cannot be leading-edge. It is the result of international negotiations, it is voluntary, and it can be implemented and operated with a good deal of latitude. However, every five years the ISO standards undergo reviews which provide an opportunity for improvements. Recently, a review of the product quality control standard ISO 9000 and ISO 14000 considered combining the two systems. The conclusion was not to combine them — they were to keep their original purpose — but to align and harmonize them so that corporations seeking registration to both standards would have less difficulty.[6] ISO 14001 was reviewed in 2001, five years after it was initially published. The Committee Draft was completed in November 2001, the Draft International Standard was published in June 2002, with the new standard to be published in

2004. EMAS has been reviewed and revised and EMAS II is now available.[7] The Sustainability Group within the British Standards Institution[8] is leading a group of partners in the SIGMA Project[9] to develop the next generation of management systems and tools, which leading-edge corporations will want to examine.

Table 2.1 ISO 14000 Series of Standards and Guides

Topic	ISO 14000 Documents
Environmental Management System Specification	14001
Environmental Management System Guideline	14004
Environmental Auditing Guidelines	14010, 14011,14012, 14015 (Now ISO 19000 series)
Environmental Labeling Guidelines	14020, 14021, 14024, 14025
Environmental Performance Evaluation	14031 (Guidelines) 14032 (Technical Report)
Life Cycle Assessment	14040, 14041, 14042, 14043, 14049
Terms and Definitions	14050
Environmental Aspects in Product Standards Guidelines	14061

There is a debate between environmental organizations and international negotiators about how rigorous ISO 14001 should be. If it were very demanding, then fewer organizations might attempt to meet the requirements. However, if it is relatively easy to achieve registration, depending upon the size and complexity of the organization, then more corporations will seek registration. It is assumed that the requirements for continual improvement and the built-in system for feedback will lead to a superior, more effective EMS.

Implementing an EMS

There is a good deal of advice available on the ISO 14001 guidelines, including a rapidly growing number of books and websites, some of which are listed at the end of this chapter. Registrations are increasing rapidly in Europe and Japan, and more recently in the U.S.A.[10] As experience is gained, design and implementation will become easier.

The advice available on websites and in the literature is largely about the specification document and how to meet the requirements. However, we have found that difficulties, if not failures, are likely if there is not adequate preparation before the design and implementation process starts. Experience has taught us that the following eight prerequisites or corequisites must be in place, or the organization must be prepared to put them in place at or near the beginning of the process, before the design and implementation starts:

- basic understanding of EMS, costs, benefits, terminology, etc.;
- scope and scale required for the EMS;
- commitment by senior management;
- a champion — delegated responsibility;
- resources (money and time);
- skills, knowledge, and expertise (a consultant if necessary);
- education and training; and
- an implementation strategy.

ISO 14001 has five basic requirements which will be met if the EMS is properly designed, implemented, and operated. If these are identified separately from the 18 specific requirements listed below for the EMS, they will help to assure stakeholders that the broader goals and objectives will be met:

- establishment and maintenance of an Environmental Management System,
- an environmental policy,
- compliance with all applicable laws and regulations,
- pollution prevention, and
- continual improvement.

Commitment

Commitment is critical throughout the entire process. Senior management of the organization must be committed to the effective design, implementation, and operation of the EMS. If not, then individuals with influence in the organization who are committed to seeing the EMS succeed should use the list of driving forces (chapter 3) to persuade senior management of the benefits of investing in an EMS.

Commitment is not explicitly recognized as an important factor in EMS standards such as ISO 14001. However, we have found that it is important to obtain firm commitment at the beginning of the process and assess commitment continually throughout the process.

There are eighteen explicit requirements for an EMS under ISO 14001:

- Establish and maintain an EMS
- Develop an environmental policy
- Planning
    environmental aspects and (potential) impacts

    legal and other requirements

    objectives and targets

    environmental management program

- Implementation and operation

    structure and responsibility

    training, awareness, and competence

    communication

    documentation

    document control

    operational control

    emergency preparedness

- Checking and corrective action

    monitoring and measurement

    nonconformance and corrective and preventive action

    records

    Environmental Management System audit

- Management review

It is important to note that the skills and knowledge required to design and implement an EMS can be different from those required to operate one successfully. Therefore, an organization must decide what skills and knowledge for design and implementation its employees should obtain, and how much it can rely on consultants. That decision will depend on implementation strategy — if the experience from designing and implementing the EMS in one unit is then going to be applied to other units, a higher level of design and implementation skills and knowledge will be required. Regardless of the strategy, the consultants must be part of a team of employees, so that the employees know what is being done and why. An EMS cannot be a *turnkey operation* that is designed and implemented by consultants and then turned over to employees for operation.

Four Key Elements of Environmental Management Systems

Effective management systems include four key elements: policy — set goals and objectives (Plan); implementation and operation (Do); audit (Check); and revise, learn, and corrective action (Act), the interactive process that leads to continual improvement (Figure 2.3). Each of these elements must be properly developed and linked in order for a system to function well.

However, before that cycle can operate, there are critical preparation and implementation steps, as shown in Figure 2.4.

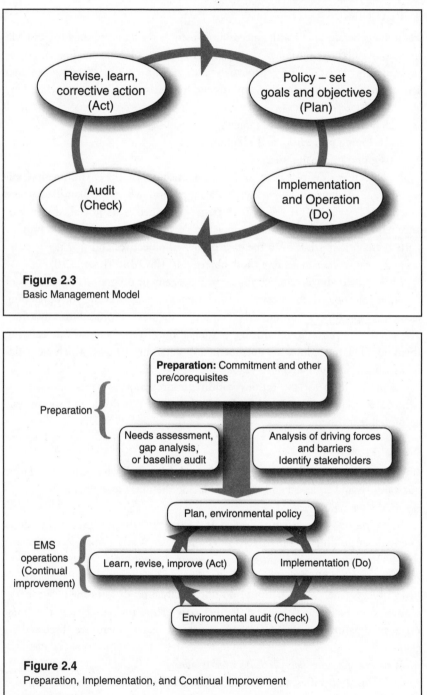

Figure 2.3
Basic Management Model

Figure 2.4
Preparation, Implementation, and Continual Improvement

1. PLANNING

Planning generally starts with a needs assessment — what is required for an EMS in the particular circumstances that apply? A somewhat less demanding and comprehensive start would be a gap analysis or baseline audit. Planning includes setting goals and determining the means and methods of realizing them. Planning should include

- identifying objectives and targets,
- developing procedures and programs, and
- assigning responsibilities.

An objective is defined as an "overall goal, arising from the environmental policy, that an organization sets itself to achieve, and which is quantified where practicable." (ISO 14001 sec. 3.7). A target is defined as a "[d]etailed performance requirement, quantified where practicable, applicable to the organization or parts thereof, that arises from the environmental objectives and that needs to be set and met in order to achieve those objectives." (ISO 14001 sec. 3.10)

As described above, an environmental management program is the process of reaching your objectives and targets. Environmental programs include developing elements, especially environmental operating guidelines and procedures and emergency response procedures, with the participation of those who will be carrying them out. The procedures are documented in detail in manuals, which are widely distributed and updated on a regular basis.

Responsibilities for the actions within the programs and procedures documents are assigned to ensure that these actions are carried out and someone is accountable for them.

Needs Assessment

An important step in developing an EMS is determining what is needed. Three questions should be asked and answered during the needs assessment.

Why is the EMS needed?

Knowing why the system is needed and what the system is expected to do is essential for guiding all other steps in the process. While it may seem obvious that EMS designers will identify why they are developing a system in the first place, this is not always the case. Therefore, even though common models of the EMS process (such as ISO 14001) do not specify a needs assessment, we feel it is important to include this as a distinct part of the process. Forces that may drive an organization's need for environmental management are discussed in chapter 3.

What specific issues does the EMS need to address?

ISO 14001 specifies what should be included in a needs assessment — the identification of environmental aspects and impacts. An environmental aspect is an "element of an organization's activities, products, or services that can interact with the environment." (ISO 14001 sec. 3.3) Aspects are environmental issues that should be considered in the EMS. An environmental impact is "any change to the environment, whether adverse or beneficial, wholly or partly resulting from an organization's activities, products or services." (ISO 14001 sec. 3.4)

Since one of the main goals of the Environmental Management System is to prevent adverse impacts, we prefer to use an adjective such as potential or possible before the word impact to indicate that these impacts are not necessarily going to take place but, rather, are possibilities that must be avoided. Note that the EMS deals with aspects and impacts under normal operations. Aspects and impacts during upsets or accidents are identified and reduced where possible through risk management (chapter 10) and handled with the emergency response plan, but still must be identified for ISO 14001.

Not all of the environmental aspects that are identified by an organization in the needs assessment stage will be followed up in later stages of the Environmental Management System. Aspects that need not be addressed later include those that are deemed to be not significant or cannot be controlled by the organization.

Methods for determining significance are not prescribed by environmental management standards. Often the best way to assess significance is to use risk assessment (chapter 10), which presents a set of systematic and credible approaches.

What environmental management initiatives and systems are already in place in the organization (current practices)?

Environmental initiatives and systems that are already in place need to be identified. As well, their effectiveness should be assessed so that successful initiatives and systems components can be continued and unsuccessful initiatives and systems can be improved or eliminated. There will also have to be an assessment of the organizational culture and other management and related systems.

Gap Analysis or Baseline Audit

Gap analysis is often a starting point for EMS implementation. It is a careful comparison of the existing Environmental Management System with formal EMS standards (such as ISO 14001) to determine what elements of a system are already in place and what pieces are missing (gaps) that are needed to complete the system. Gap analysis is not, however, as comprehensive as the needs assessment outlined above, because it does not usually consider driving forces, corporate culture, and other systems that are not part of environmental management but are related to it. Another way to start EMS implementation is to do a baseline audit to determine what is in place.

2. IMPLEMENTATION

Implementation is putting plans into action. In current EMS documents there is not much discussion of implementation. For example, ISO 14001 says that various elements within the EMS must be "established and maintained," but it does not go into detail about implementation. Yet, implementation is a critical part the EMS process.

Even if plans are well designed, there is no guarantee that they will be implemented effectively. In our experience, organizations approach implementation using one of five basic EMS strategies.

Incremental Strategy

An incremental strategy could be the best one when organizations are hesitant about an EMS, or do not have the resources to make a lot of changes in a short period of time. Follow these basic steps:

- assess and then build on current practice: waste, hazardous waste, water, waste water, energy, risk, and non-compliance;
- obtain buy-in from employees running existing EMP components and give credit for action;
- start with the most beneficial activity to show the benefit of a systematic approach and improved environmental performance; and
- gradually blend the parts of the current practices into an EMS.

Test Unit or Model Strategy

This strategy involves selecting one unit or one part of an organization, which will be used to test the EMS, and developing it as a model for other units in the organization. The basic steps are

- select a business unit as a test unit (model) based on whether it was the most positive about the EMS, would obtain the most benefits from the EMS, or had the highest risk;
- develop implementation skills and knowledge;
- implement and operate the test unit or model;
- prove the benefits of the EMS; and
- apply the model to other business units.

System-wide EMS Strategy

The system-wide strategy will succeed where there is strong commitment on the part of senior management and the resources to introduce changes throughout the organization:

- obtain instructions from senior management that the EMS will be implemented,

- prepare the eight pre/corequisites,
- ensure that corporate culture will accept the new EMS, and
- proceed with implementation throughout the organization.

Build Your Own EMS Strategy

In some diverse organizations, with a number of different business units or organizational components, there may be units that are large, independent, and reluctant to give up autonomy by having other parts of the system dictate what they use as an EMS. In these cases, allowing each of those units to build their own EMS their own way may be the most effective strategy. If so, follow these steps:

- allow each business unit to build their own EMS,
- gain buy-in for implementing an EMS from all units,
- accommodate differences between units,
- use successful units as models for others, and
- gradually harmonize the EMS throughout the organization.

Bailout Strategy

When implementation is very slow or fails, follow these steps:

- review the eight pre/corequisites to see if lack of adequate preparation is the problem,
- review the barriers to see if a specific problem can be identified and overcome, and then,
- if implementation will not work, find something else to do.

Effective Implementation Tactics

Five tactics that help ensure effective implementation of strategy are to

- remember the eight pre/corequisites and ensure that they are effectively planned and/or in place,
- select a qualified consultant and assess performance,
- provide effective leadership,
- provide training for effective teamwork,
- hold regular meetings and improve effectiveness by
    establishing a schedule and time frame,
    setting agendas and keeping detailed minutes,
    selecting action items and delegating responsibilities, and
    assessing time requirements and making sure they can be met.

Barriers to design and implementation and possible strategies for overcoming barriers are discussed in more detail in chapter 4. Implementation of an EMS should involve integration of components, including

- structure and responsibility — an organization should define, document, and communicate roles and responsibilities (chapter 7);
- training, awareness, and competence for all employees and for outside stakeholders, where necessary (chapter 9);
- communication strategy (chapter 20);
- information and documentation; and
- operational control.

3. FEEDBACK

If organizations have a policy, goals, objectives, and targets then they must have a system to provide feedback on success, or lack thereof, otherwise why bother with goals and objectives? If there are no goals and objectives, then a system to provide feedback would be meaningless. Feedback, obtained through regular, periodic audits, is the basis for continual improvement.

Checking and Corrective Action:
Auditing, Measuring, and Monitoring

What doesn't get measured, doesn't get done, is a popular management maxim. Sometimes things that are not measured do get done; however, measurement and monitoring is needed to

- evaluate environmental performance of the organization — it is important to identify successes as well as failures and to track progress over time;
- identify opportunities for improvement and set priorities;
- evaluate how well the EMS itself is functioning — this facilitates making improvements;
- ensure that responsibilities within the system are being met — there should be recognition of responsibilities that are fulfilled and corrective action where responsibilities are not met; and
- document due diligence of the organization in addressing environmental issues.

Measurement and monitoring may also be required as part of regulatory processes and obligations to stakeholders.

Measurement and monitoring have no formal definitions, unless specified under particular regulations. There are two kinds of checking in ISO 14001 — audits and other measurements including performance evaluation: Section 4.4.3 refers to management based upon measuring, monitoring, audits, and other reviews. However, the term *audit* is defined by the ISO standards and obliges corporations to use qualified professionals following a specified procedure (chapter 8). So although ISO 14001 and other tools use the term *monitoring*, the use of the term *auditing* would assure stakeholders about the process to be followed.

Revise, Learn, And Corrective Action

Auditing, or some other form of review, of each part of the management system and deciding upon areas for improvement or needed change is important to ensure that the system meets goals and objectives and continues to be suitable, efficient, and effective. Within ISO 14001, senior management is responsible for reviewing the system on a regular basis. Review and improvement can also be guided by other levels of authority within an organization, depending on their ability to affect changes in the Environmental Management System.

Continual improvement is a key concept in EMSs. (See Figure 1.3) It allows for improvement, learning from experience, and starting environmental initiatives even before the perfect system is designed and implemented.

Registration

Some organizations choose to register their EMS with the appropriate national institution representing the International Organization for Standardization or with EMAS in Europe to demonstrate that they meet those standards. There are two final requirements for registration: run the EMS through one business cycle (including continual improvement) and then obtain the approval of a registered ISO auditor.

An Environmental Management System can be registered (after the EMS has run through one complete business cycle), if a systems audit carried out by a certified auditor finds that the EMS conforms to ISO 14001. Conformance is measured to the standard for a system, not to actual environmental performance of an organization. The rationale behind this is the belief that if an EMS meets the requirements of ISO 14001 or EMAS, then good environmental performance will follow.

What is it Going to Cost?

Two of the questions asked most frequently are: "What is this going to cost and how long is it going to take?" And the answer is "that depends," because the EMS has to be appropriate to the nature of the activities, scope, and scale of the organization. A study of German companies gives some average figures that help answer the question.[11]

The survey was responded to by 25 percent of the companies registered as ISO 14001-compliant; of these, 86 percent also had ISO 9000 registration and 51 percent also were registered with EMAS. Even with that experience, to register an ISO 14001 EMS they took on average: 13 months to adopt the standard, spent 180 worker days, hired consultants for 30 days, spent U.S.$83,300 on environmental protection investments and U.S.$19,400 on other registration costs. Many of the respondents had difficulty with the concept of environmental aspects.

In broad terms, the results of the German survey are consistent with our experience. It is unclear what the costs include, but if approximately U.S.$100,000 covers the design and implemention of the EMS and investments in environmental protection equipment, then it would seem to be a reasonable average that answers the question about costs for large corporations. Clients often underestimate the time required. This confirms the need for experienced, well-qualified consultants.

However, if corporations only ask what it is going to cost, they are missing a major point of an EMS — What are the benefits? That question has to be asked and answered each time the question of costs arises. We have not been able to find a survey on benefits similar to the German survey on costs. Numerous ISO 14001 sites on the Internet and newsletters such as *Business and the Environment* (BATE) produce a good deal of anecdotal evidence about individual companies that have reaped benefits from establishing an effective EMS. The investment community now recognizes the value of an EMS (see chapter 3, Driving Forces). Although there is anecdotal evidence of the significant benefits available to offset the cost of the EMS, there is nothing definitive so far. As pointed out in chapter 15 on environmental accounting, the estimation of the benefits can be complex and can easily miss significant benefits if they are defined too narrowly. The importance of doing systematic work to outline the business case for improved environmental performance is clear.

Replacement of Regulations or Strong Complement?

Since the development of EMS standards, such as ISO 14001 and EMAS, some managers were hopeful that certification of organizations to these standards might replace government surveillance and enforcement of regulations. Programs such as the U.S. Environmental Protection Agency's StarTrack, and other programs (chapter 3, Driving Forces) have implemented or experimented with regulatory fast-tracking or lower surveillance of companies that implement an EMS which conforms to a recognized standard. Regulatory responsibilities have not yet been replaced, however, by EMS programs, and will not likely be. This is due to five factors. The most prominent reason is that standards such as ISO 14001 examine how well the EMS works, but do not require proof of regulatory compliance for a system to be certified. Secondly, experience with EMS is relatively recent and regulators and stakeholders need to develop confidence in the effectiveness of the systems. Surveillance and enforcement of regulations would still be necessary for those who did not have an EMS, did not operate it effectively or who let the effectiveness of the EMS deteriorate. There is good reason to believe that many stakeholders would not stand for a strictly voluntary system. And finally, enforcement of regulations are clearly a very important driving force, and removal of it might lead to less concern about environmental issues. The best the managers who have an effective EMS can hope for is that governments will focus resources for enforcement of regulations where they are most needed, on those organizations without one. It is likely that the only way for significant changes to the enforcement of regulations to occur is when another regulation is put in place that requires all corporations to implement an EMS, have the system audited regularly by independent auditors, have the reports on the audit verified by independent third parties, and publish the reports. Therefore, one approach to environmental regulations would be replaced by another.

EMSs and SMEs

There is anecdotal evidence that Small and Medium-Sized Enterprises (SMEs) are getting ISO 14001 registration and benefiting from the EMS. This is particularly the case when major customers require ISO 14001 registration for suppliers (Ford, GM, Toyota, IBM, and others — chapter 3) or when market access is easier (Latin American flower and fruit exporters). However, many SMEs don't understand enough about EMSs to make a sound decision about them and others falsely assume that EMSs are always large, complex, and expensive. Emphasis has to be placed on the fact that the EMS must be appropriate for the scope, scale, and nature of the organization's activities. A small organization such as a restaurant, involved in only a few activities (aspects) that could have relatively little (insignificant) impact on the environment, could have a relatively simple and inexpensive EMS. There would be benefits to the company such as reduced utility and waste disposal costs and enhanced reputation, and the public would benefit from reduced cumulative environmental impact.

Actions that would encourage and assist SMEs to implement an EMS include

- a clearer description of the cost and complexity of the EMS, as it relates to the scope, scale, and nature of an organization's activities;
- examples of SMEs in different industries that have implemented an EMS and benefited from it (time, costs, and other benefits);
- development of the business case for improved environmental performance;
- assistance from industry associations;
- assistance from governments (because the benefits of reducing the cumulative impacts of a large number of SMEs could be significant);
- how-to manuals, specifically designed so SMEs can do much of the background work before they hire a consultant; and

- sharing of resources by a group of SMEs to hire a consultant or part-time employee that they could not afford to hire independently.

Governments and EMSs

United States Executive Order 13148 *Greening of Government Through Leadership in Environmental Management*[12] requires federal agencies to implement EMSs by the end of 2005.[13] In Canada, the Ministry of the Environment is also encouraging EMSs,[14] but the Commissioner of the Environment and Sustainable Development was critical of progress and stated unequivocally, in her opening statement to the Standing Committee on Public Accounts, that the system for introducing EMSs to government was not working. Only 4 of 16 departments that were audited have EMSs that would manage and meet their commitments.[15] Governments and agencies in Japan and the EEC are taking similar actions to introduce EMSs into government departments and agencies.

At the municipal level, governments are seeking ISO 14001 registration for departments and making rapid progress on implementing EMSs. The number of institutions actively developing and implementing them is also increasing.

The roles and responsibilities of governments are much broader than those of corporations; therefore, the EMSs that they would use must be somewhat different. A comprehensive government EMS should cover three separate but related activities:

1. The activities of government as owner/operator of property and systems — water and sewer, energy, solid waste, transportation, parks, administration, meeting commitments for sustainable development, etc. This would be very similar to a corporate EMS.

2. The activities of government as regulator, policy maker, and planner — air quality, water quality, transportation systems (effectiveness, efficiency, and impacts on environmental and social systems and urban areas), forestry, agriculture, etc. The role of the EMS would be to set policy, goals, and objectives, see that they are implemented effectively, and provide feedback on success. A major responsibility would be conducting strategic environmental assessments of policies to avoid unintended impacts and to improve policy coherence by identifying and removing policy conflicts. The measures of success would be developing and using indicators and reporting on the trends in the state of the environment, especially using the Pressure State Response model. That is, this part of the government EMS would determine how well the regulations and policies are protecting the environment, identify failures, and implement improvements. This is the macro view of the effectiveness of government regulations, economic instruments (chapter 16), and policies.

3. An EMS, or subsystem of a larger EMS, should be designed to oversee the activities of the corporations and institutions being regulated. That is, how are the organizations performing? Which ones, or which industries are having the greatest negative impact? The answers to those questions are important for setting priorities for policies, economic instruments and regulations governing industries, and for deciding on the level of scrutiny and monitoring to devote to companies or industries. This part of a government EMS is important where governments have established, or are establishing, a policy of reducing scrutiny on companies with a good track record or with a good EMS. This is the micro view of the effectiveness of regulations, economic instruments, and policies.

There are government institutions developing and implementing the first type of government EMS, although experience in the operations is limited. There are efforts to use the Pressure State Response model (chapter 12, Environmental Indicators) to monitor and report on the state of the environment, the pressures that are causing undesirable trends in the state of the environment, and possible responses to relieve the pressure and reverse the trends. However, action to change that monitoring function into a formal EMS has been limited. There are activities related to the third form of government EMS, but we could find no examples where the policy has been incorporated into a formal management function. The first step would be a regulatory requirement to submit detailed reports on third party EMS audits with independent verification.

Integrating Environment, Health, and Safety

In some corporations there is pressure to integrate environment, health, and safety (EHS). A study of efforts to integrate EHS in the petroleum industry in Calgary concluded that[16]

- when integration was used as a euphemism for downsizing, results were generally negative;
- at senior management levels, a degree of integration was desirable;
- for some components of the EMS, integration was important, if not essential:
    emergency preparedness and emergency response,
    hazardous materials,
    education and some training, and
    purchasing guidelines.

However, especially at the field level, the different skills and knowledge requirements, and differing cultures meant that integrating environment, health, and safety did not produce improvements in efficiency and effectiveness.

Narrow Focus of ISO 14001

A major problem with ISO 14001 and EMAS is the tendency for the identification of aspects and impacts to be pollution-oriented — products, processes, or activities that have a significant impact on the environment. That need not, and should not, be the case. Pollution prevention, compliance with laws and regulations, and eco-efficiency are important. However, if environmental managers remember that the EMS must deal with the significant driving forces (chapter 3) and that environmental policy deals with much more than biophysical impacts (chapter 6), then it should become clear that the EMS must include a much broader understanding of what protection of the environment encompasses.

By examining the driving forces and the set of environmental management tools, it can be seen that a corporate EMS should encompass the following, in particular circumstances:

- responsibility for green spaces and natural areas, where the goal of the EMS is to set goals and objectives for the space or area and take actions to maintain it (see chapter 23, Ecosystem-Based Management);
- EIA and cumulative impact assessment (chapter 14), where the emphasis is on anticipating and avoiding impacts, or control of numerous small impacts (the tourism industry, for example);
- social impacts using EIA (chapter 14) or environmental auditing (chapter 8) where issues arise due to

    public perceptions (chapter 20, Environmental Communications), introduction of computers, health services, or adult education for employees that give them significant advantages over others in the community and therefore create tensions in the community;

- health and safety and the use of human factors as a management tool (chapter 21);
- Life Cycle Assessment (chapter 18) which could lead to environmental managers being involved in

    supply chain management — education and training of suppliers, product stewardship — education and training of customers, secondary and tertiary impacts — longer cause and effects relationships,

- corporate social responsibility and the triple bottom line which is broader than most current interpretations of aspects and impacts; and
- sustainable development, which is broader than corporate social responsibility and the triple bottom line.

The current definitions in ISO 14001 and the EMS do not prevent corporate environmental managers from including these elements in the EMS. In fact, if these factors are explicitly or implicitly in the corporate environmental policy, then they should become part of the audit criteria that provide feedback in the EMS.

It is likely that there would be objections to a broad understanding of aspects and impacts which included more than compliance, pollution prevention, and eco-efficiency. The first negative argument would be that it is impractical. However, if we look at the driving forces, the business case for improved performance and for corporate social responsibility, and the number of institutions that make commitments to sustainable development, then impracticality is not particularly relevant. Similarly, the argument that the EMS is not designed to push the envelope is not relevant, because that is up to the individual organizations and how they want to use their EMS. Specialists who still see the EMS as focused on their particular narrow interest (technology or legal compliance) will object, as will short-term profit maximizers and those who reject any commitment to sustainable development. But again, their objections are based upon narrow, short-term perspectives that do not address the reality of what leading-edge corporations are already doing.

Recommended Further Reading

The ISO 14000 documents are available from the organization responsible for national standards in each country.

Canadian Standards Association. *The ISO 14000 Essentials: A Practical Guide to Implementing the ISO 14000 Standards.* Etobicoke, Ontario: Canadian Standards Association, 1996.

Cascio, J., G. Wodside, and P. Mitchell. *ISO 14000 Guide: The New International Environmental Management Standards.* New York: McGraw-Hill, 1996.

Sheldon, C., ed. *ISO 14001 and Beyond: Environmental Management Systems in the Real World.* Sheffield, U.K.: Greenleaf Publishing, 1997.

European Economic Community. *Council Regulation (EEC) No 1836/93 of 29 June 1993 allowing voluntary participation by companies in the industrial sector in a Community eco-management and audit scheme.* Available at the EMAS website listed below.

Global Environmental Management Initiative (GEMI). *ISO 14001 Environmental Management System Self-Assessment Checklist.* Rev. November 2000. Washington DC: GEMI, 2000.

Websites

American National Standards Institute (ANSI): <www.ansi.org/public/iso14000/default.htm>

British Standards Institution: <www.bsi-global.com>

EMAS: <www.europa.eu.int/comm/environment/emas/index.htm>

Global Environmental Management Initiative: <www.gemi.org>

International Network for Environmental Management: <www.inem.org>

International Organization for Standardization (ISO): <www.iso.ch>;

Isocenter: <www.isocenter.com>

Office of the Auditor General of Canada: <www.oag-bvg.gc.ca/domino/other.nsf/html>

Project SIGMA: <www.projectsigma.com>

Responsible Care: <www.icca-chem.org/rcreport/>

Standards Council of Canada: <www.scc.ca>

CHAPTER 3

ANALYSIS OF DRIVING FORCES

Dixon Thompson and Lisa-Henri Kirkland,
Wolfwillow Environmental

D RIVING FORCES are those factors that tend to cause environmental managers and/or senior managers to make improvements in environmental management. There are three reasons why analysis of driving forces is an important environmental management tool for businesses:

- To convince decision makers to make a commitment and to start the process of implementing an Environmental Management System (EMS) or applying particular environmental management tools.[1] The driving forces provide reasons why an EMS or particular environmental management tools should be used.
- To identify benefits — cost savings, reduced risks and contingent costs, increased investment, easier financing and project approvals, access to markets, etc.
- To design the EMS so that it responds to all significant driving forces to obtain all possible benefits.

Publications about driving forces, often presented as the benefits that can be obtained from improved environmental performance, have steadily refined and expanded the list of reasons why corporations must take environmental management seriously.[2] KPMG surveyed Canadian companies in 1994 and 1996 and found 16 motivating factors.[3] This chapter provides a quick overview of driving forces. It does not attempt to cover the large volume of detailed technical literature available on each driving force.

Hoffman reviews driving forces in some detail.[4] Andriof and McIntosh discuss the business case for corporate social responsibility.[5] The Global Environmental Management Initiative (GEMI) has produced two reports: *Environment: Value to Business* and *Environment: Value to the Bottom Line* that are available in pdf from GEMI's website.[6] Berry and Rondinelli summarize driving forces in their 1998 article.[7] A broader perspective on the behavior of multinational corporations, including environmental aspects, is provided by the Organization for Economic Cooperation and Development (OECD).[8]

Analysis of driving forces is not generally accepted as a formal environmental management tool. However, all effective environmental managers use some informal analysis of driving forces to understand why they are doing things or what they should be doing, even if it is almost unconscious at times. Managers involved in formal strategic environmental management may use a formal system for identifying and analyzing driving forces, depending upon which strategic management approach they are using (see chapter 5). We have found that a more formal approach to identification and analysis of driving forces makes the process faster and less likely to miss anything significant. The generic list of driving forces appears in Table 3.1 Generic List of Environmental Management Driving Forces.[9] Figure 3.1 shows that driving forces operate from inside the corporation and outside the corporation to produce pressure to improve environmental performance. The voluntary measures are forces outside the organization until they become part of corporate environmental policy and then could be considered a set of internal forces. The generic list will be very much the same for most, if not all, Organization for Economic Cooperation and Development (OECD) countries. We discuss, in an earlier book, the driving forces that apply in Latin America.[10]

Table 3.1 Generic List of Environmental Management Driving Forces

• Laws — regulations, enforcement, and penalties	• Reduced costs
• Lawsuits for damages from accidents or from pollution	• Environmental Non-Governmental Organizations (ENGOs)
• Government policies — what governments want to achieve without regulation	• Public
	• Voluntary Environmental Management Initiatives (VEMI)
• Banks and financial institutions	• Codes of conduct
• Investors	Industry codes
• Insurers	National codes
• Accounting systems	ENGO codes
• Environmental Management Systems	Issue-specific codes
• Purchasing guidelines	• Corporate ethics and corporate social responsibility
• Markets	• Professional organizations
• Employees	• International agreements

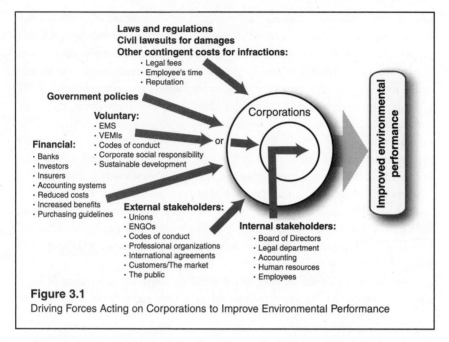

Figure 3.1
Driving Forces Acting on Corporations to Improve Environmental Performance

The generic list can be used to identify and analyze the driving forces: check each item against current operations to see if it applies. In our experience, some managers quickly dismiss all driving forces except the one or two with which they are most familiar. That is an easy way to miss significant opportunities and risks. It may take some research to determine the applicability and importance of some of the driving forces. The chief financial officer (CFO) of the organization could provide information on banks and investors and their interest in improved environmental performance. Those responsible for insurance would know, or could find out, if reduced environmental risk would lead to a reduction in insurance premiums. Marketing might know, or be able to learn, if customers are likely to introduce environmental purchasing guidelines, or if there are markets that are available only to those who can prove superior environmental performance.

The relative importance of each driving force changes with the circumstances and over time. Therefore, an important part of the identification and analysis of the driving forces is not only an attempt to determine which factors are important right now but which forces are becoming more important or are likely to become more important in the next two to five years.

It is important to note that, for any particular set of circumstances, all significant driving forces must be identified and responded to in order to optimize the benefits of an EMS and improve environmental performance. Too often, one or two driving forces are selected while others are neglected, and significant benefits can be lost. Laws and regulations are driving forces which are most often given exclusive attention. Although laws and regulations are the first driving forces discussed below, environmental managers must recognize that using an EMS to ensure compliance will not necessarily bring other benefits, especially if they adhere to the letter, rather than the spirit, of the law. However, if an effective EMS is in place to optimize benefits by responding to other driving forces, then legal compliance will almost certainly be obtained.

The internal and external environmental management structure (chapter 7) can be used to identify participants and stakeholders who might apply pressure for improved environmental performance. Strategic environmental management (chapter 5) should involve scanning of the external environment to identify and analyze possible changes in driving forces. Environmental auditing (chapter 8), indicators (chapter 12), and reporting (chapter 13) with external verification should be used to prove the level of environmental performance and report it in a credible fashion to stakeholders.

The discussion of the driving forces listed in Table 3.1 is necessarily brief. Those at the top of the list are discussed in a little more detail because their impacts tend to be more direct.

Laws and Regulations

If laws are to be effective as driving forces, three components are required: effective laws and regulations, effective and efficient enforcement, and adequate penalties. If any of these components are insignificant or missing, laws and regulations may be ineffective. To be complete, therefore, an analysis of laws and regulations as driving forces must include an assessment of all laws and regulations that apply (national, provincial/state, and municipal/local), how effective and efficient enforcement is, and what the penalties are. However, if corporate policy states that all applicable laws and regulations will be complied with, as required by ISO 14001 for example, then the level of enforcement and the size of the penalties matter less. A statement about obeying all applicable laws and regulations is rather peculiar in a law-abiding corporation. However, in some cases it is important to bring this to the attention of employees who must be familiar with the corporation's policy statement. In other cases, the environmental policy statement follows the spirit of the law, meets or exceeds all requirements, which is somewhat stronger than just doing what is required by the letter of the law.

There are three different types of legal procedures dealing with infractions by individuals and corporations:
- what non-lawyers would call criminal law;
- absolute liability where a ticket, a summons, or an administrative penalty is issued for minor infractions such as parking violations, littering, and,

increasingly, failure to comply with pollution regulations or other environmental statutes; and

- strict liability that is specifically related to environmental law, where there are provisions for a due diligence offense.

Until Canadian legislation included jail sentences and fines of up to Can$1 million for each day of an offense, penalties were small, relative to the costs of preventing infractions, so corporations often chose to pay the penalty rather then fix the problem. Jail sentences have been imposed since the early 1990s.[11] Federal and provincial prosecution statistics are available, including comparisons to those from the U.S.A.[12] Total federal government fines from 1988 to 1998 were almost Can$8 million, for Ontario provincial fines were Can$32.5 million. In the U.S.A. in 1997, EPA actions resulted in U.S.$264 million in fines and penalties and between 1995 and 1997 individuals served a total of 363 years in jail. In fiscal year 1999, the EPA imposed U.S.$166.7 million in civil fines and announced U.S.$3.6 billion in enforcement actions. Environmental criminals were sentenced to a total of 208 years in jail.[13]

In strict liability cases, the accused is innocent until proven guilty: they must be found guilty *beyond reasonable doubt*, and strict rules of evidence apply.

Absolute Liability

Absolute liability is used to enforce regulations of a relatively minor nature. A summons or administrative penalty is issued when the officer or agent finds evidence that a breach of the regulations has occurred. In these cases, parties are guilty until they prove themselves innocent, which is often hard to do. It saves the costs of legal proceedings and is administratively simple. Provisions for such administrative penalties are in place, or under consideration, in Alberta, Ontario, and other jurisdictions.[14]

Strict Liability

Strict liability involves non-compliance with environmental regulations where it is possible for the defendant to mount a due diligence defense. That is, an individual or corporation attempts to prove that they had done everything that a reasonable person would have done in those circumstances, providing evidence that they were operating at, or above, the norms for the industry, and yet circumstances led to an infraction. The defendant attempts to prove that they had been duly diligent in their efforts to avoid breaking the law. This type of defense is not permitted in other criminal cases, nor is it applicable in absolute liability cases.

Having a well-documented EMS in place is important for establishing due diligence. A recently updated environmental policy statement with evidence of corporate commitment and effective, regular audits; education and training; and use of environmental indicators and reporting, especially with third party verification, can be used to establish due diligence. The importance of an EMS in assisting corporations to be duly diligent has been recognized in environmental cases; judges have required guilty parties to achieve ISO 14001 EMS registration as part of the sentence (e.g., cases against Prospec Chemicals and the City of Calgary in Alberta and Cortech in Ontario).

In Canada, the 1992 Bata case highlighted the importance of due diligence for environmental infractions. Bata managers knew that they had a hazardous waste problem but avoided spending the Can$57,000 estimated for the cleanup. Ontario Environment prosecuted Bata for contamination of groundwater caused by the leaking chemicals. One executive proved that he had been duly diligent, by showing that, if his explicit instructions had been followed, the incident would not have occurred. Two other executives were fined, the company was fined, the contamination had to be cleaned up, and other conditions were imposed. It is likely that the total costs to Bata were as much as ten times the estimated cost for the cleanup.

It is important to note that the requirements for being duly diligent continually change because each new case can change what the courts recognize as due diligence, and the continual improvements in environmental management mean that what is required to meet industry norms change.

Innovative regulatory approaches are also being established. Environmental Protection Alternative Measures agreements (EPAM) are like administrative penalties but involve a negotiated agreement to improve environmental management and performance and to complete other tasks. EPAMs were introduced during revision of the Canadian Environmental Protection Act in 1999.[15]

In efforts to focus their attention on organizations that are most likely to be out of compliance, the U.S. EPA, and governments in Canada, Norway, Austria, and other countries are easing the scrutiny and regulatory pressure on companies that demonstrate improved environmental performance by implementing an EMS and reporting on results.

Civil Court Lawsuits for Damages

When environmental damage is caused, those who suffer financially can sue in civil court to recover their losses. This can add significantly to the costs of an infraction. The legal burden of proof for successful recovery of losses due to such damage is less in civil courts than in criminal courts. In civil courts, the decision is made on the *balance of probabilities*, rather than the criminal court's *beyond reasonable doubt*. The distinction is easily illustrated with the O. J. Simpson trial for murder, in which Simpson was acquitted, because reasonable doubt had been raised. However, in civil court, the parents of the victims were awarded U.S.$35 million against Simpson for their losses. Similarly, in the case of the Valdez oil spill, EXXON faced both types of penalties: they paid heavy fines and are still fighting billions of dollars in damages to people who had suffered losses, in addition to legal fees, and other costs.

Government Policies

Governments often have stated goals and objectives (policies) which are not enshrined in legislation and enforceable regulations. These goals and objectives are stated in many different forms: the Speech from the Throne or State of the Union message, campaign speeches, statements by the President, Prime Minister and cabinet ministers, and formal white papers or green papers in the case of environmental policies. Corporations whose activities help the government achieve their goals and objectives will likely find direct benefits in the form of grants and tax incentives, especially if the government does implement green taxes. Indirect benefits can accrue in the form of better relations with government agencies, faster approvals for projects or products, etc.

Banks and Financial Institutions

Banks and financial institutions became a significant driving force for improved environmental management when they started to suffer losses due to the poor environmental performance of people or corporations to whom they had loaned money. They are also starting to examine their roles with respect to sustainable development.[16] Initially the losses involved a decrease in estimated value of assets because of failure to understand environmental liabilities. However, with the Northern Badger case, lending institutions in Canada became more concerned about understanding environmental liabilities. Northern Badger was a small oil company in Alberta that became insolvent (bankrupt). The bank holding Northern Badger's assets as collateral for a loan wanted to liquidate the assets to cover some of the loan. However, the Energy Utilities Board in Alberta ruled that Northern Badger's remaining assets had to be used to cover the cleanup costs at abandoned oil well sites before any of those assets were released to the bank. The bank appealed the ruling to the Alberta Court of Appeals and lost. Therefore, it was established in common law that the owners of corporate assets were at least partially responsible for corporate environmental liabilities, whereas previously there was no cleanup, or the taxpayers had to cover the costs.

For real estate transactions, banks now insist on a site assessment (chapter 11) if there is any possibility that there might be environmental liabilities associated with the site. Interest rates have been reduced for borrowers who can prove that they have a superior EMS, because they pose less risk. A small reduction in interest rates for corporate loans will pay for a great deal of environmental management.

Banks now have environmental management experts to ensure that their interests are protected. This driving force is likely to increase in importance as the expertise and experience of lenders improves their ability to assess the environmental performance of borrowers.

Investors

In lay terms, there are three forms of investment strategies, all pursued for financial gain: market activity and performance, ethical investing, and value investing.

Those making investment decisions based upon market performance or activity have little or no interest in what companies do or how they do it, so environmental management is not relevant. This is a short-term strategy used by day traders and speculators.

Some investors want to avoid investing in corporations that do not share their values, or which do not have a good record in environmental protection and conservation of resources. In these cases, proving that a corporation has a good record on environmental matters is important.[17] Australian institutions have combined to publish *A Capital Idea: Realizing Value from Environmental and Social Performance*.[18] The use of this long-term investment strategy is growing.[19]

Value investing relies on efforts to understand the qualities of a corporation to determine which investments will perform well, and is coming back in favor.[20] There is a belief that superior environmental performance is an indicator of superior overall management or that superior environmental performance leads to reduced risk and, therefore, improved financial performance. The Tellus Institute is unequivocal: "Recent work by a wide range of researchers reveals consistent evidence of a positive association between a company's environmental performance and its financial performance."[21] The Conference Board of Canada states, "recent evidence indicates a positive link between corporate sustainable development (SD) practices and share price performance."[22] However, the debate about whether environmental performance provides improvements in financial performance of corporations is not yet completely resolved.

Following the interest in ethical investing and the likely link between financial performance and environmental performance, a number of investment indices, lists, and ratings are being developed, such as The Dow Jones Sustainability Group Index,[23] Portfolio 21,[24] FTSE4Good,[25] and Innovest,[26] but not everyone is happy.[27] These systems to assist investors are in the development phase and, if they mature, will become a much more significant driving force.

The bodies governing investment have recognized the importance of information about environmental liabilities. The U.S. Securities and Exchange Commission, the Ontario Exchange Commission, and others require disclosures of environmental liabilities by companies that are listed on their exchanges.

Insurers

To the extent that effective environmental management can reduce environmental risks, insurers might be convinced to reduce insurance premiums for those corporations that can prove that they have identified and reduced their environmental risks. Insurers could refine estimates of risk by requiring risk management (chapter 10) and reporting (chapter 13).

Accounting Systems

In December 1992, the Canadian Association of Chartered Accountants initiated a major change in driving forces for improved environmental management when they announced that financial statements prepared by their members must charge environmental liabilities, where they could reasonably be identified, against their assets. This extended the requirements imposed by exchange commissions to all companies. It was a bold and courageous move to state that liabilities must be identified and charged against assets, before the details of how those liabilities could be quantified were worked out.

The ruling introduces a practice that makes common sense. If a corporation has real estate valued at $100 million but it contains a contaminated site that is going to cost $20 million to clean up, then it would be fraudulent and misleading to claim property assets of $100 million.

Now that environmental liabilities must be included in financial statements prepared by chartered accountants, there has been a scramble to develop and apply environmental management tools that identify and quantify possible environmental liabilities. The usual mechanism of quantification is a realistic estimate of what it would cost to eliminate the liability. Liabilities generally take the form of contaminated groundwater and/or contaminated soil or hazardous waste that must be properly stored and disposed of. Realistic estimates of costs can be obtained from environmental engineering companies who deal with such problems, through the formal process of site assessment (chapter 11). However, many companies in Canada and the U.S.A. do not properly account for, and report, environmental liabilities and the rules are not always enforced.

Accounting systems can play another role as a driving force, as will be shown in chapter 15, Environmental Accounting. As environmental accounting systems improve, it will be easier to estimate or to show direct and indirect savings that have been, or could be, obtained from improved environmental performance. It will also be possible to make improved estimates of avoided costs or contingency costs — those costs that would be incurred if an accident were to happen. Therefore, it will be easier to show how investment in improved environmental management will provide a return on that investment, and would not be just another cost of doing business.

Environmental Management Systems

Because of the requirements for continual improvement, auditing, reporting, verification, and increased competitiveness, Environmental Management Systems are driving forces for improved performance, even though there is some variation in the different EMSs. ISO 14001 Environmental Management System, EMAS (Ecosystem Management and Auditing Scheme), and GEMI (Global Environmental Management Initiative) are discussed in chapter 2.

ISO (International Organization for Standardization) is an international NGO that is not financially supported by governments. It is user-driven. That is, ISO does not introduce an international standard or guideline until asked to do so — it does not take the initiative on developing standards and guidelines. ISO standards are also the product of negotiation by those nation members who want to take part and, therefore, controversial or demanding aspects are often eliminated, due to the need for compromise to reach agreement.

As an EU (European Union) regulation supported by governments, EMAS carries a little more weight and is somewhat stronger in certain respects than ISO 14001 (chapter 2).

GEMI is an organization of 26 large American corporations that uses example and persuasion to bring about change. Its website (www.gemi.org) is a good source of information.

Responsible Care is a management system or an elaborate code of conduct started in Canada in 1984 as a response to very negative public attitudes about the chemical industry. There seems to be a difference of opinion about whether Responsible Care is a pubic relations system to convince the public that the chemical industry is responsible or an Environmental Management System that the corporations will use to improve environmental performance and therefore improve their public image. Responsible Care now includes the chemical industries in more than 40 countries. It has the potential to be a very powerful driving force because there are provisions for members to refuse to sell to, or buy from, non-member companies and/or companies that do not do audits to prove that they meet Responsible Care requirements.

Purchasing Guidelines

In the last few years, corporations wishing to improve their overall environmental performance have started to require suppliers to prove that they too have an effective EMS, often ISO 14001 registration or equivalent (chapter 19). Unfortunately, this concern is not always reflected in equally stringent requirements on the downstream (marketing) side, although take-back legislation is changing that.

Faced with a major customer's demands to meet certain environmental performance requirements, suppliers have no choice but to improve their environmental management. In many cases, customers imposing such conditions will offer assistance to suppliers in meeting the new conditions. The use of purchasing guidelines by large corporations has risen sharply since the late 1990s and is likely to become a common practice and, therefore, a major driving force for improved environmental performance.

Part of the reason for increased use of purchasing guidelines is the increased use of Life Cycle Assessment (LCA), described in chapter 18, which can show manufacturers where the largest environmental impacts occur in the life cycle of their products. If LCA shows that large impacts occur during the production of their supplies, they may decide to use purchasing guidelines to try to reduce those impacts and, therefore, the overall impact of their product(s).

Markets

Markets are a driving force for improved environmental performance.[28] Environmentally conscientious consumers try to keep informed and buy products that are environmentally friendly from corporations that have a good environmental record. Keeping up to date and getting the necessary information is difficult and time consuming, so even those consumers with the best of intentions cannot always act on them. There is a struggle between advertisers who want to influence buying patterns and conscientious consumers who want the market to send a message to designers and manufacturers. Product labeling and consumer associations are two ways in which consumers can get information about products and the environmental performance of corporations that produce them. Consumers are also getting information from the Internet about corporations and making informed purchases to help the market send the signals about preferred products and corporate performance. A discussion of the market and its imperfections is in chapter 16.

Another aspect of markets as a driving force is the actions by governments who make market access easier for those with demonstrated EMS capabilities. Trade agreements have constrained governments from legislative requirements for environmental performance that extend outside their borders. Nonetheless, market access and product acceptance in terms of the environmental conditions that can influence product quality have become major issues.

JETRO (Japan External Trade Organization) has encouraged those who want access to markets in Japan to obtain ISO 14001 registration. Flower and fruit growers in Latin America have obtained ISO 14001 registration, in order to assure access to markets in Europe.[29]

Employees

Employees become a driving force for improved environmental performance for four reasons:

- Their personal values dictate that they do not want to be part of a system that is not doing as much as it can to reduce environmental impacts.
- They are concerned about the future for their children or their grand-children — future generations in sustainable development terms.
- They want to be proud of the job they do and the corporation they work for.
- They want to work in a clean, healthy, and pleasant environment.

Reduced Costs

There are different ways in which improved environmental performance can reduce costs. Chapter 15 discusses accounting practices for estimating costs and benefits. Direct savings include improved energy and material efficiency, reduced waste disposal costs, and lower insurance premiums. Less direct benefits are more difficult to estimate. They include less scrutiny by regulators; faster, less expensive approvals; improved image and reputation; better relationships with banks and investors; and easier access to markets.

Contingent or avoided costs are important but difficult to estimate — costs that would be incurred only if certain events occur — an accident or chemical spill for example. Like the value of preventative medicine, it is difficult to recognize, let alone estimate, the value of spending money to prevent something undesirable from happening.

Environmental Non-Governmental Organizations (ENGOs)

ENGOs have played a significant role in putting pressures on corporations to protect the environment. Clearly, different ENGOs use different strategies and tactics to apply pressure. Chapter 7, Environmental Management Structures, recommends a process for identifying and classifying ENGOs that might affect a particular corporation. The nature of the driving force will depend upon the strategies and tactics, skills and knowledge, and the resources of a particular ENGO or group of ENGOs. This driving force changes over time and with the profile of a particular issue or corporation.

The Internet is making it much easier for ENGOs to organize and to increase their effectiveness as a driving force. This has certainly been the case with respect to organizing opposition to the Multilateral Agreement on Investment, the World Trade Organization meetings in Seattle and Prague, the Free Trade Area of the Americas meeting in Quebec City, and the G8/20 meetings in Kananaskis.

Although it is difficult to predict when and how pressure will be applied by an ENGO or group and how effective that pressure will be, it is certain that this driving force will be significant from time to time, especially for those corporations that have not made a credible effort to demonstrate corporate social and environmental responsibility, and even for some who have. Some of the biggest impacts that ENGOs can have on corporations are through well-organized product boycotts and through opposition to projects.

The Public

Individual members of the public play different roles that are part of different driving forces: consumers, investors, members of ENGOs, and voters. The public's roles, as voters that governments sometimes listen to and as the body that forms public opinion, can be important. These roles as citizens in civil society produce a diffuse pressure that changes with time and circumstances. However, the attention and money paid by corporations to their image and reputation reflect a justified concern about the public as a driving force. (see chapter 20)

Voluntary Environmental Management Initiatives

The Commission for Environmental Cooperation reviewed North American Voluntary Environmental Management Initiatives (VEMIs).[30] There are different types of VEMIs:

- environmental management systems
- industry codes
- country codes for multinational corporations
- NGO codes
- issue-specific codes

Voluntary codes are not enforceable. The strength of the voluntary code as a driving force depends on the commitment of the corporation that subscribes to the code, and its willingness to use the code as environmental audit criteria and to publish the results of the audits to prove compliance. The credibility and strength of the VEMIs as a driving force varies with the transparency of the processes involved and the requirements of the VEMI to prove that stated performance improvements are being obtained.

VEMIs are taken for two very different reasons. In some cases, subscribers to the initiative are willing to make a commitment to improved environmental performance beyond what is required by government regulations, and so they voluntarily act to formalize that commitment. The other reason for taking such an initiative is that industry sees this as a means of avoiding, or at least postponing, legislated requirements by voluntarily agreeing to do what governments might have required them to do by legislation.

Where voluntary measures meet the requirements for demonstrating credibility — transparency and auditing and reporting with verification — some regulatory agencies have decided to allocate resources to those corporations that require the most scrutiny and are allowing those companies that demonstrate improved environmental performance by VEMIs more independence, fewer inspections, etc.

In Canada the Voluntary Challenge and Registry (VCR) attempted to achieve reductions in greenhouse gas emissions, which has had difficulty with credibility because too many members took little or no action.[31]

Industry Codes

Industry sectors have organized themselves into associations — mining, petroleum, chemicals, forestry, pulp and paper, agriculture, electronics, etc. — that often have environmental codes. In some cases the codes are recommended, and in others adherence to the code and a process (environmental audits) of demonstrating compliance is required for membership. Some industry codes require members to apply the same Environmental Management Systems in all their operations, regardless of where they are located. That is, the members are not allowed to have high standards at home and lower standards abroad.

The impact of industry codes as a driving force must be assessed on a case-by-case basis. They are voluntary and unenforceable. They cover a wide spectrum from ineffective public relations efforts to improve image without improving performance to credible efforts to improve performance in order to improve reputation.

National Codes for Multinational Corporations

Canada and Japan have voluntary codes of conduct for multinational corporations which were drafted as a result of concern about extensive media coverage of companies' behavior abroad. These national codes are the result of political decisions and, as such, are likely to vary with political processes and the commitment of the particular government and a specific minister. Therefore, it is unlikely that they will become a serious driving force for improved environmental performance, unless a coalition of ENGOs, corporate organizations, and politicians decide to make this form of VEMI a strong driving force.

International NGO Codes of Conduct

International non-governmental organizations have prepared codes of conduct for their members or for corporations who want to prove that they are using third party criteria to guide their international environmental performance. The World Business Council on Sustainable Development was involved in the preparations for Brazil '92 and the drafting of ISO 14000 as a set of international environmental management guidelines and standards. The 1992 UN conference in Brazil also produced *Agenda 21*, which is a much more elaborate and demanding set of guidelines for multinational corporations. The International Chamber of Commerce has an environmental code of conduct for its members. CERES

(Coalition for Environmentally Responsible Economies) has gained some high-profile members for its voluntary code.

Issue-Specific Voluntary Environmental Management Initiatives (VEMI)

There are some high-profile VEMIs that are aimed at specific environmental problems. The Voluntary Challenge and Registry is a VEMI directed at the voluntary reduction of greenhouse gases (GHG).[32] Members are required to send a letter of intent, outline an action plan, and indicate results of GHG reduction efforts. Because of the very loose voluntary nature of the agreement, there were many letters of intent but few credible results.[33] Governments had to threaten legislation before the requirements for the voluntary initiative were strengthened. ARET (Accelerated Reduction and Elimination of Toxics) is a combined effort of industry and ENGOs to systematically reduce the release of toxic materials into the environment. Several annual reports showed significant results although the long-term viability of the effort depends very heavily on the volunteers from industry and ENGOs to keep the initiative going.[34]

Corporate Ethics and Social Responsibility

Capitalist models for corporate behavior use financial performance as the only criteria for consideration in corporate performance — the (single) bottom line. Periodically, but more particularly in the last decade, some corporations started to include corporate environmental and social ethics to guide their behavior, not just the letter of the law and financial returns. Commitment to meeting social and environmental responsibilities as well as financial performance — the triple bottom line — has lead to voluntary corporate changes in what they see as their obligations and responsibilities. This could be a response to executives' personal values that they believe corporate citizens must also follow and/or their belief that meeting corporate social responsibility makes good business sense.[35]

This internal driving force will only apply when corporate culture and values lead to a commitment to the triple bottom line. If there is better evidence for the business case for the triple bottom line — accepting and implementing policies on corporate social and environmental responsibility — then it may become a driving force for other corporations that accept it for financial reasons, independent of ethics or social responsibilities.

Professional Organizations

At national and international levels, organizations of the professions involved in various aspects of environmental management have a significant impact on their members and their employers. Professional organizations that are taking specific steps to improve environmental performance by increasing the skills, knowledge, and professional practice of their members include: SETAC (Society of Environmental Toxicology and Chemistry) with respect to Life Cycle Assessment (chapter 18) and Risk Assessments (chapter 10); the AWMA (Air and Water Management Association); IAIA (International Association for Impact Assessment) (chapter 14); and the Academy of Management ONE (Organizations and the Natural Environment). At the national level, professional organizations of engineers, chemists, biologists, and others have recognized their environmental responsibilities, but the concerns remain largely within the discipline and do not extend into the area of environmental management.

International Agreements

There are more than 250 multinational environmental agreements (MEAs) that have different strengths as driving forces for improved environmental performance. Companies should review the applicable MEAs to determine where they must, or may have to, take action.

One of the most successful of the MEAs is the Montreal Protocol on ozone-depleting substances because it is to industry's advantage to substitute more expensive new products for older, cheaper products. The biggest problem here is using the available environmental management tools to demonstrate to developing countries, like China, who are committed to providing refrigeration to their citizens, that high-tech, energy-efficient, CFC-free design is the most cost-effective in the long term. That will require proving that the alternative refrigerators have superior performance and providing access to the technology and to financing for the units that may have higher initial costs.

Governments around the world, especially in Canada and the U.S.A., are struggling with the Kyoto Protocol on reduction of greenhouse gases. When an agreement is reached, governments will require improved environmental performance from corporations, including an EMS, auditing, and verification systems to prove their achievements in reducing greenhouse gases to meet the requirements of the climate change MEA.

The recent MEA on Persistent Organic Pollutants (POP) will have an impact on those companies that produce or use POPs. They will have to reduce, or preferably eliminate, release of these pollutants by changing processes, finding less persistent substitutes, and developing management tools to do so.

Recommended Further Reading

Andriof, J., and M. McIntosh. *Perspectives on Corporate Citizenship*. Sheffield, U.K.: Greenleaf Publishing, 2001.

Berry, M. A., and D. A. Rondinelli. "Proactive Corporate Environmental Management: A New Industrial Revolution." *Academy of Management Executive* 12, no. 8 (1998): pp. 38-50.

Garcia, P., J. Gonzales, and D. Thompson. "Driving Forces and Barriers to Implementing Sound Environmental Management in the Andean Region of Latin America." In *Growing Pains: Environmental Management in Developing Countries,* edited by W. Wehremeyer and Y. Mulugetta. Sheffield, U.K.: Greenleaf Publishing, 1999, pp. 132-147.

GEMI (Global Environmental Management Initiative). *Environment: Value to Business.* Washington DC: GEMI, 1998.

Hawken, P., A. Lovins, and H. L. Lovins. *Natural Capitalism: Creating the Next Industrial Revolution.* New York: Little, Brown and Company, 1999.

Hoffman, A. J. *Competitive Environmental Strategy: A Guide to the Changing Business Landscape.* Washington DC: Island Press, 2000.

Willard, B. *The Sustainability Advantage: Seven Business Cases, Benefits of a Triple Bottom Line.* Gabriola Island, B.C.: New Society Publishers, 2002.

Websites

GEMI (Global Environmental Management Initiative): <www.gemi.org>

Organization for Economic Cooperation and Development, 2000, The OECD Guidelines for Multinational Enterprises, available in pdf at <www.oecd.org>

CH A P TER

ANALYSIS OF BARRIERS

Lisa-Henri Kirkland, Wolfwillow Environmental
and Dixon Thompson

ATTEMPTS TO APPLY environmental management tools or to implement an Environmental Management System do not guarantee success. However, the likelihood of successful environmental initiatives can be greatly enhanced if problems or barriers to the process can be anticipated and strategies developed to overcome them.

Definition of Barriers to Environmental Management

Barriers to environmental management are conditions that may adversely affect the implementation or effectiveness of environmental initiatives. Analysis of barriers is an environmental management tool that ascertains specific reasons why the introduction of a management tool or system is difficult or slow, so that these barriers can be identified, reduced, or eliminated. It formalizes a process that many managers use implicitly and informally.

Although barriers to environmental management can be of significant concern, there has been little formal discussion about them in the literature. Environmental literature has concentrated on EMS frameworks and components and presented a relatively simple approach to the process of environmental management, especially the introduction and implementation phases. Recognizing and dealing with barriers requires a fuller understanding of how organizations (and individuals within them) think and act.

Work on recognizing and analyzing barriers to environmental management is in the early stages. Even so, the generic list of barriers that have already been identified is long. At present, this list cannot be distilled into a small number of key factors because
- the relationships between the barriers are not well understood, and
- a comprehensive list of barriers is a useful reference for those encountering difficulties.

The list is long and detailed but efforts to consolidate somewhat minor barriers under major headings so far have resulted only in oversimplification of a very complex and difficult set of problems. Barriers may also be complex because they may be interrelated: the presence of one barrier increases the likelihood of finding, or leading to, another.

The barriers that arise in a specific situation depend on

- the environmental management tools being used,
- the circumstances in which the tool or system is used (setting, size of organization, organizational culture, formal and informal management styles, etc.),
- individuals involved in the process, and
- the stage of development of environmental management.

Barriers will also vary from industry to industry and country to country. The generic list of barriers can be used to identify factors that might impede environmental management, so problems can be anticipated, avoided, or minimized. Potential barriers should be identified as early in the environmental management process as possible and reviewed on an ongoing basis. Some barriers may remain hidden and only start to cause problems later in the project.

The following list has been developed from our direct experience with attempts to apply environmental management tools or to introduce Environmental Management Systems. That experience has been augmented by information from the literature on environmental management and anecdotal evidence from other practitioners.

We have found that consultants or employees sometimes continue to try to implement an EMS or apply one of the management tools (e.g., audits) against significant resistance. In those circumstances where time and energy is being spent on trying to force the issue rather than the implementation, the analysis of the barriers that might be impeding progress could identify approaches that would make life easier for everyone. On the other hand, some reluctance and skepticism is normal and should be expected. In some circumstances, slow progress may be all that can be expected if it is going to take time to increase awareness and make people more comfortable with the new concepts and management systems.

Barriers to Environmental Management

Table 4.1 provides a generic list of possible barriers to environmental management. The order of the list is not intended in any way to suggest the relative importance of the barrier nor the likelihood of encountering it. The process for using the generic list of barriers is shown in Figure 4.1

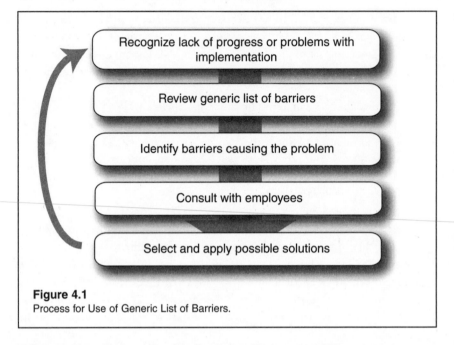

Figure 4.1
Process for Use of Generic List of Barriers.

Table 4.1 Generic List of Possible Barriers to Environmental Management

1. lack of recognition of the need for environmental management:
    • lack of awareness of Environmental Management Systems and tools,
    • lack of concern about environmental issues,
    • lack of understanding of specific environmental driving forces,
    • lack of commitment by senior management;
2. perceived cost of environmental management initiatives and underestimation of benefits:
    • no understanding of benefits and costs,
    • short-term financial thinking,
    • no amortization of costs over an appropriate period;
3. avoidance of the unknown and unfamiliar:
    • reluctance to change or innovate,
    • distrust of or lack of familiarity with, formal management systems,
    • the iterative nature of the process — preference for linear processes that have an end;
4. denial — ignore the problem and maybe it will go away;
5. crisis management — reactive not proactive management approach;
6. resistance to complexity — solutions have to be simple;

7. belief that current practice is adequate;

8. paper tigers — system looks good on paper but implementation is missing;

9. concerns about legal issues;

10. no delegated responsibility;

11. lack of skills, knowledge, and expertise;

12. lack of resources:
    - lack of funding,
    - lack of time,
    - higher priority assigned to other tasks,
    - lack of information on how to implement the EMS or tools,
    - no in-house expertise and no education and training;

13. reluctance to use external expertise (consultants);

14. lack of appropriate case studies and examples of success;

15. multiple stakeholders with conflicting interests;

16. application of inappropriate solutions:
    - poor advice,
    - oversimplifying the process,
    - making the process too complicated;

17. incompatibility with corporate culture;

18. isolation of environmental management from the rest of corporate structure — failure to integrate the EMS with the business plan;

19. lack of identification of specific environmental drivers affecting an organization;

20. loss of commitment by senior management;

21. negative attitudes of specialists;

22. territoriality;

23. employee resistance:
    - additional work with no benefits,
    - seen as a threat to security and advancement,
    - union resistance;

24. attempting to do too much too fast;

25. inappropriate timing of initiatives;

26. hidden agenda;

27. disorganized effort:
    - lack of planning for implementation,
    - lack of coherence in environmental policy,
    - corporate restructuring;

28. language and lack of communication;

29. unfavorable political climate; and

30. corruption.

BARRIERS ENCOUNTERED RECENTLY

Environmental Ideology or Idealism

Some environmental groups believe that management systems and tools are produced by industry and are unacceptable because they are designed to help industry, not primarily to protect the environment.

Rigid Bureaucracies and Guidelines

In some societies there are well-established bureaucracies that are responsible for setting guidelines for procedures and processes. These guidelines must be followed, even if they cause environmental damage and they are difficult to change.

Requests for Turnkey EMS

Clients request the consultant to design and implement an EMS on a turnkey basis — the consultant is expected to do all the work, independent of the client, and then turn over the working system. Such systems are generally doomed to failure because of lack of involvement of those who must operate the system.

Changes in the Champion

It is essential to have someone designated as the person responsible for the successful design, implementation, and operation of the EMS. Unfortunately, when such a person is very good at their job and their skill and knowledge is recognized, they sometimes are rewarded with a promotion, and the EMS then suffers for lack of leadership.

Failure to Recognize that Change is Going to be Slow

In some organizations, change is going to be slow and it may take five to ten years to finally achieve the changes necessary for a successful EMS. If the organization does not want to go through the radical upheaval that rapid change would require, then it might be necessary to accept a slow rate of change.

Failure to Keep up with Rapid Changes

The pace of change in environmental management is very rapid in some areas, and a good deal of time, money, and energy is required to keep up. When that is not possible, up-to-date systems are not possible.

Lack of Recognition of the Need for Environmental Management

A common barrier is lack of recognition of the need for environmental management. Lack of recognition may be related to

- being unaware of Environmental Management Systems or tools,
- lack of concern about environmental issues,
- lack of understanding of specific environmental driving forces, and
- lack of commitment by senior management.

This set of problems can be resolved through education and training, through analysis of driving forces to show senior management the benefits, or by outlining the exposure to risks that could threaten the corporation because it lacks an Environmental Management System. The big shock of an accident, a prosecution, or a near miss either to the corporation itself, or to a corporation that senior executives know, may be the factors that increase awareness and lead to understanding the need for an EMS and, subsequently, the commitment to build one.

The informal responsibility for dealing with this barrier often falls on those individuals who recognize the need for an EMS in an organization and want to try to increase awareness. Unfortunately, these individuals generally do not have the resources or the formal role within an organization to be effective.

Perceived Cost and Underestimation of Benefits

While many decision-makers are quick to associate environmental initiatives with cost, they are slow to recognize the benefits of the initiatives. Problems with the cost of environmental initiatives are usually related to three factors:

1. Limited experience — costs are higher where experience with the environmental management tool or EMS is limited and people using the tool or EMS are struggling up a learning curve.
2. Underestimation of benefits — the benefits that can be derived are generally underestimated. Effective environmental initiatives can result in three types of benefits:
   - direct savings, such as reduced costs of solid and hazardous waste disposal, energy, and water and savings in product losses (spills, etc.);
   - indirect savings, through improved community and stakeholder relations (image) and easier approvals; and
   - avoided (contingent) costs, such as fines, civil damages, legal costs, cleanup costs, and insurance premiums.
3. Benefits are recognized and reasonably estimated, but the costs of the initiative will appear to outweigh them.

The corporation might be preoccupied with short-term financial issues or financing and amortizing the costs of environmental initiatives may not be done over an appropriate time period. Large capital investments are impossible without proper financing and amortization. Similarly, the significant costs for an environmental initiative or EMS must be properly financed and amortized over the period that the investment in the EMS will provide benefits. For example, if design and implementation cost $50,000, that could look like a large expenditure in one year. However, if that cost were amortized over the five years that the EMS can be expected to provide benefits, then $10,000 per year would not be perceived as so expensive.

Avoidance of the Unknown and Unfamiliar

The ability of an organization to recognize the value of new, external information, assimilate it, and apply it to commercial ends is known as the organization's absorptive capacity.[1] This capacity appears to be largely related to prior knowledge. Applied to environmental management, the concept of absorptive capacity suggests that the introduction of an environmental initiative will be most difficult in organizations that have little knowledge about environmental management tools and systems.

If something is relatively unknown, the chance of it being tried depends on an organization's innovative capacity. *Innovators,* or those who are willing to try the unknown, are less common than *borrowers,* or those who follow already proven techniques. Rogers identified different levels of willingness to innovate in organizations (see Figure 4.2).[2] Kubr identified eight reasons for resistance to change in organizations: lack of conviction that change is needed; dislike of imposed change; dislike of surprises; fear of the unknown; reluctance to deal with unpopular issues; fear of inadequacy and failure; disturbed practices, habits, and relations; and lack of respect and trust in the person promoting change. He also noted the opposite problem of too much change, when managers suffer from chronic reorganization disease.[3]

Only a small proportion of organizations (less than 20 percent according to Rogers) will take the lead in implementing new concepts — the innovators and early adopters.

When attempting to introduce Environmental Management Systems and tools in circumstances where change appears to be difficult, it is recommended that efforts be made to find those individuals or units who have a positive attitude to change. Where attitudes indicate a reluctance to change (innovate), then strategies must be developed to show that others have already adopted such changes and benefited.

Innovation may be related not only to an organization's culture but also to business concerns. Innovation may be particularly difficult in the case of small and medium-sized companies where absorptive capacity is limited and where the failure of an innovation could result in the failure of the business.

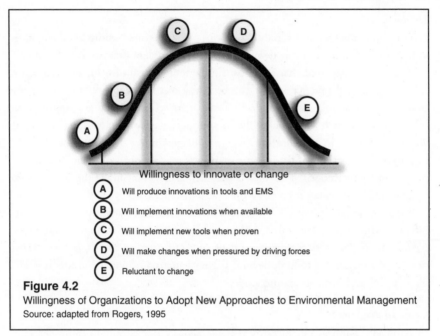

Figure 4.2
Willingness of Organizations to Adopt New Approaches to Environmental Management
Source: adapted from Rogers, 1995

Some environmental management tools are better known and more utilized than others. The most familiar tools include: environmental site assessment, environmental audits, and Environmental Impact Assessment. Other tools, such as environmental accounting, are less familiar, often because they are relatively new.

The best approach to reducing unfamiliarity, which can be a significant impediment to EMS introduction, is by providing carefully designed awareness and education programs including relevant examples of successful systems which stress EMS benefits.

Employees without education and training in formal management systems will often be reluctant to commit themselves to a new EMS in a corporate culture where existing hierarchies are not recognized as management systems, or where very strong top-down instructions obviate the need for a management system. Again, education and training, provision of reinforcing examples, and gradual change in corporate culture are required.

Due to education, personality, or corporate culture, some employees and institutions are more comfortable with linear systems that have a clearly identified starting point and end. The iterative nature of the continual improvement approach to implementation of an EMS introduces uncertainty and discomfort. Education and training, explaining the reason for using continual improvement, and giving employees time to gain an understanding and familiarity with the process may resolve this problem.

Denial

Environmental issues and suitable solutions are sometimes ignored because individuals or institutions simply deny that there is a problem that needs to be solved.

Pfeffer has suggested that the most fundamental reason for organizations not following rational practice is that the best way of managing falls outside of the point of view or focus of attention of managers.[4] Denial may also result from other processes, such as the belief that if you ignore a problem for long enough it will resolve itself. In organizations where managers move from position to position over short periods of time, some managers may ignore a problem in order to pass it on to a successor. This means that denial does not make the problem go away so much as makes it go away for that particular employee.

Environmental initiatives are often given a low priority by organizations because, while environmental initiatives usually involve short-term costs and long-term benefits, business performance is usually measured in the short-term. If an organization is unable to look beyond the next quarter's financial results it is not likely to be environmentally proactive.

Crisis Management

In corporate cultures where crisis management is the dominant approach, the longer-term issues of anticipating and avoiding environmental problems through the implementation of an EMS will be difficult. There could well be a commitment to change but it will be "as soon as we get the time," or "after we deal with the current crisis." Providing evidence of the benefits of responding proactively to driving forces, or examples of the costs of failure to do so, may reduce this barrier.

Resistance to Complexity

Although an important goal of environmental management tools is to assist in managing complex issues, individuals and organizations may, in fact, fear that environmental management will add to the complexity. Resistance to perceived complexity associated with environmental management may be particularly significant in small and medium-sized enterprises. Where they have control, these organizations tend to keep processes, products, and markets as simple as possible to match their limited capabilities. Environmental concerns, whether raised by business partners, governments, the market, ENGOs, the public, banks, investors, or other stakeholders, may be seen as unfamiliar, unnecessary, and unwelcome intrusions.

Belief that Current Practice is Adequate

Some managers may be optimistic about their company's environmental performance and believe that this performance needs no improvement.

Paper Tigers

Institutions sometimes are satisfied with producing an EMS on paper and see no need for implementation — the fact that it exists on paper is good enough.

Concerns About Legal Issues

Use of environmental management tools or the introduction of an EMS may result in the identification of issues with legal implications. For example, site assessments and audits may discover instances of non-compliance with regulations. Unnecessary fear of identifying legal issues may lead an organization to decide against using these tools.

Many jurisdictions in Canada and the United States have enacted legislation or developed policies to assure organizations that regulators will not prosecute companies on the basis of information discovered during environmental audits or investigations provided that the organization reports and deals with issues, as required under law, as soon as these issues are discovered.

Oregon passed the first environmental audit privilege law in the United States in 1993. A list of current privilege laws in the U.S. is available.[5]

Despite environmental privilege laws, many companies still feel that if they don't look for environmental problems, they won't have to deal with any. This approach is dangerous. Legal cases have established that companies must show due diligence in managing environmental responsibilities.

No Delegated Responsibility

Implementation of a significant environmental initiative may be difficult to accomplish when no one within an organization takes, or is given, responsibility for dealing with environmental matters. Problems may also occur when those responsible for environmental matters lack the resources or power to implement environmental initiatives. It has been widely recognized that new initiatives need champions within an organization.

Lack of Skills, Knowledge, and Expertise

An organization requries a minimum of skills, knowledge, and expertise to start designing and implementing an EMS or applying a particular environmental management tool such as an audit. Therefore, education and training about the EMS or the tool is a necessary prerequisite or corequisite for success. Early stages must include formal education and training programs to bring employees, especially those in critical positions, up to speed on the tasks before them. Consultants or outside education and training courses can accomplish this. Consultants are often necessary for successful implementation of an EMS because the required design and implementation skills are much more extensive and demanding than the skills required to operate an EMS once it is in place. However, the outside consultants cannot do it all by themselves.

Lack of Resources

Environmental initiatives can be hindered by management's failure to recognize or provide the necessary resources including money, time, and personnel to design, implement, and guide the initiative, money, and time. Resources may also cause problems if they are not properly allocated. Provision of inadequate resources may result from other barriers such as lack of commitment or prioritization of other company issues over environmental management.

Reluctance to Use External Expertise (Consultants)

When an organization requires the assistance of an outside consultant in introducing an environmental initiative, barriers may result from the client-consultant relationship. In discussing the psychology of clients, Kubr noted that there may be

- reluctance to admit that a consultant is needed,
- doubts about the consultant's competence and integrity,
- fear of becoming dependent on a consultant, and
- fear of excessive consulting fees.[6]

TOP TEN THINGS A CONSULTANT SHOULDN'T TELL A CLIENT

1. That was my first guess as well, but then I really thought about it.
2. You should see the hotel I'm staying at.
3. Hey, I just realized that I was in third grade when you started working here.
4. I like this office space. I'll have them put me in here when you're gone.
5. My rental car looks nicer than that junker you're driving.
6. Sure it'll work; I learned it in business school.
7. So what do you need me to tell you?
8. Of course it's right; the spreadsheet says so.
9. I could just tell you the answer, but we're committed to a three-month project.
10. And, the number one thing a consultant shouldn't tell a client: What are you, stupid?

TOP TEN THINGS YOU'LL NEVER HEAR FROM A CONSULTANT

1. You're right; we're billing way too much for this.
2. Bet you I can go a week without saying "synergy" or "value-added."
3. How about paying us based on the success of the project?
4. This whole strategy is based on a Harvard business case I read.
5. Actually, the only difference is that we charge more than they do.
6. I don't know enough to speak intelligently about that.
7. Implementation? I only care about writing long reports.
8. I can't take the credit. It was Ed in your marketing department.
9. The problem is, you have too much work for too few people.
10. Everything looks okay to me.

Excerpted by permission from *Hazardous Materials Management*

Lack of Case Studies and Examples of Success

Another barrier may occur when there is little information on, or analysis of, the application of environmental management tools or implementation of EMSs. In this case, an organization re-invents processes and is not able to learn from the experience of others. The lack of appropriate (or industry-specific) case studies also means that positive experiences in environmental management may not be properly recognized, thereby losing management's potential interest in, and commitment to, environmental management.

Multiple Stakeholders with Conflicting Interests

The success of an environmental initiative within an organization may be threatened when internal stakeholders have conflicting interests or views about the initiative.

All organizations may have important external stakeholders who present conflicting interests and demands. Local landowners, community groups, environmental groups, regulators (municipal, state/provincial, and federal), shareholders, investors, banks, suppliers, buyers, contractors, and partners may not see environmental issues (and initiatives) in the same way. As well, some environmental initiatives may not address stakeholder interests effectively and efficiently.

Application of Inappropriate Solutions

Problems can arise from attempts to apply a quick fix where a more involved solution is required, or from attempts to apply general solutions to specific cases. For example, some organizations may be tempted to apply an easy, but inappropriate, EMS instead of one that would meet their needs but would require greater effort in terms of time, money, or thought. Ashby's Law of Requisite Variety states that solutions to problems must match the complexity of the problems or else essential elements will not receive adequate attention.[7] Environmental issues pose complex problems for organizations. The approach to these issues must eventually be appropriately complex.

Inappropriate solutions could be advocated by consultants seeking to obtain work with promises that they can develop an initiative, such as an EMS, at low cost. Inappropriate solutions could also be proposed by individuals with little understanding of the environmental management tool or EMSs.

Organizations may also apply inappropriate solutions when they use templates of tools or an EMS without making necessary modifications. For example, audit protocols are not suitable if they are general and do not address environmental issues specific to their subject. Many templates of EMSs are now available, however, they often fail to meet the specific needs of organizations.

The application of an inappropriate tool or EMS can result in two negative effects. First, the organization involved usually becomes disenchanted with environmental management of any kind. Second, when stories of these mistakes circulate within an industry, resistance to the tool or EMSs within the industry increases.

Incompatibility With Corporate Culture

Studies have indicated that individuals and organizations tend to approach problem-solving using previously adopted methods.[8] Even some who advocate change as a device to overcome organizational inertia have concluded that radical shifts in organizational behavior may be difficult, if not impossible.[9] Therefore, environmental initiatives will be most effective if they are compatible with the culture of the organization in which they are being introduced.

Corporate culture can be defined by the shared values, management style, or prevailing attitudes within an organization. It is strongly influenced by the selection processes of hiring and advancement, education and training (or lack thereof), the reception or rejection of ideas, and by strong or dominant personalities. There is a strong positive relationship between innovation success and its compatibility with the corporate climate.[10]

Compatibility of an environmental initiative with corporate culture may be important in order to reduce dissonance for both organizational decision-makers and the organization itself. For example, an EMS that radically changes the way things are done may be perceived by decision-makers and other employees as a criticism of their work and meet with poor participant buy-in. Bacharach et al noted that "theories of cognitive consistency have maintained that parties often seek to avoid or reduce inconsistency even if this reduces the potential for utility maximization."[11] In other words, even if an environmental initiative will assist an organization, it may be implemented poorly if it is inconsistent with corporate culture.

Dissonance with corporate culture can be anticipated to be more significant the larger the scope of the environmental initiative. Therefore, dissonance is most critical in the case of EMSs and large environmental initiatives but may not be important for minor environmental initiatives.

Isolation of Environmental Management from the Rest of the Corporate Structure

An environmental management initiative may fail if it is not integrated with other management activities. Environmental issues are closely related to other organizational issues, such as operations, finances, profitability, and overall management. If an environmental management initiative does not interact with appropriate segments of the organization, it will, at the very least, be less effective than it could be otherwise. At the worst, an isolated initiative may not succeed.

Lack of Identification of Specific Environmental Drivers Affecting an Organization

Not identifying the specific environmental drivers affecting an organization — that is, the forces that affect an organization's need for environmental management — can result in underestimating the need for, and potential benefits of, environmental management. Resources may be wasted on issues that are of relatively little importance rather than being allocated where environmental performance can be enhanced. If problems are misunderstood, the solutions that are developed for them will be ineffective.

Loss of Commitment by Senior Management

While current models for environmental management, such as ISO 14001, recognize that environmental management involves commitment, they do not address problems related to obtaining and maintaining commitment. Without commitment, environmental management may not be initiated, resources may be inadequate, environmental management initiatives may be abandoned, or they may become an ineffective paper exercise.

Loss of commitment is liable to be more of a concern for large-scale environmental initiatives. It is easier to maintain commitment over a short period of time (for example, for a site audit) than over a longer time period (for example, for an EMS). Loss of commitment to an EMS during its design and implementation has, unfortunately, sometimes occurred. Individuals who provide the initial commitment to an EMS may lose interest in, and commitment to, introducing an EMS when they become fully aware of what is required. While continual improvement is required to allow the EMS to improve and adapt to change, iteration may be misunderstood and taken as a sign of system failure rather than strength.

Commitment may change if an organization, industry, or the economy suffers a downturn. Commitment may also be lost if the commitment is shallow and the organization shifts easily from solution to solution. Managers must be careful of fads from the latest management guru, because the time to implement it may be longer than the shelf life of the fad. Large-scale changes require several years to take hold within an organization. "When changes sink down deeply into the culture, which for an entire company can take three to ten years, new approaches are fragile and subject to regression."[12]

Negative Attitudes of Specialists

In some instances, specialists from other departments or units in the organization, who have little or no understanding of, or sympathy for, environmental management concerns, control or make decisions about information or resources that are critical to improved environmental performance. If they have negative attitudes to environmental management, then barriers will exist, because their cooperation and agreement to provide resources and/or information are crucial for success. The negative attitudes arise when specialists are unaware and unconvinced of the value of improved environmental management, when they hold narrow perspectives that do not include environmental goals and objectives, or when their educational backgrounds have led them to believe that environmental protection and conservation of resources is an option that they don't have to take seriously. If their backgrounds and attitudes are such that they believe that environmental concerns are an unnecessary expense, or too low a priority for attention, then progress will be delayed or stopped. For example, because environmental issues are poorly integrated into the majority of MBA programs in North America, the majority of MBA students are rarely exposed to environmental management issues and may conclude that the issues are unimportant.[13]

When this barrier is encountered, either the specialists must be convinced to change by persuasive arguments or pressure from senior officials, or ways must be found to move around them.

Territoriality

Territoriality is the tendency to guard one's territory and not let outsiders make changes or require changes. It results in resistance or reluctance to provide information, participate in processes, or cooperate in initiatives originating outside the unit. Territoriality can be overridden by instructions from senior officials. Convincing managers who are guarding their territory that improved environmental management was their idea is another means of getting around the problem.

Employee Resistance

Employee resistance can arise from four factors. In many cases, the additional work that an EMS, audit, or other environment management tool might impose is seen as an unacceptable burden by employees who are already very busy and under stress. This can become an issue of lack of resources, if overworked employees are expected to take on additional responsibilities. Employees may be also protecting their territory from an invasion by people who are providing unwanted assistance. Introduction of new procedures, especially those that seem to increase accountability and reporting of problems, could be seen as a threat to security and advancement. In some cases, unions may resist improvement in environmental management, but, for the most part, unions in North America and Europe have supported such initiatives.

Attempting Too Much Too Fast

In those cases where implementation of initiatives is set at too fast a pace, employees will not be able to achieve the goals and objectives, and/or mistakes will be made. In either case, the pace will have to be slowed to one that will improve the chances for success.

Inappropriate Timing of Initiatives

If there has not been adequate preparation for environmental initiatives, or if the corporate culture is set against proposed changes, then it might not be an appropriate time for change.

Hidden Agenda

On occasion, progress is slow, or change seems to be impossible, without any apparent reason. Perhaps there are important but concealed goals and objectives — a hidden agenda — that senior managers and others want to accomplish besides improved environmental management. They may want to paint the surface of the institution green without making any substantial changes in order to satisfy, or appear to satisfy external stakeholders. These hidden agendas develop when corporations make a shallow commitment to improved environmental management, when relatively independent units decide not to make needed changes, when employees decide to continue with old processes and procedures, or when there are conflicts between elements of corporate strategy or policy (incoherence).

When a hidden agenda is suspected as the barrier, the alternatives are to uncover the hidden agenda and change it, continue with a new strategy to change the hidden agenda without uncovering it, by proving the advantages of the EMS, or bail out and find something else to do.

Disorganized Effort

There are four reasons for disorganization which leads to failure of environmental management initiatives. One reason is lack of adequate planning for implementation, due to failure to understand what is required for success. Another is too great haste. A third is environmental policy that is not internally consistent, or is inconsistent with other, higher priority policies, especially short-term profits. We see a fourth reason for initiatives failing or progressing very slowly: they are attempted when the organization is being restructured. As internal units, roles, responsibilities, and lines of communication changed and were out of the control of environmental managers, the instability and uncertainty created significant difficulties.

Language and Lack of Communication

Where language problems exist, well-qualified translators must be available, terminology must be established in all languages used by personnel, employees must be educated about the new terms, and effective communications systems must be established. For example, using a corporate website is of little use to employees who are not computer literate and who do not have access to the web. Newsletters in a language that they cannot read are of little help.

Unfavorable Political Climate

In some jurisdictions the political climate, at whatever level, can be such that improved environmental management is not viewed favorably because politicians think that it is unnecessary and/or too expensive, or they are operating on an outmoded development model which dictates that economic growth must come first, and then the environmental mess will be cleaned up.

Corruption

Where corruption exists, environmental initiatives may be difficult.

Strategies to Overcome Barriers

Due to the complexity of the barriers and the variability of organizations, no one set of solutions can be developed for overcoming barriers to environmental management. A number of strategies may, however, be considered and applied where appropriate. Nine of these are outlined below.

Strategy — Identify the Environmental Driving Forces Affecting the Organization

While it seems obvious that an important factor in using environmental management tools or developing an EMS should be an understanding of what needs are to be met, organizations may not, in fact, know what these needs are. Identification and analysis of the environmental driving forces (chapter 3) affecting an organization allows for their use in obtaining the commitment to develop an environmental initiative. Particular needs will determine some of the specific elements that should be included in the EMS. Identification and analysis of the driving forces and, by implication, identification of the actors and participants are also necessary to identify the savings that are possible and the costs which could be avoided through improved environmental performance.

Strategy — Make the Business Case

It may be important to prove that improved environmental management is now part of normal business practice because it provides significant benefits to the financial strength of the corporation. The business case for improved environmental performance on an industry by industry basis is essential.

Strategy — Educate, Train, and Communicate

Barriers to environmental management can arise from lack of understanding or knowledge. Education and training are, therefore, important factors for success. (see chapter 9.) Effective communication is required to convey information and knowledge where it is needed. (see chapter 20.)

Strategy — Align the EMS with the Organization

Dissonance among environmental management, the organization, decision-makers, and employees can be avoided by aligning environmental management initiatives with the organization's culture and formal management structure. Cultural alignment can be facilitated by discussing company values and the way things are done through interviewing employees and involving them in planning and implementation. For example, an EMS can be meshed with the organizational structure by aligning the EMS with existing programs (such as health and safety or a quality program — IOS 9000) or by designing elements of the EMS using other successful programs within the company as models (incremental or model unit strategy, chapter 5).

Strategy — Phase in the Introduction of Environmental Management

Phasing in environmental management may overcome barriers involving lack of recognition of the value of environmental management and limited resources. Part of this strategy would be to start with relatively easy aspects with high potential for savings, and then move on to more difficult, less lucrative phases (incremental strategy, chapter 5).

While the full benefits of environmental management will not be realized until all the necessary elements of an EMS are in place, staging allows a company to start to do something. If a few environmental tools or elements of an EMS are successfully introduced and benefits are recognized, resistance to other elements of environmental management may be overcome.

Strategy — Encourage Employee Acceptance of Environmental Management Initiatives

Employee acceptance of environmental management is critical because employees may, consciously or unconsciously, sabotage environmental management initiatives. Acceptance may be facilitated through education, training (chapter 9), and communication with the employees (chapter 20), and the employees' participation in the use of a tool or the design and implementation of the EMS. Employee acceptance of environmental management will be greater where the tool or EMS fits the organizational culture. Attention to job descriptions, performance evaluation, and rewards is also important. Where inappropriate behavior cannot be changed, (re)moving the employee may be the best option.

Strategy — Identify Required Resources

Identifying required resources (time, money, personnel, training, etc.) for significant environmental initiatives is absolutely essential to ensure that initiatives can be carried out. Failure to identify, or underestimation of, necessary resources can lead to the delay or failure of an initiative. Overemphasis on costs should be avoided, so it is important to identify benefits and amortize the investment.

Strategy — Share Resources

Introduction of complex environmental initiatives, such as EMSs, may be especially challenging for organizations with limited resources. One way of mitigating the cost barrier is for companies to share resources. This may be done through the use of experienced outside consultants, assistance from industry associations, and sharing resources among organizations with similar needs. As a European Union regulation, Ecosystem Management Auditing Scheme requires larger organizations to assist small and medium-sized organizations with environmental management system development. (ISO 14001 does not include this requirement.) Large companies requiring ISO 14001 registration for suppliers in their purchasing guidelines often assist with education and training programs.

Organizations can also reduce their costs by cooperating with like-minded companies to share consultants (for example, combining resources to hire a consultant to design and implement an appropriate EMS) or by sharing an employee who would otherwise be too expensive for one company. Where consultants are hired to solve environmental problems, attention should be paid to having the consultant educate and train staff where appropriate.

A third option is to use cooperative study programs and graduate students for assistance where qualifications, abilities, and supervision make this possible. Given universities' increasing willingness to innovate, an increasing interest in appropriate co-op programs for graduate students, and partnerships with members of a university's community, this option is being strengthened. It offers distinct advantages to both parties of the partnership.

Strategy - Identify Innovators and Early Adopters

As was noted previously, it has been estimated that fewer than 20 percent of companies (or key individuals within those companies) are willing to take the lead in implementing new concepts. It is important to identify organizations and individuals that are willing to lead so that they can be the focus in promoting newer environmental management tools or Environmental Management Systems.

Recommended Further Reading

Garcia, P., J. Gonzales, and D. Thompson. "Driving Forces and Barriers to Implementing Sound Environmental Management in the Andean Region of Latin America." In *Growing Pains: Environmental Management in Developing Countries,* edited by W. Wehremeyer and Y. Mulugetta. Sheffield, U.K.: Greenleaf Publishing, 1999, pp. 132-147.

Kirkland, L.H., and D. Thompson. "Challenges in Designing, Implementing and Operating an Environmental Management System." *Business Strategy and the Environment* 8, no. 2 (1999): pp.128-143.

Pfeffer, J. "When It Comes to 'Best Practices' — Why Do Smart Organizations Occasionally Do Dumb Things?" *Organizational Dynamics* (summer1996): pp. 33-43.

von Hippel, E. *The Sources of Innovation.* New York: Oxford University Press, 1988.

Websites, Newsletters, and Organizations

No website, newsletter, or organization which addresses barriers to environmental management directly and explicitly has been identified. Some of the sources cited in chapter 2 (Environmental Management Systems) do so indirectly and implicitly.

CHAPTER 5

STRATEGIC
ENVIRONMENTAL MANAGEMENT

Dixon Thompson

STRATEGIC ENVIRONMENTAL MANAGEMENT is a set of processes that helps senior management address environmental issues and involves

- establishing policies and setting goals and objectives, or endorsing them, if the details are delegated to other employees and consultants;
- supervising implementation of actions to achieve goals and objectives;
- receiving feedback on success;
- making appropriate adjustments to improve performance;
- anticipating and avoiding problems; and
- scanning the external environment.

Strategies address the questions about where the organization is going (forecasting), where it wants to go (forecasting and backcasting), and how it gets there from here. Environmental managers need to understand the wide range of possible definitions to be able to recognize how strategy is defined in the organizations they work with. If environmental managers try to operate on the basis of a strategy that is significantly different from that of the rest of the organization, they will need an effective strategy to accommodate that difference or difficulties will arise.

Pearce and Robinson define strategic management as

> [t]he set of decisions and actions that result in the design and activation of strategies to achieve the objectives of the organization. It is the large-scale, future-oriented plan for interacting with the competitive environment to achieve company objectives. In a large organization, actions take place at three levels: corporate (headquarters), business (business unit), and functional (operations).[1]

Handy asserts that "diagnosis lies at the heart of effective management"[2] and defines strategy as a plan of action for allocating resources.[3] Peter Schwartz defines strategy as "setting priorities for the company's long-term development" and notes that it is a tragedy if it is left to specialists who do not communicate the strategy to the rest of the organization.[4] The Institute of Environmental Management held a set of best-practice workshops and published the results, one of which is *Being strategic: Building skills to manage for the future.*[5] Mason, Roper, and Porter present arguments for integrating environmental issues into corporate strategy.[6] Mintzberg has a definition that stresses the pattern of actions and four other views of strategy — a plan, a ploy, a position, or a perspective.[7]

If anyone were led to believe that a tidy definition could be found, Mintzberg, Ahlstrand, and Lampel outline four things that strategy does: strategy sets direction, focuses efforts, defines the organization and provides consistency.[8] They then provide seven areas of general agreement about strategy:
- It concerns both the organization and its changing environment.
- It is complex and dynamic.
- It affects the welfare of the organization.
- It involves process and content.
- It is not purely deliberate.
- It exists on different levels.
- It involves conceptual and analytical thought processes.

They also describe ten different schools of strategic management, having distinct characteristics, strengths and weaknesses:
- design school — process of conception
- planning school — formal process
- positioning school — analytical process
- entrepreneurial school — visionary process
- cognitive school — mental process
- learning school — emergent process
- power school — negotiation process
- cultural school — collective process
- environmental school — reactive process (here environment is the external environment, not social and biophysical)
- configuration school — transformation process.

In most successful organizations, corporate environmental strategy would have the following characteristics, or should be striving to develop them:
- Strategy is dynamic, because of changing driving forces and the requirement for continual improvement.
- Strategy deals with the big picture and does not get bogged down in detail (tactics), therefore documents must be relatively short.
- Strategy must match the variety of the system under its control because Ashbey's Law of Requisite Variety dictates that control can only be

obtained if the variety of the controller is at least as great as the variety of the situation being controlled[9] — if the management strategy is overly simple, then something important can be missed.

• Strategy is proactive and designed to anticipate and avoid problems.
• Environmental management strategy is integrated with corporate strategy.
• Strategy sets policy, goals, and objectives, the vision, and mission for the organization.
• Strategy has to be effectively implemented.
• Strategy provides feedback on achieving (or failing) to meet goals and objectives so that appropriate adjustments can be made.
• Strategy involves accountability.
• Strategy involves scanning the external environment so that there are fewer surprises and pitfalls.
• Strategy provides the organization with resilience if it is caught by surprise.

The 1996 Institute for Environmental Management (IEM) survey showed that environmental managers have a key role to play in overall corporate strategy:

> "...many members are now turning to the longer term, projecting future trends, and helping steer their organizations to successfully ride them. Although too many people still resist the fact that the stability of their organization ultimately depends on being in balance with the natural environment and resource base, there is no getting away from the fact that it does — and it is the environmental manager who is best placed to interpret what this does, or might, mean for the business. The environmental manager as overseer of the organization's day-to-day environmental management processes and as the individual who is best informed about the issues is ideally placed to guide the organization's management towards a sustainable future."[10]

Environmental managers must also be able to recognize the characteristics of ineffective strategies. If the strategy is an unread document on someone's shelf, then it cannot have the desirable characteristics listed above. Having no strategy is, in fact, a strategy by default — and likely that of the laggards in Roger's innovation curve (see Figure 4.1). Reactive, ad hoc strategies are characteristic of the late adopters in Roger's curve, and would not be used by leading-edge organizations or those striving for that position.

Environmental managers may find strategic environmental management intimidating, especially if they do not have much experience with the skills and knowledge required, or if the seriousness of the decisions (the future of the organization) and the "altitude" bother them. As with mountaineering, a healthy respect for high places makes good sense. If they are not intimidated by the seriousness of the risks and the exposure, then they don't really know what's going on and shouldn't be there. However, environmental managers cannot avoid involvement in strategic issues, so they should obtain the necessary education and training, seek the assistance of a mentor with experience and confidence, and build a team with appropriate skills or work with other strategists in the organization to have a team formed. With skills, knowledge, and mentor (guide) and a competent team, the intimidating nature of strategic environmental management will be reduced, but will not likely be eliminated.

Strategic Planning and Strategic Management.

Planning can be defined as a process of preparing a multifaceted set of alternatives from which to select actions for the future. Plans are directed at setting and achieving goals by preferred means. These activities and attributes are much like what has been defined and described as strategic management. Planning has much to offer managers, and managers do make and implement plans. However, while planning is part of strategic management it often lacks three essential characteristics of effective strategic management. (1) Planning is not always clear about the process of setting goals and objectives, at times because those are set by others in a political process. (2) Planning does not require feedback to ensure that goals and objectives are being met. (3) The relationships between planners and those who implement plans are different from that of effective managers, who are in touch with and involved with those who implement strategies. That is, planners make plans and pass them on to others for implementation.

Mintzberg is particularly critical of strategic planning: "The most successful strategies are visions, not plans."[11] Hambrick and Fredrickson agree: "Strategy is primarily not about planning. It is about intentional, informed, and integrated choices."[12]

Environmental managers have to understand the planning process and be able to make plans. Therefore, they should at least be able to recognize the basic types of planning and their general advantages and disadvantages. Three approaches to planning are strong on theory but weak on implementation: rational/comprehensive, process (consultation, negotiation, dialogue, building relationships), and normative (values). Three other approaches are weaker on theory but are more practical when it comes to implementation: disjointed/incremental, blueprint, and functional. At the beginning of the process, assuming that there are time and resources, managers should use a comprehensive, rational approach, which includes dialogue with stakeholders and consideration of values. However, plans that are comprehensive become too big, and consultation and dialogue, especially about values, can go on forever. So at some point, we have to stop talking, crawl out of the hot tub, dry off, and change to the more practical aspects of specific blue prints dealing with issues at a functional level. This hierarchy is followed in strategic management and carried out at three levels in larger organizations: corporate executives, the business units, and operations, with feedback linking them.

Strategic Environmental Management in Smaller Organizations

Smaller organizations do not have elaborate, formal environmental management strategies, nor should they. However, smaller organizations still require strategies with similar attributes to the desirable characteristics listed above. They need fewer formal processes for setting goals and objectives, selecting and implementing means of achieving them, obtaining feedback, and keeping track of events in the external environment. As Schwartz notes, in a small organization everyone can and should be involved in developing strategy — or at least some of it — because they will be partly responsible for successful implementation.[13]

Beyond Pollution Prevention and Eco-efficiency, on to The Triple Bottom Line, Corporate Social Responsibility, and Sustainable Development

Corporate environmental management strategies that focus on legal and regulatory compliance, pollution abatement, and resource efficiency are acceptable but a long way from the leading edge. Corporate goals and objectives now regularly go beyond controlling environmental impacts and improving efficiency. Corporations respond to driving forces (chapter 3) and establish environmental policy (chapter 6) that includes commitments to the triple bottom line, sustainable development, corporate social responsibility, and one or more of the numerous environmental codes of conduct. They have to incorporate those factors into the corporate environmental management strategy, and there have to be realistic ways of meeting those goals and objectives and of providing feedback on success. Even if a corporation only fulfills the basic requirements for an Environmental Management System (chapter 2), then strategies must set goals and objectives and meet the requirements for continual improvement.

Managers responsible for strategic environmental management must understand the fundamentals of the set of environmental management tools because that set of tools will be used to define the problems, anticipate and avoid problems, and implement the environmental strategy.

Tools for Strategic Environmental Management

Environmental managers have a set of tools for developing strategies: environmental scanning, benchmarking, forecasting, and backcasting. In each of these, managers use imagination, information, and judgement to try to see into the future (see Figure 5.1).

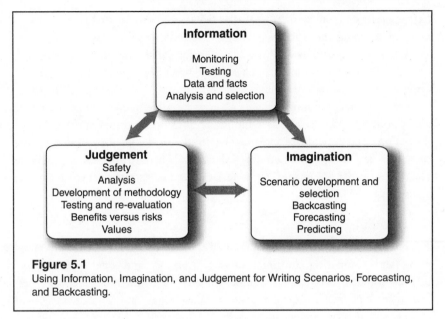

Figure 5.1
Using Information, Imagination, and Judgement for Writing Scenarios, Forecasting, and Backcasting.

Environmental Scanning

A critical role for environmental strategists is keeping track of what is happening in the external environment and what is likely to happen, as it relates to the corporation's interests in, and impacts on, the social and biophysical environment. Environmental scanning includes using those tools explicitly designed to anticipate and avoid problems — especially environmental audits (chapter 8), risk management (chapter 10), EIA (chapter 14), product and technology assessment (chapter 17), and human factors (chapter 21). Environmental scanning should take maximum advantage of the sources of information that are available through environmental communications (chapter 20).

Stafford Beer's cybernetic model for corporate management is complex but has a great deal of appeal.[14] He turned to biological models to find practical ways to manage complex systems more effectively. The human body is a very complex set of interacting systems, and yet we remain unaware of most of that activity. Think of what life would be like if it were necessary to monitor our sympathetic and parasympathetic nervous systems to keep track of how all our internal organs and functions were working. Our brain would be flooded with so much background noise from monitoring internal activities that we couldn't pay attention to our senses. Only because those systems function without our being conscious of them (unless something goes wrong) are we able to focus our attention on the outside world using our senses. The outside world is where threats and opportunities arise. Similarly, the strategic management system of the corporation must be designed to focus at least as much on external activities as on internal activities. The importance of scanning the external environment could be overstressed, but not by much. Avoiding surprises and pitfalls is a major concern for corporate strategy, and scanning the environment and keeping in touch with stakeholders are critical activities for staying out of trouble.

Environmental scanning looks for changes in pubic opinion; announcements and actions by ENGOs; activities and innovations by trend-setting corporations, institutions, and individuals; and emerging legislation domestically or in countries that show leadership on environmental issues. When environmental scanning identifies or predicts a change, strategies or other management activities must be adjusted appropriately.

Benchmarking

A benchmark is a criterion or reference point. Benchmarking is a process of measuring and comparing an organization's processes and operations against best-of-class in order to inspire improvement.[15] Benchmarking identifies performance shortfalls in comparison to other organizations that excel and encourages corrective actions to improve performance.

Crognale defines a benchmark as "(1) A permanent reference mark fixed in the ground for use in surveys, tidal observations, etc.; and (2) A reference point serving as a standard for copying or judging other things. (Webster's Dictionary)"[16]

Benchmarking is designed to find ways to improve performance; it is not just a comparison for comparison's sake. It must use more than one indicator for comparison, unless that one indicator was specifically selected as the sole purpose of a very focused benchmarking exercise. It is not the same as comparisons with standards that determine if institutions have met minimum requirements, such as accreditation of academic institutions by professional organizations, or with international standards such as ISO 14001 EMS, by environmental audits.

Benchmarking is an important tool for traditionally or conventionally structured or defined organizations in industries or activities, where there are similar organizations with varying levels of performance. Benchmarking will not work across the board for organizations that are innovative or that have unique characteristics because there will not be a suitable cohort available for comparison. If such organizations do a benchmarking exercise and compare themselves to institutions that do not share their unique characteristics then the value of the innovative attributes could be lost because they might be left out of the results of the comparison and improvements might be focused elsewhere. The purpose of benchmarking is not to impose uniformity; it must not be used to stifle innovation.

Requirements for effective benchmarking:

1. careful preparation and commitment — funding, education, and training about benchmarking and a well-qualified consultant;
2. a set of criteria for evaluation of performance;
3. a benchmark against which to compare performance; .
4. comparison of performance against the benchmark to find areas requiring improvement;
5. selection of areas for improvement; and
6. implementation of improvements.

As with most management systems and tools, the preparation phase is critical. Without commitment, funding, a clear understanding of the purpose of the exercise, education and training, and probably a qualified consultant, benchmarking is not likely to succeed.

Based upon the stated purpose of the benchmarking process, a set of criteria to be used in the comparison must be defined (see chapter 12, Environmental Indicators). Possible criteria:

• administratively simple
• cost effective
• appropriate level of detail
• responsive to change
• widely accepted, objective methodology
• not easily manipulated or misused
• does not distort goals and objectives
• suitable for comparison

There are four possible sources of best-practice or best-of-class for comparisons:

• an existing set of data from an organization (industry organization such as the Global Environmental Management Initiative (GEMI);[17]
• purchased through a consultant;[18]
• the performance of similar organizations in benchmarking partnership; or
• theoretical best-practice, developed from codes of conduct, aggregation of best-practices from surveys, conferences, etc.

Each of the four sources has inherent strengths and weaknesses. Appropriate industry organizations do not always have the data for comparison in benchmarking. When consultants have built a database for benchmarking, it can be expensive. Use of partnerships assumes that suitable partners are available and that the information needed for comparison can be shared. Best-practice surveys and codes of conduct may not have enough detail for benchmarking.

If the data for the individual organization has been gathered and there is a benchmark for comparison, the comparison should be rather straightforward. The comparison will reveal those areas in which the institution falls short of the best-practice or best-of-class. Given limited resources, the organization selects those strategic or priority areas for which improvements will be designed and implemented and proceeds with implementation.

Indicators (chapter 12) are becoming standardized or formalized (e.g., eco-efficiency,[19] toxic releases in the U.S.A. and Canada), and so benchmarking will be easier to use. Benchmarking will be encouraged as reporting becomes routine, required by legislation, or encouraged by government policies. There are more than 40 codes of conduct related to corporate social and environmental responsibilities. As more and more companies adhere to the codes and publish results proving that they do so, benchmarking will become more routine. Finally, as competition increases among corporations for markets or public institutions' resources, benchmarking will be recognized as a means of gaining competitive advantage and will be used by organizations to gain that edge. GEMI, in particular, is encouraging the use of benchmarking as a strategic element in their mission of business helping business.[20]

Strategy Involves Predicting the Future

Strategy uses information about the past and the present to try to anticipate and avoid problems in the future and identify and implement actions to reach a desirable future. Prediction of the future is uncertain, imperfect, and fraught with difficulties. Feedback on reliability of predictions and for updating them is therefore essential.

Predictions for the future can be made using a variety of techniques differing in complexity and expense: environmental scanning — looking for trends, patterns, and indicators of possible changes; trend extrapolation (the future will be like the past, at least in the short term); modeling; cross-impact analysis; and forecasting and backcasting.

Scenarios are a forecasting technique. The use of scenarios generally involves three or more possible scenarios: worst case, plausible worst case, business as usual, optimistic, conditional (particular problems, opportunities, or alternatives), etc. Peter Schwartz's *The Art of the Long View* includes a User's Guide: How to Hold a Strategic Conversation, an Appendix: Steps to Developing Scenarios, and Scenario Building: Select Bibliography.[21] These resources should help practitioners. However, practice, experience, a vivid imagination tempered by a healthy level of skepticism, and the guidance of a mentor are essential for developing the skills of this art.

Backcasting is a variation of forecasting that involves creating a scenario for a desirable future and then determining the steps required to end up at that point in the future rather than some other. Its advantage over forecasting is that, rather than predicting what the future will be, it describes a desirable future state and determines the actions necessary to arrive there.

For example, it is possible to determine trends and make forecasts about energy sources and consumption in the future. However, it is also possible to decide what sort of energy future would be desirable and then determine what would have to be done to ensure that we achieve the desired future. Backcasting defines specific roles or actions for stakeholders that can be used to discuss what would be needed to make that particular future a reality.

Forecasting attempts to describe possible futures when current strategy is applied under specified constraints and assumptions.

Backcasting describes a desirable future, likely constraints and assumptions, and then develops an appropriate strategy to reach that future. It is a process for developing a set of long-term objectives and targets and then developing and implementing strategies to achieve them.

Delphi Technique

Delphi (from the Oracle at Delphi) is a technique for producing information about possible futures but it can be expensive and time-consuming. In general terms, it involves selecting a group of experts for a particular topic. They must have appropriate, diverse disciplines and backgrounds, in order to try to avoid a herd mentality. Honorariums, if not consulting fees, are paid to get the time and full attention of busy people. A carefully designed set of questions is prepared, distributed, and the results collated but kept anonymous. The responses can be obtained by written survey, interviews, or computer conferencing. Opinions that differ from the consensus are highlighted. In some cases those who differ from the consensus are asked the reasons for the differences. The results are circulated for a second round of responses and the results again collated. More iterations can be carried out if time and money permit and if improvements are expected. The Delphi technique is out of favor and out of practice. However, given the extremely complex nature of environmental problems facing corporations and society perhaps a version of Delphi could be used to produce a consensus on the nature of the problems, approaches to them, and insights on possible innovative ways of dealing with them.

Corporate Governance.

Because the board of directors and senior corporate officers have responsibility for corporate strategy, the issue of corporate governance must be raised. In Canada, the board of directors is responsible for overseeing an organization's strategic direction, ensuring effective succession planning, evaluating risks, monitoring performance, and assuring the integrity of financial reports. Effective board governance contributes to improved organizational performance. Major international organizations such as the Organization for Economic Cooperation and Development, the International Monetary Fund, the European Bank for Reconstruction and Development, and national governments, such as Canada's, have codes or definitive statements of governance principles.[22]

It is clear that boards of directors are responsible for environmental management strategy, evaluating environmental risks, monitoring environmental performance, and ensuring that financial reports correctly disclose environmental liabilities and assets.

These issues could affect how corporate policy is formulated and implemented through corporate strategy:

- How are board members selected?
- What is the make-up of the board?
- Is there a job description for the chair and are the duties and responsibilities of the members clearly defined?
- What is the balance between short-term profits and long-term stability and corporate social responsibility?
- Is the board responsible to both shareholders and the society(ies) within which they operate?
- Does the method for compensating the members place too much emphasis on maximizing short-term profits?
- Is there an environment committee of the board that meets regularly, receives regular reports on corporate environmental performance, and recommends corporate environmental management strategy to the board?
- Do board members, especially those on the environment committee, receive regular briefings or seminars to keep them up to date on Environmental Management Systems and environmental management tools, so that they can exercise their environmental responsibilities effectively?

Corporate Strategy and Environmental Strategy

It should be obvious that a strategy to protect the environment and conserve resources is required. That strategy can include elements of keeping the organization out of trouble (what are the potential risks and threats?) but also identify opportunities provided by environmental issues. Corporate strategy and environmental strategy must be compatible and congruent, but identifying and removing conflicts and incompatibilities can be difficult. Corporate strategy could be based upon the assumption that environmental matters are an expensive imposition that must be tolerated. In that case, an environmental strategy that is designed to show that improved environmental performance is an invest-ment and an activity that uncovers opportunities will not be compatible with corporate strategy. Strategies and tactics would have to be designed and imple-mented to convince corporate strategists of the advantages of a revised corporate environmental management strategy.

Recommended Further Reading

Camp, R. *Business Process Benchmarking*. Milwaukee, Wisconsin: ASQC Quality Press, 1995.

Corporate Environmental Strategy (journal from Elsevier)

Crognale, G., ed. *Environmental Management Strategies: The 21st Century Perspective*. Prentice Hall PRT Environmental Management and Engineering Series, vol. 5. Upper Saddle River, New Jersey: Prentice Hall, 1999.

Global Environmental Management Initiative (GEMI). *Benchmarking: the Primer. Benchmarking for Continuous Environmental Improvement*. Washington DC: GEMI, 1994. Available at <www.gemi.org>

Hacker, M., and B. Kleiner. "12 Steps to Better Benchmarking," *Industrial Management* 42, no.2 (2000): pp. 20-23.

Schwartz, P. *The Art of the Long View: Planning for the Future in an Uncertain World: Paths to Strategic Insight for Yourself and Your Company*. Toronto: Currency Doubleday, 1996. pp. 219-220.

Strategic Management Journal (Strategic Management Society)

Wilson, G., and D. Sasseville. *Sustaining Environmental Management Success: Best Business Practices from Industry Leaders*. New York: Wiley, 1999.

Websites

Canadian Democracy and Corporate Accountability Commission:
    <www.corporate-accountability.ca>

Strategic Management Society: <www.smsweb.org>

CHAPTER

ENVIRONMENTAL POLICY

Dixon Thompson

THE INTERNATIONAL ORGANIZATION FOR STANDARDIZATION (ISO) defines environmental policy as a statement by the organization of its intentions and principles on its overall environmental performance, setting out environmental objectives and targets and providing a framework for action.[1]

Section 4.2 of ISO 14001 requires that an environmental policy

- be appropriate for the nature, scale, and the environmental impacts of the organization's activities, products, and services;
- include a commitment to continual improvement;
- include a commitment to pollution prevention;
- make a commitment to comply with all relevant legislation and regulation;
- make a commitment to meet other requirements to which the organization subscribes;
- provide a framework for setting and reviewing (auditing) environmental objectives and targets;
- be fully documented;
- be effectively implemented and maintained;
- be communicated to all employees; and
- be available to the public.

The ISO definition is used here because of the developing strength of the ISO 14001 standard. However, it presents several difficulties. The words goals, objectives, and policies are used differently in North America and Europe. The ISO definitions arose from the BS7750 EMS standard and so the policy is the overall statement. Section 3.7 of ISO 14001 defines an environmental objective as an overall environmental goal arising from the environmental policy. The detailed set of scientific, technical, and engineering activities designed to achieve the objectives is the Environmental Management Program.

In North America, the guiding principles, commitments, and the general plan of action are often stated in the vision statement (Where does the organization want to be in the mid- to long-term?), the mission statement (What does the organization do?), and the statement of goals and objectives. The general principles and commitments are developed as part of strategic planning and management, and more detailed policies outline how goals and objectives will be reached. It is expected that this confusion of terms will persist in the literature, so readers will have to determine from the context how the terms are being used. For example, Pearce and Robinson define policies as "directives designed to guide the thinking, decisions, and actions of managers and their subordinates in implementing a firm's strategy...previously referred to as standard operating procedures."[2]

ISO 14001 definitions of policy, objectives, and environmental management programs are not universally accepted outside the field of environmental management, especially in North America (see Table 6.1).

Table 6.1 ISO 14001 and North American Definitions of Policy, Objectives, and Environmental Management Programs

ISO 14001	North America
Policy Statement	Vision Statement Mission Statement Goals and Objectives
Objectives and Targets	Specific Policies Standard Operating Procedures
Environmental Management Program	Implementation of Policies
Environmental Audits	Environmental Audits

Regardless of what it is called, there must be a statement which
• clearly states guiding (general) principles;
• sets the direction of the organization for a plan of action;
• makes specific commitments;
• sets requirements for effective action; and
• establishes feedback, through audits, for continual improvement in achieving goals and objectives.

Cascio, Woodside, and Mitchell; Welford; GEMI; and the Canadian Standards Association provide advice on environmental policy.[3] ISO 14004, the general guidelines document for ISO 14001, provides advice on policy in Section 4.1.4.[4] The European Union's EMAS (Eco-Management and Audit Scheme) contains advice on policy in Annex I Section A.[5]

All companies and institutions have an environmental policy, because even no policy or a reactive, ad hoc approach is by default a policy. The lack of an explicit, proactive policy could create serious problems if a due diligence defense were needed in a prosecution for infringement of regulations. However, the policy statement is not an end in itself. It must be effectively implemented and appropriate indicators must be used to show that progress is being made (feedback) so that continual improvement is possible.

There are different levels of development of environmental policy statements:
- no policy, or a reactive, ad hoc policy which means that an institution will wait until external events or factors force the organization into action;
- initial development — first draft and a test period;
- continual improvement of a new policy, during which components are added or strengthened; and
- mature environmental policy, in which all necessary components are present and revisions are a matter of periodic updating and strengthening as part of continual improvement.

Table 6.2 shows how Rondinelli and Vastag categorized corporate environmental policies as reactive, proactive, crisis preventive, or strategic and compared them with respect to seven different activities.[6]

Drafting an Environmental Policy Statement

There are three fundamental prerequisites or corequisites for environmental policy development:
- the commitment to create and implement a realistic and effective policy,
- the resources to do so (time, funding, skills, and knowledge), and
- a program of education and training.

If any of the pre- or corequisites are missing or inadequate, chapter 3 on driving forces will provide some arguments about why an environmental management system and an environmental policy are important, so that those who must make commitments and allocate resources might be persuaded to do so. Chapter 4 on barriers will help those developing environmental policies to identify, reduce, or remove factors that inhibit progress on environmental policy development. Once the policy is established, it is necessary to commit resources to implement the policy through the environmental management program of pollution prevention, pollution abatement, risk reduction, and resource conservation. Figures 6.1 and 6.2 outline the policy development processes.

The decision to proceed with development of an environmental policy without adequate commitment and resources will depend on an assessment of whether the attempt will increase awareness and change the attitude to environmental policies and environmental management, or whether it would be a waste of time. In some

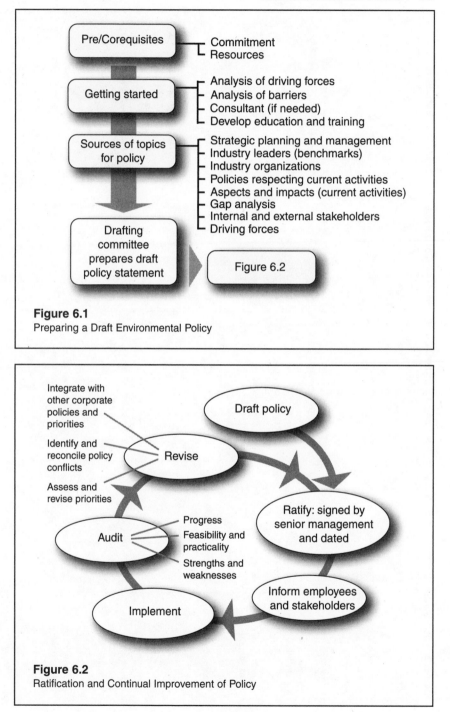

Figure 6.1
Preparing a Draft Environmental Policy

Figure 6.2
Ratification and Continual Improvement of Policy

Table 6.2 Four Strategies for Policy Development and Comparison of Different Corporate Environmental Activities.

Activity	Reactive	Proactive	Crisis Preventive	Strategic
Decision making and environmental reporting	middle-level management with consultants	senior managers at sites	senior management leadership and corporate-wide auditing and reporting	CEO and/or board of directors, corporate wide.
Driving forces	regulations and codes	anticipated changes in regulations, codes, and risks	protection of reputation	reputation management and marketing opportunities
Operational control	site guidelines and control	site control with corporate supervision	corporate guidelines, site control	corporate-level guidelines and control
Environmental management	corrective action in response to external changes	corrective action as potential risks are identified	emergency preparedness	continual improvement
Training	training for middle-level management	corporate-wide environmental training for senior and middle management	corporate-wide specific training for senior and middle management	training for top management and board of directors, specific training for senior and middle management, and awareness training for all employees and suppliers
Nature of environmental improvements	monitoring and end-of-pipe treatment	technologies to reduce pollution and reduce waste	emergency prevention and response and green communication and marketing	pollution prevention, green labeling, environmental communications, continual improvement
Environmental technologies	conventional technologies that meet regulatory requirements	state-of-the-art for pollution reduction, reliable technologies for risk reduction and fail-safe systems		state-of-the-art pollution prevention technologies

Source: adapted from Rondinelli and Vastag, 1996.

cases, policy development without commitment of senior management could be done to raise awareness and to start the process of education and training.

There are several different strategies that institutions can use to draft an environmental policy statement:

- Senior decision makers draft and endorse the statement, and then inform employees and other stakeholders about it and their responsibilities, roles, and obligations under the policy.
- Senior decision makers make a commitment to the concept of an environmental policy statement and its implementation but pass the responsibility for the initial draft to a small group. The draft statement is prepared in consultation with stakeholders and sent to senior decision makers for revision, ratification, and signature(s).
- A process of wide consultation is used to gather ideas for the policy statement, which are edited by a committee, circulated for comment, and then revised and sent to senior managers for ratification and signature(s).
- Policy makers enlist the help of their industry organization, if that organization has an active environmental management element, which has drafted model environmental policies for their sector.
- The organization adopts and adapts the policy of an industry leader in environmental management.
- Environmental issues of concern to the institution are identified and the statements about how the issue is to be handled are drafted.

Policy should be drafted early in the development of an EMS because all personnel who work on environmental management should use the policy as a touchstone. Policies must be laudable but achievable because there is expectation that progress will be made. The regular revision of the policy statement allows changes to be made so that what is achievable will be changed to meet improved abilities and greater expectations.

Given the importance of the environmental policy in the EMS, it is surprising how little detailed advice there is for corporations on policy development. GEMI's *ISO 14001 Environmental Management System Self-Assessment Checklist* provides advice in an annex,[7] as do other EMS 14001 handbooks. However, this advice tends to be general because policies must be appropriate for the nature, scope, and scale of the corporation's activities and the nature of the impacts on the environment. As stated above, the policy will also be heavily influenced by corporate strategy with respect to environmental management. Therefore, it will likely be difficult, if not impossible, to develop international standards for environmental policies but it would be very practical to develop model (benchmark) policies for industry sectors.

We cannot provide specific advice on topics for all environmental policies, aside from repeating those required by ISO 14001. However, the following seven methods can be used to identify topics or issues that could be, or should be, incorporated in an institution's environmental policy statement:

1. Use brainstorming with employees to develop a list of topics.
2. Use other environmental management tools such as goals and objectives from strategic environmental management, analysis of driving forces, and assessment of stakeholders from environmental management structures to identify elements that must appear in the policy.
3. Examine the general principles that the company might want to adhere to when implementing and operating its EMS, such as product stewardship, eco-efficiency, or sustainable development (see Table 1.2, Concepts and Principles).
4. Analyze the aspects — activities that might have an adverse impact on the environment — and impacts — activities that do have an impact on the environment — as required by ISO 14001 which will identify topics for inclusion in the policy statement.
5. Use gap analysis with the assistance of a consultant to compare current corporate activities with what is expected by a management standard such as ISO 14001 or GEMI, and identify those elements that are missing from the current set of activities that should be added to the policy statement.
6. Use the incremental approach to gather the separate policy statements, or even the implicit policies, followed by different units in the corporation (solid waste, water and energy, hazardous materials, etc.), and bring them together to form a single statement. This would have to be followed by a gap analysis.
7. Use a model policy statement from an association or corporation in the same industry. This approach is based upon selection of best-practice (benchmarking) for the model.

Policy imposed by membership in an organization such as the International Chamber of Commerce, World Business Council for Sustainable Development, Coalition for Environmentally Responsible Economies, and Responsible Care may determine what is contained in a policy statement. Employees are also sources of elements in the policy statement because of their personal values and/or the obligations they hold as members of professional associations.

Brainstorming

Brainstorming can help identify environmental issues of concern to an institution. A more participatory means of gathering ideas is to have a brainstorming session (of all employees or their representatives) in which everyone contributes words or phrases for ideas or topics that could be addressed in the environmental policy statement. The normal rules for brainstorming are followed, so there are no criticisms of the suggestions and all ideas are recorded. The group then separates the ideas into three categories. The first category includes those ideas about which hard statements can be made because there is an external obligation which must be met (such as regulations) or the organization is certain about the commitment it wants to make and can therefore make a clear and definitive statement. The second category would be softer because firm commitments or decisions on specific actions could not be made. These soft statements include words like develop, build, improve, where feasible, etc. These parts of the statement could become firmer as experience is gained, skills and knowledge improve, and revisions are made. A third category of ideas would be very soft (squishy) where there is some interest in the topic but no agreement can be reached on a specific statement or not enough information is available to make a concrete statement. Words like initiate, investigate, explore, etc. appear here. With revisions, squishy statements are either made firmer or are dropped.

Use of Other Tools

The use of other environmental management tools can make the process of drafting the environmental policy statement easier. The goals, objectives, and plans of action produced by strategic planning and management (chapter 5) can be critical inputs. Where the list of driving forces (chapter 3) has been used to identify those driving forces that affect the organization, information will be available on to whom the environmental policy statement must respond, and what an appropriate response might be. The list of internal and external stakeholders (see chapter 7) will also be useful in drafting the statement. Understanding who would read it and how they might respond is important. The drafters of the statement could use the list of environmental management tools to decide which tools should be referred to in the policy statement, whether there is a commitment to use the tool or to develop the ability to do so, for example, audits (chapter 8), indicators (chapter 12), reporting (chapter 13), and EIA (chapter 14).

General Principles

In chapter 1 there is a list of general principles which could be included in the statement: efficiency, green design, design for environment, sustainable development, pollution prevention, product stewardship, precautionary principle, etc.

Aspects and Impacts

Identification of the aspects of an organization's activities, what an organization does that might affect the environment positively or negatively, and the impact on the environment of those activities is useful in deciding what kind of commitments and statements should appear in the policy. This exercise would be part of the iterative process of continual improvement, which is required by ISO 14001, but would also be a useful part of any formal EMS. That is, a policy is formulated and used to guide activities during the business cycle. At the end of the cycle, progress is measured and the environmental policies are revised in light of the experience that has been gained.

Gap Analysis

Gap analysis is a means of identifying important components of environmental management which are not being addressed, or which are not being addressed adequately. Gap analysis is generally carried out by outside consultants who examine an EMS, or current practices and operations, to identify the gaps and determine how they compare to what would be considered a complete and cohesive system in the particular circumstances.

Incremental Approach

An incremental approach is the development of environmental policy by gathering and consolidating policies on existing activities. That is, most organizations, if not all, will have some sort of policy with respect to energy and energy conservation, water and water conservation, waste water, solid and hazardous wastes, safety, etc. The process of building an overall environmental policy on these initiatives provides three distinct advantages: it acknowledges initiatives that have already been taken; it improves buy-in by those who have to implement the new or revised policy; and it demonstrates that an environmental policy is not a new set of responsibilities imposed by someone who doesn't understand the institution.

Model from Industry Association or Benchmarking (Best-Practice)

Many industry associations have constitutions that impose on members specific obligations to protect health, safety, and environment and to conserve resources. This is the case in many countries for mining, forestry, energy, and petroleum. Although these requirements are often not enforced or are unenforceable, they should appear in the environmental policy statements of all members. Industry associations may have developed a model policy statement for adaptation by their members, which would be an obvious choice where this applies.

It might also be possible to select, as a model, the policy statement of a corporation that is respected for a high level of environmental performance. The environmental policy statement for such a corporation would be a public document and should be easily obtained. A more formal mechanism would be to start or to join a benchmarking exercise to determine who has demonstrated leadership and has established best-practice.

Policy Imposed by Obligations of Association Membership

Existing international organizations, such as the International Chamber of Commerce, or organizations that were created specifically to improve their members' environmental performance, such as the World Business Council for Sustainable Development and the Coalition for Environmentally Responsible Economies, impose specific environmental codes which must be incorporated into their members' environmental policies. These memberships are obviously voluntary and the only sanction for failure to comply would be expulsion from the organization. However, when these codes of conduct are reinforced by the use of other tools (such as regular environmental audits, environmental indicators, and reporting) with external, third party verification, they become credible and carry significant weight.

Employees Provide Input to Environmental Policies

Employees may, individually or collectively through their employee association or union, ask that environmental factors be included in the environmental policy statement. This is particularly the case with issues related to health and safety. However, those concerns could arise from their individual values, concern about the world their children or grandchildren may have to live in, or concern about the reputation of their employer. Employees who are members of professional associations — accountants, engineers, biologists, chemists, etc. — may also have obligations imposed by the code of conduct and ethics of their profession. Obviously, if the employer's environmental policy statement does not have all the elements that are in the employees' codes of conduct, then there is going to be a conflict.

Drafting the Environmental Policy Statement

Once the topics have been identified using one or more of these methods, the difficult part begins — drafting the environmental policy statement, that is, selecting specific words to define clearly what the corporation intends to do with respect to each particular issue.

One way to start is to divide the topics into three categories:

1. **Hard policy statements** — those topics where the intentions are clear, the corporate stand on the issue is unambiguous, the objectives and targets have been, or can be, set, and the indicators for measuring progress are available. Deciding on wording for these statements is often less controversial than the other two categories. Legal requirements, the requirements of industry or association codes, and a formal EMS such as ISO 14001 or EMAS appear here.
2. **Soft policy statements** — those topics where there is agreement that the topic should be included, but there are problems with how specific

the commitment should be, what the objectives and targets would be, what specifically could be done to implement the policy, and how progress would be measured.

3. **Very soft (squishy) policy statements** — those topics where there is agreement that something should be said, but where disagreement on priority, practicality, or problems prevent development of objectives and targets or measurement of progress makes even a soft statement impossible. Lofty principles often end up in this category — sustainable development, precautionary principle, etc.

The process of continual improvement should produce a gradual hardening of policy statements as knowledge, skills, and experience improve.

A Living Document

The environmental policy statement must be a living document that is continually updated for three reasons. First, the requirements for a successful due diligence defense will change because each new ruling in environmental prosecutions and improvements in what is normal practice will change the expectations of what is required to be duly diligent. Second, the non-regulatory components of the external environment (the driving forces) will change and so policies must be adjusted in light of those changes. Third, there are expectations of, if not requirements for (ISO 14001), continual improvement which will also require changes in the environmental policy.

It is recommended that the date(s) of revisions to the policy be recorded so that it is easy to see when the revisions were made, particularly the latest. Each revision must be ratified and signed by senior management. The policy should include a statement about when and how revisions will be made.

Difficulties in Developing a Clear Policy Statement (Statement of Goals and Objectives)

Difficulties arise when trying to draft an environmental policy statement

- if the pre- and corequisites (commitment, resources, education, and training, etc.) are missing or inadequate;
- because policies can be influenced by fads (the flavor of the month);
- when not all policies are explicit statements: corporate culture can produce attitudes which are, in effect, policies or which heavily influence policies, but which are never written down and are not explicitly available either inside or outside the institution;
- when there are conflicting corporate policies, with no clear indication of how to resolve conflicts (e.g., profitability and speed of work versus care and caution);

- if general principles are stated in such a way that it is difficult to understand what action should be taken and how to measure progress;
- when there is a conflict between the need for the statement to be short, clear, and concise and the need for enough detail to specify meaningful action and to identify measures of progress (indicators);
- if compromises are made to resolve conflicting views to the point where the statements become meaningless and the commitments are vague;
- if environmental policies can be corrupted by bad legal advice such as advice not to make commitments, not to do audits, or not to agree to reveal information about the corporation;
- if development of policy can be thwarted by excessive corporate secrecy;
- if development of environmental policy becomes a public relations exercise — making the right noises — it can lead to policy statements which are not supported by the firm commitment and the resources for effective implementation; and
- in cases where corporate culture includes a reluctance or aversion to change, the development and introduction of any new policy will be difficult.

Chris Ryley analyzed the contents of 130 North American corporate environmental policy statements in 1995.[8] He concluded that there were 12 themes that were required and 16 themes that were recommended. Ryley's work used the North American wording for goals, objectives, and policies, so the tables would read somewhat differently if revised to reflect the ISO 14001 definitions. In light of changes in knowledge and practice which have occurred in the six years since that analysis was done, eight themes have been added to Ryley's list of required themes for complete policy statements in Table 6.3. Table 6.4 presents 12 themes that are recommended for environmental policy statements.

Layering of Detail

In moving from policy to goals and targets to management programs, in ISO 14001 terms, or from vision and mission statements to goals and objectives to policies in North American terms, the level of detail and specificity increases. At the one end of the spectrum, the need for short, clear statements precludes detail. However, with increasing specificity, indicators would be developed to measure the progress on achieving goals and targets through the management program. If the Pressure State Response model for indicators and reporting (chapters 12 and 13) is used, then the goals, targets, and management program (goals, objectives, and policies in North America) might have three indicators (the state, the pressure, and the response). At the very least, the goals and targets must be worded so that it is clear how progress will be measured.

Table 6.3 Twenty Required Themes for Complete Environmental Policy Statements

Theme	Comment
Dates and Updating	Important to policy process. Date of most recent versions and of previous updates must be identified. Explicit commitment to update regularly.
Continual Improvement	Required in order to keep up with rapid change in environmental management issues.
Mission/Vision Statement	Outlines the philosophy or approach used in dealing with environmental issues.
Commitment and Accountability	Signature(s) of senior executive. Must identify officer or committee accountable for implementation of the policy.
Management Responsibility	Specific accountability on the part of the Board of Directors and Environmental Managers (including job descriptions and appraisals) is important.
Environmental Goals	The goals drive the environmental policy. An explicit commitment to review and revise these goals must be made. (In ISO 14001 terms the words goals and policies would be changed.)
Legal Commitments	Regulatory requirements must be met.
Education and Training	All employees must be educated about the policies and their roles. Training for specific duties must be provided.
Indicators and Reporting	Indicators must be developed to allow progress to be monitored. Internal environmental reports are necessary, external reports are optional.
Environmental Auditing	Regular environmental audits are required.
Risk Management	Critical where products or processes pose risks to internal or external stakeholders.
Emergency Response or Preparedness	Where materials or processes pose a hazard, emergency preparedness or an emergency response plan is essential.
Environmental Scanning	Scanning attempts to predict changes in external driving forces so that a proactive approach can be used on anticipated changes.
Strategic Planning	Environmental considerations must be part of the overall strategic planning process for effective and proactive environmental management.
Integration with Other Systems	Although developed and operated relatively independently from other parts of management, the EMS must be integrated with the rest of the institution's management system.
Environmental Impact Assessment	EIA is a critical tool for anticipating and avoiding problems with projects and policies.
Energy Management	Offers savings through improved efficiency, conservation, and reductions in GHG emissions, including transportation and employee commuting.
Waste Minimization	Solid waste reductions (3Rs) offer savings and image enhancement.
Hazardous Materials and Waste Management	Specific programs must be developed for hazardous materials and for reduction of hazardous wastes. Required for NPRI (National Pollutant Release Inventory) in Canada and TRI (Toxic Release Inventory) in the U.S.A. Cost reductions possible. ISO 14001 requires commitment to pollution prevention.
Water and Waste Water Management	Water conservation and reduction of waste water are becoming increasingly important.

Source: adapted from Ryley, 1995.

Table 6.4 Recommended Themes for Environmental Policies

Benchmarking	Comparison of corporate performance to others in the industry is essential for institutions stating that they will be leaders.
Product and Technology Assessment	Increasingly important for designers, manufacturers, marketers, and purchasers to reduce waste and improve stewardship with supply chain or products.
Purchasing Guidelines	Important for minimization of waste and overall impacts.
External Environmental Reporting	Done by leaders in environmental management to inform all stakeholders of environmental performance, including good aspects and bad.
International Legal Concerns	Operations should meet the same high standards regardless of location.
Business Relationships	Business partners, contractors, suppliers, etc. must be required to understand and adhere to corporate environmental policy.
Employee Relations	Education and training must be provided and job descriptions must state roles and responsibilities with appropriate reward system. Suggestions should be received, evaluated, and utilized. Whistle-blower protection might be important.
Community Stakeholders	Provide external stakeholders opportunity for meaningful two-way discussion. Involvement in emergency response is critical.
Full Cost Accounting	Helps the organization understand what the real environmental impacts are and helps to anticipate possible changes to internalize externalities.
Research and Technology Transfer	Helps to develop or to introduce efficiency improvements and pollution prevention.
Sustainable Development	Often included but must be stated to clarify what the organization is committed to. The Natural Step helps in this respect.
Advisory Organizations	Could be part of community involvement and risk communication system.

Source: adapted from Ryley, 1995.

Different Forms of Policy

It is essential for readers to understand that policies come in many different forms. Further, unless there is a sophisticated policy analysis system, which is unusual, there will very likely be conflicts between different forms of policies from different sources within the organization. Obviously, policies that emerge as explicit statements are ratified and signed by senior executives. However, policy is also established, in a sense, by statements in annual reports and shareholders meetings, press releases, speeches and writing by executives and corporate lawyers, in public relations efforts, and by public statements. Unwritten policy is also set by corporate culture. If the written environmental policy statement conflicts with corporate culture, it is unlikely that it will be effective. Annual review of policy statements should identify and remove conflicts.

Public policy on the environment is a very large topic related to, but different from, corporate environmental policy. How public policy is formulated and implemented is very important for corporations because it is a major driving force. Corporations also spend time and effort attempting to influence public policy and participate in public policy development processes. A discussion of public policy is beyond the scope of this work. Readers are referred to Doern[9] and Smith[10] for examples of analysis of public environmental policy.

Recommended Further Reading

Cascio, J., G. Woodside, and P. Mitchell. *ISO 14000 Guide: The New International Environmental Management Standards.* New York: McGraw-Hill,1996. Chapter 5, Environmental Policy.

Canadian Standards Association. *ISO 14000 Essentials: A Practical Guide to Implementing the ISO Standards Plus 14000.* Etobicoke, Ontario: Canadian Standards Association,1996: pp. 22-27.

Global Environmental Management Initiative (GEMI). Rev. Nov 2000. *ISO 14001 Environmental Management System Self-Assessment Checklist.* Washington DC: GEMI, 1996. Available in pdf at <www.gemi.org>

Welford, R. *Corporate Environmental Management: Systems and Strategies.* London, U.K.: Earthscan Publications,1996.

CHAPTER 7

ENVIRONMENTAL MANAGEMENT STRUCTURES

Dixon Thompson

THE ENVIRONMENTAL MANAGEMENT STRUCTURE for a corporation is the organization of people and corporate units, a description of their responsibilities (job descriptions), the flows of information, the decision-making processes, and the relationships with internal and external stakeholders.

The environmental management structure (*structure* from here on because it cannot be called the EMS due to confusion with the Environmental Management System) must include internal and external structure (relationship to stakeholders outside the corporation or institution), formal and informal relationships, and must include all stakeholders, participants, and actors. The internal, formal structure is often represented in an organization chart showing the relationships and titles of people in the organization. However, because such relationships and titles change in the dynamic structures of management, the organization charts are often out of date. Further, such charts generally show neither informal relationships, which can be very important, nor external relationships. Practitioners should note that corporate telephone directories reflect the corporate structure to a degree. Since they must be kept up-to-date to maintain effective corporate communications, they are sometimes better sources of information on corporate structure than an out-of-date organization chart. Organizational structure is sometimes defined as how tasks are formally divided, grouped, and coordinated: the structure shows the building blocks of the organization.

There is an enormous volume of literature on organizational structure that is too large and too detailed for review here. However, general texts on management and especially those on strategic management provide more detailed descriptions of structural options. For example, Mintzberg, Quinn, and Voyer[1] and Pearce and Robinson[2] provide good descriptions of structural options and their functions. Beer approaches organizational structure from a managerial cybernetics perspective.[3] *The Academy of Management Journal* has published a "Special Research Forum on New and Evolving Organizational Forms."[4]

Recently, Mintzberg and Van der Heyden argued that organization charts do not really show how corporations work and proposed a new model using sets, chains, hubs, and webs as the means of describing internal structures.[5] Thirty years earlier, Stafford Beer had applied managerial cybernetics to the same problem and produced the *mulitnode* as a means of showing how organizations really work.[6] The multinode is an elaborate assemblage of elements (patterned after neurons in the brain) that accommodates the reality that managers are not hard-wired like machines, according to the organization chart. They have all sorts of informal sources of information and means of communication. The organization chart is helpful but must be recognized as a formal, over-simplified representation. To understand what's really going on, managers must look at the corporation as an organic, social organization rather than a bureaucratic structure. These alternative views of corporate reality might improve the managers' understanding of how the organization really works, but the organization chart, even out of date, would still be useful to external stakeholders who are trying to understand how the organization works.

It is important to understand the structure of an organization in order to know who makes decisions, how those decisions are made, and how they are, or can be, influenced. This understanding is essential in order to get information from, or provide information to, an organization. It is also important to know the existing structure when designing an EMS and developing an effective communications strategy. The external structure will inform decision makers about who could be affected by corporate activities and who could affect the corporation. In this respect, understanding those relationships and possible relationships is important for environmental scanning.

Internal Structures

The internal structure of an organization is determined by size, the presence or absence of a formal management structure, the stage of evolution or development of the organization's Environmental Management System, the corporate culture, and the preferences of senior managers.

Handy describes the different structures used by organizations of different sizes, from single proprietor, through partnerships, to more complex structures required by larger organizations.[7] Small organizations do not need, and cannot often afford, formal management structures. They are small enough that most employees know each other, their responsibilities, the organization's operations and activities, and often have a personal stake in, or commitment to, that organization. A formal environmental management structure would be overkill. However, allocating responsibilities, formally defining responsibilities in job descriptions, and providing the necessary, ongoing training and education are important. When it is not possible to have all the needed expertise within a small organization (and that is often the case) there are three options available to make up for the lack of resources to hire full-time environmental specialists. One option is to hire consultants, to keep those consultants on a retainer, and/or to share the consultants with other similar groups to share the cost. A second option is to hire the needed expertise on a part-time basis, particularly if other organizations can be persuaded to take the rest of that expert's time (five companies take one day per week). A third option is to obtain assistance from an industry association.

In larger organizations, the formal structure helps people understand who to see when they have a concern or need information. Where no such structure exists in a small company, the job title and description must play the role of directing people to the proper employee when environmental issues arise.

Formal structures of larger organizations can be described in at least eight different forms: centralized, decentralized, matrix, modified decentralized (corporate group), production teams formed through re-engineering, ad hoc (reactive, fragmented, unorganized), task forces, and advisory groups. The first five are formal management structures for large organizations; the last three are less formal, often temporary, structures.

Figures 7.1, 7.2, 7.3, and 7.4 show four types of formal environmental management structures which are used by large organizations: centralized, decentralized, matrix, and modified decentralized (staff function). Each of the four has advantages and disadvantages and none of them can be considered the best environmental management structure in all circumstances.

Centralized Structure

The centralized structure (Figure 7.1) places all employees working on environmental issues within one unit in the organization. This provides the advantages of group coherence and teamwork, profile within the organization, and leadership with specific responsibilities for the success of the group. Resources (budget, employees, equipment) are allocated specifically to the unit. Much of the environmental information is centralized, but not all of the information needed by the environmental management group may be held by that group. Critical information may be the jealously guarded property of other departments. Another disadvantage of this structure is the relationship of the environment unit to other parts of the organization which might see the efforts of environmental managers as unnecessary interference. Further, employees within the unit might not have an adequate understanding of the details of other operations and therefore not be effective in their efforts to have environmental factors given due consideration.

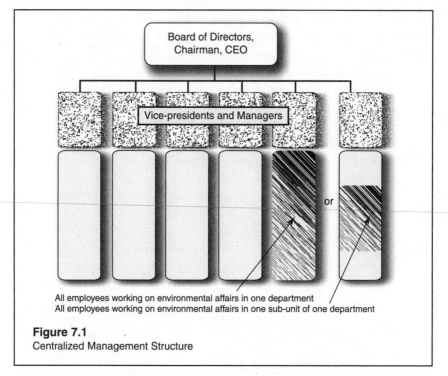

Figure 7.1
Centralized Management Structure

Introduction of an EMS in a centralized structure could be relatively straight-forward once senior management makes the commitment to proceed and provides the resources. A potential source of difficulties is the need to establish effective working relationships with other units in the organization.

Decentralized Structure

The decentralized structure (Figure 7.2) distributes employees with environmental responsibilities throughout the organization, where they work directly with those involved in operations where problems are created and solved. Employees with environmental skills and knowledge, whose job descriptions include responsibility for specific environmental matters, are spread throughout the organization at the grassroots level. This generally creates better working relationships at the operations level, although at times the relationships become so close that environmental quality is compromised. This is because employees in the decentralized structure have a divided loyalty: to the operations unit to which they are attached and to their environmental responsibilities. There is no group that can support them, although there are often committee meetings. There is no senior group responsible for setting goals and objectives, establishing corporate policy, and receiving feedback on the effectiveness of implementing the policies to achieve the

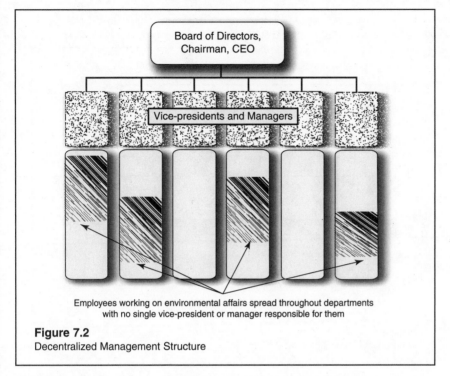

Figure 7.2
Decentralized Management Structure

goals and objectives. Often there is no leadership on environmental issues because no senior company official is charged with responsibility for protection of the environment. Communication among those responsible for environmental matters is often informal because no formal channels for environmental information exist. Funding for environmental matters is buried in other budgets.

In those circumstances in which senior management and corporate culture support a high level of awareness of, and willingness to act on, environmental issues, the disadvantages of the decentralized structure are considerably reduced, because there is no problem of divided loyalties.

Introduction of an Environmental Management System in a decentralized structure could be difficult, even when commitment is made and resources are provided by senior management. This is because some means must be found to establish the leadership for the EMS and organize the individuals and small units that are dispersed throughout the organization. The EMS would have to centralize some of the previously decentralized structure.

Matrix Management

The matrix management structure (Figure 7.3) is a complex structure designed to handle the complexities of large organizations. The matrix can be based upon

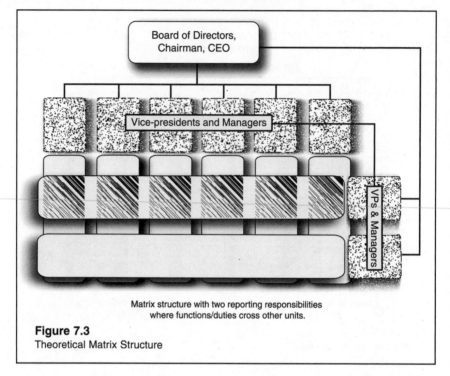

Board of Directors,
Chairman, CEO

Vice-presidents and Managers

VPs & Managers

Matrix structure with two reporting responsibilities
where functions/duties cross other units.

Figure 7.3
Theoretical Matrix Structure

function and geography, function and product line or activity, or different aspects of operations and support functions (legal, finance, accounting, environment personnel, etc.). The structure suffers from breaking the one-person-one-boss rule because loyalties are formally divided by the matrix. However, this structure formally recognizes the complexity of large organizations and can reduce the problems of divided loyalties by formally recognizing them. Although the matrix structure is currently out of favor, it does have some strong theoretical merits, which might be realized in a practical sense as complexities increase and our abilities to manage them improve.

Staff Group: Modified Decentralized

The modified decentralized structure (Figure 7.4) has a staff group which is a centralized, senior body that reports to senior management. It is responsible for strategic planning and management, formulating corporate policy, and ensuring that policies are implemented effectively. However, most of the employees with environmental responsibilities are decentralized: they are spread throughout the organization in the places where they are thought to be most effective. There are formal channels for information to be collected from and disseminated to individuals and appropriate groups. There is a senior spokesperson on environmental

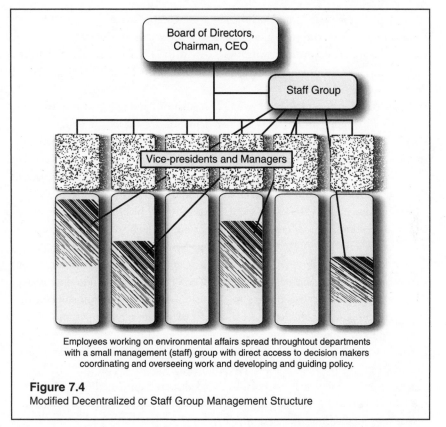

Employees working on environmental affairs spread throughtout departments with a small management (staff) group with direct access to decision makers coordinating and overseeing work and developing and guiding policy.

Figure 7.4
Modified Decentralized or Staff Group Management Structure

matters who can fight for budget allocations and act on behalf of employees who have concerns. There is a division of loyalties, but, as with the matrix, it is formalized and less of a problem. This structure has found considerable favor with large organizations because it is a satisfactory combination of the strengths of the centralized and decentralized structures without the management complexities of the matrix structure.

In this structure, environmental strategy, especially environmental scanning, and policy formulation are centralized but are done in consultation with workers in the various units. Functional and operations decisions are decentralized but the corporate group is kept informed.

This structure has many, if not all, of the components required for a formal EMS, so implementation of one would be easy relative to the other structures.

Re-engineering and Downsizing

If downsizing is defined as reducing the number of employees but not reducing the amount of work to improve efficiency, productivity, and profits (at least temporarily), then the impact on the environmental management structure will depend upon where the cuts take place. It is a perversion of the resource conservation slogan, Doing more with less. As with all activities in downsized organizations, environmental management will suffer if fewer employees have to do more work.

Some of the arguments about reducing regulations and red tape arise from the demands for higher productivity. Other demands are the result of downsizing where the remaining employees simply can no longer cover all the requirements. In these cases, the suggestion that voluntary systems can reduce the need for regulation and enforcement will only make sense if there are adequate resources in the downsized organizations to make the voluntary systems work effectively.

Re-engineering, on the other hand, is an effort to place employees in teams related to products or services by taking them out of the boxes or silos that previously housed only specialists.[8] This often improves productivity because the teams understand the entire process, rather than just a small segment of it related to their area of specialization. Re-engineering does not necessarily include downsizing. There are very distinct advantages to the teamwork approach compared to the sequential process of completing isolated special studies (economics and financing, engineering, design, and marketing) before introducing environmental factors. That sequence often results in one of two unfortunate results: very expensive changes are required, or the environmental factors are deemed to be too expensive and are ignored. This can be avoided if environmental factors are considered in parallel with the other factors such as economics and financing, marketing, engineering, and design.

Interdisciplinary teamwork is often stressed as a key to successful environmental science and management. Therefore, the interdisciplinary team approach, which is at the core of re-engineering, when re-engineering is not a euphemism for downsizing, fits well with environmental management.

Ad Hoc, Reactive Approach

The ad hoc, fragmented, unorganized structure tries to react to environmental issues as they arise. No formal structure is, by default, the organization's structure. For example, an organization will always have to use energy and water and will generate wastes. When efforts are made to reduce energy and water consumption and waste, environmental management has started, in a sense. The unorganized efforts are better than nothing but are generally less desirable in terms of effectiveness and efficiency.

This reactive approach was found in the survey work carried out by KPMG[9] and by Kirkland and Thompson[10] and is reflected in statements indicating the organization responded as needed when environmental problems arose.

The ad hoc approach does have the merit of allowing those who are cautious or reluctant about taking action on environmental issues to attack problems in small, manageable pieces, where costs appear to be lower and are directly related to something that is clearly identified. However, problems are dealt with in a reactive rather than proactive fashion, which is generally more expensive and can't anticipate and avoid problems. It is management by the seat-of-the-pants, or bush firefighting, rather than a systematic approach. It also means exposure to high cost risks.

The unorganized approach to environmental management can become a systematic approach by bringing the pieces together into a coherent structure which would gradually become a formal structure as part of an EMS. By now almost all organizations have taken some action on various environment and resource conservation issues. Generally, organizations have various licenses which have to be obtained and maintained by reporting according to requirements. At the same time, we know that most small organizations have no formal EMS. Amalgamating the parts of a company which are responsible for different environmentally related activities and melding them into a coherent structure will be one of the major strategies for creating an environmental management structure and eventually an EMS.

Task Forces

Task forces are also used by organizations to bring expertise to bear on a problem quickly. They are often effective in the short term, but since membership is short-term and there may not be any long-term commitments and little follow-up, they must be considered as temporary structures within a larger structure. Task forces can be important in starting action on environmental management but they are no substitute for a permanent structure which is appropriate for the organization's scale and activities.

Advisory Committees

Advisory committees can play important roles in receiving and distributing information, formulating policy, and maintaining links with important stakeholders, community groups, and NGOs. In some cases, an environmental advisory committee is the only formal structure with specific environmental responsibilities. In some cases, a committee is used as an excuse for not taking any further action. Like a task force, it is no substitute for a permanent environmental management structure. Members are assigned committee responsibilities on top of their existing duties, the committee often does not have direct access to the resources necessary to solve or prevent problems, and therefore, action is often slow and ineffective. Further, an advisory committee can only advise and has no power to formulate policy or implement possible solutions.

Why Do Structures Change?

As stated above, there is no best structure, although the modified decentralized structure has found some favor. Nonetheless, corporations may change environmental management structure for five different reasons.

- The management structure of a corporation is often determined by senior management; therefore, new management may change the structure to reflect their preferences.
- If priorities change significantly, management structures may have to accommodate the increasing size and importance of some units relative to others.
- The evolution and maturation of the corporation leads to changes in structure. A corporation with an unorganized approach to environmental management may formalize a decentralized structure by recognizing employee responsibilities in job descriptions, corporate publications, and statements by senior executives. While corporate policy on environmental issues strengthens, the structure could become a more centralized system as employees with environmental responsibilities are grouped together to gain the advantages of a centralized system. That approach could evolve into a decentralized structure in which senior management commitment, support, and corporate culture make it the best approach; or it could change to a modified decentralized structure (staff function) in which components of the centralized structure move to a staff function and the remaining environmental management employees move to the appropriate operations groups.
- A significant change in company size can cause a change in corporate environmental management structure. At some stage of growth, structures that worked well at the smaller scale are no longer adequate for larger enterprises. This can happen gradually or as a result of mergers or acquisitions.
- At times changes in management structures (job descriptions, positions within the corporations, reporting and decisions making systems) are required in order to make other changes. That is, it is possible to change corporate goals and policy with respect to an issue like the environment; however, inertia and corporate culture make changing goals and implementing new policies impossible, so a real shakeup of corporate structure is needed.

Integration

The level of integration of the environmental management structure with the rest of corporate management structure requires careful consideration. On the one hand, it's possible to have a centralized structure with all employees with environmental responsibilities in one isolated, ineffective structure. On the other hand, there could be a centralized structure with full commitment and support of senior management, an information management and communication system, and a corporate culture which makes that centralized unit well integrated with the rest of management. The same set of problems could be posed for employees in a decentralized structure. Either of those can be well, or badly, integrated.

The modified decentralized structure and the interdisciplinary teams formed as a result of re-engineering have a much greater potential for good integration into the overall management structure. Again, the integration can be done well or badly.

The term *fully integrated* is used in two different ways. In one sense, it means well integrated into the overall management structure of the corporation, in the sense that well integrated is used in the above paragraphs. In another sense, fully integrated is used to mean that the environmental management structure is completely absorbed into the larger structure. If this absorption means that environmental specialists, as such, disappear, then it is difficult to understand how the technical details would be handled and how continual improvement would take place. It does not seem reasonable to assume that all employees would informally accept the responsibilities and have the resources to operate the (absorbed) Environmental Management System at an optimum level. Therefore, if some expertise is required for a sound EMS, then complete absorption, full integration, would not seem to be desirable.

There has been a trend to integrate health, safety, and environment units on the basis of perceived similarities and in the interest of improved efficiency. Some aspects of health, safety, and environment can and should be integrated. Emergency response and management of hazardous materials must be dealt with in an integrated structure. However, the corporate cultures and the skill and knowledge sets of the three units are different, and so integration might not lead to efficient and effective management.

Regardless of what the management structure is, it must be able to facilitate the roles and responsibilities of environmental managers, as shown in Figure 7.5. The decentralized model is the only one that might have significant weaknesses: unless the Environmental Management System is well established, the corporate culture accommodates it completely, and environmental managers operate effectively without any need for some form of centralized authority.

Management Philosophy

Theory X (top down), Theory Y (bottom up), and Theory Z (consultation, etc.) are three management styles described by Ouchi that will influence formal and informal corporate structure.[11] ISO 14001 is clear that commitment of senior

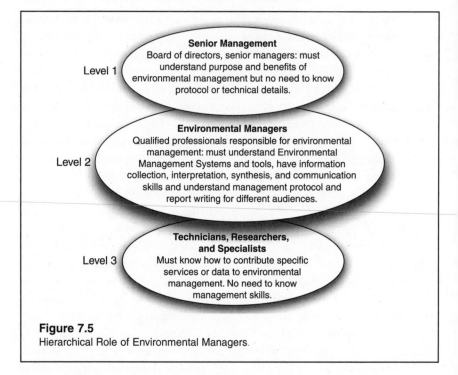

Figure 7.5
Hierarchical Role of Environmental Managers.

management is essential for effective action at significant levels, but that does not mean that ISO 14001 requires a top down (Theory X) approach. It is also clear that in many organizations there is a great deal of work being done at the grassroots level (Theory Y), but it is less effective and efficient than it could be and should be because of lack of understanding and support from above. That leaves us with structures and systems which include a commitment of senior management with buy-in at the grassroots level. On the other hand, given downsizing and the general increase in workloads for individuals in many organizations, it may not be realistic to expect the grassroots, all employees at the operations levels, to enthusiastically take on additional responsibilities for environmental matters. It may not be realistic to seek the resources for education and training to bring all employees to a sophisticated level of understanding of environmental issues. A balance of understanding and support from senior management and the grassroots, with a sophisticated and effective group of experts, is likely better. That is, there should be a corporate policy which ensures that there is a basic level of education about the environment (basic concepts, principles, and corporate policy) and about the impacts and aspects of the company's operations. Training about the company's environmental goals, objectives, and policies and about activities that involve employees (safety and health, waste minimization and recycling, energy and water conservation) is necessary. All employees have to become committed to act when their corporate responsibilities require it. Senior executives do not need to know the details of Environmental Management Systems and the use of environmental management tools. However, they need a broad understanding of the issues, particularly as they relate to corporate activities, the driving forces, the benefits of a sound EMS, and their responsibilities for providing the necessary resources and support.

Those technicians, researchers, and other employees whose specific duties include environmental responsibilities require training, and regular retraining, in their particular technical specialties.

The environmental managers' roles (see Figure 7.5) are to inform senior management at an appropriate level of detail and to assist with the formulation of corporate policy. They transmit that policy to technicians and researchers and guide their activities. They receive detailed information from technicians and researchers, translate it, and present it at an appropriate level of detail for senior management and others in the company.

External Structures

As noted in the Introduction (Figure 1.2), it is important to identify and characterize or understand external stakeholders, actors, and participants. The internal structure involves descriptions of roles and responsibilities, relationships, flows of information, and influences on decision making. The same applies to external structures.

Table 7.1 List of Possible Stakeholders, Actors, and Participants

Formal Relationships	Informal Relationships
regulators (international, federal, provincial, municipal)	local communities
suppliers	ENGOs
customers	politicians
partners	the media
subcontractors	educational institutions
labour unions	the market
professional associations (engineering, accounting, biology, chemistry, medicine, law, auditing, human factors)	future generations
investors and financial institutions	the global community
insurance agents	health and safety professionals, the competition, the environment

Informal, External Relationships

Understanding the people outside the organization who could influence performance positively or negatively is important for strategic planning and management. It helps managers understand the external environment, how it might change, and provides insights into how to respond to changes. Communications with external participants is critical, so understanding what information a corporation needs from outside, and what information outsiders need must be assessed on an ongoing basis (see chapter 20). Many of the influences of stakeholders, actors, and participants are described in chapter 3.

Participants and stakeholders can be either allies or adversaries. When influential groups are identified, they should be assessed with respect to their likely perspectives and impacts on corporate environmental management. Such groups are not homogeneous, so, for example, lumping all ENGOs together would be an error. Some ENGOs will be unimportant or unconcerned; others may want to work with corporations to help solve problems; others will be critics but will not work cooperatively. Extremist groups are uncontrollable, unpredictable, and probably outside the limits of effective communication.

It is also important to note that the organization's relationship to a particular ENGO may change with different issues. A group might take an uncooperative hard line on one issue but be willing to work cooperatively on another.

Formal, External Relationships

Formal relationships involve some kind of legal, contractual, or other written agreement. Increasingly those agreements include references to environmental issues and how they are to be handled. Those agreements can impose major changes on environmental management within corporations. For example, in December 1992, the Canadian Institute of Chartered Accountants ruled that proper accounting procedures must include a statement of environmental liabilities as a charge against assets, which is similar to requirements by the securities and exchange commissions in the U.S.A. and Canada. After that ruling, environmental managers had to provide the accounting department with estimates of the environmental liabilities, so that the accounting department could inform the board of directors, banks, investors, etc. Other professional organizations of engineers, biologists, chemists, environmental auditors, and, soon, environmental scientists place explicit environmental, ethical, and professional requirements on their members. Employers must understand that such professional employees are bound by those environmental obligations.

Other professional organizations such as the American Society for Quality, the Canadian Environmental Auditing Association, the International Association for Impact Assessment, the Air and Waste Management Association, and the Society for Environmental Toxicology and Chemistry are working to improve standards and the quality of professional practice.

Industry Organizations

The Canadian Chemical Producers Association, the Canadian Association of Petroleum Producers, the Mining Association of Canada, and many other industry associations now have environmental codes of practice, which they expect members to know and respect. The Responsible Care code of the chemical industry started in Canada in 1984 and is now subscribed to by the chemical industries in more than 40 countries. The International Chamber of Commerce, the Coalition for Environmentally Responsible Economies, the Global Reporting Initiative and the World Business Council on Sustainable Development also have environmental guidelines, codes, or charters which members must understand and respect. Non-members should become familiar with them to understand what will likely become normal expectations with respect to environmental codes.

Purchasing Guidelines

Purchasing guidelines, described in detail in chapter 19, are a major external influence on suppliers. For example, in a letter to 950 suppliers, IBM encouraged suppliers to meet ISO 14001 requirements and to pursue registration as part of IBM's overall ISO 14001 strategy.[12] Casio, Woodside, and Mitchell state that "an organization must ensure that its suppliers and contractors understand its requirements so that they do not unwittingly cause the organization to compromise its own EMS."[13] Thus, suppliers must expect environmental concerns on the part of their customers, and buyers should indicate their level of concern to their suppliers.

More Complex Views of Organizational Structure

Most of the large volume of literature on organizational structure focuses on formal, internal structure. It is important for environmental management, but, as outlined above, the external formal and informal structures are also important.

McKinsey's consulting company developed "Seven S's": structure, strategy, systems, skills, style, staff, and shared goals,[14] as shown in Figure 7.6. Handy divides the seven elements into the cold triangle (structure, strategy, and systems) and the warm square (skills, style, staff, and shared values or superordinate goals).[15] To the seven S's, I would add four more: size (how big is the organization?), setting (where is it located?), substance (what does it do?) and stakeholders (who does the organization work with and interact with?). These additions link the internal structure to important elements outside the organization (Figure 7.6).

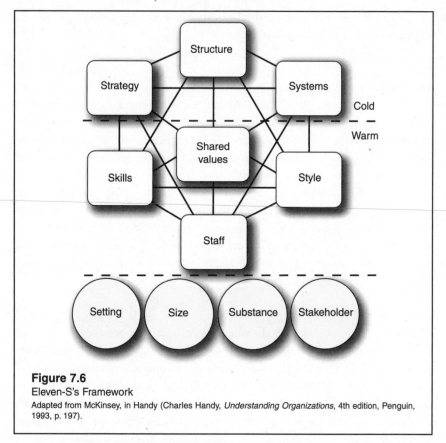

Figure 7.6
Eleven-S's Framework
Adapted from McKinsey, in Handy (Charles Handy, *Understanding Organizations*, 4th edition, Penguin, 1993, p. 197).

In a more esoteric approach to structure, at least at the time it was being applied in Chile, Stafford Beer used cybernetics to develop a decision-making model in which senior management was primarily concerned with the external environment (our senses, our sympathetic nervous system which informs us about opportunities and threats in the external environment).[16] In Beer's model, senior management did not want to be informed about performance of the various internal units, as long as things were working normally. Only when some aspect of operations went outside specified norms did the structure alert senior management. The human system analogy is persuasive. If each of us had to constantly monitor and adjust heart rate, digestion, body temperature, enzyme function, immune system activity, etc., we would never be able to think. When those functions are normal, carry on.

It is important to pay constant attention to changes in the external environment that need attention because they offer opportunities or pose threats. This is the environmental scanning obligation and strategic planning and management responsibilities of senior management. Beer's work in Chile, before the assassination of President Allende, did not have access to the very small and powerful computing capacity easily and cheaply available today. In terms of strategic decisions and understanding the impact of the external environment, Beer's approach should be re-examined.

Recommended Further Reading

Beer, S. *Brain of the Firm: The Managerial Cybernetics of Organization.* London, U.K.: Allen Lane Penguin Press, 1972. Chapter 11 Corporate Structure and its Quantification, and Chapter 14 Multinode – System Five.

Handy, C. *Understanding Organizations.* 4th ed. London, U.K.: Penguin, 1993.

Mintzberg, H., J. B. Quinn, and J. Voyer. *The Strategy Process.* Englewood, NJ: Prentice Hall, 1995. Chapter 6, Structure and Process, pp.133-167.

Pearce, J. A. and R. B. Robinson. *Strategic Management: Formulation, Implementation and Control.* 6th ed. Chicago: Irwin, 1997: pp. 339-352.

ENVIRONMENTAL AUDITING

Mel Wilson, PricewaterhouseCoopers LLP

E NVIRONMENTAL AUDITING is a systematic and periodic documented verification process of objectively obtaining and evaluating evidence to determine whether specified environmental activities, events, conditions, management systems, or information about these matters, conform with audit criteria and communicating the results of this process to the client.[1]

The ability of the organization to objectively assess its environmental performance is a necessary component of an effective Environmental Management System (EMS). There are different ways of collecting environmental performance information, from quantitative data collection, such as air emissions monitoring, to routine physical inspections by on-site personnel. However, one of the most widely used and effective means of comprehensively collecting, assessing, and reporting environmental performance and management information is through environmental auditing. Figure 8.1 illustrates the position of the audit program within an EMS.

Environmental Audit Definitions

Of the several definitions of environmental auditing, the most widely accepted is that of the International Organization for Standardization (ISO).[2] The following are brief definitions of the keywords used in the ISO definition.

Systematic: the audit process follows a logical and rigorous methodology that meets basic audit standards as defined by industry and recognized standard setting bodies.

Verification: an assessment to determine whether the activities or conditions of the audited organization meet specific standards and expectations.

Audit criteria: the specific standards against which performance is compared. These can be legal or voluntary requirements.

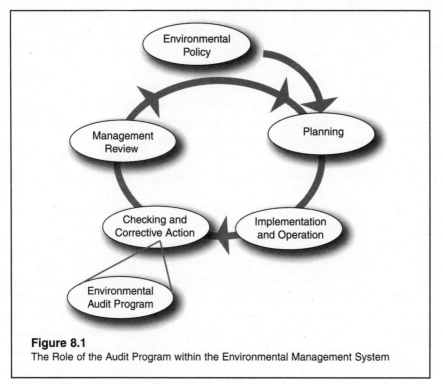

Figure 8.1
The Role of the Audit Program within the Environmental Management System

A Brief History of Environmental Auditing

Environmental auditing began in the 1970s in the United States. According to Greno et al, it was during this time that "a few industrial companies, working independently and on their own initiatives, developed environmental audit programs as internal management tools to help review and evaluate the status of the company's operating units."[3] For the first few years, auditing did not gain significant attention outside of those few companies. According to Reed[4] and Cahill and Kane,[5] the crystallization of environmental auditing as a recognized environmental management practice occurred during the years 1977–1980 when the United States Securities Exchange Commission (SEC) required three large industrial companies to conduct environmental audits of all holdings in order to disclose the environmental liabilities to shareholders more accurately.

Environmental auditing continued to gain prominence as an effective management tool during the 1980s in the U.S.A. This momentum was boosted by the recognition of environmental auditing by the U.S. Environmental Protection Agency (EPA). In 1986, the EPA published "Environmental Protection Agency: Environmental Auditing Policy Notice," clarifying its support for environmental auditing:

> "It is EPA policy to encourage the use of environmental auditing by regulated entities to help achieve and maintain compliance with environmental laws and regulations, as well as to help identify and correct unregulated environmental hazards."[6]

Environmental auditing also developed and grew in Canada throughout the 1980s in a similar fashion. The first major examination of environmental auditing in Canada was John Reed's "Environmental Auditing: A Review of Current Practice" completed in cooperation with Environment Canada.[7] This study surveyed Canadian companies on the state of environmental auditing in the early 1980s.

In 1988, Environment Canada issued "Canadian Environmental Protection Act: Enforcement and Compliance Policy." Among other things, this policy recognizes the contribution of environmental auditing to effective environmental management by identifying "compliance problems, weaknesses in management systems, or areas of risk." Another important part of this policy is the commitment by Environment Canada not to demand or confiscate environmental audit reports from regulated companies except under unique circumstances where the environmental information can not be obtained in any other way. This reduces the Canadian companies' fear that the environmental audits could be taken and used against them by regulators.[8]

Environmental auditing has now gained international prominence as an effective environmental management practice. In 1996, the International Organization for Standardization (ISO) issued three audit-related standards: *ISO 14010: Guidelines for Environmental Auditing — General Principles*,[9] *ISO 14011: Guidelines for Environmental Auditing — Audit Procedures — Auditing of Environmental Management Systems*,[10] and *ISO 14012: Guidelines for Environmental Auditing: Qualification Criteria for Environmental Auditors*.[11]

The ISO standards must be reviewed and revised every five years. The ISO's technical committee on environmental management (TC207) noted that the ISO 9000 series on quality management was being revised and many companies that have implemented both ISO 14000 and ISO 9000 were concerned about the lack of consistency between the audits required for the two standards. To update the ISO 14000 auditing guidelines and to make them more consistent with ISO 9000, a single auditing standard has been established — *ISO 19011 Guidelines on Quality and Environmental Auditing*, which replaces the ISO 14011 guideline.[12]

TYPES OF AUDITS

Audits are typically categorized along three dimensions:

Criteria:

(Legal) Compliance (e.g., federal, state, provincial, and municipal regulations)
Corporate policies and standards
Industry standards
Management system standards (e.g., ISO 14001, Responsible Care)

Topic Scope:

Biophysical: solid waste, hazardous waste, air, water, energy, etc.
Focus: environmental performance, management system effectiveness

Organizational Scope:

Narrow focus (e.g., one facility, one division)
Wide focus (e.g., multiple facilities or divisions, cross-organizational)

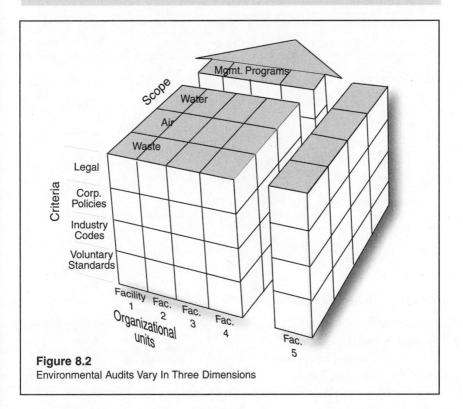

Figure 8.2
Environmental Audits Vary In Three Dimensions

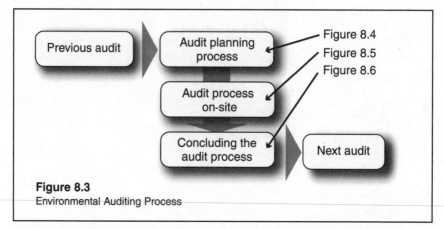

Figure 8.3
Environmental Auditing Process

CATEGORIES OF ENVIRONMENTAL AUDITS

COMPLIANCE — comparison of operations and performance against legal or other requirements.

ENVIRONMENTAL MANAGEMENT SYSTEM — assessment of EMS against established EMS standard, for internal purposes or as part of the EMS certification process.

DUE DILIGENCE — examination of practices to determine whether due care is taken to prevent environmental problems.

Specialty audits

Specific topics (e.g., waste audits, air quality audits)
Specific facilities (e.g., pipeline audits, waste storage area audits)
Specific technical criteria (e.g., fire code, PCB, regulatory audits)

Multidisciplinary

Environment, health, and safety
Environment and quality

Types of Environmental Audits

As auditing evolved, many categories of environmental audits developed. They all share the same basic audit process but differ in their scope, criteria, and purpose. For example, when the scope is limited to waste management it is typically referred to as a waste audit; and when legal requirements are the criteria it is typically called a compliance audit. A gap analysis is sometimes considered as a baseline audit conducted to determine the areas where an organization's EMS does not conform with ISO 14001. Examples of different categories of audits include:

- Compliance audits — an audit of an organization or operation to determine the degree of compliance with applicable legal requirements. Compliance audits often include assessment of conformance with specified company and industry standards in addition to legal requirements.

- Environmental Management System audits — an audit of an organization's Environmental Management System either to determine the degree of conformance with a specified EMS standard (such as ISO 14001) or to assess the effectiveness and efficiency of the system against internal standards.

- Due diligence audits — an assessment of an organization to determine whether the organization has implemented policies and practices that, in the auditor's judgment, are in keeping with industry standards and would be sufficient for the organization to establish a due diligence defense, if necessary in a court of law.

- Specialty audits — an audit confined to a specific environmental topic area, such as waste audits, air quality, water, energy, and greenhouse gas emission reduction, which focusses only on the generation, handling, storage, and disposal of waste products and may address compliance, management practices, and due diligence.

- Specific facilities/structures (e.g., pipeline, refinery, chemical plant) — an audit of one facility or group of facilities. For example, a pipeline company could initiate a compressor station audit program which does not cover other pipeline facilities.

- Specific technical criteria (e.g., transportation of dangerous goods, fire code) — a compliance audit of a specific regulation or other requirement.

- Multidisciplinary audits — audits done concurrently on more than one major corporate activity in order to obtain consistent audit results and improve the efficiency of audit teams. These audits would have been done separately in the past: environment, health, and safety; environment and quality control.

Although the audit category, scope, or focus may be different the basic audit process remains the same.

The Environmental Audit Process

Overview

Every environmental audit follows a standardized systematic process consisting of three stages of activity: Audit Planning, On-site, and Post-audit. For example, while compliance audits and management system audits focus on different issues and will result in different reports, the process for conducting the audits follows the same three-stage process.

DO YOU REALLY WANT AN AUDIT?

Clients sometimes ask for an audit when they really want or need something else — such as a site assessment, a gap analysis, program development, or risk assessment.

Audit Planning Stage

Before the auditors visit the site, much work must be done to prepare the auditors and the site for the audit. These steps, described below, are often carried out in a parallel and iterative manner.

Select the facility(s) to be audited

The audit manager (typically the client and not the auditor), must determine what facility(s) will be audited. While this may be easy for an organization with a small number of operating facilities, it can be problematic for an organization with many operating sites spread out over a large area. In the latter cases, managers often employ risk assessment techniques to help identify which sites would benefit most from an audit. Factors to be considered include:

- nature of activities at the facility,
- size and complexity of operation,
- location,
- age of facility,
- regulatory environment, and
- environmental track record.

Determine the objectives of the audit

The audit manager must decide very early the goal of the audit. Is it to assess compliance with regulations? Assess management practices from a due diligence standpoint? Evaluate the Environmental Management System against some specified standard? Audits are typically conducted within the context of an

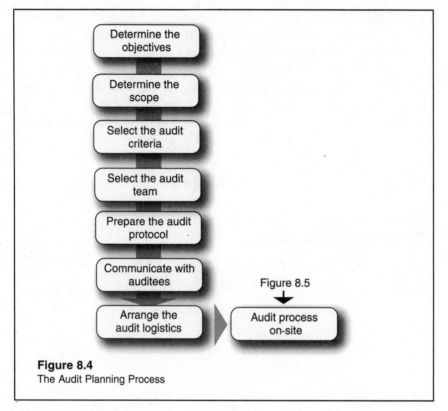

Figure 8.4
The Audit Planning Process

overarching audit program and these questions are addressed in the planning of the audit program. However, from time to time companies conduct stand-alone audits which address these questions for the individual audit.

Determine the scope of the audit

The audit manager must determine the audit's scope which provides boundaries for the audit. This includes operational scope (e.g., the specific operations at the facility that will be audited), the topic areas to be included (e.g., waste management, water quality, air quality), and the time period to be assessed (i.e., how far back in time will the audit research). A typical audit includes all operations at a facility, all environmental topic areas, and performance over the past two to four years. However, the audit manager must determine the scope of each audit by considering various risk factors.

Select the audit criteria

In the case of compliance audits, the audit manager must determine what regulations are applicable to the operation and should be included in the audit. In the case of EMS audits, the audit manager must identify the EMS standards to be used. This function is sometimes delegated to the audit team leader.

Auditors may be asked to audit against best management practices. This can be problematic, however, because an audit should be based on specified and accepted standards (such as regulations) and not the auditor's own criteria. Auditing against best-practice typically results in the auditor comparing the organization's operations against his preconceived notions of good management, which may not be appropriate for the audited operation.

AUDIT CRITERIA

- Laws and regulations (federal, state or provincial, local)
- Licenses, permits, and approvals
- Corporate policies and procedures
- Industry association or other codes
- Environmental Management System standards (ISO 14001, EMAS, GEMI)
- Stakeholder concerns
- Previous audit results

Select the audit team

The audit manager or team leader selects the audit team which may consist of external auditors (i.e., consultants), internal auditors (i.e., corporate environmental staff), or a combination. However, in no case should an employee responsible for environmental management at the facility act as an auditor of that facility, as this will put the person in a conflict of interest. Even if the person performs the audit objectively, there will be perceived conflict that could taint the credibility of the audit report.

Prepare the audit protocol

The audit team, under the direction of the team leader, collects and reviews relevant information, obtained through consultation with the client, prior to the site visit. This often includes environmental information such as copies of licences and permits, monitoring data, operations drawings and blueprints, procedures and manuals, accident reports, organizational charts, site maps, and facility history.

The audit team must then prepare the necessary audit tools, often called the audit protocol. These are the documents that will guide the auditors during the interviews, site inspections, and document reviews.

Experienced auditors often believe that they can perform audits without such protocols — that they can simply walk around the site and take notes. While it may be possible for the highly experienced auditor to do this, it is considered unprofessional practice because the auditor has no documented evidence indicating the criteria covered by the audit. If, after the audit, an environmental problem is discovered that was not reported, the auditor would be unable to prove his audit was appropriately thorough.

Communicate with the auditees (the customer)

Under no circumstances should an environmental audit be a surprise to those being audited. Such audits are almost guaranteed to fail, either through lack of cooperation by the auditees or because of difficulty in locating or accessing necessary information. Auditees should always be notified well in advance of the upcoming audit.

Some may argue that this would give facility management an opportunity to fix problems and clean things up before the auditors' arrival. This often is the case, and is usually acceptable because those same items will have to be fixed and cleaned up after the audit in any event. In addition, any corrections performed before the auditors' arrival will most likely be for small housekeeping items. It is unlikely that the site will be able to correct any major problems, such as poor waste management practices, on short notice.

However, the auditors must always thoroughly check any areas at the facility that appear much newer than the rest of the site. For example, if the auditors find fresh gravel at the site, it is possible that it has been placed there to cover evidence of an oil spill.

Arrange the audit logistics

The audit manager and audit team leader must ensure that the logistics (e.g., travel arrangements, accommodations, audit schedule) are managed; otherwise the audit may be hindered and less effective than necessary due to simple problems.

On-site Stage

Every audit includes a visit by the audit team to the audited facility. The length of the site visit depends on the size and complexity of the facility and the size and complexity of the audit. Site visits can range from half a day (small facility, simple audit) to weeks (complex site and complex audit). Environmental audits of government departments can require months to complete.

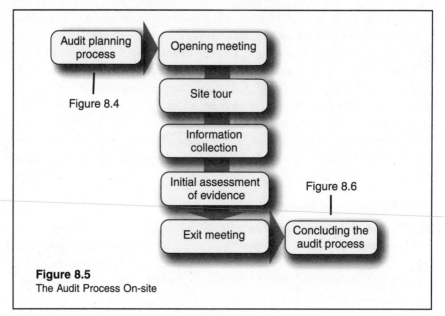

Figure 8.5
The Audit Process On-site

While at the site, the following activities are carried out:

Opening meeting

When the auditors arrive at the site, the first activity is a meeting with key facility representatives including management, environmental staff, and others (e.g., union representatives, health and safety representatives). The purpose of this meeting is to

- Introduce the audit team and the site representatives.
- Review the purpose, scope, and, methodology of the audit.
- Schedule interviews and other meetings.
- Discuss health and safety risks at the site.

Site tour

After the opening meeting, it is often a good idea for the audit team and site representatives to quickly tour the facility together. This tour achieves three goals:

- It allows the audit team to identify areas requiring future detailed inspections.
- It allows the audit team leader to assess the amount of effort required to complete the audit and to determine whether the planned schedule is achievable.
- It allows the audit team to become familiar with the health and safety issues and standards at the site.

Notes may be taken during the tour, but the auditors should refrain from completing the protocols during the tour.

Information collection

The primary goal of the audit team while on-site is the collection of relevant and credible information. All audits rely on three basic means of information collection:

- Carry out site inspections, using prepared checklists and protocols.
- Review relevant documents, such as environmental monitoring data and summary reports.
- Conduct structured interviews with selected facility personnel.

These three information sources are sometimes referred to as observation, documentation, and conversation. Generally speaking, the order presented reflects the reliability of the information: information collected through direct observation is generally more reliable than information obtained from documents, which is more credible than information collected through interviews. This is not to suggest that interview evidence is not important; rather, it recognizes that people's memories are not infallible and sometimes the interviewee innocently provides erroneous information. In all cases, audit information should be cross-checked to ensure it is correct.

Initial assessment of evidence

While on the site, the audit team typically reviews the collected information and prepares a preliminary summary of the audit findings (areas where the facility's practices or conditions do not meet some specified standard). This summary may be given to the site representatives in written or verbal form during the exit meeting; however, it is considered to be unofficial until the audit report is issued.

Exit meeting

The site visit typically ends with an exit (or closing) meeting, again between the audit team and the site representatives. The purpose of this meeting is to

- Review the purpose, scope, and methodology of the audit.
- Provide an overview of how the audit went and comments on the nature of the audit findings.
- Review the findings, stressing that these are preliminary and are subject to change during the preparation of the final report.
- Discuss the findings to ensure they are based on correct information.
- Discuss the next steps (e.g., preparation of the report and an action plan).
- Thank the site personnel for their cooperation and hospitality.

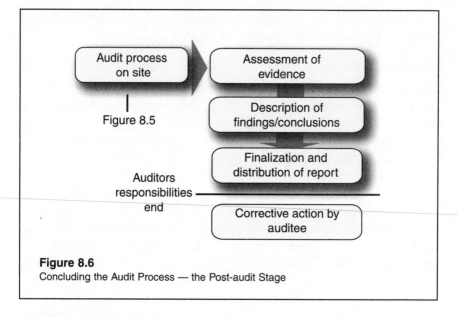

Figure 8.6
Concluding the Audit Process — the Post-audit Stage

Post-audit Stage

Final assessment of evidence

Once the audit team leader returns to his/her office, he/she will perform a more thorough review of the findings to ensure they are accurate and backed by supporting evidence. The other audit team members may be consulted for information during this process. It is considered inappropriate to contact the audited facility for additional information unless the missing information is essential to a significant finding or if such a call was discussed and agreed upon with site management.

Drafting of audit report

It is considered good practice to submit a draft report to the audit manager for review and comment rather than submitting a final report directly. Decisions on the distribution of the audit report are made by the audit manager.

Typically the reviewers of the draft report are given one to two weeks to review the draft and make comments. If no comments are received within the specified period, the audit team leader assumes there are no comments, and the report is finalized.

Finalization and distribution of audit report

Once the comments on the draft report are returned and addressed, the audit team leader submits the final report to the audit manager and to others as identified by the audit manager. In some cases the audit team may be asked to present the report in a formal presentation to senior management.

The audit team leader, not the audit manager, should always retain final editorial control of the report. For this reason, the team leader should only provide electronic versions of the report to the audit manager after he has obtained assurance that the findings and conclusions will not be modified.

Corrective Action Phase

An environmental audit program typically consists of two main phases: the audit phase, which we described above, and the corrective action phase, which consists of three main stages.

Action Planning

Management from the audited operation reviews the audit report and prepares a response to each audit finding. Because the typical audit finding is reported as a deficiency, the usual response is some type of corrective action. To be effective, someone, usually at the audited facility, will be assigned responsibility for designing and implementing each corrective action. A target date for completion is often set. In cases where the audit has identified numerous findings, the findings and corrective actions are prioritized to ensure that the most important deficiencies are addressed first. The action plan is often documented in a memo or report and included as part of the audit file, though not as part of the audit report.

Implementation and Monitoring

Once responsibilities for corrective action have been assigned, those responsible will have to complete the work satisfactorily, by the target date. The status of the corrective action is often tracked or monitored by site management or by the organization's environmental management department to ensure that the target date is met and to provide assistance if necessary.

Completion and Sign-off

Once the corrective action has been satisfactorily implemented, management of the audited site and/or the organization's environment department must verify completion through site inspection, interviews, or document review and sign off that the deficiency has been appropriately remedied.

The time required for the corrective action phase depends upon a number of factors: available people with skills and knowledge, budget, time, and the urgency of resolving the deficiency. In some cases, corrective action will occur over a number of years as budget resources become available.

The adequacy of implementation of the corrective actions is often evaluated in subsequent audits.

Why Audit?

Environmental auditing has become a standard environmental management tool in Canada. Most organizations that have environmental impacts or are subject to environmental regulations have developed environmental programs to help them manage these risks. Implementing an environmental audit program has been shown to provide significant benefits to organizations, including

- greater assurance to senior management that the organization's environmental risks are being controlled;
- overall improved environmental performance;
- cost-savings through avoidance of environmental problems, litigation, and fines;
- improved compliance with legal requirements;
- improved environmental management processes;
- increased awareness of environmental issues at the operating sites; and
- improved stakeholder relations.

The Professional Practice of Environmental Auditing

Over the past twenty years environmental auditing has gone from an informal management process implemented by a small number of large corporations to an internationally recognized and standardized discipline. Whereas in the mid 1980s the practice of environmental auditing was rudimentary and auditors often had little training and experience, today auditors are expected to have significant familiarity with the process through formal training and direct hands-on experience.

In 1991 the Canadian Environmental Audit Association /Association canadienne de verification environmentale (CEAA/ACVE) was founded by professionals interested in, and practicing, environmental auditing in Canada and was incorporated as a non-profit organization in 1994. The Mission of the CEAA/ACVE is to encourage the development and the discipline of environmental auditing and the improvement of environmental management of Canadian public and private organizations through an auditor certification process and the application of environmental auditing ethics, principles, and standards. The association's membership is multi-disciplinary, including engineers, scientists, accountants, and lawyers, all with a common interest in environmental auditing.[13]

The CEAA/ACVE's main functions include

- providing input to provincial and federal policies related to environmental auditing (for example, Canadian Standards Association Document

Z751: *Guidelines for Environmental Auditing: Statement of Principles and Practices*; ISO Technical Committee 207, which is responsible for developing and reviewing the ISO 14000 standards).

- managing a national certification program for environmental auditors that meets the requirements of ISO 14000. The CEAA/ACVE also developed *Qualification Criteria for Certified Environmental Auditors* and assisted the Coalition for Sustainable Forest Management to develop similar *Qualification Criteria for Certified Sustainable Forest Management Auditors*.
- developing and upholding a Code of Ethics for environmental auditors. All certified auditors must agree to abide by this code.
- providing for a discussion of environmental auditing issues, through the publication of the *Auditorial*, a quarterly newsletter, and through an annual general meeting and technical conference.
- developing international perspectives and linkages in the field of environmental auditing and environmental management through ongoing communication with other environmental auditing associations.

As mentioned, one of the key developments in the area of environmental auditing in the 1990s was the establishment of the environmental auditor certification process by the CEAA/ACVE. While certification is not mandatory for environmental auditors, it does serve to indicate to clients that the auditor's experience and skills have been reviewed and accepted by peers, and that the auditor is bound by the CEAA's Code of Ethics which is as follows:

Each CEAA member will endeavor to

- be honest and candid, and perform professional services with integrity and due care;
- be competent, having the required skills, knowledge, and experience to perform the services undertaken;
- continually seek to maintain and improve professional knowledge and skills;
- serve the client in a conscientious, diligent, and efficient manner;
- hold in strict confidence, except as required bylaw, all information concerning the business and affairs of the client acquired in the course of the professional relationship, and not use this information for personal gain ;
- remain free of any influence, interest, or relationship that impairs professional judgment, independence, or objectivity, while providing professional services;
- commit to honest, thorough, and straightforward communication in the performance of professional duties;
- not be associated with any report, statement, or representation known to be false or misleading;

- not advertise in a misleading manner or in a manner that is injurious to the profession; and
- conduct himself or herself toward other professional auditors with courtesy and good faith and endeavor at all times to enhance the public regard for the profession.

Recently, the U.S. EPA commissioned the National Academy of Public Administration to do a year-long study to assess the effectiveness of the registration process for ISO 14001. The study provided a long list of recommendations but concluded that the current system is fundamentally sound although more attention has to be paid to gain public confidence in the system, through implementing the recommendations. The recommendations were presented to the American National Standards Institute and the Registrar Accreditation Board that administer the ISO 14001 accreditation program in the United States. They included standardization of the registrars' interpretation of the standard, institution of a peer review process, and a requirement for certification for EMS auditors and consultants similar to the process for certified public accountants.

Other countries would do well to consider similar changes, because the credibility of the auditors will determine how much confidence stakeholders such as the public, investors, banks, and regulators can have in audit results.

PricewaterhouseCoopers reports that the International Accounting Standards Committee is working with organizations such as the International Organization of Securities Commissioners, the European Union, and G7 governments to develop global accounting standards.[14] Although the focus will be on financial accounting, the global standards should influence, if not include, environmental auditing standards.

WHO AUDITS THE AUDITORS?

Conclusion

Environmental auditing has become a fundamental environmental management tool for organizations in Canada and internationally. Many companies have found it to be an effective tool for assessing compliance with regulations and other obligations, and for evaluating the integrity of management systems and practices.

The environmental audit methodology has become standardized in North America and Europe, and internationally accepted standards for conducting an audit now exist. While each audit will differ in the details, all audits follow a basic process consisting of three stages: pre-audit activities, on-site activities, and post-audit activities. Any deviation from this basic methodology results in the exercise not being a true audit (i.e., may be considered as a review or assessment.)

Auditors in Canada can now become certified through the Canadian Environmental Audit Association (CEAA). The process for achieving certification is rigorous and requires a review of experience and a demonstration of knowledge through a written examination, which is evaluated by peers. The CEAA has developed a Code of Ethics for all certified auditors to ensure a consistent level of integrity and quality for its practitioners.

Recommended Further Reading

Cahill, L. B. *Environmental Audits*. Rockville, Maryland: Government Institutes Inc.: 2001.

Robertson J., and W. Smieliauskas. *Auditing and Other Asssurance Engagements*. 1st Canadian Edition. Toronto: McGraw Hill Ryerson,1998.

Thompson, D., and M. Wilson. "Environmental Auditing: Theory and Practice." *Environmental Management* 18, no.4 (1994): pp. 605-615.

Standards

CAN/CSA. *ISO 14010 – 96 Guidelines for Environmental Auditing: General Principles*. Rexdale, Ontario: Canadian Standards Association, 1996.

CAN/CSA. *ISO 14011 – 96 Guidelines for Environmental Auditing. Audit procedures: Auditing of Environmental Management Systems*. Rexdale, Ontario: Canadian Standards Association, 1996.

CAN/CSA. *ISO 14012 – 96 Guidelines for Environmental Auditing: Qualification Criteria for · Environmental Auditors*. Rexdale, Ontario: Canadian Standards Association, 1996.

Websites

American Society for Quality: <www.asq.org>

American Society for Testing and Materials: <www.astm.org>

The Auditing Roundtable: The Professional Organization for EHS Auditors: <www.auditear.org>

Board of EHS Auditor Certifications: <www.beac.org>

Canadian Environmental Auditing Association: <www.ceaa.acve.ca>

International Accounting Standards Committee (Board): <www.iasc.org.uk>

EDUCATION AND TRAINING

Dixon Thompson

EDUCATION AND TRAINING are essential tools for effective implementation and operation of Environmental Management Systems. They are also critical for successful application of environmental management tools, continual improvement, and establishing due diligence. Education and training must explain what environmental policy is and why particular actions are being taken in order to get buy-in from stakeholders.

The words education and training are often used interchangeably, as synonyms. Here we will use education and training to refer to both processes, but the individual terms education and training will be used differently. The Air and Waste Management Association makes these same distinctions in their education programs and training programs.[1]

Education instills knowledge about general principles and basic concepts as they relate to the institution's activities, the environment in which it operates, and the environmental issues that are of direct concern. General principles and basic concepts do not change much over time, so refresher seminars, courses, and updating are required, but not re-education. All inside and many outside stakeholders should be educated, at an appropriate level of detail, about the corporation's environmental policies and activities, the components of the environment that are, or could be, affected by its activities, and its environmental performance. (See chapter 13, Environmental Reporting and chapter 20, Environmental Communications.)

Training relates to techniques or technologies required for a specific task. Only those doing a particular task require training to do it. As techniques and technologies change, retraining is required. Training generally involves employees; however, some other environmental management tools may involve training of suppliers (purchasing guidelines), and product stewardship may require training of customers. Emergency response plans certainly require training of anyone who might be involved in an emergency situation.

The attention that education and training has received in the environmental management literature does not reflect the critical role they must play. *Greening People Part 3 Training and Skills towards Environmental Improvement*,[2] especially the chapter by Milliman and Clair[3] and one of the case studies, address this issue. Two chapters in *ISO 14000 and Beyond*, one by Crognale[4] and one by Wells[5] provide basic advice. MacLean provides strategies for building a strong professional development program.[6] His article in *EM* is followed by a case study showing that education improves regulatory compliance for hazardous materials handling.[7]

Most professional associations related to Environmental Management Systems and tools offer education programs, or at least annual conferences, which provide education and training opportunities (Air and Waste Management Association, Society of Environmental Toxicology and Chemistry, International Association for Impact Assessment, Global Environmental Management Initiative, etc.), so it is possible to get information on courses, seminars, and conferences from those organizations. A web search will provide a long list of private sector organizations that provide education and training programs for environment, health, and safety.

If education and training proceed successfully but there is no change in the institution and the setting in which stakeholders find themselves, then those who have been educated and trained will likely be frustrated by the incongruity between what they have learned and the setting in which they must operate. Therefore, institutions have to learn.[8]

This chapter addresses seven main topics: the importance of education and training, educating internal stakeholders, training internal stakeholders, educating external stakeholders, training external stakeholders, learning institutions, and certification and accreditation.

Education programs include informal means to provide information through reports, CD Roms, videos, and websites; attendance at conferences, seminars, and discussion groups; and formal means where evaluation and certification take place. Training is generally more specific but varies from training on energy conservation, greenhouse gas emission reduction, and waste minimization to formal training in health, safety, and environmental protection techniques and technologies, often required by regulations or codes.

Education and training are critical whether the corporate environmental strategy is proactive or reactive. A proactive strategy may require more sophisticated skills and knowledge and therefore more education and training.

A large city made a commitment to design and implement an Environmental Management System. Responsibilities were assigned to individuals in the departments involved and a series of meetings were organized to start the design and implementation process. However, the individuals involved in the meetings were not given adequate education and training, so the scheduled meetings lacked direction and progress stalled. Failure to train employees given responsibility for the design and implementation of the EMS resulted in failure to complete the project on schedule, wasting time and money.

The Importance of Education and Training

Education and training play a critical role in obtaining the benefits that an Environmental Management System can provide. ISO 14001 EMS requires education and training as part of the EMS. Section 4.2(e) requires that policy is communicated to all employees and Section 4.4.2 addresses awareness and competence.[9] ISO 14004, the guidance document for ISO 14001, elaborates on awareness and motivation in Section 4.3.2.4 and knowledge, skills, and training in Section 4.3.2.5.[10] EMAS (Eco-management and audit scheme) has a short part of Annex 1 Part B that mentions awareness, competence, and training.[11] The CSA[12] and GEMI[13] also provide advice on awareness and training.

We have identified education and training as one of eight prerequisites to help guarantee success that must be in place before implementing an EMS:

1. basic understanding of ISO 14001, vocabulary, costs, benefits, etc.;
2. scope and scale of EMS needed;
3. commitment — by whom, how;
4. champion — delegated responsibility;
5. resources — time, money;
6. skills, knowledge, expertise (consultants if necessary);
7. education and training; and
8. implementation strategy.

Benefits of Education and Training

There are six main benefits to be obtained by well-designed education and training programs: cost savings, reduction of risk and contingent costs, due diligence, continual improvement, credibility, and EMS efficiency and effectiveness.

Cost Savings

Those institutions that do not use energy or water and do not generate any waste won't need education and training programs. Neither will corporations that are unaffected by the rapid rate of change in the field of environmental management. All other corporations and institutions can obtain benefits and/or avoid costs through programs for education and training. At the very least, even for those institutions with very low environmental risks, education and training can assist in conservation of energy and water and reduction of waste to obtain direct savings.

As the level of energy, water, and material consumption increases and as environmental impacts and risks increase, the benefits that can be obtained from education and training also increase. If all employees are educated about how much, and what kind of, energy is used and what the options are for savings, then a set of training programs can be introduced to reduce energy consumption and therefore contribute to reduction of greenhouse gas emissions, which could provide an economic benefit in marketable emission reduction credits. Education and training can reduce water consumption and waste water generation and is an essential component of solid and hazardous waste minimization and recycling programs, resulting in significant cost savings.

Some training is required by law, for example, where employees are exposed to hazardous materials. Emergency response and safety programs have comprehensive training components. Any system in which employees need certification will require formal education and training. There are cost savings in less employee lost time and lower insurance costs when staff is properly trained.

Reduction of Risk and Contingent Costs

Costs imposed by spills, accidents, or unanticipated events can be reduced by education and training for those institutions that have identified risks. Costs of emergency responses, cleanup of spills and other accidents, fines, lawsuits for damages, legal fees, and increased insurance premiums can add up. These costs are harder to quantify and it is more difficult to convince decision makers of the value of avoiding them. Improvement of compliance with laws and regulations and subsequent reduction of contingent costs are two of the greater benefits of education and training.

Training is an essential component of risk control in risk management (chapter 10) and is closely linked to human factors (chapter 21) as a management tool for reducing risks, improving quality of the workplace, and reducing errors that create waste or cause accidents.

Due Diligence

The standards that must be met for a successful due diligence defense continue to change. Three criteria for due diligence undergo constant change: previous court rulings, the understanding of what a well-informed individual would have done in the circumstances, and industry practice. Education and training must be used to keep employees up to date about how those three criteria are changing with respect to their particular responsibilities. If corporate officials establish an excellent environmental policy but fail to educate and train employees to effectively implement it, then it is likely that they would not have been duly diligent. In a 1998 case in British Columbia, the court found that although the company had an advanced EMS, among other problems "there was a breakdown in the implementation and training."[14]

Continual Improvement

Continual improvement (Figure 1.4) is required by the ISO 14001 Environmental Management System and is necessary for any EMS that is not doomed to stagnate and become out of date. Continual improvement depends upon education and training, therefore they are crucial components of any EMS that requires continual improvement.

Credibility

An effective education and training program is essential to maintain credibility with both internal and external stakeholders. Keeping them up to date about activities, initiatives, and indicators of success (or failure) is important. Chapter 20, Environmental Communication, addresses the issue of the importance of maintaining credibility.

EMS Effectiveness and Efficiency

Institutions have voluntarily chosen to try to improve environmental performance, or have been pushed into it by outside forces. However, these initiatives sometimes fail because those handed the responsibility for design and implementation of an EMS, or the use of a particular environmental management tool such as an EIA or an environmental audit, are not adequately educated and trained.

Media and Processes

Instructional materials for education and training come in a wide variety of options: brochures, pamphlets, newsletters, environmental reports, websites, videos, CD ROMs. Because the materials will likely be used to reach several different audiences, the same information can be presented at different levels of detail, with different vocabularies. Chapter 20, Environmental Communication, discusses the importance of communications strategies for all stakeholders. Chapter 7, Environmental Management Structures, outlines processes for identifying actors, participants, and stakeholders who would make up the various audiences which a communications strategy must address.

The Importance of Professional Judgment

ENGOs, the public, corporations, and practicing professionals are justifiably concerned about issues of objectivity and subjectivity in the design and implementation of EMSs and the application of environmental management tools. Qualified professionals have to make professional judgements on predictions of impacts, selection of options from possible alternatives, and setting of priorities. They have to make decision on whether components, impacts, or aspects are appropriate, significant, acceptable, or harmful. It is important to note that qualified professionals have specific education, experience, and a code of ethics to guide their judgment which makes that professional opinion more objective, or at least less subjective, than one by someone without those qualifications. The importance of those professional opinions is a critical reason for maintaining high quality education and training for environmental professionals and for professional development (continuing professional education).

Environmental education and training programs can make use of a wide variety of educational processes:

- informal, passive processes in which stakeholders are provided with information to be absorbed if, and when, they want to put in the time and effort;
- self-learning packages used by employees and others but with some form of evaluation to check on how much had been learned;
- seminars and workshops where formal instruction takes place but without testing and evaluation;
- attendance at conferences;
- seminars and workshops with a testing and evaluation process;
- courses on specific topics (safety, WHMIS, H2S, CPR, first aid, etc.), which are required for employment in certain positions;
- formal courses with certification (e.g., AWMA, SETAC, CEAA);
- formal courses at universities and technical schools;
- specific degree requirements for particular positions, such as engineering, biology, chemistry, accounting;
- ongoing (continual) professional education and upgrading;
- awareness building by educating employees about issues and putting them in touch with nature; and
- team building.

Stakeholders — Internal and External

Educating Internal Stakeholders

Employees and board directors must be educated about the corporation's environmental policy. Because the policy should be updated periodically, the education program must be able to bring everyone up to date. All employees should be educated about the adverse impacts that the company has on the environment and the procedures to reduce those impacts. A positive environmental record could be a tool in retaining valuable employees. The best 35 employers in Canada invested an average of 40 hours per year per employee in education and training. They all offered 100 per cent tuition reimbursement for job-related courses, 11 offered tuition reimbursement for non-job-related courses and 8 offered paid sabbaticals.[15] If there are particular environmental concerns such as climate change, the ozone layer, water pollution, air pollution, or hazardous wastes, then programs should educate employees about those issues and why they are of concern. The progress (or lack thereof) made by the corporation in reducing impacts should be a feedback component of the education program. Programs to conserve water and energy, minimize and/or recycle waste should also be part of the education program because awareness and participation by everyone is necessary to optimize results. Once the education programs provide the basics and raise awareness, then training programs on employees' responsibilities and duties must follow.

Educating External Stakeholders

Some external stakeholders could require the same education as internal stakeholders, if there is a formal (contractual) relationship that brings them under corporate environmental policies. Contractors and suppliers could be included here.

Other external stakeholders (employees' families, local communities, customers, ENGOs, etc.) can be educated through informal, passive systems (provision of information in suitable forms) or through more formal systems such as workshops and seminars, depending upon the environmental communication strategy.

Training of Internal Stakeholders

It is essential that individual employees, or groups of employees, receive training on their specific tasks or equipment. As techniques or technologies change, retraining must take place. Training about health and safety issues, hazardous materials, first aid, and CPR must be repeated depending upon legislation and regulations and rules governing insurance coverage, certification requirements, etc.

Emergency response (chapter 10, Risk Management) and environmental communication (chapter 20) impose special training requirements.

Where employees use, or contribute to the use of, other environmental management tools, they must be adequately trained, according to their roles. Site assessments, Environmental Impact Assessments, risk management, environmental audits, purchasing guidelines, life cycle assessment, and environmental accounting practices all require special skills and knowledge. Even when outside consultants are used, some training of employees might be important to ensure that inputs to the process are of a suitable quality, and that the results can be applied to the best advantage.

Training of External Stakeholders

Where emergencies could affect local communities or other members of the public, it may be essential to train external stakeholders about emergency response.

Where purchasing guidelines are introduced to reduce upstream environmental impacts by suppliers, corporations have supported programs to assist suppliers, especially smaller companies, with education and training to help them meet the requirements. The Center for the New American Dream and TerraChoice, the consultant supporting Canada's eco-labeling program, hosted a conference on purchasing and the Centre sponsors free bi-monthly conference calls on a variety of green purchasing topics.[16] Where product stewardship is part of corporate policy, training programs, or at least information, should be available for customers.

Learning Institutions

Institutions must also be able to adjust to changing circumstances — they must become learning institutions. Oliver Sacks, the renowned abnormal psychologist,[17] has defined a normal person as someone who can tell their story and identify threats in their current environment. This definition can be extended to corporations and institutions which are normal if they are able to tell their own story (i.e., knows their history) and are able to identify things that threaten them. Using these definitions and the requirements for learning, it can be concluded that to be normal and to be able to learn, individuals and corporations must have memory (to know their history, their story), and there must be feedback so that experience can be gained. Experience is essential for determining whether plans were successful and for analyzing whether the plan was flawed, whether it was badly implemented, or both.

Peter Senge describes the five disciplines required for learning institutions and, therefore, for the individuals within them in *The Fifth Discipline* and in the workbook *The Fifth Discipline Fieldbook*:[18]

- building shared vision
- mental models
- team learning
- personal mastery
- systems thinking

If this system of corporate learning is to work, employees must have opportunities to play roles in setting the vision and mission statements and setting goals and objectives, to use North American terms, or in setting the corporate policy, in ISO 14001 terms.

These five requirements also mean that employees must be provided with specific skills and knowledge: teamwork skills, interdisciplinary skills, and communications skills. Teamwork skills are not the same as interdisciplinary skills: a team of engineers, or lawyers, or biologists needs teamwork and communication skills but does not need interdisciplinary skills. This is because they all belong to the same profession and so must have similar education, experience, language, mental models, and basic assumptions. A team made up of engineers, lawyers, biologists, and others must have teamwork skills, interdisciplinary skills and communications skills because they do not share common technical language, mental models, education, and experience.

An EMS should introduce some aspects of a learning institution: strategic environmental planning and management require systems thinking, and environmental audits provide feedback, because audit criteria must include corporate policy. Documentation required by ISO 14001 provides memory.

Being a learning institution implies a willingness to change as a result of that learning. Any institution with a reluctance to change cannot really be a learning institution. Rogers' Innovation Curve,[19] (see Figure 4.2) suggests that, for some people, there may be an inherent reluctance to change and, therefore, a reluctance to learn in a significant proportion of corporations.

Strategy for successful education and training would necessarily be different, and more difficult, in those institutions in which innovation and change is not encouraged. Therefore, before designing and implementing an education and training program, some sense of corporate culture and attitudes to learning and change would be important.

Similarly, individuals have different attitudes to learning. Depending upon hiring practices and educational background, employees will be active learners who are seeking opportunities to learn, or passive learners who will learn to various degrees if placed in an appropriate situation, and some will be resistant.

The willingness to learn (actively or passively) may also vary with the topic (interested or disinterested) and the corporate culture: education and training is important and part of career advancement versus it is only something we do because we have to.

Certification and Accreditation: Qualifications of Professionals

Because of the increasing importance of EMS and environmental management tools, the control of the quality of professional practice is becoming more important.

There is the need to maintain the credibility of the profession, for employers to hire qualified professionals and for professionals seeking employment, and for individuals and institutions seeking professional help. Maintenance of the quality of professional practice lies with

- legislators and regulators who control some aspects of professional practice,
- the professional bodies (associations) that have been given responsibility for professional practice by legislation,
- individual professionals,
- national and international professional organizations, and
- international organizations dealing with issues of certification and registration.

There are five types of certification or similar qualifications:

- restricted practice — the right to practice the profession is stipulated by legislation and controlled by the professional organization;
- restricted activities — professionals doing tasks which require specific skills and/or training have to be evaluated;
- right to title — legislation gives control of the right to use the title to a professional organization but no right to control the practice (biology, chemistry, etc.);
- member of a professional association — membership is open to those who meet the organization's requirements with no legislative support (AWMA, SETAC, IAIA etc.); and
- certified practitioner — organizations certify practitioners who meet their requirements but there is no legislative support (QEP, Qualified Environmental Professional by the AWMA; CCEP, Canadian Certified Environmental Professional by the Canadian Environmental Certification and Assessment Board; certified environmental auditors, and registrars, etc.).

All professions require aspirants to meet three qualifications:

- education in the profession's skills and knowledge to a specific level in all required topics;
- experience in applying those skills and knowledge for a specified time, often under the guidance of a qualified professional supervisor; and
- adherence to a code of professional ethics (although enforcement can be problematic).

Legislation uses three different models to define a profession. Legislation governing restricted practice and restricted activities dictates that the profession sets the criteria and standards and controls the admission to the profession by issuing a license or other document to people meeting the necessary qualifications. Therefore, people who are not licensed can be charged with practicing without a license if they attempt to operate as a professional in those fields. Professionals under restricted practice and restricted activities in the fields of law, medicine, accounting, and engineering make important contributions to environmental management. However, so far, there are no examples of legislation that apply to environmental management. The legislation allows members, and only members, to use the title after their name, e.g., M.D., P. Eng.

A less rigorous level of legislated professionalism is right to title. Unless practitioners can prove that they meet the designated professional organization's qualifications (education, experience, ethics), they cannot claim to be a member of that profession. The legislation allows members of the profession to use a title after their name (e.g., Professional Chemist, P. Chem. or Professional Biologist, P. Biol.).

In the above cases related to professional practices in environmental management, continuing professional development is being required in order for practitioners to keep up to date and to retain the right to practice or the right to title.

Membership in a professional organization is a type of involvement in a profession that is not established by legislation and is much less formal. There is no legislated designation or title but these organizations are crucial for advancing the state of the art and keeping members up to date in fields that play critical roles in environmental management: AWMA, SETAC, IAIA, ONE of the Academy of Management, etc. These organizations are increasingly becoming international and, in some cases, multilingual (AWMA's editorials are now in English, French, and Spanish). They are improving the quality of professional practice, advancing the state of the art, harmonizing practice internationally, and providing advice to governments. They inform their members and add to the relevant bodies of knowledge through annual meetings, conferences, education and training programs, newsletters and journals, websites, and working groups.

The fourth type of professional qualification is certification for particular skills. At present, this type of certification has been confined mainly to environmental auditing. This may be the result of the close relationship between financial auditing where certification of financial auditors or accountants has been required for a long time. In the case of auditing for registration of companies under ISO 14001, national organizations are responsible for certification of registrars — for example, the Registration Accreditation Bureau in the U.S.A. and the Canadian Standards Association. Certification of lead auditors and auditors rests with the American National Standards Institute and American Society for Quality and the Canadian Environmental Auditing Association.

Professional Standards and Qualifications at the National and International Levels

In developed countries and many developing countries, there are national and state/provincial institutions involved in maintaining the quality or standards of professional practice related to environmental management. Almost all countries have an institution that is responsible for the application of ISO standards.[20] There is concern that some of these institutions are very weak and that certification may only involve paying a fee, rather than meeting specific standards. This concern will be resolved if: there is stricter control of registration and certification by appropriate international bodies, international assistance is provided to improve the education and training capacity in developing countries, and people hiring professionals carefully scrutinize their qualifications and work.

At the national level, umbrella organizations have been established for environmental management: the Institute of Environmental Management and Assessment in the U.K.,[21] the Environmental Institute of Australia,[22] and the Canadian Council for Human Resource in the Environment Industry.[23]

At the international level, the International Organization for Standardization has set the qualifications for environmental auditors in ISO 19012 (ISO 14012). They have established methodologies for other environmental management tools such as Life Cycle Assessment, but not the qualifications for practitioners. However, the ISO has little, if any, control over the application of the standards.

Internationally there are organizations working to maintain and improve international auditing, certification, and registration standards. Some of these are not yet working directly on environmental issues but their work will indirectly affect environmental standards or will expand into that area. The International Auditing Training and Certification Association (IATCA)[24] is dedicated to improving business performance. The International Accreditation Forum (IAF)[25] is dedicated to facilitating trade and commerce in accordance with WTO policies. Presumably, as the WTO includes environmental issues in its considerations, the IAF would include environmental management standards. The International Auditing Standards Committee[26] of the International Federation of Accountants is working to improve auditing internationally. Because of the requirements to include environmental liabilities in financial audits, environmental audits will also be improved.

The Certification Monitoring Network is a group of environmental and consumer organizations that polices advertising claims made in connection with ISO 9000 and 14000 standards, EMAS, and others.[27]

Increasingly international activity will be directed at improving the capabilities of professionals doing environmental audits and environmental impact assessments, where there are now concerns about poorly qualified practitioners or outright fraud. The demand for improved education and training and establishment and maintenance of high standards will increase. This will require international cooperation and capacity building in education and training in developing countries and countries in transition, with contributions from professional organizations and registrars around the world.

Recent work by Stephen Hill at the University of Calgary has shown that education and training only partly solve the problem of improving environmental performance because knowledge is only one of four factors that influence how managers assess environmental risks. The other three factors are salience (how close is the issue — is it going to have direct and immediate impact?), an emotional or spiritual connection to nature, and feelings about the resilience of nature.[28] People use experience (experiential knowledge) and feelings (emotive knowledge) in addition to theoretical knowledge to assess situations. Therefore, institutions wanting to improve employees' analysis of, and response to, environmental problems have to consider all four factors and how they can assist each other.

Salience is the directness of the relationship of the individual to environmental issues. How much damage is caused to you or could be caused to your children? Is the problem immediate or remote? Where there is no salience, increasing empathy would be one way of increasing the significance of this factor. Empathy could be enhanced by visiting sites where environmental damage has occurred or problems have arisen and talking directly to those affected, suggesting that employees put themselves in the place of those affected. Environmental problems may not be salient for corporate executives who live and work in another country. Where empathy does not increase salience, other driving forces could do so by hitting executives or employees where it hurts — fines for infractions, civil law suits for damages, and the application of other economic instruments.

Opportunities to spend time in a natural environment might increase the feeling of a connection to nature.[29] Providing opportunities for direct experience and understanding of the resilience of nature would be more difficult. It may be that education about the stability of ecosystems and climate, thresholds for radical change (flips of apparently stable systems — rapid change between stable or relatively stable states) is the only avenue with respect to this factor.

Recommended Further Reading

Crognale, G. "Training; Preparations for Maintaining Effective Environmental Management Systems." In *ISO 14000 and Beyond: Environmental Management Systems in the Real World*, edited by C. Sheldon. Sheffield, U.K.: Greenleaf Publishing, 1997.

Senge, P. *The Fifth Discipline: The Art and Practice of the Learning Organization.* New York: Currency Doubleday, 1994.

Wehrmeyer, W., ed. *Greening People: Human Resources and Environmental Management, Part 3: Training and Skills towards Environmental Improvement,* Sheffield, U.K.: Greenleaf Publishing, 1996.

Wells, A. "Training and Environmental Management Systems." In *ISO 14000 and Beyond: Environmental Management Systems in the Real World,* edited by C. Sheldon. Sheffield, U.K.: Greenleaf Publishing, 1997.

10

RISK MANAGEMENT

*Lisa-Henri Kirkland, Wolfwillow Environmental
and Dixon Thompson*

The revolutionary idea that defines the boundary between modern
times and the past is the mastery of risk: the notion that the future
is more than a whim of the gods and that men and women are not
passive before nature.[1]

WHEN RISK MANAGEMENT was first developed in the 1800s, it was applied to
finances. In the past century, risk management techniques have been
adapted and broadened so that risk assessment and risk management of environmental issues are now well-recognized fields in environmental management. Since
the early 1980s, risk management has emerged as an environmental management
tool that has influenced regulations, decision making, and policy.

What is Risk?

The Oxford dictionary defines risk as "the chance of hazard, bad consequences,
loss, etc." Risk is the likelihood of an undesired effect.

The Canadian Standards Association defines environmental risk as "the chance
of injury or loss as defined as a measure of the probability and severity of an
adverse effect to health, property, the environment, or other things of value."[2]

Risk is often defined according to one of three approaches: the engineering
approach, the (eco)toxicological approach, and the actuarial approach of the
insurance industry. These are distinctly different methods of risk assessment which
use different terms and models. Managers should understand that one is not more
correct or better than the other — the differences arise from the varied approaches of the three professions to assessment of risk.

In the engineering approach, risk is defined in terms of probability and
consequence:

risk = probability x consequence

Both probability and consequence must be present in order for a situation to present any risk. If there is zero probability or zero consequence, then risk is zero. As probability and/or consequence increases, then so does the risk. There are, therefore, two options for controlling risk — reduce the probability and/or reduce the consequences.

Toxicologists often define risk in terms of three components: stressor (or source of contaminant), pathway(s) (or route), and receptors (or target). In this definition, a stressor (a contaminant that can cause an adverse effect) travels along a pathway to reach a receptor (a target that can be affected). All three components must be possible in order for a risk to exist.

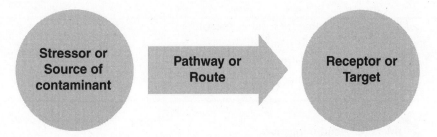

Risk may be perceived, financial, or a quantitative or comparative scientific estimate. Although perceived risk is more subjective than objective, it affects people's responses to a situation. In fact, perceived risk may often overshadow the understanding of real risk in a situation. Therefore, perceived risk cannot be rejected because it is not scientific and must be recognized and carefully considered in risk management. Some scientists make the mistake of suggesting that public perceptions are wrong when they differ from the scientific estimate. Perceptions are not wrong, but they can be different and are a very important part of understanding risk and the public's response to it. (Risk perception is discussed more fully in chapter 20.)

Sometimes environmental risk is defined narrowly within the context of human well-being. However, environmental risk should be considered in a broader context, especially with respect to threats or risks to renewable resources such as agriculture, forestry, or fisheries, or as they relate to global risks such as global warming, loss of biodiversity, or endangered species.

What is Risk Management?

There is no single, precise definition of, or model for, risk management. Risk management can be defined in terms of its activities: "Risk management is the systematic application of management policies, procedures, and practices to the tasks of analyzing, evaluating, controlling, and communicating about risk issues."[3]

It can also be defined in terms of its goals: "Risk management is the process of identifying, evaluating, selecting, and implementing actions to reduce risk to human health and to ecosystems. The goal of risk management is scientifically sound, cost-effective, integrated actions that reduce or prevent risks while taking into account social, cultural, ethical, political, and legal considerations."[4] The U.S. Presidential/Congressional Commission on Risk Assessment and Risk Management identified six stages in risk management, as shown in Figure 10.1.[5] The Canadian Standards Association's risk management model includes the steps shown in Figure 10.2.[6] Although feedback is not clearly indicated in these models, monitoring and evaluation are important in improving the risk management process.

The use of either model requires specialists who are familiar with it and its applications. The relevant standards should be consulted. In larger and more complex cases, teams of specialists will be required.

Risk management can be divided into six general components:
- risk identification
- risk assessment
- risk control and mitigation
- emergency response
- risk communication
- risk perception

Risk Identification

Before risks can be assessed and managed, they must be identified. Some risks may be quite obvious, while others may be more difficult to identify. Developing a complete list of potential risks is important in analyzing a situation because some unrecognized risks may be significant. Focussing on the most obvious may result in resources being spent on less serious risks.

Risk identification can pose two major problems. One problem may occur when members of the public perceive a risk that is not recognized as such by government or industry, so they have a difficult time getting that particular risk on the public agenda. There are few readily accessible, formal means for concerned citizens to bring their perceptions of risk to government agencies. A second problem may occur when the formal mechanisms for monitoring adverse impacts, which suggest that risks exist, are not effective, so adverse impacts go undetected until numbers accumulate to the point that someone raises an alarm. Recent examples include prescription drugs, vehicle or tire safety, and food and water contamination with E. coli H: 0157.

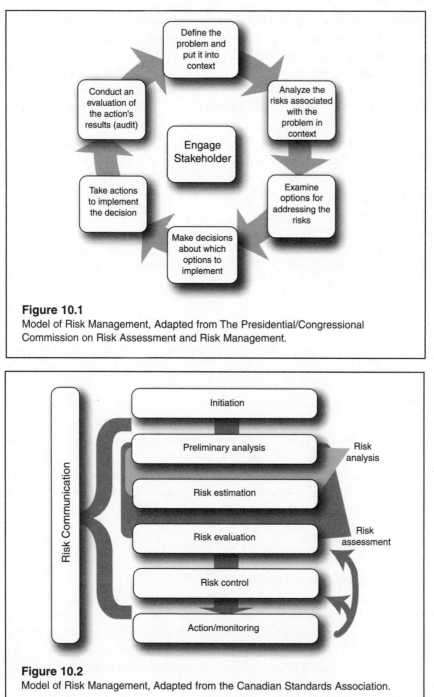

Figure 10.1
Model of Risk Management, Adapted from The Presidential/Congressional Commission on Risk Assessment and Risk Management.

Figure 10.2
Model of Risk Management, Adapted from the Canadian Standards Association.

Risk identification can be carried out th rough a variety of means including
- review of regulatory requirements — regulatory requirements may refer to specific risks associated with an activity or situation;
- analysis of inputs and outputs in a process — knowing what goes into and comes out of a process or system may indicate the risks associated with it;
- process analysis — looking at various parts of a process may assist in identifying risks;
- analyzing possible stressors, receptors, and pathways in a system;
- job hazard analysis — observing people carrying out tasks can help identify risks in those tasks (chapter 21);
- brainstorming — convening a group of people familiar with the situation to identify risks in it;
- environmental impact assessment (chapter 14);
- product and technology assessment (chapter 17);
- environmental scanning of the press and stakeholders for emerging concerns (chapter 20);
- epidemiology;
- anecdotal evidence; and
- disasters, accidents or near misses (chapter 21).

Use of more than one method of risk identification often identifies risks that a single method may miss or underestimate.

Risk Assessment

Risk assessment is the estimation or calculation of the likelihood of undesired effects due to a risk. It can be used to screen out trivial issues, to gauge how significant a risk is, and to prioritize issues.

"Risk assessment is the determination of the kind and degree of hazard posed by an agent, the extent to which a particular group of people has been or may be exposed to the agent, and the present or potential health risk that exists due to the agent."[7]

Kaplan and Garrick note that a risk assessment seeks to answers three questions: What can happen, what can go wrong? How likely is it that it will happen? If it does happen, what are the consequences?[8]

Some risk assessments may be more normative than others and include consideration of human values and socioeconomic issues as well as physical effects. For example, the Canadian Standards Association definition includes both risk analysis and risk evaluation as components of risk assessment. It also includes softer stakeholder issues: "Risk evaluation: the process by which risks are examined in terms of costs and benefits, and evaluated in terms of acceptability of risk considering the needs, issues, and concerns of the stakeholders."[9]

As with risk management, there is no universally accepted process for carrying out a risk assessment. The methods and sequences in carrying out a risk assessment vary, depending on

- the kind of risk,
- the requirements and accepted methods in various jurisdictions,
- the background and experience of the assessors, and
- the purpose of the risk assessment (internal or external stakeholders).

Risk assessment approaches can be seen as falling into one of two types based on the definition of risk one uses: an (eco)toxicological approach or an engineering approach. Some risk assessment involves a combination of the two approaches.

The (Eco)Toxicological Approach to Risk Assessment

Based on the key concepts of stressors, pathways, and receptors, the biological or (eco)toxicological approach to risk assessment involves the steps shown in Figure 10.3.

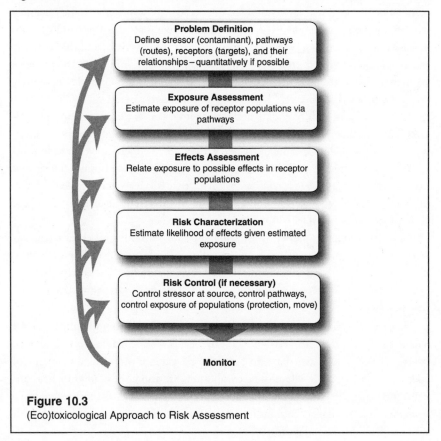

Figure 10.3
(Eco)toxicological Approach to Risk Assessment

Problem Definition

During problem definition, an understanding of the system or site is developed, goals of the assessment are outlined, and working hypotheses are defined. Problem definition includes identifying stressors (sources of contaminants), pathways (routes), and receptors (targets).

Exposure Assessment

Exposure assessment estimates "the extent of adverse effects likely to result from given levels of exposure to a risk agent are then estimated."[10] Factors that may be considered in the exposure assessment include

- size of population affected,
- types of population exposed (young, healthy adult, pregnant and lactating, elderly, sick, etc.), and
- duration, timing, and magnitude of exposure.

It is essential to understand the characteristics of hazardous materials and contaminants to assess risk in the (eco)toxicological approach. When acutely poisonous chemicals are involved, it is critical to guarantee that leaks and spills do not occur, that there is a very good emergency response system, and that employees are well trained and protected. The use of cyanide in mining or the presence of high concentrations of hydrogen sulfide in sour gas are examples of acutely toxic chemicals that pose very high risk if not handled carefully.

It is important to differentiate between chemicals that decompose in the environment and those that are persistent and accumulate in the environment and in animal tissues (including human tissue). Heavy metals (mercury, lead, cadmium) and persistent organic pollutants (some pesticides, PCBs, and other chlorinated compounds, etc.) can eventually accumulate to toxic levels even when fugitive emissions are below detection limits. Releases of these substances must therefore be kept as low as possible, if not eliminated altogether.

Another important aspect of assessing risk is determining whether chemicals have no threshold for toxicity — that is, all exposures cause harm and all exposures carry a risk. For those chemicals that have a threshold — that is, harm is unlikely below that threshold concentration — then exposures below that level are low risk (see Figure 10.4).

Trace nutrients are chemicals which are essential for plants and animals. If the diet is too low in the trace nutrients, disease occurs — anemia due to lack of iron, scurvy due to lack of ascorbic acid (vitamin C), thyroid problems due to lack of iodine, etc. Most, if not all, of these compounds are also poisonous at higher concentrations, so there is a range of concentrations that is essential for health while at higher or lower concentrations in the diet there is risk. This results in an inverted J curve as shown in Figure 10.5.

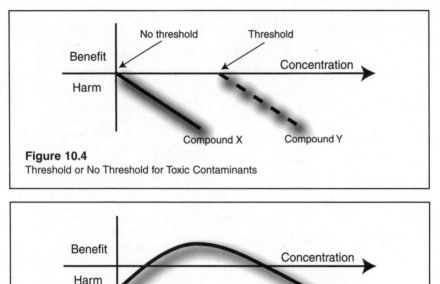

Figure 10.4
Threshold or No Threshold for Toxic Contaminants

Figure 10.5
Inverted J Curve for Trace Elements

Effects Assessment

In this step, the effect(s) (impacts) a contaminant may have on receptors is assessed. Depending upon the goals of the risk assessment, the effects considered may pertain to the health of human populations or ecosystems or both.

Ecological risk assessment commonly uses Environmental Impact Assessment (see chapter 14) and monitoring to assess potential hazards to ecosystems.

Table 10.1 Possible Effects of Contaminants and Sources of Data

Possible Human Health Effects	disease (e.g., cancer) illness reproductive and genetic abnormalities death
Possible Ecological Effects	loss of habitat deaths species extinction other ecosystem damage

Data on effects may be drawn from a number of sources:

Epidemiological Studies	Epidemiology is the determination of the causes of diseases in humans.	Provides a direct way of learning about effects on humans: if the level of exposure to the agent of interest and the exposed population can be well-defined and if the study is sufficiently sensitive to detect small changes in risk levels in a population.
Toxicological Studies	Toxicology involves the study of varying exposure levels on test animals in order to predict effects on humans.	Difficulties may be encountered in applying animal models to human beings. Costs of study may require that fewer animals are tested at high exposure levels thereby bringing statistical validity and low-dose effects into question.
Structure-Activity Studies	Evaluation of toxicity based on an agent's chemical structure.	This method can have a poor predictive capacity due to uncertainties about molecular structure and toxicity.
Exposure Data and Exposure Modelling	Identifying pathways (inhalation, ingestion, absorption) of the agent and doses, then estimating effects.	Simulation models are used when reliable human exposure data is not available

Risk Characterization

The (eco)toxicological approach characterizes risk as the combination of exposure and effects and offers three options for control: reduce the amount of exposure by reducing or eliminating the sources of the contaminant, interrupt or block the pathway or route of the contaminant, and/or protect the receptor or target.

The Engineering Approach to Risk Assessment

The engineering approach to risk assessment centers on probability and consequence and generally involves following the steps shown in Figure 10.6.

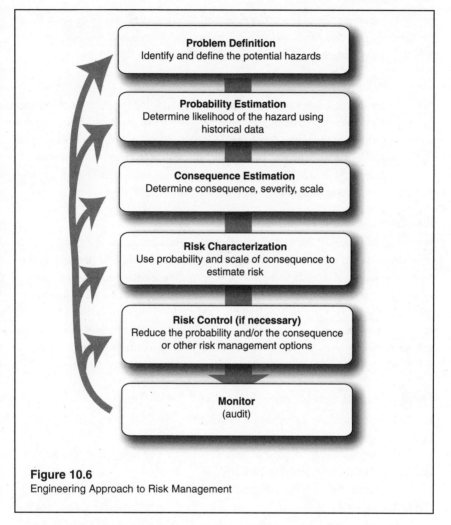

Figure 10.6
Engineering Approach to Risk Management

Problem Definition

When an engineering approach is applied to risk assessment, the problem is defined in terms of an event and outcome with associated probability and consequence. Sources or situations with a potential for harm are called hazards.

Probability Estimation

The likelihood or frequency of an event may be estimated through a number of means. Probability may be discovered through the use of statistical records of past similar events. Experience with near misses and similar events may indicate how likely something is to occur in a specific situation. People familiar with the process being evaluated may be able to offer expert opinion on an event's likelihood. Fault tree analysis and other formal mechanisms are highly technical methods for calculating probability, but are not dealt with in this chapter.

Consequence Estimation

Methods for determining the consequence of an event (or the severity of its outcome) include: detailed toxicological analysis, analysis of statistics indicating the severity of probable outcomes (explosion, fire, hazardous material spill, etc.), and the estimation of consequence, by a group of people familiar with the process being evaluated. Scenarios are often used to gain an understanding of possible consequences — worst-case scenario, plausible worst case, etc.

Risk Characterization

When the engineering approach is used, risk is characterized as the combination of probability and consequence. Therefore, in this approach there are two opportunities to reduce risk: reduce the probability and/or reduce the consequences.

For example, in the case of risk due to storage tanks filled with petroleum products, the probability of a spill can be reduced through education and training, sound maintenance and inspection programs, and fail-proof controls on valves. The consequence of a spill can be controlled (reduced) through adequate dykes or berms around the tanks and a good emergency response plan.

Qualitative and Quantitative Assessment

Risk assessment and the presentation of risk evaluation results may be qualitative or quantitative. A qualitative, professional judgment determines whether there is a significant probability of adverse effects. Quantitative risk assessment seeks to quantify risks (often in terms of probability).

Comparative risk assessment considers the risks that have been derived for several agents and orders them by size. There can be two levels of comparative risk assessment: specific risk comparison and programmatic comparative risk assessment. Specific risk comparison "refers to side-by-side evaluation of the risk (on an absolute or relative basis) associated with exposures to a few substances, products, or activities." Programmatic comparative risk assessment "seeks to make macro-level comparisons among widely differing types of risks, usually to provide information for setting regulatory and budgetary priorities for hazard reduction."[11]

Levels of Risk Assessment

Risk assessment may involve three levels of investigation. These are in order of increasing complexity and effort required:

Table 10.2 Levels of Risk Assessment

Screening (also known as Level 1)	Involves only existing data, conservative assumptions and is deterministic. *
Phase 1	Involves the gathering of additional data and may be deterministic or probabilistic. *
Phase 2	Involves more detailed data gathering and is probabilistic. *
* Deterministic assessment combines average, conservative, high, and worst-case scenarios to develop conservative point estimates for exposure and risk. Probabilistic risk assessment uses input variables as random variables in probability distributions to develop a distribution of risks.	

Looking at risk assessment from a broader perspective, a range of models may be applied:

- conceptual models
- statistical models
- physical models
- mechanistic mathematical models

The most robust assessments use several types of models that provide multiple lines of evidence for the assessments' conclusions and recognize that risk assessment is a complex process. Triangulation can be used to narrow in on a value or to verify that it can be derived using several approaches.

Uncertainty

Since risk involves probability, professional judgments, and predictions based on historical information, which may be incomplete, inaccurate, or very recent, it inherently involves uncertainty. Uncertainty in risk assessment may result from

- uncertainty in the inputs used to estimate probability,
- variability in situations or those being affected,
- inability to understand and characterize situations,
- variability in response in ecosystem health,
- limited ability to measure and model uncertainty accurately, and
- lack of historical records.

Uncertainty in risk assessment must be recognized and factored in so that the results can be understood in terms of their confidence level. Where uncertainty is significant and confidence levels are low, more research may be needed before confident estimates could be produced.

Risk Control and Mitigation

Managing risk involves determining what levels of frequency and consequences are acceptable. Some risks may be considered acceptable without any further risk management. Others may require risk control or mitigation. If a risk is found to be at an unacceptable level (high risk), it should be reduced by decreasing probability and/or severity or by controlling contaminant, pathway, or receptor.

The Canadian Standards Association has outlined six broad strategies for controlling risk:[12]

- avoiding the exposure altogether;
- reducing the frequency of the loss (e.g., through training, monitoring and maintenance programs, and use of higher quality materials);
- reducing the consequence of the loss (e.g., emergency response plans and capability, wearing of protective equipment);
- separating exposures (e.g., separating pesticides from food);
- duplicating assets, including creating redundancies in safety systems (e.g., keeping important supplies in several different locations, backup systems); and
- transferring the obligation to control losses to some other party through a contractual agreement.

To this list, we would add

- education and training, including incentives and disincentives;
- proactive maintenance and inspections; and
- pollution prevention programs.

When selecting options consider

- how well the option addresses the problem,
- ease of application of the option,
- costs and benefits of the option,
- distribution of costs and benefits,
- acceptability to the decision maker,
- acceptability to stakeholders,
- public perceptions,
- residual risk, and
- legal issues.

Emergency Response

An effective emergency response plan is an essential component of risk management because it plays a critical role in reducing the consequences of an accident.

Risk Communication

Risk communication, discussed in depth in chapter 20, is required in order to manage risk properly.

Risk Perception

Risk perception, described in chapter 20, must be considered in selecting risk control options, understanding the possible response of stakeholders to risk, and designing an emergency response plan.

From Risk Assessment to Risk Management

Over the past decade, risk assessment has come into relatively common use as an approach to dealing with environmental problems. As risk assessment has matured, it has been seen in a broader context that recognizes its role in managing environmental issues. Risk assessments often act as the input into environmental management.

According to the American Chemical Society there are three essential tasks in risk management:[13]

- determining what hazards present more danger than society (as represented by its government, ENGOs, etc.) is willing to accept,

- considering what control options are available, and

- deciding on appropriate actions to reduce (or eliminate) unacceptable risks.

A fourth step should be evaluating the actions to control risk, with appropriate mechanisms for feedback. As in other types of environmental management initiatives, evaluation (auditing) is needed so that the success of initiatives can be determined, learning can take place, and improvements can be made where necessary.

When Should Risk Management Be Carried Out?

Risk assessment and management are applicable to a wide variety of situations including

- deciding to proceed with a project,
- selecting a site,
- planning and designing a facility,
- operating a facility,
- remediating a site (chapter 11),
- monitoring a site,
- decommissioning facilities,
- introducing new products or technologies (chapters 17, 18, 19), and
- responding to stakeholder concerns (chapter 20).

Within ISO 14001, the evaluation of environmental aspects and the determination of which aspects are significant are forms of risk assessment.

Standards

It is important for environmental managers with risk management responsibilities to know the standards that apply in the jurisdictions in which they operate. If a standard does not exist in a particular jurisdiction, select one that would be most appropriate under the circumstances. Environmental managers should contact appropriate federal and state or provincial environment and health departments and agencies and ENGOs to ensure that they have the most current standards or guidelines, which are generally available on the organization's website:

- U.S. EPA risk assessment and ecological risk assessment guidelines,
- Society for Environmental Toxicology and Chemistry,
- Canadian Standards Association requirements and guidelines for risk analysis and risk management,
- Health Canada,
- Environment Canada, and
- Canadian Council of Resource and Environment Ministers

Trends and Issues

In the past, risk management has been carried out generally in reaction to issues that have already been identified. For example, a risk analysis might be initiated after a specific deleterious substance was found in an area or after health complaints were received. However, the current approach to risk is to be more proactive. To be effective, a proactive assessment would become part of an environmental and risk communication strategy (chapter 20). Screening assessments are now sometimes carried out at the beginning of projects. This signals a movement towards looking at risk in a broader context than was traditionally the case.

Risk assessment and management are, unfortunately, often disconnected from other environmental management activities. For example, a remediation program for a contaminated site (see chapter 11) may be developed without a risk assessment having been carried out.

Properly applied, risk assessment offers a systematic, transparent, defensible way of evaluating risks that is as objective as qualified professionals can make it. However, risk assessment is occasionally subverted by people who try to force assessment, or the people doing it, to reach a conclusion of no risk or acceptable risk, even when significant risk may be present. The attempt to eliminate or downplay risk by underestimating or misreporting its significance is known as *risking away a problem*. In fact, such attempts to risk away a problem may increase the risks, should they be significant and result in damage. Attempts to risk away problems result in distrust in other credible risk work.

Risk Assessment and Safety

Risk management should be as objective and as transparent as well-qualified professionals can make it. However, risk assessment and management do not determine what is safe, although they greatly contribute to that decision. What is considered acceptable risk (safety) changes with the benefits received by taking that risk. As shown in Figure 10.7, people will accept a higher level of risk, if they receive benefits by doing so. For example, chemotherapy for cancer and the drugs for HIV are very toxic; however, the benefits obtained of curing or controlling the diseases make the risk of taking toxic chemicals acceptable. We accept the risks of driving because of the perceived benefits. Societies will accept situations which involve risk if the benefits are necessary or desired.

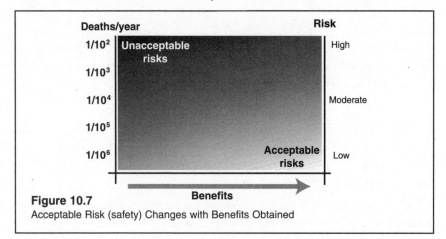

Figure 10.7
Acceptable Risk (safety) Changes with Benefits Obtained

Deciding what is safe involves trade-offs in which the scientific assessment of risk is part of the input to the decision along with political and economic factors, as shown in Figure 10.8. When politics and economics enter into the determination, it is no longer scientific.

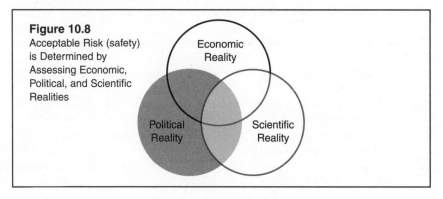

Figure 10.8
Acceptable Risk (safety) is Determined by Assessing Economic, Political, and Scientific Realities

In *Lessons from Longford*, Andrew Hopkins examines the findings of the Royal Commission into the Esso gas plant explosion at Longford, Victoria, in September 1998.[14] Risk managers have numerous lessons to learn from this unfortunate accident in which two people were killed and the natural gas supply to the state of Victoria and city of Melbourne was cut off for two weeks.

The Royal Commission's analysis showed that the reasons were complex and inter-related, including

- absence of engineers on the site due to cost-cutting,

- communications failures,

- failure to carry out a HAZOP (Hazardous Operations Assessment),

- maintenance backlog and poor maintenance priorities,

- poor auditing, including reluctance to convey bad news to the top of the organization,

- failure of the incident reporting system, and

- inadequate training and processes.

Recommended Further Reading

There are many textbooks on risk management written for different audiences and from different perspectives (engineering, management, (eco)toxicology, etc.). We recommend checking with major publishers in science, engineering, and management and the information sources found in the websites listed below.

Canadian Council of Ministers of the Environment. *A Framework for Ecological Risk Assessment: General Guidance*. PN 1195. Winnipeg, Manitoba: CCMF Subcommittee on Environmental Quality Criteria for Contaminated Sites, 1996.

Canadian Standarads Association. *Risk Analysis Requirements and Guidelines*. CAN/CSA Q634 M91. Etobicoke, Ontario: CSA, 1991.

Canadian Standards Association. *Risk Management: Guidelines for Decision-Makers*. Etobicoke, Ontario: CSA, 1997.

Hopkins, Andrew. *Lessons from Longford: The Esso Gas Plant Explosion*. Arcadia, NSW, Australia: CCH Australia, 2000.

The Presidential/Congressional Commission on Risk Assessment and Risk Management. Framework for Environmental Health Risk Management. Washington DC, 1997.

U.S. Environmental Protection Agency. *Final Guidelines for Ecological Risk Assessment*. EPA 630/R-95/002F. Washington DC, 1998.

U.S. Environmental Protection Agency. *Guidelines for Health Risk Assessment of Chemical Mixtures*. Washington DC, 1986.

Websites

Canadian Council of Ministers of Environment: <www.ccme.ca>

Canadian Standards Association: <http://www.csa.ca>

Environment Canada: <http://www.ec.gc/envhome.html>

EPA: <http://www.epa.gov/ngispgm3/iris/glossary.htm>

EPA - Integrated Risk Information System (IRIS): <http://www.epa.gov/iris/>

EPA's Office of Air Quality Planning and Standard: <http://www.epa.gov/oar/oaqps/>

Health and Environment: <http://www.sra.org/>

Health Canada: <http://www.hc-sc.gc.ca>

Network for Environmental Risk Assessment and Management:
   <http://www.eng.uwaterloo.ca/irr>

Risk World: <http://www.riskworld.com/>

SETAC Society for Environmental Toxicology and Chemistry: <http://www.setac.org>

Society for Risk Analysis: <http://www.sra.org/glossary.htm>

Toxicology Excellence for Risk Assessment: <http://www.tera.org/>

ENVIRONMENTAL SITE ASSESSMENT

Lisa-Henri Kirkland
Wolfwillow Environmental

There is only one kind of event that can create a negative value in a property and that is environmental risk. Any other kind of loss, however catastrophic (an earthquake, for instance), can only carry the asset value down to zero. Environmental contamination can create liability where there had previously been equity.[1]

E NVIRONMENTAL SITE ASSESSMENT is a systematic investigation to characterize and evaluate environmental liabilities that may stem from past and/or current uses of a specific site. Part of the assessment is to select and implement appropriate solutions where problems are identified. Environmental site assessment is often used to determine whether such liabilities may exist on a property and to characterize and assist in remediation of these liabilities.

Although the term *assessment* is often confused with the term *audit*, they differ in focus and methodology. An assessment focuses on physical conditions at a site; an audit looks at processes at a site that can affect its physical condition or surroundings. (Audits are discussed more fully in chapter 8.)

Environmental site assessments normally focus on potential contamination from past and current property use, whereas audits center on environmental compliance of current property uses.[2]

Environmental site assessment can involve varying types and degrees of investigation. Most commonly, environmental site assessment is classified as Phase I (preliminary or screening level), Phase II (verification, characterization, and physical extent of contaminants), and Phase III (corrective action and cleanup). Phases

I and II can yield negative results (no potential liabilities or concerns) and lead to a decision that no further action is required. Each successive phase should provide more detailed information about the site, demonstrate that there are no liabilities, or lead to remedial action that would decrease or eliminate those liabilities. Figure 11.1 illustrates the three-phase approach to environmental site assessment.

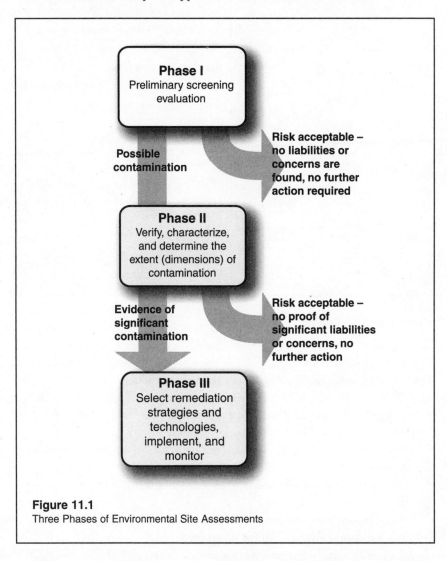

Figure 11.1
Three Phases of Environmental Site Assessments

The terminology applied to environmental site assessments is, unfortunately, often quite confusing. Some of the many terms that may be applied to an environmental site assessment are shown in Table 11.1.

Table 11.1 Terminology Used for Phases of Site Assessment

Type of Environmental Site Assessment	Other Commonly Used Terms
Phase I Environmental Site Assessment	Pre-Acquisition Site Assessment
	Preliminary Environmental Site Assessment
	Screening-level Environmental Assessment
	Transactional Environmental Assessment
	Initial Assessment
	Property Environmental Liability Assessment
	Environmental Site Investigation
Phase II Environmental Site Assessment	Subsurface Investigation
	Intrusive Investigation
	Site Characterization
	Initial Site Characterization
Phase III Environmental Site Assessment	Remediation
	Remedial Investigation
	Final Site Characterization

Phase I Environmental Site Assessment

The most common type of environmental site assessment is a Phase I Environmental Site Assessment. The Canadian Standards Association states that a Phase I Environmental Site Assessment (ESA) is the systematic process, as prescribed by this Standard, by which an Assessor seeks to determine whether a particular property is or may be subject to actual or potential contamination.[3]

Phase I seeks to answer the following questions:

• What activities have been, or may have been, carried out on the property (and adjacent properties)?
• Are these activities likely to have caused environmental liabilities or concerns?
• Are there conditions evident on the property that might suggest that there may be environmental liabilities or concerns?

An environmental site assessments is initiated for a variety of reasons. Most often, it is driven by real estate transactions. In Canada, court cases such as Northern Badger[4] have established that environmental liability comes before other lender liability, interests, or obligations. Previously, owners or lenders often liquidated assets and left the public responsible for environmental liabilities. When the small oil company Northern Badger went into receivership, it was ruled, and supported on appeal, that remaining assets should first go to well site cleanup before lender or creditor claims were met.

In the United States, the Comprehensive Environmental Response, Compensation, and Liability Act (CERCLA) requires that "all appropriate inquiry into previous ownership and uses of a property" should be carried out prior to a property transaction in order for a property owner to establish a defense of innocent ownership.[5]

These legal considerations, as well as experiences where the value of properties have been found to be less than the costs required to address their environmental problems, have prompted more and more property buyers and their lending institutions to seek a Phase I Environmental Site Assessment before finalizing a purchase or providing a loan on a property. A Phase I assessment may also be carried out in order to establish baseline conditions at a site at a point in time. For example, a Phase I Environmental Site Assessment may be carried out before a property is sold so that the seller can establish the state of a property at the time of sale and not be liable for environmental problems created later.

In the United States, a transaction screen process may be undertaken prior to deciding to proceed to a full Phase I Environmental Site Assessment. The transaction screen process includes

• completing a questionnaire about current and past property usage;

• inquiring into municipal, state, and government records regarding hazardous waste activity on or near the property; and

• a visual inspection of the site to complete an environmental observation checklist.[6]

A Phase I Environmental Site Assessment involves three steps, shown in Figure 11.2: a record and historical review, site reconnaissance, and report preparation. Because it is a preliminary assessment, a Phase I site assessment does not involve intrusive sampling (this is done in a Phase II site assessment).

The record and historical review

• provides an understanding of the past uses of a site and adjacent properties;

• helps identify conditions or events that could have adversely affected the site (e.g., possible tank leaks, hazardous materials releases, fires, explosions, environmental non-compliances);

- facilitates site inspection and, if necessary, site sampling and remediation; and
- may reveal problems at a site that are not apparent in a site inspection.

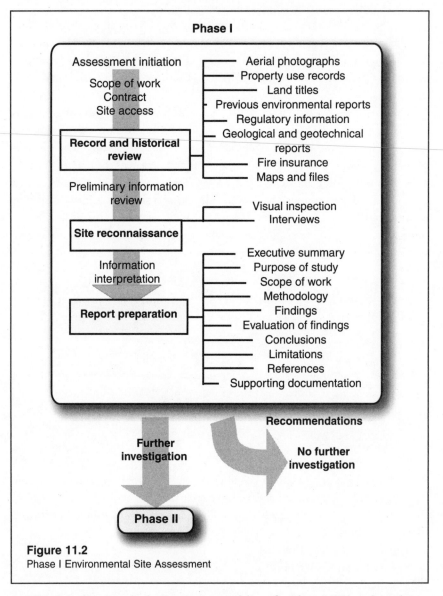

Figure 11.2
Phase I Environmental Site Assessment

The Canadian Standards Association guidelines for Phase I ESA and good professional practice, require that the following sources of information be reviewed during the record and historical review:

- aerial photographs
- property use records
- title search and assessment rolls
- previous Phase I ESA reports
- company records
- geological and geotechnical reports
- regulatory information

Other sources of information can include:

- geological and soils maps
- topographic maps
- land use maps
- public health documents
- utility company records
- fire insurance maps and records

In theory, the record and historical review should be carried out prior to site reconnaissance, and must include a comprehensive set of records, if they are available.[7] In practice, however, site inspection often takes place before all of the historical material is obtained and reviewed.

Site reconnaissance involves visual observation, olfactory (odor) detection, and a record review limited to those records that were only available on site. Often, site assessors use a well-defined protocol or checklist in order to identify issues they should examine on site and to document their visit.[8] Photographs of the site can provide evidence of site conditions.

The CSA outlines issues and conditions that can be examined at a site:

- property use
- structures on the site
- topographic, geologic, and hydrogeologic conditions
- wells
- hazardous materials
- unidentified substances
- stains
- above ground and underground storage tanks
- storage containers
- odors
- potable water supply
- asbestos-containing materials
- lead

- polychlorinated biphenyls (PCBs)
- ozone-depleting substances
- radon
- urea formaldehyde insulation
- drains and sumps
- waste water and sewage disposal
- pits and lagoons
- fill materials
- dumps and landfills
- state of vegetation
- adjacent properties

If available, neighbors and personnel familiar with the site may be interviewed in order to corroborate or provide additional information.

The standards require that in reporting, the site assessor "evaluate the findings obtained in the records review, site visits, and interviews and present such information in a manner designed to help the client understand the significance of the findings."[9] Phase I Environmental Site Assessment reports often function as legal documents.

The cost of a Phase I Environmental Site Assessment may range from one thousand to several thousands of dollars, depending on

- size and complexity of the site,
- degree of development of the site,
- level of investigation of the site,
- quality of information available in documents,
- length of time that the site has been developed, and
- nature of activities on the site — fuels, pesticides, hazardous materials.

Greenfield sites, or sites that have never been developed, cost less to characterize than brownfield sites, where industrial or other activities have taken place. Brownfield sites are "abandoned, idled, or under-used industrial and commercial facilities where expansion or redevelopment is complicated by real or perceived environmental contamination."[10]

The perceived cost of a Phase I Environmental Site Assessment sometimes leads to resistance to carrying out an assessment. However, the perceived costs are often small relative to the value of a Phase I Environmental Site Assessment in reducing risks and contingent costs (costs that would be incurred if there were liabilities that were not identified and reduced). Reluctance to do an assessment is also sometimes due to fears of discovering environmental concerns on a property.

The philosophy of What you don't know can't hurt you is completely wrong. Failure to find out if environmental liabilities exist is now seen as incompetence and lack of due diligence.

An environmental site assessment will progress from Phase I to II if Phase I results indicate that conditions on the site warrant further investigation. The Canada Mortgage and Housing Corporation suggests that a Phase II Environmental Site Assessment be carried out if one or more of the following potential hazards is identified during Phase I:[11]

- underground storage tanks present on the property,
- leakage from PCBs from light ballasts or transformers,
- evidence of landfilling on the property,
- long history of industrial use,
- evidence of less-than-desirable industrial housekeeping practices,
- hazardous chemicals use on property,
- visual and/or olfactory evidence of soil/groundwater contamination,
- evidence of upgradient, off-site sources, and
- significant industrial activities within 1000 m (3281 feet) of the subject property.

Triggers for a Phase II Environmental Site Assessment may be more or less stringent than the above criteria, depending on the standards applied to a site and the level of acceptable risk, as determined by intended development on the property. For example, if residential development were proposed, the standard of cleanup would be much higher than if another industrial activity were intended.

A Phase II investigation may sometimes be carried out without prior Phase I work when there is already sufficient evidence of contamination or when a specific area of a site has a high probability of being contaminated, such as in the case of removing an underground storage tank from a site. The absence of a Phase I investigation, however, usually hampers Phase II work. It is difficult to determine where sampling should be carried out on a site if its history is unknown.

Phase II Environmental Site Assessment

Phase II Environmental Site Assessment involves intrusive investigation to

- verify the presence of contaminants,
- characterize contaminants, and
- provide a preliminary assessment of their extent.

A Phase II Environmental Site Assessment generally focusses on specific areas of concern identified in Phase I, so that sampling is focussed on areas where contamination is likely. Occasionally it may be carried out on a screening level where Phase I did not provide enough information about where contamination occurred.

Sampling and analysis within aPhase II Environmental Site Assessment can vary with the

- scope and complexity according to potential issues on a site,
- quality of the information provided by Phase I,
- amount of certainty required about the environmental status and intended use of the site, and
- funds available for site investigation.

A Phase II Environmental Site Assessment can involve

- soil sampling (test pitting, grab samples, drilling, or soil vapor analysis),
- geophysical analysis (magnetometer and conductivity),
- surface water sampling,
- groundwater sampling (installation of observation wells or piezometers),
- air sampling (indoor or outdoor),
- materials sampling (e.g., asbestos surveys),
- sediment sampling,
- vegetation sampling,
- fauna sampling, and
- risk assessment.

Sample gathering techniques will depend on

- the nature of suspected contaminants (gas, liquid, solid, hazardous, non-hazardous),
- the location of suspected contaminants (water, soil, air, building materials, etc.),
- accessibility of the material to be sampled, and
- the quality of information that is desired.

In most Phase II Environmental Site Assessments, samples are usually taken off-site for laboratory analyses, although some analyses may be performed in the field. Field screening analyses can be used to guide decisions, such as the selection of further sample points, made during the Phase II investigation.

Phase II may take place in stages, with screening activities or sampling over a site being followed by more detailed sampling and analysis.

Costs of a Phase II Environmental Site Assessment are highly variable depending on the method of investigation, the number of sampling points, and the types of analyses carried out. Costs can range from Can$5,000 to Can$100,000 or more.

If a site is found to be contaminated during Phase II work, regulators must be notified and may become more actively involved in further assessment work.

The Phase II Environmental Site Assessment process is summarized in Figure 11.3.

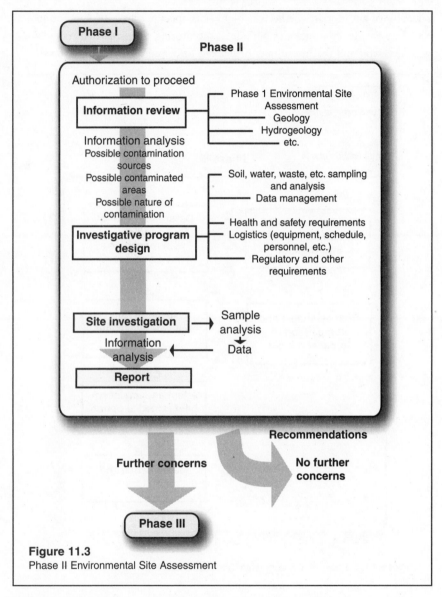

Figure 11.3
Phase II Environmental Site Assessment

Phase III Environmental Site Assessment

Although not defined by standards, Phase III Environmental Site Assessment usually refers to further site characterization, remedial investigation, cleanup, corrective action, and remediation. Phase III Environmental Site Assessment generally follows Phase II when concerns on the site warrant further investigation or remediation. Providing standards for Phase III would be difficult because the selection of appropriate methods is highly site-specific. Phase III Environmental Site Assessment often includes periods of monitoring to ensure that remediation was successful and that no sources or pockets of contamination were missed.

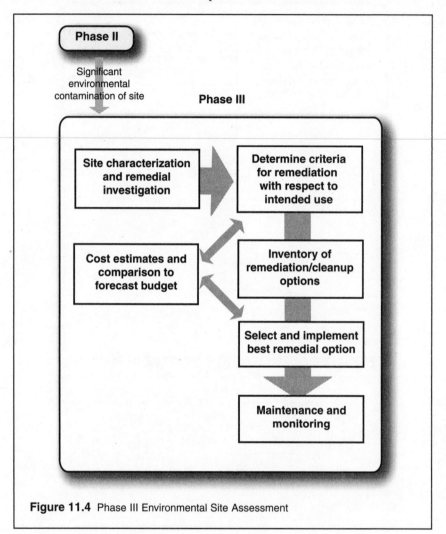

Figure 11.4 Phase III Environmental Site Assessment

The purposes of a site characterization and remedial investigation are to
- determine criteria for cleanup (remediation) of the site,
- identify feasible approaches to clean up the contamination, and
- allow remediation costs to be estimated.

Activities can include further sampling and analysis, treatability studies, feasibility studies, and design of remediation systems.

Remediation techniques include:

Air Sparging: injection of air into contaminated soil, forming bubbles that rise and carry trapped and dissolved contaminants to the surface where they are collected for further treatment.

Bio-remediation: breakdown of organic contaminants into harmless substances by micro-organisms, such as bacteria, by injecting bacteria, air (if aerobic), and nutrients.

Chemical Dehalogenation: conversion of contaminants containing halogens to less toxic substances through controlled chemical reactions that remove or replace halogen atoms.

Containment: use of walls, liners, or other means to contain contaminant in a restricted area.

Deep Well Injection: disposal of contaminants in deep wells.

Dig and Dump: removal and disposal of contaminated material into a suitable, legal landfill or waste containment area.

Encapsulation: enclosing contaminated materials so that they cannot become mobile.

Excavation: removal of contaminated soil for treatment or disposal off-site.

In Situ Soil Remediation: flooding contaminated soils with a solution that moves contaminants to an area where they can be extracted then recovered or treated.

Natural Attenuation: decrease of contaminants over time due to natural processes.

Phyto-remediation: using vegetation to take up contaminants from the soil.

Pump and Treat: bringing contaminated groundwater to the surface where it is treated then injected back into the water table.

Soil Vapor Extraction: removal of contaminant vapors from soil through the use of vacuum extraction wells.

Soil Washing: using water or a washing solution and mechanical processes to remove contaminants from soil.

Solvent Extraction: separation of hazardous organic contaminants from oily wastes, soils, sludge, and sediments to reduce the volume of hazardous waste that must be treated.

Stabilization: incorporating contaminants into stable solids to render them inert or immobile.

Thermal Desorption: heating contaminated soil to vaporize contaminants.

Treatment Walls: placing a filter in the ground to capture contaminants in groundwater flowing through it.

An important consideration in Phase III Environmental Site Assessment is that it should be designed in accordance with the requirements of pertinent regulators,

with due consideration to the wishes of stakeholders, and with careful consideration of the intended use(s) of the site.

Standards and Accreditation

A number of guidelines and standards have been developed for environmental site
assessment. Phase I standards include

- Canadian Standards Association (CSA), 1994, Z768-94 *Phase I
  Environmental Site Assessment,*
- Canada Mortgage and Housing Corporation (CMHC), 1994, *Phase I
  Environmental Site Assessment Interpretation Guidelines,*
- American Society for Testing and Materials, 1997, E-1572-97, *Standard
  Practice for Environmental Site Assessments: Phase I Environmental Site
  Assessment Process, and*
- American Society for Testing and Materials, 1996, E1572-97, *Standard
  Practice for Environmental Site Assessments: Transactional Screen Process.*

Large organizations that carry out extensive Phase I Environmental Site
Assessment programs often develop their own specific company standards. As
well, regulators, financial institutions, and others who receive site assessment·
reports may have their own expectations about methodology and reporting.

Because of their complex nature, many standards and guidelines pertaining to
Phase II Environmental Site Assessment are method-specific. General standards
for, and guides to, Phase II assessment include

- Canadian Standards Association (CSA), 2000, Z769, *Phase II
  Environmental Site Assessment,*
- Canadian Mortgage and Housing Corporation (CMHC), 1993, *II 99-7-
  03 Environmental Site Investigation Procedures: Phase II Environmental Site
  Assessment,*
- Environment Canada, 1994, Model Terms of Reference for an
  Assessment Study of a Contaminated Site,
- Canadian Council of Ministers of the Environment (CCME), 1994,
  Subsurface Assessment Handbook for Contaminated Sites,
- Canadian Council of Ministers of the Environment (CCME), 1993,
  *Guidance Manual on Sampling, Analysis, and Data Management for
  Contaminated Site, and*
- U.S. EPA, 1991, *Site Characterization for Subsurface Remediation,*
  EPA/625/4-91/026.

Regulators within specific jurisdictions may subscribe to particular guidelines
and criteria for Phase II investigation. More than one jurisdiction could be
involved, so ESA activities must be designed to meet all applicable criteria in the
most efficient way possible. These criteria should be identified prior to carrying

out Phase II investigative work or the site investigation may not address necessary questions.

Detailed information on the environmental and health hazards and risks associated with specific contaminants should be obtained from appropriate publications and websites. Toxicologists should be consulted if the risks are not absolutely clear and those doing the assessment are not certain of the assessment of the risks posed by the contaminants during or after remediation.

Internet sites providing useful information on contaminants include:

<www.huduser.org/publications/pubasst/enviro>
The U.S. Housing and Urban Development (HUD) site provides a summary of various contaminants and concerns associated with residences.

<www.ccohs.ca>
The Canadian Centre for Occupation Health (CCOH) site includes a description of various hazardous materials and their risks.

<www.cdc.gov/niosh/ipcs>
The National Institute of Occupational Safety and Health (NIOSH) site provides International Chemical Safety Cards describing the risks associated with specific chemicals, suggested storage and handling procedures, and spill response.

Practitioners and Accreditation

Currently, there is no mandatory program in Canada or the United States to accredit environmental site assessors. Practitioners are often accredited by professional organizations, such as engineering and geological associations (e.g., A.P.E.G.G.A. in Alberta), professional chemistry or biology associations, or other groups (e.g., the Qualified Environmental Professional [QEP] designation granted by the Air and Waste Management Association). The Society for Environmental Toxicology and Chemistry is an important source of information. The Environmental Assessment Association (EAA), a growing voluntary international organization, provides information and educational programs on environmental inspections, testing, and hazardous material removal, primarily aimed at real estate professionals.

Trends and Issues

While Phase I Environmental Site Assessment can be an important tool in identifying environmental issues, it is often treated as a commodity product. In most geographical areas, consulting firms that carry out Phase I assessments compete largely on the basis of cost. Few people hiring environmental site assessment consultants select Phase I environmental site assessors on the basis of quality of work. As well, because of cost competition and because Phase I Environmental Site Assessments are usually perceived to be easy, Phase I work is often used as a training ground for new environmental practitioners. Junior and inexperienced practitioners carry out most Phase I Environmental Site Assessments. When junior employees are not under the careful supervision of an experienced senior practitioner, these two factors can lead to poor quality Phase I assessments. With no regulating body to govern Phase I Environmental Site Assessment, poor practice is usually policed unfortunately only in the most extreme situations when legal action evolves.

Although a number of organizations offer some form of accreditation for environmental professionals, there is no single comprehensive qualification program for environmental site assessors. This presents a problem for those writing contracts for environmental site assessments. It can be difficult for non-practitioners to judge and compare the qualifications presented by assessors. Those seeking environmental site assessment often have little prior knowledge of what an environmental assessment is or who could best assist them with one, so they may default to price considerations.

The quality of Phase II and III work tends to be more consistent than that of Phase I site assessment work. Because Phase II and III work requires specific technical expertise and equipment, it is usually carried out by individuals who are qualified through professional practice bodies (such as engineering, geology, and agrology associations). However, the International Organization for Standardization has prepared ISO 14015 Environmental Assessments of Sites and Organizations, which may help standardize site assessment when it is finally released.

Another issue encountered in environmental site assessment is that it is often carried out late in the management process. For example, companies may own properties for some time before they decide to start assessing their environmental issues. A Phase I Environmental Site Assessment is often initiated at the end of a real estate transaction when there is pressure to close the deal. It should be carried out at the beginning of the transaction, when there is more time to carry out an appropriate assessment and to give the results careful consideration in evaluating the situation.

Recommended Further Reading

American Society for Testing and Materials (ASTM). *E-1528-96 Standard Practice for Environmental Site Assessments: Transactional Screen Process*. West Conshohooken, PA: ASTM, 1996.

American Society for Testing and Materials (ASTM). *E-1572-97 Standard Practice for Environmental Site Assessments: Phase I Environmental Site Assessment Process.* West Conshohooken, PA: ASTM, 1997.

Building Operators and Managers Institute (BOMI). *Environmental Site Assessments.* Arnold, MD: BOMI, 1994.

Canadian Council of Ministers of the Environment (CCME). *Subsurface Assessment Handbook for Contaminated Sites.* Winnipeg, Manitoba: CCME Publications,1994.

Canadian Standards Association. *Z768-94 Phase I Environmental Site Assessment.* Etobicoke, Ontario: CSA, 1994.

Canadian Standards Association. *Z769-00 Phase II Environmental Site Assessment.* Etobicoke, Ontario: CSA, 2000.

U.S. Department of Housing and Urban Development. *Environmental Assessment Guide for Public Housing.* Washington DC: U.S. EPA, 1991.

Websites

U.S. Environmental Protection Agency (EPA) website on brownfields: <www.epa.gov/swerosps/bf/index>

U.S. Environmental Protection Agency (EPA) website on remediation options: <www.clu.in.org/products/citguide/intech>

ENVIRONMENTAL INDICATORS

Christine Schuh, PricewaterhouseCoopers LLP
and Dixon Thompson

INDICATORS ARE quantitative or qualitative forms of feedback that deliver concise, scientifically credible information in a manner that can be readily understood and used by various audiences to assess the achievement of goals and objectives. Feedback provides information about a situation after a purposeful action has been initiated to indicate success or failure of the action. Feedback is necessary for organisms and organizations if they are to survive. Financial measures have traditionally been used because the goals and objectives of the organization have been expressed in financial terms. Many organizations have goals and objectives dealing with non-financial issues because they recognize that the financial health is intrinsically linked to other aspects of the operations. Consequently, indicators are measures that are used to provide managers with information on progress towards goals and objectives. If organizations have goals and objectives other than financial, as with triple bottom line, corporate social responsibility, and sustainable development, then non-financial indicators are essential.

This chapter is closely linked to the following chapter on reporting, because reports are prepared by gathering appropriate subsets of indicators. The corporate pioneers in environmental reporting have had to develop their own indicators and will continue to do so as they expand their reporting into areas such as the triple bottom line, sustainable development, and corporate social responsibility. Corporations must use indicators for internal use and must meet the reporting requirements of external stakeholders. If organizations are committed to continual improvements, as required by ISO 14001 EMS, and/or regard themselves as learning institutions, then those organizations must have a set of indictors to help them to improve and learn.[1]

Most corporations will use indictors developed and tested by others or participate in collaborative efforts to do so. This is because of the expense and difficulty of developing and testing effective indictors and the need for compatibility and comparability within and between industry sectors and internationally. Therefore, the following discussion of indictors is provided not in the expectation that many organizations will use it to develop their own indictors but because

- Corporations have to understand the basic characteristics of indicators, how they are developed, and their uses.
- They should understand why they should not naively strike off on their own.
- They may be involved in collaborative efforts to develop indictors, which will be facilitated by a basic understanding.
- They have to understand the basics in order to assess critically the indictors available from various sources as they select appropriate indicators.

It is important to distinguish indictors that monitor the state of the environment from those that monitor the performance of the organization. Environmental performance indicators measure the progress towards operational goals and objectives and focus on the efficiencies of the system being measured. Environmental condition indicators measure the progress towards a particular state of being and focus on the quality of the environment. An example of the difference between a performance and a condition indicator would be the measurement of greenhouse gas production per unit production from a facility (performance) versus the concentration of greenhouse gases in the atmosphere (the state). Both are required to give an accurate picture of the situation, but organizations tend to focus on performance indicators because they generally have direct control over the contributing factors and these indicators provide information on the organization's performance. Corporations would use condition indictors where they are responsible for an area because of ownership, to distinguish aspects from impacts (where their activities produce a change in the environment) or where regulations require them to monitor the state of the environment (receiving waters, for example). This chapter will focus on the performance indicators in the context of an individual organization and will use the term indicators to refer to environmental performance indicators in general.

Standards and/or Legislation

Although there are no standards for developing environmental indicators, there are standards that suggest which indicators to use, and regulations often specify what to measure, how to measure it, and how to report. In the international arena, the The Global Reporting Initiative (GRI) has become the leading environmental reporting standard.[2] The GRI publishes a list of suggested indicators that organizations could include in their report, tailored to meet their audience and business activities. Other reporting requirements have driven the requirement corporations to use certain indicators, such as the Voluntary Challenge Reporting (VCR) on greenhouse gases program, Toxic Release Inventory (U.S.A.), National Pollutant Release Inventory (NPRI in Canada), and Statistics Canada. In Canada, collaborative efforts have been directed at the development of eco-efficiency indictors based on the principles and framework developed by the World Business Council for Sustainable Development,[3] indictors through the National Round Table on the Environment and the Economy.[4] However, the intention was to develop "widely accepted, quantifiable, verifiable, and transparent indicators."[5] The three core eco-efficiency indicators were energy intensity (total energy consumed [MJ] per unit of production or service), waste intensity (total waste [kg] per unit of product or service), and water intensity (total water intake [m³] per unit of product or service), which were to be supplemented by complementary indicators and by total energy and water consumption and waste generation. Currently companies are allowed to make independent decisions about indicators to be used, project boundary, reporting period, and appropriate denominators, consequently comparability of indicators can be uncertain. More important is the fact that external stakeholders have to read the fine print on reports to determine how the values had been calculated, so usefulness is very limited. These indicators also deal only with biophysical inputs and outputs and so do not reflect biophysical impacts on the state of the environment or the social and economic aspects of sustainable development and corporate social responsibility. They do not represent the complete picture, so must be used as a subset. The methodology, application, and acceptance of these eco-efficiency indicators are evolving.

Criteria

The indicators that a company uses are usually developed from already established indicators; however, it must take care that these are of acceptable quality and applicability. Some may be adapted to suit the needs of the company. It must establish agreed-upon criteria to aid in choosing or changing indicators. These criteria may vary from company to company. A set of general criteria that apply to all indicators is shown in Table 12.1. They are separated into five dimensions: purpose, scientific, political, economic, and communication. It is important to recognize the many of these criteria are at cross-purposes with one another, and for these reasons a perfect indicator cannot be developed. There are always compromises, such as the need for conciseness and comprehensiveness. The need for high quality data, which is usually expensive, is compromised with the need with a reasonable cost/benefit ratio.

Table 12.1: Common Performance Indicator Criteria

Dimension	Criteria	Characteristics
Purpose	• relevant	• related to goals and objectives • represents key variables • fulfills information needs of users
	• comprehensive	• set of indicators • portrays linkages
	• shows trends • evolves as company evolves	• periodically reviewed
Scientific	• sound scientific reasoning and technology	• well-established, verifiable theories • best available science • reliable and consistent procedures • cause and effect relationship well understood
	• high-quality data	• reliability • accuracy • verifiable • current • non-deterministic
	• appropriate indicator behavior	• no time delay • leading or current trend information • broad range of response • change in indicator reflects change in measured phenomenon
Political	• international recognition • stakeholder interest and acceptability	• international consensus of validity • desirable for long-term interests of stakeholders • developed with stakeholder input
	• media acceptance	• attractive to use • not easily distorted or misused
	• company acceptance	• fits with company structure • drives policy and practice in right direction • assigned accountability • integrated into reward system • based on measures that company has control over
Economic	• reasonable cost/benefit ratio	• uses accessible information • uses existing measurement systems • cost-effective collection • cost-effective analysis • links to other economic, forecasting, and information systems • can be aggregated • can be adapted for different audiences

Communication	• adequate documentation	• definitions of performance indicators and terminology • defined use and limitations • description of linkages • clear results • anecdotes are not necessary to communicate purpose of indicator

	• scientific clarity	• compare against
		  • thresholds
		  • benchmarks
		  • targets and
		  • other indicators.
		• normalized data

	• conciseness • appearance	• short list of indicators • charts, graphs, and pictures • format

There are five factors to consider when selecting the appropriate indicator from the list of potential indicators:

- Use what is required (licenses, TRI/NPRI, codes etc.).
- Use what others use.
- Use what is available.
- Use what is available and apply criteria.
- Use what is needed (develop your own).

Using indictors that others have developed has advantages:

- They have been evaluated and tested — the validity of the indicators has been proved.
- It allows comparisons.
- Savings occur because the development process for indicators does not have to be done.
- The introduction requires less effort when the audience is already familiar with the indicator.

However, caution must be used in selecting indicators developed by other organizations because it is assumed that the selection criteria and framework are valid.

Most organizations, especially those who are just developing and implementing an EMS, will not have the skills, knowledge, funds, and other resources to develop their own indicators. Therefore, they will have to use the following nine main sources of indicators developed by others:

- Review licensing and regulatory requirements to determine what data you are already required to report.
- Review the reports published by leading-edge corporations in your industry to determine what they report.

- Check with your industry association to discover if they have recommendations about environmental indicators.
- Check for collaborative efforts outside formal industry associations, because in some industries, corporations with experience using indictors have joined together to assist each other with further development.
- Check with employees to find out what they do report as part of internal operations feedback or could report with some additional time and resources.
- Examine the proposed indictors for eco-efficiency.[6]
- Review the reporting requirements of the Global Reporting Initiative (GRI).[7]
- Hire a consultant with experience in environmental indicators and reporting. Determine if the cost of the consultant can be shared with other companies, your industry association, or supported by government.
- Consult with stakeholders to determine what information they would like to have.

The resulting list will include indictors for which you already have, or can relatively easily obtain, data of acceptable reliability; indicators that you do not have at present but could set up measurement systems to obtain the data at a reasonable cost; and indicators that you would like to have but cannot obtain at present. Once you have defined and described the indictors that you might use, including the methodologies for measuring and analyzing them, circulate that information internally for comment on practicality and utility. Revise the indicators and/or methods in light of comments received, revise and re-circulate, including external stakeholders, if practical. Obtain comments and revise as appropriate.

Suncor Energy published a hard copy of their 2001 *Report on Sustainability: Our journey toward sustainable development,* which is also available on their website at www.suncor.com. The table of contents shows that they report on the following:

Company Profile
President's Message
Vision and Strategy
Executive Summary
Stakeholder Relations
Policies, Organization, and Management Systems
Auditors' Report (note – external verification)

Environmental Performance	Air
	Water
	Land
	Energy Efficiency
	Regulatory Compliance
Economic Performance	Operating Performance
	Contributing to Prosperity
Social Performance	Health and Safety
	Employee Relations
	Community Relations
Integrated Performance	
Sustainable Growth	
Performance Indicators	Suncor Energy
	Oil Sands
	Natural Gas
	Sunoco

Whether or not they call them environmental indicators, most corporations use various forms of indicators because of legal requirements (NPRI, TRI, and reporting spills) and conditions of licenses (emissions, effluent quality, etc.). Corporations that do environmental audits use forms of indicators and formal Environmental Management Systems that require the use of indicators. To demonstrate the benefits of investing in improved energy and material efficiency, reduced solid and hazardous waste disposal costs, and reduced waste water treatment, etc. corporations use indictors linked to their environmental and operations accounting systems. If countries ratify the Kyoto agreement, there will be requirements for calculating GHG emissions and tracking reductions using indictors.

Specific indicators include
- total water consumption and consumption per unit of production
- total energy consumption (of different forms) and energy consumption per unit of production (energy intensity)
- total material consumption and material intensity (efficiency – material consumption per unit of production)

- total waste and hazardous waste production and waste production per unit of production
- total volume of chemical spills and number of spills
- total greenhouse gas emissions and emissions per unit of production

The details of how these calculations are done may be specified by the regulations which require reporting, national or international agreements, industry codes, or individual corporate policies.

Units of Reporting

Different forms of measurement can be used for indicators:[8]

- absolute
- nominal (ranking)
- ordinal (rank ordering)
- compound (combining absolute and ratio categories)
- interval (equal scale distances with arbitrary zero)
- ratio (equal scale distances with a known zero)
- group (data for related factors)

Absolute or direct indicators are expressed in the units of the measured quantities: MJ of energy, m^3 of water, number of spills, dollars of expenditures, kilograms of waste, etc. Ratio or relative indicators rate a measure against another amount — normalizing, using a variety of reference values — per unit of production, benchmarks, standards, targets, and averages.

Uses of Indicators

The major goal in the development of indicators is a translation, by a scientifically defensible method, of many components of the environment into an optimum number of terms with maximum information content.[9] Indicators can be used in a variety of ways to

- measure the success (or failure) of achieving goals, objectives, and targets; assist in driving behavior in the desired direction, as specified by strategies and policies;
- define scope and context of the organization's operations in the environment;
- provide information to assist in decision making about environmental issues;
- aid in integration of environmental concerns with other company aspects;
- identify valid interventions;
- communicate to people within the organization what environmental issues are important;
- provide evidence to external stakeholders that the organization is addressing certain environmental concerns; and

- demonstrate compliance with regulations, internal and external standards, and guidelines.

Measuring Different Types of Phenomena

There are four types of phenomena: continuous, periodic, discrete, and event. We have found it useful to differentiate among different types of phenomena because a continuous phenomenon occurs all the time: measurements of carbon dioxide in the atmosphere, water levels of the ocean, temperature, humidity, etc. Periodic phenomena occur with a regular frequency, with lapses or a significant reduction of the phenomena between times of activity: diurnal and seasonal changes; air flow rates in building with heating, ventilating, and a air-conditioning systems; waste production from a production line, etc. Discrete phenomena occur often but do not have a specific frequency or interval associated with them: car accidents, power failures, natural gas flaring, etc. An event phenomenon occurs with no regular interval and a large period between events: Union Carbide's Bhopal chemical release, Exxon Valdez's oil spill, Mount St. Helens' eruption, extreme climatic events, etc. Indicators can measure continuous and discrete phenomena but periodic and event phenomena are more difficult to measure. Problems with measuring periodic and event phenomena include

- determining the type of measurement to take (continuous, snap-shot, long sample),
- determining the number of samples and when to take them,
- determining whether the measurement was taken during a period of activity or inactivity, and
- deciding how to translate that data into meaningful information (maximum, mean, time-weighted average).

If the frequency of a particular periodic phenomenon is known, it is possible to take measurements. However, it must be clear what this data will be used for — worst-case scenarios, average conditions — so that the measurement method can be determined. Developing indicators for event phenomena that can be used for predictions is practically impossible.

Steps in Developing Indicators

Figure 12.1 outlines the steps involved in developing indictors which follow the classic management cycle. Some of these steps are more applicable to performance indicators that will be used by the public; however, all the steps are necessary.[10]

As usual, the first and most critical step is the commitment by senior management to develop and use indicators and provide adequate resources.[11] With this commitment, the process follows the cycle outlined in Figure 12.1.

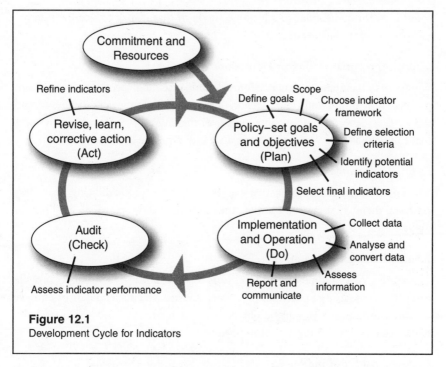

Figure 12.1
Development Cycle for Indicators

Policy — Set Goals and Objectives (Plan)

Planning includes defining goals, scoping, choosing an appropriate indicator framework, defining and identifying selection criteria, identifying appropriate indicators, and choosing the final set of indicators. Careful forethought during the planning stage can mean fewer adjustments after implementing a set of performance indicators and starting the continual improvement cycle.

Define Goals

The goals of the indicator system express the values of the organization.[12] Defining goals may consist of a gap analysis, such as determining the differences between a model, benchmark, or customer expectations and what the company delivers, and setting priorities and strategies to close the gap. However goals must not be static: the process is cyclic and goals must be updated.

Scoping

Scoping identifies: the target audience, the number of indicators that properly measure the phenomenon, the time frame over which the indicators are to be measured, and the geographic area the indicators will cover. Scoping is different from defining the selection criteria because it bounds the problem. However, the result of scoping is similar to selection criteria in that it may reduce the number of indicators for consideration.

Choose Appropriate Indicator Framework

Frameworks maintain consistency, provide guidance, and focus the development process. More importantly, the selection of the indicator framework dictates certain assumptions as to the purpose and end-use of the indicators. Different frameworks that can be used in developing performance indicators are discussed below.

Define and Identify Selection Criteria

The selection criteria for indicators will depend on the problem being addressed; however, there are some common features to most indicators, which are listed in Table 12.1.

Identify Potential Indicators

Literature reviews and reports on indicators used in similar circumstances provide easily accessible lists of potential indicators. Experts and stakeholders often have potential indicators that can be obtained through surveys, in-depth interviews, workshops, and reviewing lists of indicators used by other organizations.

Choose Final Set of Indicators

Evaluating the potential indicator list against the indicator criteria is used to select a sub set of indicators by eliminating those indicators that do not fit the criteria.

Implementation and Operation (Do)

Implementation usually requires the formation of an implementation team to link indicators to databases and information systems and to communicate about indicators to stakeholders throughout the organization.

Collect Data

Data collection is the first step in development, because raw data is not an indicator but must be analyzed and interpreted and sometimes combined with other information to produce the final indicator. (See Figure 12.2.) The data collection methods should reflect the indicator criteria for data reliability. These may include a quality assurance and control program.

Analyze and Convert Data

This stage combines the raw data and other information such as guidelines and industry standards, conversion factors, and value weighting methods to obtain the performance indicators.

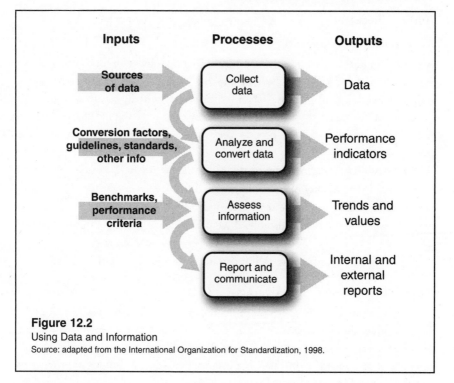

Figure 12.2
Using Data and Information
Source: adapted from the International Organization for Standardization, 1998.

Assess Information

The focus of the analysis should be on the trends of indicators (changes over time). When the process has just started, initial measurements will establish baseline values but cannot reveal trends. Trend information improves as more collection periods are conducted. The value of the performance indicators can occasionally be benchmarked or compared to established performance criteria. Data collection and analysis difficulties should be recorded so that this information can be used to improve the performance indicators.

Report and Communicate

The environmental report is the main method of communicating the quantities and trends of the indicators, internally and externally (see chapter 13, Environmental Reporting). For clarity, the report should also contain information about the meaning of each indicator and its linkages, why it is important, the historical trends or anticipated changes, and an evaluation of whether the indicator is showing movement and in what direction.[13] The data collection difficulties recorded in the previous step should also be documented in the report.

Audit (Check)

Assess Indicator Performance

Assessing indicator performance improves the usefulness of indicators to the Environmental Management System and has ramifications for all steps of the indicator development process. When indicators are initially set up, assessing the indicator performance should be frequent. However, once the indicators are confirmed and established, this process may occur less often. The development process may include

- determining costs and benefits derived from the use of the indicators,
- assessing the quality of information provided,
- determining if there a better indicator available,
- assessing whether the indicators drive performance in the right direction, and
- making sure that they are well integrated into the organization's EMS.

Revise, Learn, and Corrective Action (Act)

Corrective action must be taken on problems identified in the development cycle. One possible result is to change an indicator but this usually meets with some resistance because trend data may be lost. However, the alternative is the continuing use of a poor indicator. There is a balance between continuous improvement and the value of the trend information.

Frameworks

A framework is a conceptual model that aids in the selection and organization of performance indicators in order to maintain continuity, define the scope, and identify the limits of the measurement system. More fundamentally, the choice of indicator framework brings with it a series of assumptions as to the purpose and use of the indicators.[14]

There are three classifications of frameworks: scope, location, and process.

- Scope frameworks organize the topics that the developers of the indicators consider important. Common frameworks of this type divide the topics into environmental-societal-economic (domain) categories, goals, or issues.
- Location frameworks divide the topics into areas based on geographic boundaries, administrative-political boundaries, or ecosystems.
- Process frameworks assume that underlying rules govern the operation of the system, which include the causal or Pressure-State-Response model, linked human well-being/ecosystem model, economic models, and capital flow models.

Although a framework is helpful in providing a theoretical foundation for indicator development, in practice, a mixed framework approach is often used, e.g., one central framework is used that incorporates characteristics from other frameworks. They all have their individual strengths and weaknesses, and by combining characteristics of each framework the weaknesses may be reduced although complexity will likely increase. The following section provides a description, advantages and disadvantages, and examples of specific frameworks.

Scope Frameworks

Goal Framework

The goal-based framework uses corporate policy statements, goals, objectives, and targets with respect to issues such as compliance, emissions, and resource consumption. Although this framework gives direct information about the success in achieving goals, it sometimes neglects the more complex and/or interrelated issues.

Issue Framework

An issue framework concentrates on developing indicators for concerns of the corporation and stakeholders. It may be easier to construct and understand but may not have a direct connection to goals and may not express the interrelationship between different goals.

Domain Framework

The domain framework separates the goals and objectives into dimensions. For example, the development of indicators for sustainable development under this framework would use the dimensions of environment, economy, and society. Indicators are identified for each dimension. Dimensions can be linked through indicators that show the relationships and dependencies between each of the dimensions. However, the link between the goals of the organization and the indicators may be weak.[15]

Location Frameworks

The location framework is primarily used in government but could conceivably be used in large organizations with clear divisions. Indicators are developed based on the divisions within the organization. A municipal government would develop separate indicators for each department, agency, or service.[16]

Process Frameworks

Input-Process-Output Framework

The input-process-output framework has its roots in evaluating production line efficiencies where these components are clearly defined and indicators can be developed for them.[17] In one model, economic indicators measure the inputs, efficiency indicators measure the process, and effectiveness indicators measure the outputs. Another form of the input-process-output framework considers quality and efficiency as separate dimensions.[18] A third form of this framework consists of input, output, impact, and effect indicators, which is also known as the life cycle framework.[19] The problems associated with this framework include difficulties in distinguishing between input, process, and outputs in a complex system and in developing links between inputs, processes, and outputs. The input-process-output framework is the precursor of the causal framework. The main difference between the two frameworks is the addition of value components in the causal framework.

Pressure State Response (Causal) Framework

Pressure State Response (PSR) frameworks use the concept of cause and effect to develop indicators[20] (Figure 12.3). This framework develops three types of indicators (pressure, state, and response) for each issue. State indicators gauge the quantity and quality of the components in the system. Pressure indicators measure the human activities that affect the system. Response indicators measure the performance of society's efforts to change pressures which are causing undesirable

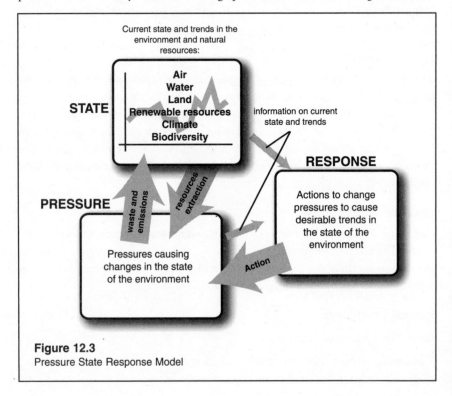

Figure 12.3
Pressure State Response Model

trends in the state. Problems with the causal framework include difficulties in differentiating between pressure, state, and response indicators and clarifying the cause and effect relationships.

Using the Pressure State Response model, Schuh developed a hybrid model in which indicators not only played the conventional role of providing information but also moved the users of the model to specific action through the response indicators. That is, the model not only provided information about the performance of the organization or system and the state of the environment under consideration where appropriate, but also guided the organization to specific actions to change pressures and trends in the state.[21]

ISO 14031

The International Organization for Standardization (ISO) has drafted an international standard for Environmental Performance Evaluation (EPE) (ISO 14031) to be used in conjunction with their Environmental Management System standard (ISO 14001), but it can also be used as a stand-alone document. EPE is an internal management process that uses indicators to compare an organization's environmental performance with its environmental performance criteria. ISO 14031 describes two categories of indicators: environmental performance indicators (EPI) and environmental condition indicators (ECI). EPIs can further be broken down into two subcategories: management performance indicators (MPI) and operational performance indicators (OPI). These categories are interrelated, as shown in Figure 12.4. ISO 14031 combines the input-process-output

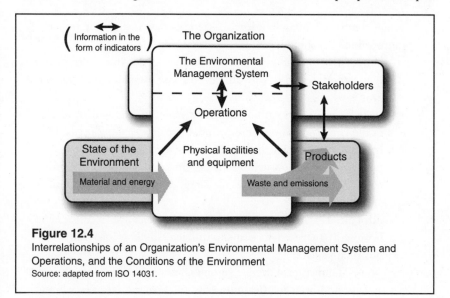

Figure 12.4
Interrelationships of an Organization's Environmental Management System and Operations, and the Conditions of the Environment
Source: adapted from ISO 14031.

and causal frameworks and has many of their advantages. One significant advantage is that it is part of a required portion of a certifiable Environmental Management System. However, it still suffers from the problem of determining cause and effect relationships.

Risk-Based Frameworks

Indicators may be developed on the basis of one of four risk-based frameworks — probabilistic, human health, financial, and sustainability — which target different issues in an organization.[22] Probabilistic frameworks examine the magnitude and probability of damage. A human health risk-based framework is concerned about long-term health of the employees. The costs of problems are reflected in a financial risk-based framework. The sustainability risk-based frameworks concentrate on problems occurring in the three dimensions of sustainable development: economic, environmental, and social.

Current Problems

Indicators are one of the most important management tools and yet may be the tool that faces the most problems due to

- lack of knowledge, technology, or funds;
- uncertainty about what to measure, often due to poorly defined goals and objectives (e.g., sustainable development);
- not knowing how to make measurements, due to lack of technology;
- failure to adequately assess costs and benefits, including intangible benefits;
- lack of comparability on four levels — temporal, spatial, within industry, and within the economy
  - temporal comparability involves examining the indicators over a long period, which can be difficult because measuring technologies evolve;
  - spatial comparisons within a geographical location or with other sites of the same company, whose boundaries or ownership fluctuate;
  - comparability is made difficult by lack of agreement on priority areas for measurement, on definitions of terms and measurement protocols, and problems with using single operations as the unit of analysis;
  - difficulties arise in environmental performance measurement because of the need to evaluate different kinds of qualitative and quantitative data;
  - abuse of indictors to produce meaningless or misleading results such as false improvement (learning how to meet the measure without

improving performance), selection (replacing low performers with high performers), and suppression of information; and

- trade-offs between simple measures, which can be easily understood and used but may not capture a complete picture of performance, and more complex ones with the opposite characteristics.

Our ability to create and disseminate measures has outpaced our ability to separate the few measures that contain information about future performance from those that do not. We are suffering from information overload due to a failure to be able to design indictors which produce useful information but do not mislead organizations to make bad decisions. This is the case with overemphasis on Gross Domestic Product, profits, and productivity as the only measures of corporate and social well-being. This is exacerbated by a tendency to maintain old indicators for their own existence and not for important information.

Indicators have been developed for isolated components of the system. However, to get a better view of changes in the system, a more holistic approach is needed. This problem is compounded by our lack of knowledge about the cause and effect linkages within subcomponents of the system. There is a focus on condition indicators and not on true indicators of performance. Monitoring the state of the environment is not usually beneficial to an organization because it is not the only contributor to the condition (i.e., measuring carbon dioxide concentrations in the atmosphere). Indicators show how effective or efficient the organization conducts its business (i.e., carbon dioxide emissions per unit production).

People have a fascination with things that they can measure, monitor, and control. Combined with our need to have as much information as possible to make decisions, the future of indicators remains bright. However, as the previous section on current problems with indicators suggests, there is much work to be done in determining how environmental systems work, which indicators to keep, and which ones to throw away. It is essential to negotiate agreements across industries and economies as to which indicators to use. Concepts such as triple bottom line and sustainable development are encouraging organizations to consider integrated and more holistic indicators.

Work on indicators for corporate and government Environmental Management Systems must be complemented by work on state of the environment indictors on biophysical, social, and economic aspects of individual and social well-being. This set of indicators must include the global commons and not just the biophysical conditions under the control of individual nations. Such state of the environment indicators and the resulting reports are necessary to better understand cause and effect relationships and to define problems and priorities.

Recommended Further Reading

International Organization for Standardization. *Environmental management - Environmental performance evaluation - Guidelines* (ISO 14031). New York: International Organization for Standardization, 1998.

Maclaren, V.W. "Urban Sustainability Reporting." *Journal of the American Planning Association* (1996): pp.184-205.

Meadows, D. *Indicators and Information Systems for Sustainable Development.* Hartland Four Corners, VT: The Sustainability Institute, 1998. <http://www.sustainer.org/resources/index.html>

Skillius, Å., and Wennberg, U. *Continuity, Credibility and Comparability: Key Challenges for Corporate Environmental Performance Measurement and Communication.* Lund: European Environment Agency, 1998. <www.eea.eu.int/ESS09/en/ccc.pdf>

ENVIRONMENTAL REPORTING

Mel Wilson and Christine Schuh, PricewaterhouseCoopers LLP
and Dixon Thompson

I N ITS BROADEST SENSE, environmental reporting refers to the issuance of any report containing information of an environmental nature, from corporate emission levels to national state of the environment reports. However, within the context of organizational environmental management, environmental reporting typically refers to the voluntary communication of formalized information about an organization's environmental policies and objectives, management systems, and measured environmental performance to the organization's stakeholders.

Private sector companies and public sector/government agencies issue environmental reports. However, while corporate and government environmental reports may be similar in content and format, the driving forces for reporting may differ. Corporations report for both stakeholder accountability and business reasons (and in some jurisdictions, because of regulatory requirements). Governments report primarily for reasons of stakeholder accountability; reporting to the public on the state of the environment for which the government is responsible. Some governments, including Canada, require departments to report on progress with respect to the government's commitments to sustainable development in reports which should be similar to corporate reports. This chapter focuses primarily on corporate environmental reporting, although many of the ideas and concepts presented here will also apply to government environmental reports.

Background

Stand-alone corporate environmental reports were first released in the early 1990s when a small number of companies, including Monsanto in the U.S.A. and Norsk Hydro in Norway, issued reports on their emissions.[1] Prior to this, corporate environmental reports (CERs) were limited mainly to estimates of environmental liabilities included as part of annual financial reports, and glossies — corporate publications focusing on values, policies, case examples, and pictures but with little actual performance information. Corporations issued these early reports for a number of reasons: responsibility for the environment, public image and reputation, competitive advantage, and legal compliance.[2]

Early forms of CERs contained little hard data, but recent studies of international environmental reporting by groups such as KPMG[3] and Stratos[4] indicate that there has been a dramatic transformation in the scope and quality of CERs in the past decade. The evolution of environmental reporting continues. The stages of environmental reporting, shown in Figure 13.1, are adapted from the United Nations Environment Programme's 1994 report.[5] Most report makers are currently at stages 1 or 2 with few companies reporting at a stage 3 level. Because of the learning involved and the need to gain experience with preparing reports, it is better to start with the easier, earlier formats before attempting the more advanced and difficult. In 1996, the Global Environmental Management Initiative released *Environmental Reporting and Third Party Statements.*[6] They concluded that, at that time, a balanced tone and the use of credible environmental indicators were more important than third party statements. Bennett and James edited *Sustainable Measures: Evaluation and Reporting of Environmental and Social Performance* which provides a useful overview.[7]

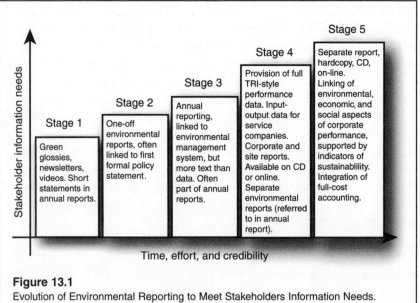

Figure 13.1
Evolution of Environmental Reporting to Meet Stakeholders Information Needs.
Source: adapted from United Nations Environmental Programme, 1994.

Throughout the 1990s, CERs evolved significantly in two directions:
- detail: as companies improved their performance measurement processes, the reports began to include more performance indicators and quantified information; and
- coverage: corporate reports expanded their focus from just biophysical environment to include health and safety information and, more recently, social, ethical, and economic performance.

The inclusion of more detail, especially with respect to the quantified performance information, was driven by a desire amongst stakeholders and corporations themselves for meaningful and comparable indicators to track performance, identify trends, and compare performance to peers. The expansion in coverage coincided with the trend by companies to merge their environmental and health and safety management systems. The addition of social, economic, and ethical performance information started to appear in the last few years of the 1990s, spurred on by publications such as John Elkington's *Cannibals with Forks*, which caused a renewed corporate interest in sustainable development.[8] In fact, few companies now issue environmental reports; most now issue integrated reports combining information on environmental, health and safety, social, ethical, and economic performance. These reports are often referred to as environment, health and safety; sustainable development; sustainability; triple bottom line; and even corporate social responsibility reports. However, for the purpose of this chapter, we will use the term corporate environmental report (CER) unless otherwise stated.

Companies making a commitment to prepare and release a public report will follow a similar evolutionary path as shown in Figure 13.1, starting with a report dealing largely with the biophysical environment. Figure 13.2 illustrates the process of report preparation.

Corporations must prepare and disseminate reports, or segments of reports, on various environmental issues:
- environmental liabilities in financial reports;
- environmental audits and site assessments for financial institutions;
- reports to regulators on accidents, spills, and release of toxic materials (NPRI in Canada and TRI in the U.S.A.);
- voluntary reports on environmental issues; and
- journal articles, speeches by executives, and press releases.

The issue is not whether to report, but to whom, why, what, and how, and how to do it most effectively and efficiently.

Once a draft is completed it must be approved and signed by senior management. If external verification is part of the strategy, it must be reviewed and signed off by an independent, external auditor.

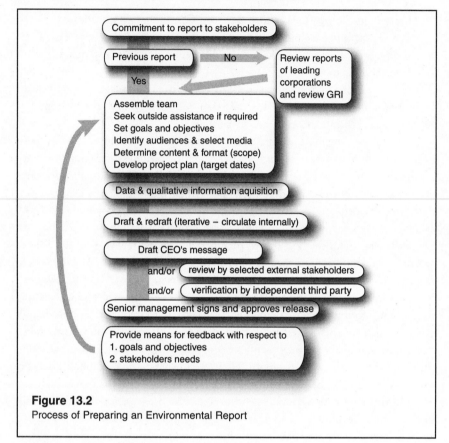

Figure 13.2
Process of Preparing an Environmental Report

Driving Forces for Environmental Reporting

Required Reporting

Denmark, the Netherlands, France, and Italy have requirements for corporate environmental reporting.[9] The Minister of Environment in the U.K. has threatened corporations with regulations if voluntary measures don't work, and the Government of Australia has produced guidelines for CERs. In Japan, the Keidanren, a government/industry organization, reports on the performance of Japanese corporations and organizations.[10] Legislation requiring organizations to report their environmental effects include: the Toxic Release Inventory and right-to-know legislation in the U.S.A., pollution registers (U.K. and France), pollution control boards (India), and the National Pollution Release Inventory (Canada). Generally accepted accounting practices have requirements for environmental disclosure.[11] Securities and exchange commissions require specific environmental information be released as part of stock exchange filings.[12]

Voluntary Reporting

Driving forces for voluntary environmental reporting by corporations have remained more or less constant since the early 1990s. The driving forces can be divided into two main types, *normative* and *business*.

Normative Driving Forces

Normative driving forces are arguments based on the concepts of moral rights and duties and basic societal values, norms, and beliefs. These arguments typically work in conjunction with each other to create a bundle of driving forces. When the bundle gets sufficiently large and accepted, external stakeholders begin to feel empowered to voice their demands for CERs and corporations begin to feel obligated to disclose more information.

The normative driving forces include:

- **Corporate accountability** The corporation and its stakeholders believe that the company is morally obligated to account to its stakeholders for its actions. This belief may be driven by the company itself (e.g., the Body Shoppe approach[13]) or led by the stakeholders (e.g., Talisman Energy in Canada[14]). The main argument of this driving force is that companies have a *moral obligation to account* to its stakeholders on how its operations affect society. In return for reporting, society extends the company's *social license to operate*. This driving force is based on social contract theory and is consistent with stakeholder theory in that corporate management is viewed as an agent of all stakeholders, not just shareholders.
- **Stakeholder rights** This driving force is based on the argument that the stakeholder has a *right* to know how the company is affecting individuals, society, and the planet. This is similar to the accountability driving force, except that the focus is on the stakeholder rather than the reporting company. The accountability and stakeholder rights driving forces are compatible and mutually reinforcing.
- **Societal control** This driving force is based on the belief that companies have gained significant influence over many aspects of society, and government and civil society need to have controls to prevent companies from using that influence only to their own benefit. One such control is to demand (and in some jurisdictions, require) that companies disclose comprehensive information on how they are using their corporate power and the social and environmental impacts of their operations.
- ***True picture* argument** This driving force is based on the belief that many stakeholders, such as investors and consumers, need the environmental information to make informed investing and purchasing decisions and therefore have a right to it. Traditional financial reports of companies (the

single bottom line reports) do not provide an accurate picture of the company's value because its non-financial assets and liabilities, and the financial costs borne by external groups, are not included. This true picture is needed by all, especially those who incorporate their personal values in their consumer and investment decisions. The most efficient way for stakeholders to get that information is to have the company itself supply it publicly. There is increasing concern on the part of securities and exchange commissions that changes have to be made so that investors can obtain the true picture.

- **Continuous improvement** This argument holds that measuring and reporting on environmental performance is necessary to drive improvement in corporate environmental performance. Conversely, companies that do not report on their environmental performance do not have to take a critical view of their own performance, and therefore are unlikely to see a need to improve, to reduce risks, and to take advantage of related business opportunities.
- **Urgency** This driving force, referred to as salience by Hill,[15] is based on the belief that current environmental (and social and economic) conditions are unsustainable, and, therefore, there is an urgent need for corporations to start measuring their impacts and providing this information to stakeholders so that possible solutions and corrective actions can be identified and shared. There is not much urgency attached to concerns for sustainable development and future generations. However, for many people, the level of urgency or salience changes when future generations are identified as their children and grandchildren.
- **Inherency** This driving force is based on that argument that corporate transparency and disclosure is *inherent* in the concept of being socially responsible. In other words, no matter what the actual impacts of its operations, a corporation can only be *fully* socially responsible, and therefore a good corporate citizen, if it issues credible environmental reports.

Business Driving Forces

Business driving forces are those arguments for environmental reporting which stem from the understanding that there is a real or potential commercial reward for companies that issue environmental reports. These rewards may be direct benefits, such as increased sales and investment, or indirect, such as enhanced corporate reputation and continuance of the social license to operate. These driving forces tend to work in conjunction, thereby mutually reinforcing each other, similar to normative driving forces. The business-based arguments for environmental reporting include:

- **Stakeholder relationships** This driving force is based on the argument that reporting on environmental performance in a credible, transparent fashion (in addition to having sound environmental performance) will strengthen relationships with stakeholders who care about environmental issues, such as certain customers, investors, employees, regulators, and environmental non-governmental organizations. This can result in various business benefits such as revenue generation, cost reduction, and cost avoidance. Regulators in North America and Europe have stated that they will reduce the scrutiny of corporations that have a good track record, which can be established in part through credible reporting, and focus their attention on those that do not.

- **Corporate reputation** The reputation argument holds that improved stakeholder relationships will have a positive impact on overall corporate reputation, which can have a positive impact on share value. When a company accounts for its environmental performance information in a proactive manner (i.e., before stakeholders demand the report), the company can gain significant reputational leverage. It can also help the company retain and extend its *social license to operate* by building public trust and preventing the delays and associated costs that result from stakeholder challenges.

- **Market differentiation** Companies will often report on their environmental performance in an effort to differentiate themselves from their competitors, thereby obtaining an advantage with respect to market share, access to resources, and ability to charge premium prices. With increasing consumer skepticism and cynicism, this driving force will become more important.

- **Ethical investments** This driving force stems from the growing interest in ethical investing by many individual investors and fund managers.[16] Reporting on environmental performance is often a requirement in screening criteria used by ethical funds.

- **Investor confidence** There are two approaches to making decisions on investments. Investing on the basis of market behavior has been popular until recent bear markets caused significant losses for investors. In this investment approach, CERs have little or no value. The other investment approach, which is regaining popularity, is value investing in which a detailed understanding of corporate strengths and weaknesses is important. The argument here is that value investors and investment analysts are concerned about corporate risk. Environmental reporting is one means of communicating to these groups that the company is aware of, and managing, its social and environmental risks effectively.

- **Justifying environmental investments and expenditures** Environmental reporting is a means of showing that resources devoted to effective environmental management are not just a cost of doing business, but that they produce quantifiable and qualitative benefits. Although producing a CER can be expensive, the cost could be small relative to the total budget for environmental management and could be important in demonstrating that the expenditures were worthwhile.

- **Efficiency** Corporations have to provide information on environmental issues related to corporate activities to different stakeholders. A corporate environmental communications strategy (chapter 20) should be developed so that information is documented, assembled, and distributed to stakeholders in an efficient manner. Responding to each request for information in an ad hoc, reactive fashion will likely be less efficient than designing and implementing a program for reporting to various audiences.

- **Benchmarking** For those companies that strive to gain recognition for leadership in corporate environmental management and social responsibility, benchmarking is essential to validate claims for superior performance (chapter 5, Strategic Environmental Management). Benchmarking will be greatly facilitated among those corporations that use a credible, standardized format to put information about their performance in the public domain.

- **Corporate governance** Corporate governance is coming under increasing scrutiny and there are demands for reform of a system, which is out of date. It is likely that, at least with leading-edge corporations, the composition, skills and knowledge, education and training, structure, and operations of boards will change. Those changes could include appointing board members with particular expertise and responsibilities in environmental and social issues, and establishing subcommittees to deal with corporate social responsibilities. Such committees would meet regularly and require regular reports and they would likely want credible CERs prepared and distributed.

Characteristics of Corporate Environmental Reports

Because of their wide distribution, CERs are one of the higher profile components of a corporation's communication strategy. For this reason it is important that the reports be of high quality and credibility. Key characteristics of quality CERs include[17]

- relevance
- reliability
- understandability
- comparability (including some form of normalization)

- timeliness
- verifiability
- credibility
- trends

Relevance

Relevance refers to whether the information being reported meets the stakeholders' decision-making needs. Information needs will typically vary from stakeholder to stakeholder. For this reason, it is important that the corporation endeavor to identify the report's audiences and their different information needs. Ensuring relevancy is challenging for two reasons. First, the report audiences can be quite diverse, and, as a result, their information needs may be broad and difficult to ascertain. Second, there may often be situations where the stakeholders' information needs are known but difficult to meet because the required information is not available or it is expensive to obtain.

Deciding on the level of detail, vocabulary, form, and format for information and medium (hard copy, brochure, low speed Internet, high speed Internet, etc.) is difficult. Until the recent evolution of websites and desktop publishing, producing appropriate hard copy reports for different audiences was prohibitively expensive not only in terms of time and money but also in terms of paper consumption, with the attendant environmental impacts. Now it is possible to design websites with layering of information so that stakeholders can seek the level of detail they want. The sites can be edited and updated on a regular basis without the costs of paper and printing.

Reliability

Reliability refers to whether the reported information is sufficiently accurate, complete, and objective to be relied upon by decision-makers. Authors of CERs must assess the quality of available information carefully because it will vary. Reported information does not need to be 100 percent accurate, complete, and objective to be useful for decision making, but it cannot be misleading either, or else it will adversely affect the outcome of the decisions based upon it. This problem can be somewhat resolved by a credible commitment to transparency and to continual improvement which would allow stakeholders to understand the reasons for uncertainty in the data and the fact that there is a corporate commitment to improve the quality of data over time.

Determining the reliability of information takes into consideration the concept of materiality which is a fundamental concept of financial auditing based on orientation of financial statements to user needs. In other words, "there will be a failure of communication, if the statements contain a material error, misrepresentation, or omission."[18] In this respect, materiality criteria derive from the information user's needs, rather than from the reporting organization's opinion. Materiality in the context of environmental reporting would be similar.

Ensuring reliability of data can be challenging, especially when reporting on new performance areas. It may be necessary to combine hard data with rough estimates to give a full picture, but unfortunately this erodes the overall accuracy of the data. Again, a commitment to transparency and continual improvement helps deal with this difficulty. While it is not imperative that corporations report 100 percent accurate information, they should have an understanding of the margin of error in their measurements, and this should be disclosed in the report. For example, calculations of carbon dioxide emissions using formulae and emission factors for combustion processes have an inherent margin of error, so it is not possible to obtain emissions data that is 100 percent accurate.

Understandability

Understandability refers to the clarity of the reported information and the appropriateness of the communication to the audience's familiarity with the topic, level of interest, time, skills, and knowledge. Simplicity is often the key, but, in many technical reports, it is not always possible to avoid technical terms and phrases. In some cases environmental reports may include a glossary or additional explanatory information in the margins or in footnotes to explain technical terms or to interpret complex measurements and trends.

Ensuring understandability can also be challenging. For example, in financial reporting there is an unstated understanding that the primary users of the information — investors — will have a reasonable knowledge of financial accounting. However, it is difficult to identify the primary users of environmental reports and their level of technical knowledge on environmental issues. For example, if it were assumed that one of the primary users of environmental reports is the investment analyst community, to what degree could one assume the analysts understand the science and relevance of NOX or VOC emissions?

Comparability

Comparability refers to the ability to meaningfully compare and contrast two or more sets of performance information. Comparability is necessary to allow for charting of performance and predictions on future performance within an organization. It also allows information users to compare the performance of different companies when making decisions to invest, purchase, or to increase or decrease regulatory scrutiny.

Comparability requires consistency in definitions, measurement methodologies, and presentation of the information. However, it is recognized that environmental reporting is still evolving, so it is expected that some changes in these three areas will occur in subsequent reports. These changes should be described and, where possible, the old data reconciled so as to be comparable with the new data.

Prior to the Global Reporting Initiative (GRI),[19] it was difficult to compare environmental reports from different companies because of the varying parameters, definitions, and methodologies for measurement. The GRI should help ensure greater consistency in the parameters reported and their definitions, although it does not specify the measurement methods that should be used.

Timeliness

Timeliness refers to the frequency of the environmental reports. Many companies now release their reports annually or bi-annually, so that the information is reasonably up to date. However, because environmental reports are voluntary, there is no requirement that they be issued on a specified reporting cycle.

Verifiability

Verifiability relates to how well the reported information will hold up to examination by an objective third party. With respect to quantitative information, this characteristic is closely linked to reliability, in that if the data is *reliable*, it should normally be *verifiable*. However, qualitative information (e.g., information on a company's values or goals) may be wholly reliable but next to impossible to verify because of its inherent nature. Throughout the 1990s there were mixed reports on the value of external verification of environmental reports; however, recent publications[20] now recognize that external verification contributes to a report's credibility.

Trends

It is important that the reports show trends in performance — is it improving or not. Therefore, wherever possible, information for the current period must be complemented by comparable information from previous reports to show whether corporate policies and practices are being effective. Showing trends in performance is essential for demonstrating that continual improvement is taking place.

Standards for Environmental Report Contents

The Global Reporting Initiative

Unlike in Europe where several countries have legislated reporting requirements, there is no legislation that governs corporate environmental reporting in North America; hence, there are no legal requirements stipulating the scope, quality, or regularity of CERs. However, there have been efforts by non-governmental organizations to standardize environmental reports throughout the 1990s, starting with an initiative by the United Nations in collaboration with SustainAbility.[21] One of the most popularly referenced reporting standards now is the *Sustainability Reporting Guidelines on Economic, Environmental and Social Performance*.[22] The GRI is an international group of organizations representing companies, government agencies, professional services firms, ENGOs, and the UN that has prepared reporting guidelines for sustainable development (e.g., economic, environmental, and social) reports. The format of indicators for reports are under development. The GRI suggests that there is a high degree of consensus on environmental indicators, some agreement on social and economic indictors, but relatively little consensus on indicators that might integrate the three areas. Most companies do not try to report on all the performance indicators but select from the GRI list to report those relevant to the company. More information is available on the GRI from their website: <www.globalreporting.org>

The GRI guidelines identify three classes of performance-reporting elements:
- categories — the broad areas of economic, social, and environmental issues of concern to stakeholders;
- aspects — general types of information related to each category (greenhouse gas emissions, energy efficiency, child labor, etc); and
- indicators — the specific measurements that can be used to track performance.

Indicators are designed to report absolute amounts that are required to understand the potential impacts. At the same time, ratios and normalized factors should be presented to facilitate interpretation and understanding. They can be used to show trends in performance and make comparisons.

The GRI states that the report should consist of the following:
- statement by the CEO
- profile of the reporting organization
- executive summary and key indicators
- vision and strategy
- policies, organizations, and management systems
- performance
  - overview
  - environmental performance (general) — energy, materials, water, emissions effluents and waste, transport, suppliers, products and services, land use — biodiversity, and compliance
  - Economic performance — profit, intangible assets, investments, wages and benefits, taxes, community development, suppliers, and products and services

○ Social performance — workplace, health and safety, wages and benefits, human rights, suppliers, and products and services
○ Integrated performance
  • Systematic — links micro (corporate) performance to macro (regional, national, global) performance
  • Cross-cutting – bridges two or more of the three categories

Selecting Indicators for the Report

The GRI guidelines can be considered a menu of performance indicators from which the reporting organization can choose. The choice is strongly dependent on two primary factors:
  • reliability of the parameter measurement processes and the resulting performance data, and
  • relevance of the issue to the organization's various stakeholders.

Reliability of the data

At any time in a corporation, different performance measurement processes will be at different stages of development. Some measurement processes will have been in existence for some time and as a result will be mature and robust and will generate consistent and reliable information. Performance measurement processes for other areas will be relatively new or under-managed, and the resulting data will be relatively unreliable, either because the data consists of rough estimates or because the performance data is measured in different ways across the organization and cannot be readily consolidated at the head office level. When the performance data is not considered reliable, reporting on performance in that area will be problematic, and in some cases not possible. (See Figure 13.3.) As a result, most companies report on their policies, goals, and objectives rather than actual performance for areas with emerging systems. Generally speaking, measurement processes that are required by regulations tend to be more reliable, while voluntary measurement processes tend to be weaker.

PricewaterhouseCoopers has assisted a number of client companies in preparing CERs or in providing external assurance for the reports. This experience has provided insights into the type of information that can, and should be, included in the reports. This experience also led to an understanding of the different types of assurance currently being offered by external assurance providers and the factors that influence the type of assurance provided.

Whereas an assessment of the data's reliability guides what indicators *can* be reported, an assessment of relevance to stakeholders influences which indicators *should* be reported. If the company has a sound environmental communications strategy and stakeholder consultation process (chapter 20), the company should understand which environmental topics are of greatest concern to the various stakeholders. For those, reporting is worthwhile and should be pursued. For topics of low interest to stakeholders, reporting does not add value and therefore should not be pursued, unless there is some other compelling business reason for doing so.

When these two dimensions are combined, they form an environmental reporting frame of reference, as shown in Figure 13.4. This frame of reference can be used as a screening tool to determine which indicators should be reported or how they should be defined in the report.

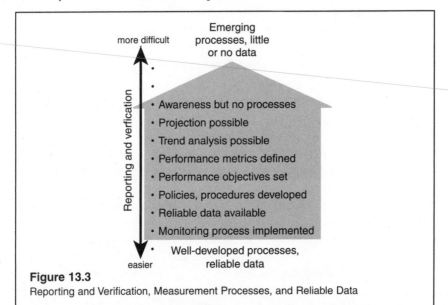

Figure 13.3
Reporting and Verification, Measurement Processes, and Reliable Data

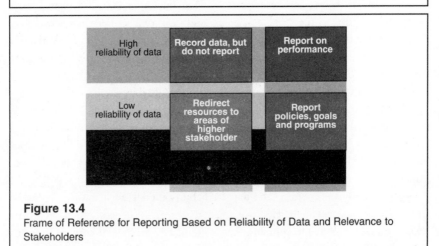

Figure 13.4
Frame of Reference for Reporting Based on Reliability of Data and Relevance to Stakeholders

Audiences for Environmental Reports

There are many users or audiences of CERs (see Table 13.1). In targeting their audiences, report makers may often address the noisiest stakeholders. Others consider their employees as their main audience but also target environmental campaigners, shareholders, and local communities. Stakeholders are identified in chapter 3, Driving Forces; chapter 7, Structures; and chapter 20, Environmental Communications.

Table 13.1: Audiences for Environmental Reports

- Shareholders
- Employees
- Consumers
- Special interest groups:
    - Consumer organizations
    - Environmental organizations
    - Other non-governmental organizations

- Investment analysts, investors
- Financial institutions
- Neighboring communities
- Media
- Government:
    - Enforcement agencies
    - Environmental departments

- Industry associations
- Peer organizations
- Others:
    - Benchmarking organizations
    - Educational institutions
    - International community
    - General public

External Assurance of Environmental Reports

Companies such as Shell International,[23] Suncor Energy,[24] Talisman,[25] and BP,[26] have engaged external groups to review and provide assurance on their environmental reports. The goal of this service is to provide reasonable (not absolute) assurance to the users of the report that the information is sufficiently reliable to be used for decision making. The external assurance providers base their conclusions on a thorough review of the evidence underlying the assertions in the environmental report, including the methodologies for data generation and calculations. If the underlying evidence is satisfactory, the external verifiers will often provide an attestation statement (also called an auditor's report or verification statement) which indicates that the reported information has been checked by an independent entity and found to materially reflect the company's actual performance.

A recent trend in corporate environmental reports is the inclusion of statements prepared by an organization independent of the reporting company. This assurance statement is typically designed to specify that the information contained in the report has been reviewed and found to be reliable, thereby providing assurance to the reader that the information reflects the corporation's actual environmental performance, similar to the auditor's report prepared by chartered accountants, which is included in corporate year-end financial statements.

The field of external assurance for CERs is still evolving and, as a result, numerous terms are used to describe the practice (e.g., external assurance, independent assurance, external verification), the players (e.g., auditors, verifiers, external reviewers), and the products (e.g., assurance statements, attestation statements, verification statements, auditors' reports, etc.). The term verification has been commonly used in popular literature on the subject; however, the term is now discouraged by a number of groups, including the Global Reporting Initiative Verification Working Group, because it implies a degree of exactitude, conformity, and certainty that is not necessarily intended or expected.[27] For the purpose of this chapter, the terms external assurance, assurance provider, and assurance statement will be used.

While the overall goal of external assurance for CERs is similar to financial audits — enhancing the credibility of the reports — the assurance processes differ. In financial auditing, the external auditor examines the processes the corporation used to generate, manipulate, and report its financial data and determines whether they conform with Generally Accepted Accounting Principles (GAAP). If the corporation's accounting practices are in accordance with GAAP, the auditor provides an Auditor's Report stating that GAAP were followed and therefore the resulting data should be reliable in all material respects. In environmental reporting, there are no environmental performance accounting procedures equivalent to GAAP. As a result, the external assurance provider must carry out a number of practices in order to assess the reported information, including

- for quantitative performance information, assess the appropriateness of the measurement or calculation processes; and
- for qualitative performance information, assess the credibility of the underlying evidence provided by the corporation.

At the end of the process, the external assurance provider issues an assurance statement that the qualitative and quantitative assertions in the report are reliable based on an examination of the underlying procedures and evidence.

Despite the difference described above, it appears that over time external assurance for CERs will come to more closely resemble financial auditing in terms of process, outputs, and terminology. Several groups, such as the Global Reporting Initiative Verification Working Group[28] and the European Federation of Accountants (FEE),[29] have drafted standards for providing assurance for environmental reports based largely on the financial audit model. Basing the practice on the financial audit model should accelerate the development process, clarifying and standardizing terminology and process, and ensuring a strong degree of rigor and discipline.

Driving Forces for External Assurance

The driving forces for external assurance can be described as value-added driving forces, in that they relate to improving the reports and therefore increasing their value in some way. These driving forces can be grouped into primary and secondary driving forces. The primary driving force behind external assurance of corporate social responsibility (CSR) reports is the desire for credible information by both the stakeholders and the reporting company:

- Stakeholders want assurance that they can rely on the information presented in the reports. Given the increasing importance of corporate environmental information in areas such as value investing and ethical investing, there is a growing incentive for companies to present only the favorable performance details in their reports, so stakeholders are more skeptical about the information. External verification is one way of giving the reader reasonable assurance that the information is reliable.

- Corporate management also benefits from the verification exercise in that they also receive assurance that the information being reported was checked by an independent third party before release, thereby minimizing the chances of embarrassment. In addition, corporate management wants to ensure not only that the information is reliable, but that it is *perceived* as reliable by the readers. Reporting companies do not want their reporting efforts to be in vain (only those who have prepared such reports can appreciate how much effort goes into their preparation).

There are four secondary driving forces behind the growth in demand for external assurance:

- **Demand for critique of company performance** Some stakeholders are requesting that the environmental reports include comments and criticisms from respected environmental experts on the quality of the company's environmental performance. Providing this qualitative assurance helps the reader determine whether or not the company's performance is as good as it should be. This is a unique type of assurance in that the focus is not on the reliability of the reported information, but on the relative quality of the corporation's environmental performance and the reputation and respect for the expert by various audiences. There is a potential problem here in that different stakeholders will have radically differing views of the way an endorsement by experts should be interpreted.

- **Demand for verification that the company's environmental management system meets external standards** Some stakeholders demand assurance that the company's environmental management system meets a specified standard, such as ISO 14001. The qualifications for doing such a review and the processes to be followed are clearly specified. This type of assurance gives stakeholders confidence that the company is well managed and will proactively manage its environmental impacts, risks, and opportunities. This information should be included in the corporation's environmental report.

- **Demand for interpretation of performance data** Some stakeholders want external analysis and interpretation of the corporation's environmental performance data, such as a comparison of the corporation's performance to that of its peers or across industry with respect to certain parameters (benchmarking, in chapter 5). For example, some readers may want to know how one petroleum company compares to other petroleum companies with respect to greenhouse gas emissions.

- **Demand for reliable data** Some stakeholders, and management itself, may want to ensure that the data reported by the company is accurate. Data with large margins of errors are not useful when one is trying to track small incremental improvements. For example, a company may determine that its carbon dioxide emissions are 300 tonnes/day, +/-15 percent. The fact that the data is +/-15 percent makes it difficult for the company to determine whether it achieved small reduction; apparent reductions may be attributed to measurement errors.

The type of assurance provided about environmental reports is a decision made by considering the needs and concerns of the reporting company, the stakeholder audience, and the assurance provider. However, the nature of the assurance will ultimately be dependent on two main factors:[30]

- The nature of the information being reviewed: is the information mainly qualitative, quantitative, or some combination?
- The nature of the auditors' professional opinions: are the assurance providers giving personal opinions (they include their values in their opinion) or

objective opinions (professional judgment based on education, experience, and professional ethics on whether reported information is factual).

When these two factors are combined, the following four types of assurance become possible:

- **Review and endorsement of company policies and performance** What does the external reviewer think of the company's performance, its policies, and its programs? This type of assurance is typically provided by auditors who are willing to express their own beliefs on how companies should perform. These reviews are most often provided by NGOs, academics, and celebrities (opinion leaders), who may or may not have skills, knowledge, and experience related to auditing and reporting.

- **Verification that management systems meet external standards** Does the company's Environmental Management System meet a specified standard, such as ISO 14001? This type of assurance is credible when provided by consultants and auditors holding special qualifications (education, training, and experience under qualified leadership) in Environmental Management Systems. A qualified external auditor can then provide evidence to appropriate bodies for registration of the EMS (see chapter 2, Environmental Management Systems).

- **Interpretation of performance data** What does all this environmental data mean? How does this company compare to peer companies? This type of assurance is typically provided by consultants with industry expertise, academics, or watchdog NGOs with access to similar performance data from other companies.

- **Verification of data integrity** Are the reported environmental data accurate and complete (e.g., reliable)? This type of assurance is typically provided by accounting and engineering companies with expertise in assessing quantified information and measurement methodologies.

These four types of external assurance are shown in Figure 13.5.

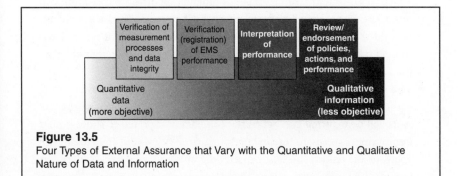

Figure 13.5
Four Types of External Assurance that Vary with the Quantitative and Qualitative Nature of Data and Information

The Barriers to Environmental Reporting

The barriers to environmental reporting can be grouped into normative and business arguments, like those with the driving forces.

Normative arguments against CERs

There are three main normative arguments that could be used to discourage environmental reporting:

- **The agency theory/private property argument** The belief that corporate management is accountable only to shareholders, not external stakeholders, and, as such, there is simply no ethical obligation to report on environmental performance publicly (although they may do so if it were in the best interest of the shareholders).
- **The right to privacy/protection against self-incrimination argument** One of the values of our society is that people (and other legal entities) all have a right to privacy, and, even more importantly, should not be required to provide self-incriminating information. Using this argument, companies (and undoubtedly their legal counsel) could state that voluntarily releasing environmental information would be dangerous because critics of the company could then use that information against the company in lawsuits, boycotts, and other reputation-damaging ways.
- **The power argument** Some pro-business groups may view environmental reporting as giving in to social groups, which could be interpreted as a sign of weak management, a betrayal of basic fundaments of capitalism. The argument states that once companies capitulate, the capitalist economy will begin to unravel, because the power will have shifted to those without a financial stake in the business.

Business Arguments against CERs

There are three main business arguments that could be used to discourage CERs:

- **The cost argument** Issuing an environmental report does cost money in terms of time and printing costs, especially if external assurance is included, and the financial benefits are difficult to measure. As a result, environmental reporting can appear to some as an expense rather than an investment.
- **The slippery slope argument** Some may argue that the cost of preparing and issuing an environmental report is just the tip of the iceberg: the real costs will be incurred later when the company is expected to show regular improvement in environmental performance. They would argue that once you issue the report, you raise expectations amongst your stakeholders that there will be follow-up reports that demonstrate improvement. You may

also inadvertently create demand for other types of corporate disclosure that will add more costs.

- **The scam argument** Finally, there are undoubtedly some business executives who would argue that the whole environmental reporting movement is a scam created by consultants, academics, and other special interest groups in an effort to create a lucrative consulting market. In their view, *they* will not be duped: they will watch their competitors throw good money away trying to meet society's unrealistic expectations.

Future

As the evolution of environmental reporting continues, there are important trends including

- CERs will continue to become more stakeholder-oriented through dialogues with stakeholders about the presentation and content of the CER.
- Stakeholders, especially consumers, environmental non-governmental organizations (ENGOs), and investors, are becoming more cynical and skeptical of corporations, so the credibility of reports will become more important.
- Standardization of report content, using GRI guidelines at least until international standards are established, will allow organizations to more easily benchmark their reports and their environmental performance.
- The format of CERs will change to become more user-friendly through the use of web pages, standardized formats, and common language (chapter 10 and chapter 15). In fact, corporate reports may become web-based instead of printed.
- Through regular reporting and benchmarking, organizations will continue to improve their abilities to evaluate their environmental risks and liabilities and concisely and effectively report on them to investors, consumers, and other stakeholders who will use that information in their decision making.
- The scope of CERs will continue to expand to include information on social and economic performance (the triple bottom line, sustainable development, and corporate social responsibility).
- External assurance on CERs will become more common and will continue to evolve.

Recommended Further Reading

Bennett, M., and P. James, eds. *Sustainable Measures: Evaluation and Reporting of Environmental and Social Performance*. Sheffield, U.K.: Greenleaf Publishing Limited, 1999.

Eccles, R. G., R. H. Herz, E. M. Keegan, and D.M.H. Phillips. *The Value Reporting Revolution*. New York: John Wiley & Sons, Inc., 2001.

Elkington, J., and F. van Dijk. "Socially Challenged: Trends in Social Reporting." In *Sustainable Measures*, edited by M. Bennett and P. James. Sheffield, U.K.: Greenleaf Publishing, 1999.

Global Reporting Initiative Verification Working Group. *Overarching Principles for Providing Independent Assurance on Sustainability Reports.* Global Reporting Initiative, 2001.

Greene, G., S. Meyer, J. Moffet, and J. Pezzack. *Stepping Forward: Corporate Sustainability Reporting in Canada.* Ottawa, Ontario: Stratos, 2001. Available at http://www.stratos-sts.com/pages/publica010.htm.

Hess, D. "Regulating Corporate Social Performance: A New Look at Social Accounting, Auditing, and Reporting." *Business Ethics Quarterly* 11, no. 22 (2001): pp. 307-330.

SustainAbility. *The Global Reporters.* London, U.K.: SustainAbility and United Nations Environment Programme, 2000.

Wheeler, D., and J. Elkington. "The End of the Corporate Environmental Report? Or, the Advent of Cybernetic Sustainability Reporting." *Business Strategy and the Environment* 10 (2001): pp. 1-14.

Wheeler, D., and M. Sillanpaa. *The Stakeholder Corporation.* London U.K.: Pitman Publishing, 1997.

Wilson, M., and C. K. Schuh. *Auditing Corporate Sustainability Reports.* Vancouver, BC.: Canadian Environmental Auditing Association Annual Technical Conference, 2001. Proceedings available at <http://www.ceaa-acve.ca/WilsonP.pdf>

Websites

AccountAbility: <http://www.accountability.org.uk/>

Association of Chartered Certified Accountants: <http://www.nextstep.co.uk/PDF/Guide.pdf>

Canadian Institute Of Chartered Accountants (CICA): <www.cica.ca>

Chartered Association Of Certified Accountants (ACCA): <www.abacca.com>

Coalition For Environmentally Responsible Economies (CERES): <www.ceres.org>

Environmental Reporting Clearinghouse: <http://cei.sund.ac.uk/envrep/index.htm>

Global Environmental Management Initiative (GEMI), <www.gemi.org>

The Global Reporting Initiative: <www.globalreporting.org/>

The International Corporate Environmental Reporting Site:
   <http://www.enviroreporting.com/>

Investor Responsibility Research Centre (IRRC): <www.irrc.org>

Keidanren: <www.keidanren.or.jp>

OECD: <www.oecd.org>

Social and Ethical Reporting Clearinghouse: <http://cei.sund.ac.uk/ethsocial/orgs.htm>

Stratos: <http://www.stratos-sts.com/pages/publica010.htm>

SustainAbility: <http://www.sustainability.com>

The Sustainability Report: <www.sustreport.org>

UNEP Industry & Environment Programme Activity Centre: <www.unepie.org>

World Business Council For Sustainable Development (WBCSD): <www.wbcsd.ch>

C H A P T E R

ENVIRONMENTAL IMPACT ASSESSMENT

William. A. Ross, University of Calgary
and Dixon Thompson

THE UNITED NATIONS ENVIRONMENT PROGRAMME (UNEP) has described Environmental Impact Assessment (EIA) as an examination, analysis, and assessment of planned activities with a view to ensuring environmentally sound and sustainable development.[1] The Canadian Environmental Research Council offers insight into how EIA is carried out professionally: EIA is a process that attempts to identify and predict the impacts of human activities on the biophysical environment and on human health and well-being. It also interprets and communicates information about those impacts and investigates and proposes means for their management.[2]

The recognition that, environmentally as well as economically, there are both costs and benefits of development projects led to the idea that we should examine developments for their environmental consequences when they are proposed, not after they are constructed. This "Look before you leap" approach is the basic idea behind Environmental Impact Assessment. The intent of EIA is to allow people to adjust development projects to enhance their benefits and to minimize their environmental costs. In addition, where it is discovered that the adverse effects of developments are likely to be so adverse as to make the costs greater than the benefits, such projects can be rejected by the proponent or refused approval by regulators or financiers. In this sense, EIA is a planning and management tool for choosing developments wisely. Sadler has described EIA as "one of the more successful policy innovations of the 20th century," noting it is "used in more than 100 countries and organizations to help decision makers consider the environmental consequences of proposed actions."[3] The National Environmental Policy Act of the United States, implemented in 1970, is recognized as the first EIA process.

EIA is a planning tool that predicts impacts before they occur, not one that measures them after they occur. It is an assessment tool because the impacts are interpreted, which means that EIA, while having a substantial scientific component to it, is very much based on human values.[4] It is a management tool because it also involves proposing means for managing the impacts of the project, both biophysical and socioeconomic, although the latter is not universally included. Another inference here is that information about the impacts and their meaning must be communicated to both decision makers and the public who might be affected by the proposed developments. Finally, the process requires management. During implementation, monitoring is carried out to discover if predictions and mitigation measures were adequate, and appropriate adjustments are made where needed.

In the 1960s it became apparent that large construction projects were causing major adverse environmental impacts. Because of increasing environmental awareness due to Rachel Carson's *Silent Spring*,[5] the work of Barry Commoner,[6] Garret Hardin,[7] and others, and events such as Earth Day on April 22, 1970, attention became focused on what could be done to avoid the most obvious damage. As a result, more than 100 countries passed legislation requiring environmental impact assessments before projects are approved.

In the 1970s the life sciences were the focus of many EIAs, because the most obvious impacts were changes in habitats and fish and wildlife populations. Furthermore, EIAs require an extensive inventory of the environment that could be affected by the proposed project, so an inventory of the biological and hydrogeological systems involved occupied a great deal of the time, effort, and budgets. However, as baseline data became established, further biological studies were less essential because existing databases could be used. The focus then shifted to the quality of the impact predictions, secondary and tertiary impacts, and socioeconomic impacts.

In addition to EIAs, special types of impact assessments were developed, or evolved, as components of EIA: Social Impact Assessment, Historic Resources Impact Assessment, Visual Impact Assessment, Strategic Environmental Assessment, and Cumulative Effects Assessment.

The formation of the International Association for Impact Assessment as an international professional association was a significant step for improving impact assessment, harmonizing the practice of EIAs, and publishing research results.[8]

Generic Process of Environmental Impact Assessment

EIA is normally implemented by governments (state, provincial, or national) and by lending agencies such as the World Bank and other development banks, in an attempt to make better development decisions. The private sector must understand the EIA requirements in order to meet them proactively. The basic steps in any generic EIA process are: screening, scoping, impact prediction and assessment, mitigation, and follow-up studies undertaken for those projects that proceed to the implementation phase.

Screening

For any project proposal, screening is the determination of the level of EIA to be applied to the proposal. In order for an EIA to be undertaken efficiently and effectively, projects with trivial impacts must be excluded from the EIA process, while major projects with likely significant impacts must be examined in detail (a full EIA). Projects with modest impacts should be subject to a focused EIA directed at issues of concern to decision makers. The need for screening is identified clearly by the UNEP where Principle 3 (see below) requires that the EIA should be focused on projects with potentially significant impacts.[9] The determination of the appropriate level of EIA, called screening, is the responsibility of the institution accountable for the EIA process. Screening is usually carried out by inclusion lists (lists of projects for which EIA is automatically required), exclusion lists (lists of projects automatically exempt from EIA requirements), and ad hoc reviews of the projects to see what their impacts are likely to be (for projects not on either list). The use of lists has great administrative simplicity, while the ad hoc reviews have the ability to identify unusual projects at the cost of requiring trained reviewers.

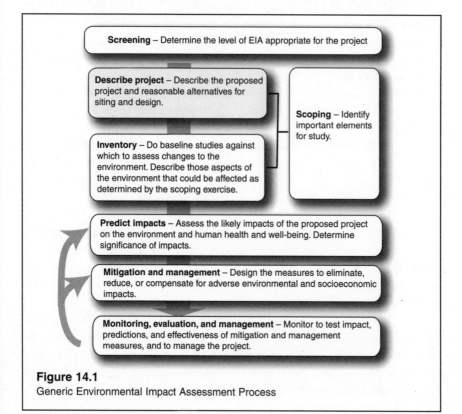

Figure 14.1
Generic Environmental Impact Assessment Process

Note that often projects with major impacts are excluded from EIA as a matter of history, political influence, and policy, especially in forestry, agriculture, and urban development.

Scoping

For those projects requiring an EIA, it is essential to focus the EIA on those impacts that will make a difference to the decision about the project. This procedure of identifying the issues and determining their priority for the EIA process is called scoping. The UNEP describes the need for scoping in Principle 5.[10] In the EIA process the relevant significant environmental issues should be identified and studied at an early stage. Scoping is undertaken through consultations with scientific and technical specialists, with members of the affected public, interest groups, and the project proponent. These consultations seek to determine views about what impacts are the most important in carrying out the environmental impact assessment, those that will influence the project decisions.

While many participants contribute to scoping, the final determination of what will be addressed in the environmental impact assessment must be that of the responsible administering authority.

There are three requirements for effective scoping:

- Identify scoping participants early in the process (if they appear too late, impacts are missed or are provided too late).
- Make sufficient information about the project available early in the review (otherwise, how could participants judge the likely impacts?).
- Make use of existing information (such as studies of similar projects, EIAs for similar projects, and existing generic guidelines for similar projects).

According to Sadler, scoping is one area in need of strengthening in the EIA process.[11]

Impact Prediction and Assessment

Impact prediction and assessment is complex and is influenced substantially by the scoping results. The possible impacts identified in the terms of reference determine what sort of impact prediction expertise is required. Methods for predicting impacts are extraordinarily varied, reflecting the wide variety of issues and tasks needed for an effective EIA.[12]

One general point can be made, however. The predicted impact for a particular component of the environmental and social systems is the difference between what the component would be with and without the proposed project. This is not necessarily the same as the difference between the prediction for that component and its baseline condition, because, even without the project, the condition of that component can change.

Having predicted the impacts, their significance must be determined. The UNEP's Principle 2 identifies the need to determine whether an activity is likely to significantly affect the environment.[13] The choice of which impacts require mitigation to make the project acceptable can only be decided through a determination of the significance of impacts. Insignificant impacts should not generally require mitigation, but significant adverse impacts usually should be mitigated. Significance may be determined by considering such factors as

- the nature and extent of impacts (e.g., type, duration),
- likely adverse effects on the receiving environment (e.g., sensitive areas, land use, community traditions),
- magnitude of impacts (e.g., low, moderate, high),
- options for impact mitigation (e.g., reduction, avoidance),
- reversibility,
- availability of compensation or offsets, and
- social and ecological value of affected resources.

The determination of impact significance is the second of the four areas that should be strengthened.[14]

Mitigation

For those impacts that are significant and adverse, it is important, and often imperative, that they be mitigated. This is most commonly done through changes to the project so that the impacts do not occur, are reduced in severity, or are otherwise managed to become less significant. Project redesign or adjustments to project operation are the usual tools of mitigation. Compensation can also be used to overcome impacts. Compensation can be in kind, for example, creation of new wetlands to replace wetlands lost due to the project, or financial (or equivalent) to people who lose valued resources due to the project, for eample, building a new facility in a community subject to socioeconomic disruption. Mitigation can also take the form of enhancing positive impacts to offset negative impacts, for eample, commitment to a greater percentage of local hiring to enhance the financial well-being of those most affected by a project.

Follow-up Studies

For those projects that proceed to the implementation phase following an Environmental Impact Assessment review, it is essential to ensure that the good environmental management plans developed for the project are actually implemented. Otherwise, the whole EIA exercise will have been wasted. The United Nations Task Force on Environmental Impact Assessment Auditing observed that follow-up studies are a very effective and necessary means of continuing the EIA process into the implementation phase of approved projects. Such studies, the

Task Force on Environmental Impact Assessment Auditing concluded, are valuable both for environmental management of the approved project and for EIA process development.[15]

Environmental management of the project involves monitoring selected attributes associated with the project, evaluating the results to see what they mean, and adapting project environmental management depending on the findings — adaptive environmental management. The basic principle here is that the information collected will be information essential for managing the project by the proponent or for regulating the project by regulators. This would involve compliance monitoring (ensuring that the project is constructed, operated, and decommissioned in accordance with the environmental management plans developed during the EIA process and required of the proponent), reviewing predicted impacts for management of risks and uncertainties, and dealing with unpredicted impacts (environmental surprises).

The EIA process development involves learning lessons from the project for application to future projects. This can involve determining the accuracy of impact predictions and the effectiveness of mitigation measures in order to transfer this experience to future projects of the same type, or it can involve determining the effectiveness of environmental management for the project in order to apply it to future projects. A credible requirement for follow-up can help to reassure those concerned about possible impacts.

Principles of Environmental Impact Assessment

The UNEP identifies thirteen principles of EIA:[16]

1. Examine environmental impacts.
2. Define criteria used to determine significance of impacts.
3. Screen proposals to select projects deserving attention.
4. EIA documents must contain project description, affected environment, description of alternatives, description of mitigation measures, identification of knowledge gaps, transboundary concerns, and a short summary.
5. Scoping to decide which issues require study.
6. Carry out independent review.
7. Involve the public.
8. Provide adequate time for considerations of EIA input (comments and submissions).
9. Document the decision on the project in a written, public statement.
10. Monitor, evaluate, and manage the project's impacts.
11. Transboundary impacts: notify, provide information, and consult.
12. Transboundary impacts.
13. Implement EIA procedures.

Principle 1 Examine environmental impacts

Governments should not undertake or authorise projects (activities in the UNEP document) until the environmental effects (impacts) are examined. This is a reminder that, if EIA is to avoid problems, it needs to be applied early in the planning process, not after projects are approved.

Principle 2 Define significance

The criteria used to determine the significance of impacts must be clearly defined. This is essential if the EIA is to focus on important impacts but this principle is difficult to apply.

Principle 3 Screening

Concentrate efforts on projects likely to cause significant impacts, which stresses the importance of good screening.

Principle 4 Content of EIA documents

A high quality EIA document should contain: a project description, a description of the environment in which the project is proposed, a description of alternatives considered for the project, an assessment of environmental impacts, a description of mitigation measures to be used to avoid or reduce further impacts, identification of knowledge gaps, transboundary concerns, and a short summary of the full document.

The phrase *description of the environment* seems to invite excessive descriptive details. One of the problems of EIA practice is excessive detail on description and too little effort on predicting and assessing impacts.

Assessment of alternatives is important because there may be alternatives that offer the same benefits at less cost or with smaller impacts. Alternatives include policy interventions, other projects, and alternatives within the project.

The need for identifying knowledge gaps arises from the virtual certainty that, for major projects, one will never fully understand the impacts. Thus, it is important for decision makers to understand what may be missing and how that influences understanding of project impacts.

Transboundary impacts are those caused in a receiving country by a project in the country undertaking the Environmental Impact Assessment (the country of origin).

The summary of the EIA document is essential for those who do not have the time or ability to read the full document: primarily members of the public and decision makers.

Principle 5 Scoping

The issues must be identified early. EIAs should be focused on matters that will affect project decisions.

Principle 6 Independent review

EIA information must be reviewed by people independent of the project proponent. The concern is that the proponent may be biased and may, even with the best of intentions, not assess the impacts in a fair and impartial manner. Even when a third party (e.g., an independent consultant) carries out the assessment, it is essential to have an independent review.

Principle 7 Public involvement

Public involvement is necessary prior to the decision about the project. While it is conceivable that experts behind closed doors could carry out an EIA, it should not to be done in that manner. Major benefits of public involvement are: moral and ethical obligations to the public, access to better information and different perspectives, and better chances of public acceptance of approved projects. The moral and ethical obligations simply reflect that people who will be affected by proposed developments have a right to be heard before the development is approved.

Principle 8 Consider EIA input

Time must be allowed to consider the input made by participants in the review, a principle of natural justice and procedural fairness, which is intended to force decision makers to take the EIA seriously.

Principle 9 Document project decision

The project decision, taken as a result of the environmental assessment, should be a public document, to enhance credibility in the process and to help ensure that conditions and mitigation measures will be reflected in any approvals.

Principle 10 Monitoring, evaluation, and management

Monitoring, evaluation, and management should be applied during the implementation phase of approved projects as appropriate.

Principles 11 and 12 Transboundary impacts

Transboundary impacts ought properly to be dealt with in the same fashion as impacts within the country where the project is proposed. Principles for dealing with transboundary impacts are notification, the provision of information, and consultation. The notification involves the country of origin advising the receiving country (or countries) about the proposed project. The provision of information involves the country of origin providing information about the project and its likely impacts while the receiving country provides information about its environment. The consultation involves the EIA review considering, on an equal footing, concerns in both countries.

Principle 13 Implement EIA

EIA procedures should be implemented.

Professional Practice of EIA

There are many roles for EIA professionals: field work to complete the inventory, predicting and determining significance of impacts, designing and implementing mitigation and management measures, EIA administration, reviewing EIA documents, reviewing projects subject to EIA, project decision making, and the preparation of EIAs.

EIA consultants normally start their work by obtaining a detailed understanding of the proposed project in order to determine the scope of the EIA. It is also essential for the EIA consultant to work closely with project designers. The EIA practitioner can identify environmental problems early, so that project designers can revise the project to mitigate impacts of concern. Project designers can also alert the EIA practitioners to project changes, and resulting possible changes in impacts. This close working relationship is very important for an effective EIA. When the EIA is carried out after the project design is completed, it is difficult and more expensive to deal effectively with identified impacts.

Well-qualified EIA consultants will seek information from the project proponent concerning experience with similar projects. These can provide excellent information concerning impacts to be expected, especially when there has been an effective follow-up program.

EIA consultants will have access to a variety of literature concerning environmental impacts: previous EIA documents, consulting reports for governments and industry, follow-up studies from existing projects, and academic publications concerning the prediction and assessment of impacts. Effective means of mitigating and managing impacts are also essential information. The project designers are aware of project alternatives, which is another sound reason for the EIA practitioner to have a good working relationship with them.

The EIA consultant needs to know people from whom essential information can be obtained. Good working relationships with government sources are important for obtaining a detailed understanding of EIA processes and procedures. This does not mean inappropriate interactions, just a fair and professional exchange of information about projects under review. Similarly, knowing researchers and consultants will allow the EIA practitioner to call them for advice, and perhaps to employ them as sub-consultants.

In large consulting firms, most expertise may be available in-house. But in smaller firms, and even in large firms when other staff are busy on other projects, qualified professionals must be accessible. They will have expertise relevant to the project under review, as well as the knowledge and skills needed to work effectively in interdisciplinary problem-solving teams. The final product will be the joint effort of a team and it should be coherent if it is to be effective in leading to better design and development decisions.

The interdisciplinary nature of the teams that carry out EIAs is of critical importance. The team must have access to the complete set of expertise necessary to carry out the inventory, make predictions of impacts and assess them, propose mitigation and management measures, and design follow-up procedures. If important skills are lacking, critical impacts or possible mitigation measures can be missed. It is folly to study only those aspects represented on an incomplete team. To be successful, team leaders and members will need teamwork skills, interdisciplinary skills, and communications skills.

Fieldwork is an expectation of many EIA practitioners, but because field studies can be quite expensive, they should only be done as a last resort. One should first make every reasonable effort to use existing studies that might provide the same (or equivalent) information. Field visits, as opposed to research, are essential. They enhance credibility, provide a better feel for the location than can be obtained from documents, and may contribute to better predictions of impacts and design of mitigation measures. Field visits also provide an opportunity to consult with local people about their concerns and local knowledge.

An EIA consultant achieves the assessment goals by creating effective mitigation and management measures. Proponents often believe the myth that solving environmental problems is very expensive. In collaboration with project designers, well-qualified EIA practitioners are often able to devise mitigation and management measures that not only reduce or eliminate impacts, but also reduce project costs. Mitigation and management plans can reduce construction and operating costs of projects that might be adversely affected by environmental problems.

Cumulative Effects Assessment

If there are several projects proposed for an area, then independent assessments might miss those impacts that result from interactions between projects or that would be insignificant if the other projects were not there. To overcome this problem, some legislated EIA processes require that the cumulative effects, not just the effects of the project alone, be assessed.[17] This is referred to as cumulative effects assessment (CEA). Assessing cumulative effects should improve environmental impact assessment for projects because the information so developed will be more useful to decision makers because it deals with the true consequences (impacts) of proposed projects.[18]

The introduction of cumulative effects assessment into EIA has not been without its critics. The reason for the concern is that project proponents are forced to predict and assess not only the impacts of their own projects, but also those of others, sometimes competitors, from whom it is difficult to obtain adequate information. Moreover, occassionally when EIA practitioners do predict cumulative impacts correctly, the regulators lack authority to deal with the most important impacts because they are caused by projects outside their jurisdiction. There are four requirements to develop greater proficiency in doing cumulative effects assessment:

1. Identify valued ecosystem components (VECs) affected by the proposed project (scoping).
2. Determine what other past, present, and future human activities have affected or will affect these VECs.
3. Predict the impacts on the VECs of the project in combination with the other human activities, and determine the significance of the impacts.
4. Suggest how to manage the cumulative impacts.

A second concern about cumulative impacts is referred to as destruction by insignificant increments, or damage creep, where no individual action produces significant damage, but, at some point, the cumulative effect of many similar actions produces a significant impact. This is the case with litter, hiking in fragile areas, impact of scuba divers on coral reefs, etc.

EIA for Strategic Purposes

Two other aspects of Environmental Impact Assessment need to be mentioned: strategic EIA and private sector EIA. Both are strategic in the sense that they are not done to assess a proposed project for regulatory purposes. Strategic environmental assessment is the environmental assessment of policies, plans, and programs which encourage, initiate, or guide projects. EIA applied to projects comes after policies, plans, or programs are approved and this is too late for effective control of environmental impacts. That is, by predicting and mitigating adverse impacts of policies, plans, and programs, the environmental impacts of projects that result from the policies, plans, and programs will be reduced.

Sadler's principles of Strategic Environmental Assessment[19]

The guiding principles of strategic environmental assessment are:
- Initiating agencies are accountable for assessing the environmental effects of new or amended policies, plans, and program.
- The assessment process should be applied as early as feasible.
- The scope of assessment is to be commensurate with the proposal's potential impact or consequence.

- Objectives and terms of reference should be clearly defined.
- Alternatives to a proposal should be considered.
- Socioeconomic factors should be included as necessary and appropriate.
- Evaluation of significance and determination of acceptability should be made against policy framework of environmental objectives and standards.
- Provision should be made for public involvement, consistent with potential degree of concern and controversy of proposal.
- Public reporting of assessment and decisions is required, unless explicit limitations on confidentiality are given.
- Environmental factors must be included in policy making.
- Processes should relate, where possible, to subsidiary strategic environmental assessment and project EIA — that is, EIA for projects as part of a policy, plan, or program should take into consideration the findings of the strategic environmental assessment for the policy, plan, or program.
- Include monitor and follow-up measures.
- Independent oversight of process implementation, agency compliance, and government-wide performance is required.

Running a business encompasses a wide variety of activities, not least of which is the management of potential risks associated with failure to handle environmental matters adequately. Industry does this by managing its environmental affairs with due care and by being increasingly eco-efficient, taking account of scientific, technical, and economic factors, and the requirements of environmental legislation as a starting point. At the heart of sound environmental management is the assessment of effects, real or potential, on the environment as a consequence of business activities and the planning and implementation of measures to avoid or mitigate that damage. Environmental assessments can assist companies in their quest for continuous improvement in both financial and environmental performance by:

- facilitating and speeding approval of proposed projects,
- reducing risks and liabilities,
- avoiding expensive changes to proposals late in the process,
- reducing waste and emissions in new projects, and
- demonstrating a sense of social responsibility to customers and neighbors.

Companies are starting to use EIA as an environmental management tool independent of the regulatory need to do so. Similarly, Mason et al note that "businesses should be considering impacts not only because it is best for our world, but also because there is increasing evidence that it may well be the most profitable approach as well."[20]

Success of EIA

EIA has been described as one of the more successful policy innovations of the 20th century. That success is reflected in the fact that it has been widely adopted around the world. But it would also be less than fair to suggest EIA is an unqualified success. EIA can be quite ineffective if not used properly:

- if proponents undertake EIA after the project is designed,
- if decision makers fail to use EIA results in making development decisions, or
- if the implementation of projects subject to EIA fails to follow through effectively with the sound environmental management plans developed through the EIA process.

In spite of the problems, it is important to note how effective EIA has been. A study in the Netherlands indicated that over 70 percent of EIAs resulted in significant improvements to the projects for which they were done.[21] Practitioners routinely demonstrate cost savings for developers as a result of Environmental Impact Assessment. And, most importantly, better environmental protection has been achieved through EIA.

EIA and Other Environmental Management Tools

The EIA processes and documents are means to an end (resource conservation and protection of the environment), not ends in themselves. The UNEP's Principle 3 states the importance of focusing on important projects. Therefore, where experience with a type of project in well-known areas has shown that impacts can be predicted and mitigated, it should be possible to replace an EIA with a binding commitment to regular audits and public reports on them. This would provide the same results as an EIA but avoid costs to all parties: regulator, public, and the proponent. The substitution of audits for EIAs of less important projects could only proceed if interested parties agreed. It would, however, allow regulators and proponents to meet or exceed the spirit of the law at a lower cost.

The UN Task Force on EIA Auditing noted the importance of auditing for follow-up and improvement (feedback) but the audit provides additional benefits in that less significant projects are still scrutinized but at less cost.

The expansion of a commercial recreation facility required the purchase of government land which would have been stopped or delayed by regulators if there were objections from the public or ENGOs. The proponent's consultants had done a thorough EIA, including detailed mitigation measures. The proponent promised concerned citizens that they would do regular audits and report the results to the public. The representatives of the public agreed that these provisions were adequate and approval was granted. Unfortunately there was no binding agreement so not all conditions were met. This example teaches two lessons: EIA can facilitate approvals, but follow up is necessary.

There are no clear dividing lines between EIA, Life Cycle Assessment (chapter 18) and product and technology assessment (chapter 17). To emphasize the fact that EIA should include project life cycles, the Pembina Institute has developed a process it refers to as Life Cycle Impact Assessment.[22]

The overlap among these tools can be seen in the case of solar and wind power systems. They might be exempt from an EIA through scoping but be assessed by Product and Technology Assessment to optimize benefits and reduce costs and minor impacts. However, at some scale of solar and wind power arrays, an EIA or a cummulative impact assessment might be required because of the scale and cumulative effects. Note that wind systems can generate noise pollution and are lethal to birds that try to fly through them. Solar systems will have a finite lifetime, if aging decreases efficiency or replacement technology is more efficient. At that point, disposal and/or recycling of complex mixtures of exotic materials would be an issue.

Compensation in Lieu of Complete Mitigation

In some project proposals it is impossible to mitigate all significant impacts on the site. In those cases, proponents might seek approval by compensating for the loss at some other location. This can be the case in jurisdictions where projects affecting fish must meet the requirement for no net loss of fisheries. Approval might be granted if the proponent can enhance fish production in similar parts of the watershed to meet the requirement.

In other cases, corporations might seek approval to expand existing activities or introduce new activities in a protected natural area (provincial/state or national park or reserve). It is conceivable that proponents could enhance the possibilities of approval by finding means of significantly expanding the size of the protected area as compensation for unmitigated impacts. This could be done by buying deeded land adjacent to the area and turning it over to the government to become part of the protected area. Where all adjacent land is unprotected government land, land swaps might be arranged for deeded property elsewhere, or the proponent could purchase the government land and then return it to become part of the protected area.

Of course, serious objections could and should be raised to ensure that the benefits of the compensation are sufficient to justify approval.

Abandonment

Before we leave this chapter, the topic of abandonment must be addressed in a little more detail than references to scoping and life cycles. Around the world, communities face the costs of cleaning up abandoned sites: contaminated industrial sites, mining and petroleum installations, tailings ponds, and other sites that pose health, safety, and environmental risks. Most, if not all, governments have learned, or should have learned, that approval of new or expanded projects should never be granted without a binding commitment to carefully designed, clearly acceptable plans for abandonment. This should include provisions for ongoing monitoring and auditing where necessary.

To make the commitment binding, governments have required the proponent to post a bond that is returned when proof is provided that all commitments have been met, or it is used to cover the cost of rehabilitation. Where proponents argue that the proper abandonment plans or the requirements for bonds are too expensive, approval should not be granted. They are seeking approval to profit at public expense.

Recommended Further Reading

Canter, L. W. *Environmental Impact Assessment.* 2nd ed. Toronto, Ontario: McGraw-Hill Ryerson, 2001.

IAIA Journal: *Impact Assessment and Project Appraisal*

IAIA Newsletter

Petts, J., ed. *Handbook of Environmental Impact Assessment.* 2 vols. Oxford, U.K.: Blackwell Science, 1999.

Porter, A. L., and J. J. Fittipaldi. *Environmental Methods Review: Retooling Impact Assessment for the New Century.* Fargo, ND: The Press Club, 1998.

Walthern, P. *Environmental Impact Assessment: Theory and Practice.* New York: Routledge, 1992.

Websites

Australian EIA Network: <http://www.erin.gov.au>

Canadian Environmental Assessment Agency: <http://www.ceaa.gc.ca>

International Association for Impact Assessment: <http://www.ext.nodak.edu/IAIA>

United States Council on Environmental Quality: <http://ceq.eh.doe.gov/CEQ>

World Bank: <http://www.worldbank.org>

ENVIRONMENTAL ACCOUNTING

*Stephen Hill, University of Calgary
and Dixon Thompson*

E NVIRONMENTAL ACCOUNTING is the collection, estimation, organization, and presentation of environmentally related financial information for decision makers. They can be managers within an organization or company, politicians and managers within a government, investors or bankers considering an investment or loan, or stakeholders and community groups interested in a company's environmental performance.

The discipline of accounting deserves credit for providing environmental management with many of its systems and tools. The traditional accounting control system is fundamentally similar to an ISO 14001 Environmental Management System (i.e., plan – do – check – act). Environmental auditing derives many of its techniques from financial auditing, and many of the concepts surrounding environmental reporting and indicators stem from annual reports and financial performance indicators. (Performance measurement and environmental reporting have often been considered a part of environmental accounting.) The more environmental accounting improves, the easier it will be to demonstrate better environmental performance.

Environmental accounting has a great deal to offer in terms of information provided to internal and external decision-makers. However, significant difficulties can also arise because

- there is no standardization of terms — sometimes the same term has different meanings, different terms have the same meaning, or similar terms have the same meaning, or with very subtle differences;
- there is a lack of standardization and credibility for auditing;
- there is a lack of cooperation among different professionals who have or need information; and

- there can be significant costs for changing accounting methods to provide environmental accounting information.

Environmental accounting has started to receive more attention in the environmental management literature. For instance, Bennett and James[1] and Schaltegger and Burrit[2] have produced books which help greatly in understanding a difficult, complex, technical set of issues. The UN has commissioned three workbooks on environmental management accounting — *Environmental Management Accounting Metrics, Procedures and Principles, Improving Governments' Role in Promoting Environmental Management Accounting,* and *Policy Pathways for Promoting Environmental Management Accounting.*[3] The EPA has produced a report on three case studies: *Enhancing Supply Chain Performance with Environmental Cost Information.*[4] Wilmhurst and Frost have examined "The Role of Accounting and the Accountant in the Environmental Management System."[5] In contrast, Buonicore and Crocker have criticized corporations for being too slow to develop the needed skills.[6]

Environmental accounting can provide information to decision-makers in a variety of contexts (Figure 15.1). This chapter outlines and clarifies these contexts and examines some of the more import applications and techniques of environmental accounting. It also examines how environmental information and costs can be incorporated into traditional accounting practices.

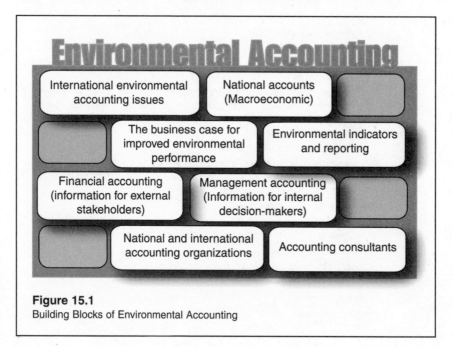

Figure 15.1
Building Blocks of Environmental Accounting

Table 15.1 Components of Environmental Accounting

International concerns

- the value of natural capital, the environment, biodiversity, and natural productivity
- taxes for access to the global commons for maintenance and protection
- measurement of well-being for international comparisons

National accounts (macroeconomic)

- Gross Domestic Product and adjusted GDP
- discount rate and the future value of resources
- internalization of negative externalities
- determining the value of natural capital and the environment
- measurement of national well being

Corporate accounts (microeconomic)

- Financial environmental accounting (information for external stakeholders)
  - environmental expenditures — capitalized or expensed?
  - environmental liabilities and contingent costs
  - environmental assets
  - emission trading certificates
  - indicators and reporting
- Environmental management accounting (information for internal decisions)
  - energy and materials accounts — utilities and waste disposal
  - environmental cost accounting
    - direct costs
      - capital (buildings, equipment and installation, utility connections, project engineering)
      - operation and maintenance expenses/revenues, raw materials, utilities (energy, water, sewer) labor contractors, revenue from recovered material, internal energy generation (some of these may be hidden in pooled or overhead accounts)
    - indirect/hidden costs
      - permitting, reporting, monitoring, education and training, record keeping and documentation, emergency preparedness, health and safety, EMS, and auditing (if not capitalized) insurance
    - liabilities and contingent (risks) costs
      - fines, jail sentences, penalties, civil damages claims, cleanup costs, legal fees, time lost for employees and equipment, increase insurance premiums
    - reputation/image costs
    - opportunity costs
    - investment appraisal/total cost assessment
    - life cycle costing
    - external costs

In the regional or national context, national accounts provide information and indicators such as the Gross Domestic Product (GDP). While these traditional indicators are useful for some things, they often show progress when the environment and/or human well-being are actually being damaged or resources are being wasted. For example, when the Exxon Valdez spilled its oil off Alaska, the ecological damage was not reflected in the GDP. However, all of the money spent on legal fees and to clean up the accident contributed to a growing GDP.

Some authors include non-monetary information in the form of environmental indicators and reporting as part of environmental accounting.[7] Because those topics are covered in chapters 12 and 13, they will not be considered here.

Figure 15.2 shows the relationships between the components of macroenvironmental accounting issues at the national and international levels, and corporate environmental accounting issues. National and international accounting organizations are involved in setting standards and the qualifications for accounting professionals, so they are included as significant elements. Consultants play major roles in applying accounting processes and interpreting the international standards, so they too are included.

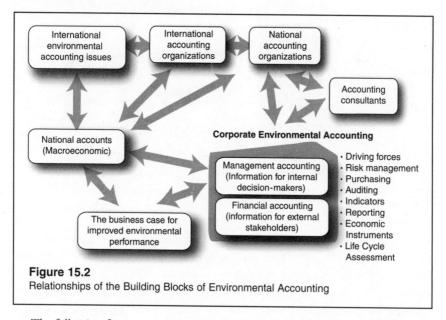

Figure 15.2
Relationships of the Building Blocks of Environmental Accounting

The following five accounting issues related to national accounts are important because, as they change, corporate environmental accounting and environmental management will be affected:

• an adjusted GDP — the measurement of national well-being
• internalization of negative externalities

- use of the discount rate to determine the value of resources in the future
- placing a value on natural capital
- ensuring national economic/financial security

These five national accounts issues are important for sustainable development policies — the triple bottom line for governments. Strategic managers in corporations must understand these issues, monitor and hopefully anticipate changes, and adjust corporate strategies accordingly.

Figure 15.3 shows the major components of national accounts and corporate accounts related to environmental accounting.

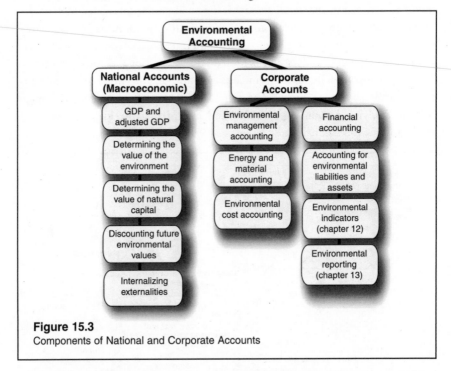

Figure 15.3
Components of National and Corporate Accounts

Within an organization, environmental accounting can be addressed from three perspectives (Figure 15.4): management accounting (i.e., the use of internal accounting information in management decisions), financial accounting (i.e., the measurement and reporting of an organization's financial performance, particularly to external audiences), and the business case (financial and other benefits) of improved environmental management. These three environmental accounting issues use data about four different issues: risks, liabilities and contingent costs; costs and benefits (direct, less direct, and intangible); capitalization of investments and amortization of those costs, if appropriate; and determining the value of environmental assets.

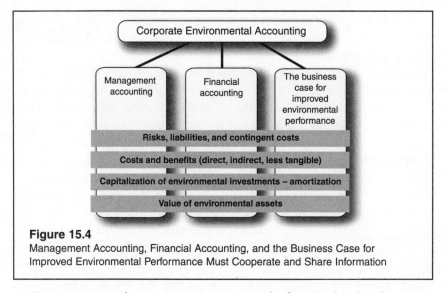

Figure 15.4
Management Accounting, Financial Accounting, and the Business Case for
Improved Environmental Performance Must Cooperate and Share Information

For environmental management accounting, the focus is placed on how environmental information can improve decision making at the strategic and operational levels of an organization (e.g., product design and costing, capital investments, process design and costing, strategic planning, purchasing). In financial accounting, the focus is on how to obtain and report environmental information (both financial and non-financial) to external audiences and stakeholders. For instance, changes to the Generally Accepted Accounting Principles (GAAP) require that firms include environmental liabilities (e.g., contaminated sites) in their financial statements. This has had a tremendous impact on the identification, assessment, and cleanup of contaminated sites (chapter 11).

The third part of corporate environmental accounting is essential but sadly neglected — making the business case for improved environmental performance. Environmental accounting has, for some reason, focused on the costs and not paid enough attention to the benefits. These consist of reduced direct, indirect, and contingent costs, improved benefits, and reduced costs through reputation management. If perceived costs of improved performance are larger than the immediate benefits, (e. g., the cost of design and implementation of an EMS), then a form of amortization of those costs should be used to show the costs over the period of time when the investment provides benefits. This is a normal process for large capital costs.

Financial Environmental Accounting

Financial environmental accounting is the term that describes how organizations report on their financial performance to shareholders and stakeholders, generally through quarterly and annual reports and websites. To ensure consistent reporting and comparison of financial information among different firms and over time, the Generally Accepted Accounting Principles (GAAP) include specific rules, practices, and procedures.

The Canadian Institute of Chartered Accountants (CICA) issued a research report that identified two categories of environmental costs: environmental measures and environmental losses.[8] Measures are the actions taken to prevent, abate, or remediate environmental damage or to conserve resources. Losses refer to the impairment of a traditional asset because of environmental concerns (e.g., site contamination) or other environmental costs for which there is no benefit (e.g., fines, damages). In Canada, companies issuing financial reports are required to provide for the cost of site cleanup and reclamation. The costs of cleaning up past environmental damage must be included when they can be reasonably determined. To estimate these costs, a team of scientists, engineers, accountants, and even regulators may be required to use the techniques outlined later in this chapter for contingent costs. If the work required for completing this cost assessment is deemed unreasonable, then the liability may exist but not be included in the financial books — a worrisome thought for many investors.

Securities and exchange commissions impose similar requirements on reports to investors or potential investors, so that they can more accurately assess the corporation they are considering. The International Auditing Standards Commission is working with the International Association of Security Exchange Commissioners to improve auditing standards. Indirectly, that will require an improvement in environmental auditing and accounting.

Environmental Management Accounting

Environmental management accounting provides information for making decisions that will affect the business and the environment. Managers have a great deal of latitude, compared to the GAAP's procedures, in how they organize management accounting information. Unfortunately, many environmental managers have had little direct experience with accounting practices and concepts. It is important, therefore, for environmental managers to work with experienced accountants.

Managers face common strategic and operational decisions that will have some impact on the natural environment, such as

- product and service decisions (e.g., product mix, product design, manufacturing inputs, product pricing);
- capacity decisions (e.g., to break even or target profitable production volumes, expand an existing facility or build a new facility and decommission existing one);
- technology decisions (e.g., capital investment to improve technology);
- design, implementation, and operation of an EMS; and

- applications of various environmental management tools.

Moreover, managers may also face decisions that deal directly with environmental protection such as how and whether

- to invest in pollution prevention technology;
- to redesign a product with a lower environmental impact;
- to improve resource harvesting techniques (e.g., forestry, agriculture, or mining);
- to invest directly in environmental mitigation with no direct bearing on the product or service (e.g., carbon offsets, pollution treatment devices, ecosystem protection);
- to set priorities for environmental initiatives;
- to abandon an activity with high risk (high contingent costs); and
- to abandon a product or activity when activity-based accounting shows that it involves high costs.

Traditionally, management decisions have ignored environmental performance information and concentrated on financial impacts. Environmental protection decisions have often been driven by regulatory requirements and are not thought of in financial performance terms. However, as environmental protection costs continue to increase (i.e., as externalities become internalized to the firm) and managers realize that internal cost-savings can be found from improved environmental performance, the integration and redefinition of these techniques becomes more important.

Techniques are available to analyze environmental cost information and assist with environmental performance decisions:[9]

- cost analysis: activity-based costing, quality costing, full environmental cost accounting;
- investment analysis: total cost assessment, multiple criteria assessment, environmental impact/risk assessment; and
- performance evaluation: environmental performance indicators, environmental multipliers, environmental indices.

The following section presents four environmental management accounting techniques:

- activity-based accounting,
- quality costing,
- full environmental cost accounting, and
- investment analysis and appraisal.

Activity-based Accounting

Not all products and services create the same internal environmental costs. A particular product or activity may be disproportionately responsible for environmental impacts. Unfortunately, traditional costing systems often fail to accurately track these costs because they become hidden in overhead (pooled) accounts.[10] Activity-based accounting or costing is a method for tracking the cost of activities and allocating them not to a department or overhead account but to a specific product or service. In order to accomplish this, activities required to produce a particular product or service are analyzed. Costs related to an activity are determined and then allocated to the product or service. Activity-based costing allows potentially hidden internal environmental costs such as permitting, waste disposal, and environmentally related labor, energy, and water to be allocated to the product or service that created the cost. This information helps managers modify or eliminate activities that create the greatest environmental cost, perhaps by using economic instruments to ensure that one product does not subsidize another.

Quality Costing

Quality costing techniques have been applied to environmental accounting just as the concepts of total quality have been applied to environmental management.[11] Quality costing defines and measures three types of costs:
- prevention: the costs associated with preventing environmental damage, including pollution prevention, control, or mitigation.
- appraisal: the costs of inspecting and identifying environmental damage such as environmental risk assessments, life cycle assessments, and environmental audits.
- failure: the costs associated with environmental damage, especially contingent costs. Often, failure costs are divided into internal and external costs. The scope of these costs is debatable but, in keeping with the spirit of total quality, should likely include the full costs of externalities.

Quality costing is intended to highlight the cost of environmental failure in order to motivate managers to prevent it. Some believe, that in the long run, the cost of appraisal and prevention will be much less than the cost of failure.

Full Environmental Cost Accounting

Many have argued that an essential aspect of integrating ecological and economic information is getting the price right[12] (see chapter 16). Environmental assets provide the life-support system for the planet, yet remain largely unvalued in the market. As a result, organizations will either ignore or undervalue them in their decisions. To correct this and to better understand their impact on the environment, some proactive organizations have attempted to estimate the economic value of the environmental resources and services they depend upon and consider these costs in managerial decision making.[13] By incorporating these externalities into decision making, firms will be able to make more informed decisions about the full environmental costs of their activities. Life cycle assessment is one tool that provides the environmental impact information for a product or process needed to determine full environmental costs, sometimes referred to as life cycle costs (see chapter 18).

Investment Analysis and Appraisal

Investment in new capital assets requires an understanding of the future benefits that each asset will provide. In traditional capital budgeting techniques, a discounted cash flow analysis is used to compute the value of expected cash inflows and outflows for a proposed investment. If the investment exceeds an internal hurdle rate or has a present value greater than zero, it is considered a good investment.

A 1996 study at a Dow Chemical facility showed that pollution prevention strategies could eliminate 500,000 lbs. of waste, shut down a hazardous waste incinerator, and save the facility more than U.S.$1 million per year. Still, these incentives were not enough for the programs to be implemented. The savings did not outweigh other corporate priorities, and the managers feared that shutting down the incinerator might cause a loss of future business.

Had there been a regulatory requirement to reduce this waste, the projects would have proceeded without any capital investment appraisal. However, because they are voluntary, the pollution prevention opportunities need to do more than create a win-win situation — they have to do better than other capital investment options.[14]

However, it must be pointed out, that in this case, there was no value attributed to the reduction of risk and contingent costs.

Total cost assessment and multiple criteria assessment are two techniques used in investment analysis. Total cost assessment includes environmental costs in capital investment decisions. Most of the work in this area restricts environmental costs to those that are internal to the organization, although some have argued for the consideration of external costs. Total cost assessment includes elements that are normally not considered in traditional discounted cash flow analysis.

The Tellus Institute has developed a model and computer software package (P2 Finance available from the U.S. EPA at no cost) to level the playing field for environmentally related investments.[15] Their model improves traditional investment appraisal by helping to identify internal environmental costs and risks. Pollution prevention projects tend to be more favorably treated using total cost assessment than with traditional investment analysis. Total cost assessment has been well reported in the research literature and the EPA computer model makes much of this work accessible to business. Unfortunately, the majority of companies have yet to adopt this valuable tool and software package.

Some firms use a qualitative technique called multiple criteria assessment to deal with the inherent difficulties of predicting future cash streams from environmental capital investments (i.e., the benefits are often intangible, qualitative, or outside of the market). Multiple criteria assessment is a systematic process to evaluate alternatives against multiple criteria that are measured on different scales.[16] Ontario Hydro has used this process to compare private economic costs and external environmental impacts for different energy planning strategies.[17]

Types of Environmental Costs

Before we discuss some of the tools and techniques of environmental accounting, it is important to have some understanding of the types of environmental costs and benefits. For an organization, costs and benefits are either internal or external.

Internal costs can be described as
• direct (conventional)
• indirect (hidden)
• reputation (image)
• contingent

External costs, while no less real, are costs to society or the environment for which the organization is not yet accountable, and they do not yet have any immediate financial consequence for the firm but will, if economic instruments are applied by governments to internalize these costs. The boundary between external and internal costs is often very gray, particularly with rapidly changing regulations and market requirements to protect the environment. These changes are tending to internalize many previously external environmental costs.[18] As a result, it is becoming very important for corporations to know and understand what their external costs are. (see Figure 15.5)

Energy and Material Costs

This is probably the best understood aspect of environmental accounting — the direct costs of energy and materials used by the corporation and any savings through conservation.

Direct Costs

Direct costs tend to be straightforward costs such as equipment, materials, utilities (e.g., energy, water), and labor.[19] These are the well-understood costs that are tracked and allocated within traditional accounting systems. Problems arise in accessing information and linking it to decisions within the EMS.

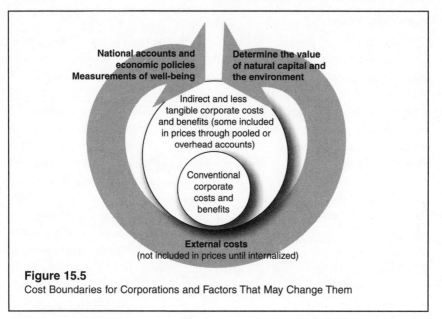

Figure 15.5
Cost Boundaries for Corporations and Factors That May Change Them

Indirect or Hidden Costs

Indirect and less tangible costs (hidden) costs are indirect internal expenses that firms do not measure, account for, or actively consider when making management decisions. They are often lumped together with overhead (pooled) accounts (e.g., energy and water consumption may be pooled together with other building costs). Examples of hidden costs include the costs of compliance (permitting, reporting, tracking, waste handling, record keeping, etc.), raw material lost during production, spill preparedness, and emergency response.[20] Organizations are beginning to realize that these hidden costs can be significant and should not be overlooked. In a series of five environmental accounting case studies published by the World Resources Institute, internal environmental costs were shown to range from 3.2 to 22 percent of operating costs.[21] As companies realize that these potentially hidden environmental costs can be significant, techniques for uncovering and allocating them such as activity-based accounting become increasingly important.

Reputation (Image) Costs and Benefits

Reputation costs and benefits are those that are difficult to quantify but still have an impact on a firm's financial performance. They include image and relationship costs, improved product or service quality, employee productivity, and increased market share. These costs are difficult to accurately track and account for. Despite this, it remains important to consider them, even qualitatively, when making management decisions.

Contingent Costs

Contingent costs are costs that may occur in the future if a particular event takes place. The Environmental Protection Agency outlines six broad categories of potential liabilities: compliance obligations, remediation (existing and future), fines and penalties for non-compliance (including legal fees), compensation to private parties for damage or loss, punitive damages for gross negligence, and obligations to pay for natural resource damage.[22] Examples include the cost of emission permits and credits, cost of lost sales due to product boycotts, and the cost of repaying a community for health damages. Methodologies for determining future risk or contingent costs are typically based on predicting the cost and probability of the future impact. Techniques include engineering estimation, fault tree and decision analyses, predictive modeling, scenario and sensitivity analyses, forecasting, and professional judgment. In Canada, the Canadian Institute of Chartered Accountants requires firms to provide for contingent liabilities if there is a greater than 50 percent chance of their existence. In practice, many of these contingent costs are ignored because of the work required to estimate them.

Efforts and expenditures to reduce risks will reduce contingent costs. This is an area of accounting where the potential benefits could be large, for example, avoidance of a major accident or spill (see chapter 10). However, there are no widely accepted, credible systems for estimating those avoided costs and including them in environmental accounts. This area of environmental accounting requires a good deal of attention.

External Costs and Benefits

Perhaps the most difficult aspect of environmental accounting involves identifying and allocating environmental and social externalities. Many industrial activities produce unmeasured side effects and impose hardship on society. When the costs of these side effects are not included in prices of goods or services, they are called external costs (negative externalities). External costs can be captured within the market or associated with environmental damage that is outside the current market.

As an example of an externality, when a firm pollutes the air, the community may be uncompensated for the increase in health costs (i.e., external costs within the market) and damage to buildings and vegetation (i.e., external cost that is typically outside of the market). Ontario Hydro studied the impact of the external costs on the people and government of Ontario.[23]

As governments move to internalize negative externalities, the prices of goods and services will increase, and corporations must therefore take those expected increases into account in strategic planning. (See Figure 15.6) Corporations should be trying to reduce the costs they impose on the environment, but pressure to do so will increase when those cost are internalized. As corporations find ways and means to reduce those costs, prices will decrease and/or profits will increase.

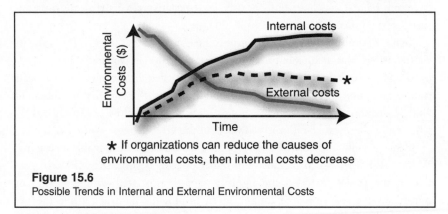

Figure 15.6
Possible Trends in Internal and External Environmental Costs

National Income Accounting

There are five national accounts issues, which can be important for environmental management, especially with respect to corporate strategy:
- an adjusted GDP
- internalization of negative externalities
- use of the discount rate to place a value on resources in the future, placing a value on natural capital
- ensuring national economic and financial security

An Adjusted GDP

The GDP has long been recognized as a poor indicator of national well-being for three reasons:
- direct costs of damage increase the GDP — fatal car or aircraft accidents or the cleanup and legal costs of environmental damage all contribute to an increase in GDP;
- over-exploitation of resources temporarily increases GDP, making policies that promote unsustainable harvesting of resources appear to be beneficial; and
- the environmental cost of damage to the environment and health by soil degradation; air, water and soil pollution; accumulation of persistent pollutants, etc. does not appear on national accounts.

The Gross Domestic Product (GDP) has been the primary indicator for the last 50 years of how well a country's economy is performing. The System of National Accounts is an international agreement that measures the total consumption or throughput in the economy, including many goods and services that may not add to human welfare. Each time a dollar changes hands the GDP goes up. Unfortunately, consumption and economic throughput (i.e., money changing hands) can have both positive and negative effects that are not captured in the GDP.

Two economists failed in an attempt to demonstrate that the GDP, despite its shortcomings, was a suitable proxy for measuring human welfare.[23] They developed a Measure of Economic Welfare (MEW) that took into account market costs such as pollution, health care from air pollution, and the benefits of household work. Instead of proving their hypothesis, they found that the per capita MEW, while still rising, was significantly lower than the GDP.

Herman Daly and John Cobb proposed an Index of Sustainable Economic Welfare (ISEW)[25] which included a number of costs beyond the MEW. In particular, the ISEW included the significant costs associated with depletion of non-renewable resources and long-term environmental damage. While the per capita GNP rose approximately two percent each year since 1970, the ISEW remained constant and even declined somewhat.

Cobb and Cobb argue that the accounting system used to measure well-being is a reflection of society's values. While they would feel some small victory in replacing the GDP with an indicator like the ISEW, their overarching concern is the "avenues by which the type of values implicit in [a new] index can be expressed through the political process."[26]

As societies move toward ecological sustainability, governments will increasingly rely on more robust economic indicators and adjusted GDPs, such as the ISEW. Policies with respect to resource conservation and pollution will change when information from an adjusted GDP is used. Therefore, corporations must be aware of these possible changes and be prepared to adjust strategies accordingly.

An international agreement on an adjusted GDP will take many years to finalize but governments could use an adjusted GDP as an internal measure for sustainable development policy formulation. Corporations would have to adjust to policy changes before an international agreement were reached.

It could be argued that nations could not afford to make such changes for the same reasons that it was argued that corporations could not go beyond the letter of the law with respect to corporate and social responsibilities. The argument that they would not be competitive has not been proven. Similarly, governments would likely find that appropriate sustainable development policies based upon an adjusted GDP would provide advantages nationally and internationally.

Internalizing Negative Externalities

When environmental managers want to understand the external environmental costs their organization is creating, they will need to establish a small team of people with environmental science and environmental economic backgrounds to conduct a study of the externalities. The team would base their study on three broad categories of techniques:

- Direct Cost Approach (defensive expenditures): determining or estimating actual expenditures required for complete mitigation. For example, health costs related to pollution, travel costs to an environmental resource, and prevention and appraisal costs such as impact assessments or pollution control.
- Hedonic Pricing: determining revealed differences in market values between ecosystem services of different environmental quality. For example, determining property values near clean versus contaminated sites, while attempting to hold other factors constant.
- Contingent Valuation: estimating the value of an environmental service through surveys and questionnaires. People are asked to indicate their willingness to pay to protect an environmental service or their willingness to accept a reduction in a service.

Although these techniques are well-developed and frequently used in social cost-benefit analysis, there are significant limitations on our ability to put a dollar value on environmental values. Difficulties in developing economic values for the environment include[27]

- inter-temporal issues — benefits that are incurred in one time period may create costs in another (see the section in this chapter on discounting);
- risk and uncertainty — the science surrounding cause-and-effect relationships and nature's ability to provide services and sustain impacts remains difficult;
- irreversibility — the possibility of irreversible changes or flips in the natural environment[28] are difficult to acknowledge in economics; and
- substitutability — substituting between natural and manufactured capital.

Because of these difficulties, many assumptions and uncertainties surround environmental cost studies. Assumptions tend to reflect a particular set of values and beliefs rather than being strictly objective and uncontroversial. As a result, findings from an economic valuation should be considered not in isolation but in concert with the assumptions and methodologies used in the study. Further, it is likely best to think of economic valuation as being partial, rather than comprehensive, and indicative or suggestive, rather than definitive.[29]

Value of Natural Capital

By reallocating certain property rights and creating a market for environmental goods many of these externalities can be corrected. Environmental economists distinguish between three types of capital: natural, manufactured, and human or labor.[30] Natural capital provides ecosystem services including climate and water regulation, water supply, soil formation and retention, waste treatment, and nutrient cycling among many others.[31] The capacity of natural capital to continue to provide these services is dependent on the resiliency of the ecosystem[32] and the pressures that are put to bear on it.

A study published in the journal *Nature*[33] looked at the value of ecosystem goods and services to human welfare, excluding non-renewable fuels and minerals. Compiling a vast number of environmental cost studies, they arrived at a minimum global estimate ranging from U.S.$16 to 54 trillion (i.e., 10^{12}) per year with an average of U.S.$33 trillion. The total value of human throughput (i.e., global GNP) in the world economy is U.S.$18 trillion per year. It is clear that the market is not entirely adequate at capturing the value of the natural environment to human welfare.

Organizations receive free services from the natural environment. If they choose to mismanage and oversubscribe to these services, they risk impairing or losing them forever. These ecosystem services have option values that can be exercised in the future if they are protected. The greater the protection, the greater the number of future options.[34] A green GDP places a value on these services and would reflect damage to natural capital — our current GDP does not.

Discounting and Future Environmental Values

Determining the future value of natural capital presents a difficult problem. With traditional types of capital, the discount rate is taken to be positive to reflect people's preference for benefits today over equivalent benefits tomorrow (known to psychologists as impulsiveness). As well, manufactured capital is productive: a dollar invested today returns more in the future. Finally, future generations are assumed to be better off than today's generation, making the value of current assets less in the future. The higher the rate of discounting, the greater the importance placed on near-term benefits. The lower the rate, the greater the importance of long-term values. There are two major shortfalls associated with discounting future environmental benefits and costs:

- With discounting, all assets would have an economic value of nearly zero in 15 to 25 years (at a ten percent discount rate). As a result, many argue that natural capital critical to human survival (i.e., soil, biodiversity, breathable air) should not be discounted to maintain the value of future options, as required by sustainable development.

- The preference that lower discount rates give to megaprojects (e.g., nuclear plants, hydroelectric dams) that may offer environmental complications of their own poses a further complication for discounting.[35]

In essence, discounting should normally only be used in situations where environmental impacts are reasonably certain and can be monetized, and costs and benefits do not extend over a few decades. In difficult cases, environmental concerns should be addressed outside of economic discounting procedures.[36]

Barriers to Environmental Accounting

Environmental protection is a challenge to the private sector because it requires many types of innovation. While evidence suggests that business is pursuing some win-win environmental protection initiatives, there are still opportunities that are overlooked. Firms may miss profitable environmental protection measures for two reasons: internal organizational barriers and improper external incentives. A Resources for the Future study tentatively concludes that organizational barriers were less important than proper external incentives; however, the absence of environmental initiatives within industry is likely some combination of these two.[37] Organizational barriers include a lack of information, accounting distortions, a lack of managerial experience with the environment, and a need for proper employee incentives. More specific examples include

- poor integration of environmental functions with other activities of an organization,
- lack of economic and accounting knowledge by environmental managers,
- lack of knowledge of potential environmental costs (conventional, potentially hidden, contingent, intangible, and external) by accountants, and
- managerial compensation tied to short-term performance.

The majority of organizations will begin to use many of the tools outlined here only when they become an absolute necessity. The current business and economic system does not require most organizations to fully consider environmental performance. While a few organizations are proactive environmental leaders, society needs to take steps to make the environment as important as the economy before business truly integrates environmental and economic issues. As this happens, these barriers will slowly be overcome.

Recommended Further Reading

Bailey, P. E. and others. *Valuing Potential Environmental Liabilities for Managerial Decision-making: A Review of Available Techniques.* Washington DC: U.S. Environmental Protection Agency, 1996. EPA 742-R-96-003.

Bennet, M., and P. James. "Environment-related Management Accounting: Current Practice and Future Trends." *Greener Management International* 17 (spring 1997).

Bennett, M., and P. James. *The Green Bottom Line: Environmental Accounting for Management: Current Practice and Future Trends.* Sheffield, U.K.: Greenleaf Publishing, 1998.

CICA. *Environmental Stewardship: Management Accountability and the Role of Chartered Accountants.* Toronto, Ontario: CICA, 1993.

Ditz, D., J. Ranganathan, and R.D. Banks. *Green Ledgers: Case Studies in Corporate Environmental Accounting.* Washington DC: World Resources Institute, 1995.

EPA (Environmental Protection Agency). *An Introduction to Environmental Accounting as a Business Management Tool: Key Concepts and Terms.* Washington DC: Office of Pollution Prevention and Toxics, 1995. EPA 742-R-95-001.

Epstein, M. *Measuring Corporate Environmental Performance.* Burr Ridge, IL: Irwin Professional Publishing, 1995.

Epstein, M.L. and others. *Tools and Techniques of Environmental Accounting for Business Decisions.* Hamilton, Ontario: Society of Management Accountants of Canada (CMA), 1997.

Gray, R.H. *The Greening of Accountancy: The Profession after Pearce.* London, U.K.: ACCA, 1990.

Gray, R.H., K.J. Bebbington, and D. Walters. *Accounting for the Environment: The Greening of Accountancy, Part II.* London, U.K.: Paul Chapman, 1993.

Gray, R.H., D.L. Owen, and C. Adams, eds. *Accounting and Accountability: Social and Environmental Accounting in a Changing World.* Hemel Hempstead, U.K.: Prentice Hall, 1996.

Owen, D.L. *Green Reporting: The Challenge of the Nineties.* London, U.K.: Chapman & Hall, 1992.

P2/FINANCE Version 3.0, Pollution Prevention Financial Analysis Cost Evaluation Spreadsheet Software Application (December 1996). This is a spreadsheet system for conducting financial evaluations of current and potential investments. It runs with either Lotus 1-2-3 Version 3.4a for DOS or Microsoft Excel Version 5.0 for Windows. (EPA 742-C-96-001/002).

Rubenstein, D.B. *Environmental Accounting for the Sustainable Corporation: Strategies and Techniques.* Westport, CT: Quorum Books, 1994.

Scahltegger, S., and R. Burrit. *Contemporary Environmental Accounting: Issues, Concepts and Practice.* Sheffield, U.K.: Greenleaf Publishing, 2001.

White, A.L., M. Becker, and D.E. Savage. "Environmentally Smart Accounting: Using Total Cost Assessment to Advance Pollution Prevention." *Pollution Prevention Review* (summer 1993): pp. 247-259.

Websites

Asia-Pacific Centre for Environmental Accountability: <www.accg.mq.ecu.au/apcea>

CSEAR, U.K.: <www.gla.ac.uk/departments/accounting/csear>

IUCN The World Conservation Union, The Green Accounting Initiative: <www.iucn.org/places/usa/literature.html>

Office of the Auditor General: Commissioner for the Environment and Sustainable Development. Sustainable Development Accounting Project: www.oag-bvg.gc.ca/

U.S. EPA Common Sense Initiative: Environmental Accounting Project: <www.epa.gov/opptintr/acctg/resources.htm>

CHAPTER

ECONOMIC INSTRUMENTS FOR ENVIRONMENTAL MANAGEMENT

Stephen Hill, University of Calgary and Dixon Thompson

E CONOMIC INSTRUMENTS are a means of guiding behavior towards environmentally responsible activity and away from undesirable actions through economic incentives and disincentives. They can be applied to integrate environmental consequences into economic decision making. They help correct market imperfections and direct consumers, companies, employees, or governments to consider environmental costs that might not otherwise be included in the traditional marketplace.

Negative externalities are a significant market imperfection. They are a form of subsidy when the prices of goods and services do not include all the costs. Economic instruments are designed to internalize the environmental costs of a product or service that are created by one institution but borne by someone else.

Five types of economic instruments will be introduced in this chapter:
- fees, taxes, or charges
- tradable permits
- deposit-refund systems
- grants, loans, tax relief
- removal of subsidies (perverse subsidies) that support undesirable environmental behavior

Economic instruments are useful for formulating government policy, but they can also be important in assisting organizations and businesses to achieve their environmental goals. In general, economic instruments have been underutilized as an environmental management tool at all levels of society. We hope that by better understanding how, where, and when economic instruments can be applied they will be considered more often to protect the environment or conserve natural resources.

In theory, economic instruments should be preferred to the other two means of controlling behavior (laws and regulations and voluntary measures) because they can be used to

- improve the practical application of economic and market theory;
- achieve environmental goals with greater economic efficiency;
- encourage research and development, innovation, and improvement in ways and means of achieving environmental improvements;
- raise revenue that can be specifically targeted at environmental problems or to reduce taxes on desired activities; and
- remove the subsidy that results when goods and services are sold at a price that does not include all the costs.

Economic instruments are applied for other social purposes. They have wide, varied, and innovative application in other policy areas such as research and development, technology transfer, resource development, and employment. When applied as an environmental management tool, they internalize externalities and help to correct market failures: they use the market to achieve environmental goals by moving the market toward full-cost pricing with no externalities (i.e., an imperfect market with externalities directs behavior in undesirable directions).

Economic instruments, in theory, are more economically efficient in protecting the environment than command-and-control regulations. This arises because different groups have different abilities to improve their environmental performance: the groups who are more efficient gain economic advantage which creates an incentive for less efficient organizations to improve or leave the market. However, in spite of having been studied extensively and the fact that some progress has been made in Europe, governments, especially in North America, have not exploited the possibilities extensively.

International organizations and governments have produced numerous studies of the application of economic instruments for environmental purposes: the OECD,[1] World Business Council for Sustainable Development,[2] The International Institute for Sustainable Development,[3] UNEP,[4] U.S. EPA, Sweden,[5] Canada,[6] Ontario,[7] and British Columbia.[8] The Pembina Institute has made the *Proceedings from Second Annual Global Conference on Environmental Taxation Issues, Experience and Potential* held in 2001 available on their website[9] and Sustainable America has published the Environment-Friendly Taxes Organizer Kit.[10]

Corporate environmental managers must understand economic instruments for six reasons:

- to ensure that the prices of their individual products and services do not include cross-subsidies by applying activity-based accounting (full-cost accounting),

- to use incentives and disincentives internally to encourage desired behavior of business units and individuals,
- to use trading systems of emission credits internally to optimize efficiency,
- to be prepared to respond appropriately as governments take action to internalize negative externalities,
- to support the use of economic instruments by governments and institutions to adjust the economic and market framework within which they have to operate to facilitate corporate goals of corporate social responsibility and sustainable development, and
- to remove inconsistencies between market/economic theory and reality, improve economic efficiency, and provide correct market signals to all.

EXAMPLES OF APPLICATIONS OF ECONOMIC INSTRUMENTS

- The province of Alberta applies a Can$4 tax on new tires that is directly targeted at finding ways to recycle used tires.
- In British Columbia there is a Can$5 fee charged by industry when paint is purchased to cover the cost of disposal.
- Ontario Hydro carried out a study of full-cost accounting for their decision making which has been published as a case study by the U.S. EPA's Environmental Accounting Project.[11] It showed that Ontario Hydro should have added 0.4 cents per kilowatt-hour of electricity produced to cover the costs of negative externalities related to their air emissions.[12] Of course, the increased revenue would have had to be returned to the people who suffered the damage, or at least to the government to offset increased social and environmental costs.
- Husky Injection Molding gives GreenShares as financial incentives to employees who walk to work, buy energy-efficient appliances and use manual lawn mowers.[13]
- BP has committed to a ten percent reduction in greenhouse gases below 1990 levels by 2010. To meet this goal, the company has established an internal emissions trading system in which all business units must participate. The intention is for each unit to have the most flexibility to find innovative and efficient ways to reduce their production of greenhouse gases.[14]

Economic Instruments as an Environmental Policy Instrument

Organizations and governments have a suite of policy instruments at their disposal for improving environmental quality and conserving natural resources.

Organizations have obligations (see chapter 3, Driving Forces) to protect the environmental resources under their control. For organizations, environmental control of employees, suppliers, and customers can be achieved through direct formal means (e.g., developing policies and procedures for employees to follow), informal control (e.g., organizational culture and norms,), or by using economic instruments (e.g., linking pay to environmental performance, incentives and disincentives, bonuses, and deposit-refund systems within an organization).

There is no right policy instrument — instead, the choice and mix of environmental policy instruments should depend on the nature of the situation. There are, however, some general criteria against which policy instruments should be judged.

- Environmental effectiveness — is the instrument achieving the environmental outcome or goal that is desired (this implies that the outcome is monitored and regular feedback to policy makers provided)?
- Economic efficiency — does the instrument create unnecessary economic inefficiencies (this implies that the cost of various instruments can be measured or, at least, estimated)?
- Equity and fairness — does the instrument place an unfair burden on some members of society or the organization?
- Adaptability, dynamic response, and ability to continually improve — as conditions change and learning occurs, can the instrument be modified to fit the new circumstances?
- Administration, information requirements, and enforcement — is it feasible to collect the information required to administer and enforce the policy instrument?
- Political acceptability — will the policy instrument be accepted by stakeholders such as organization members or the public, or is education and training necessary?

It is difficult, if not impossible, to create an environmental policy instrument that would satisfy all of these criteria. However, they do help guide the selection of the most appropriate instruments. Of critical importance is the rigorous monitoring of the instrument's success in meeting its objectives in order to provide feedback for improvement.

The market, in theory and in practice, has a very important role to play in environmental management. However, there are two major sets of problems: market imperfections, which mean the market cannot do in practice what theory says it should; and, limitations on what the market can do, especially with respect to delivery of public goods and services.

Market Imperfections

There are at least seven significant imperfections which mean that the market cannot deliver in practice what it is supposed to deliver in theory:

- The value of natural capital is largely excluded from the market. For example, Costanza et al found that approximately U.S.$33 trillion dollars in ecosystem services were not included in conventional markets.[15]
- The market allows environmental externalities to be imposed onto others and future generations. Compensating for the damages related to externalities remain difficult, if not impossible.
- The time frame for market decisions can be inconsistent with environmental and biophysical relationships — myopic markets. If the corporate strategy is to maximize short-term profits regardless of long-term damages, the market cannot work.
- Information in the market is inadequate and not perfectly communicated.
  - Inadequate information. For market theory to apply optimally, adequate, if not perfect, information is required and that is seldom available.
  - Inadequate communication. For the market to function, information must be communicated effectively, if not perfectly.
  - Lack of skills, knowledge, and time for consumers. For the market to function, consumers must have the skills, knowledge, and time to participate effectively.
  - Lack of consumer complaints. Consumers must complain effectively about product deficiencies or the market cannot work.
  - Sellers, and manufacturers, refusal to report complaints. If producers will not record and report consumer complaints, the market cannot work.
  - Advertising. If advertising does not present complete, objective information, and creates perceived needs from wants, the market has been distorted.
- Consumers and corporations in the market are not rational decision-makers, as most economic theory and models assume. For instance, advertising can be overly persuasive in influencing market decisions.
- Damages are sometimes not compensatable. If damages are inflicted that cannot be adequately compensated then the market cannot work. If people die or are permanently injured, the market cannot provide adequate relief.
- Compensation not available. If the damage is known and seller is known but will not pay for the damages or product failure, then the market cannot work.

What can be done? The above list is a long one, but much is known about how to fix, or at least start fixing, the imperfections:

- Use economic instruments and other means to internalize negative externalities.
- Facilitate the activities of consumer groups to balance their strength and resources with that of corporations.
- Establish effective labeling standards, which consumers and purchasers can rely on.
- Establish effective processes for product and technology assessments.
- Carry out product monitoring, especially in those cases where there may be irreversible, non-compensatable damages.
- Increase the use of civil suits and class actions to recover damages and internalize the costs of those causing the damage.

Limitations on what the market can do

The market, in theory and practice, plays an important role in allocating private goods and services: where there is a yes-or-no choice about the purchase and where there is a choice among suppliers. However, it does not do a good job in allocating resources for public goods and essential services, such as education, health, and a clean environment. This is because

- The market is not democratic.
- The market cannot deal with questions of equitable distribution of essential services.
- The market has no interest in, or ability to measure well-being.

What can be done? These are difficult problems, especially at a time when government influence is under attack and the private sector is thought to be able to deliver everything more efficiently. However, increasingly the limitations of the market in delivering public goods is being acknowledged, and a balance between providing private goods efficiently and providing and protecting public good effectively is being recognized. Appropriate roles for governments, corporations, and civil society are being redefined.

Types of Economic Instruments

We classify economic instruments into five main categories. Although the theory and literature on economic instruments can be detailed and difficult, understanding the basic attributes of these instruments is important for environmental managers. The following categories of instruments are discussed: taxes, fees, or charges; tradable permits; deposit-refund systems; grants, loans, tax relief;

and removal of subsidies supporting undesirable environmental activity (perverse subsidies).

Taxes, Fees, or Charges

Taxes, fees, or charges are applied for three main reasons: to internalize external environmental costs, to change the behavior of individuals or organizations, and to collect funds for environmental protection activities. They help support the "polluter pays principle" by placing an economic cost on an environmental resource or service.

Environmental fees and taxes can be revenue neutral. That is, any environmental tax or fee can be offset by an equivalent price reduction in another, perhaps more environmentally friendly area. In this way, the market adjustment does not necessarily need to penalize the consumer, only those consumers that choose to continue buying undesirable products. For governments facing an electorate that thinks it is overtaxed, this is important: Any environmental tax can be offset by a reduction in income, corporate, labor, or sales tax. The adage applied is Don't tax what you want, tax what you don't want.

An environmental tax may not necessarily be progressive (i.e., the rich pay a higher proportion than the poor) but can be made so through actions such as rebates for low-income groups or graduated fees depending on income (e.g., a threshold for consumption of basic needs such as water might have to be met before a fee was levied, with increasing charges for higher levels of consumption).

To change behavior, environmental fees need to be sufficiently high to change well-established habits. The amount will depend on the reliance of a person or organization on a product and how many options there are (i.e., what economists refer to as elasticity). If a consumer has many other product options (presumably with a lower environmental impact), then a small tax could induce consumers to buy other items. If there are few other viable or desirable alternatives, then a fee must raise the price high enough to make it worthwhile for consumers to actively search out other options and for companies to develop these alternatives.

There is a wide range of options available for countries to increase fuel efficiency, reduce local air pollution, and reduce greenhouse gas emissions which have been exercised more in Europe than in North America. In Germany, taxes on fuel are high, registration fees for automobiles are based upon engine displacement, and insurance fees are based upon engine power. The net result is that people drive much smaller, fuel-efficient cars, and standard transmissions are used instead of less efficient automatics.

In January 1991, Sweden applied a carbon dioxide tax to reduce emissions of CO_2 which was made revenue neutral by a reduction in labor taxes. Because Sweden is highly dependent on international trade, carbon dioxide taxes had to be carefully designed so as not to disadvantage Sweden's trade competitiveness. The taxes vary according to the carbon content of various fuels but are applied differently to basic users and industrial users. The industry rate is about one-quarter of the basic rate. These tax changes were part of Sweden's overall energy policy, which has goals of stabilizing 1990 levels of CO_2 and then reducing them, phasing out nuclear energy by 2010, protecting unharnessed rivers from hydroelectric development, and supporting conservation and renewable fuel sources. Sweden's high CO_2 tax has demonstrated that environmental taxes can be successful in stabilizing a country's emissions and increasing demand for renewables.[16]

An environmental tax can be applied either by the government, a company, or collectively by an industry association. As an example of the latter, a government directive requiring producers to take back packaging and products at the end of its useful life (as has been the case in Germany and under consideration in more than 20 countries) might lead an industry association to use a product charge in response to this directive. The industry association, in order to pay for a collaborative and more efficient collection system, could collect a product charge from each of its members. The charge could be related to the number of products sold and the weight or volume of the products and associated packaging. Members would benefit from the industry association's capacity and economies of scale at collecting and redistributing packaging and their products — it would be cheaper for them to pay the charge to the industry association rather than attempt to collect their own products and packaging.

A study of environmental taxes in France, Germany, the Netherlands, and the United States examined the practical aspects of their use and concluded that[17]

- environmental taxes have been applied primarily to raise revenue for environmental protection activities, and
- most taxes are not large enough to influence behavior or environmental performance.

For environmental taxes to become an effective environmental management tool, they must be sufficiently large enough to change people's purchasing habits and companies' production methods. Environmental taxes should not be a tax grab but should be part of a broader restructuring of the economy to encourage job creation, resource conservation, and pollution prevention.

An environmental tax or fee can be applied at a variety of points in a product's life cycle: from raw material extraction, manufacturing, marketing, sales, and use to disposal or recycling (chapter 18, Life Cycle Assessment). Such a fee might be referred to as an extraction tax, product fee, user charge, administrative fee, or effluent or disposal fee or tax. Different application points will affect different groups within the life cycle and will have different impacts on both the environment and the economy. Each stage of a product's life will have different environmental impacts — a life cycle assessment will help to identify these impacts — and a fee should be applied at the stages where the greatest environmental improvement, with the least cost, can be found. It is important to consider potential side effects and unanticipated consequences of an environmental fee, by doing an Environmental Impact Assessment of the policy (see chapter 14).

Tradable Permits

Tradable permits can be used to improve the efficiency of controlling the emission of pollution or the extraction of a natural resource (e.g., fishery quotas). Under this system, different companies, regions, countries, or organizations are given a permit to pollute (within a specified limit or cap) or harvest resources. If they cannot meet the limit, they must buy the right for the amount in excess from another permit holder. If they do not need or want their full allotment, they can sell their permits or portions of them to others.

Tradable permit systems can be used by governments in situations where no previous market existed or to complement traditional command-and-control regulations. Placing an upper limit on pollution or resource consumption achieves the same end as a command-and-control approach — it is the means that are different. The creation of a market for trading emissions or natural resource extraction requires three things:

- the establishment of a ceiling or upper limit through regulation or agreement,
- the initial allocation of permits to participants within the market (often auctioned or allocated based on historical emissions or resource extraction), and
- a set of prescribed rules and an institutional framework for guiding the trading of permits.

Trading can occur at many levels: between or within countries (see chapter 22, Joint Implementation and the Clean Development Mechanism), within large companies, and between companies within an industry or trading association. Currently, trading systems are most commonly being established at national and international levels, although many of these are pilot projects.

Using Tradable Permits

Imagine that two companies emit a certain pollutant. There are two legislative approaches to reduce emissions: fixed reductions for all parties (command-and-control) or a tradable permit system. Under a command-and-control regime, each firm would be required to reduce emissions by a fixed amount or percentage, generally below some cap or ceiling. However, different companies would have different abilities to reduce pollution — some are more efficient than others. By allowing companies to trade pollution permits, those companies that are better equipped to reduce pollution would do so. Those that are less efficient at reducing pollution would pay others for their permits, unless that was too expensive and then they might go out of business. There is the disadvantage that there may be problems of local pollution near those companies that have purchased emission credits. On the other hand, the public or ENGOs could enter the market to reduce emissions by purchasing credits and reducing the total emissions available for industry.

Economic Benefits of Tradable Permits

A simple example can illustrate the financial benefits of a tradable permit system. Imagine that a government establishes an upper limit for carbon dioxide and allocates emission permits to industrial users based on a percentage of historical emissions (i.e., the grandfathering approach). For company A, the cost of reducing carbon dioxide emissions is $100 per tonne. For company B, the cost of reducing carbon dioxide emissions is $50 per tonne. If both companies were required to reduce emissions from 20 to 15 tonnes (a command-and-control approach), the total economic cost would be $750 [(5 tonnes x $100/tonne) + (5 tonnes x $50/tonne)]. To achieve the identical goal of 10 tonnes of reduction under an emission trading regime, both company A and B could be allocated permits for 15 tonnes of carbon dioxide emissions, assuming each had equal historical emissions. If company B were able to reduce emissions by 10 tonnes (at a cost of $50/tonne or a total cost of $500), they could trade five of their credits to company A for, say, $50 plus $25 profit for each credit. Company A would then pay $375 (5 tonnes x $75/tonne) to company B making company B's net cost for reducing pollution $125 (i.e., $500-$375). The table below summarizes the costs from the previous discussion.

Table 16.1. Summary of the Relative Theoretical Costs of Reducing Pollution Under Two Policy Approaches

	Company A	Company B	Total Economic Cost
Cost of Reducing Pollution per Tonne	$100 / tonne	$50 / tonne	
Cost of Meeting Command-and-Control Requirement	$500 to reduce emissions by 5 tonnes	$250 to reduce emissions by 5 tonnes	$750 to reduce emissions by 10 tonnes
Cost of meeting Requirement under Emissions Trading	$375 to buy 5 tonnes of reduction	$125 net cost ($500-$375) for 5 tonnes of reduction	$500 to reduce emissions by 10 tonnes

Trading Permits over Time

A further extension of permit trading involves the trading not only within or between firms or countries but over time. This type of trading is often referred to as *banking*. For instance, a firm may plan on upgrading its factory to significantly reduce pollution three years from now. If the rules of trading allowed for inter-temporal trading, the firm could use the knowledge of the future reductions to trade future credits for current permits. Conversely (and likely more appropriately), a firm could bank any credits for current reductions for use in the future. To achieve their goals, environmental groups could buy permits and bank them to reduce the release of pollutants.

There are dangers with trading permits over time. Science plays a significant role in determining whether inter-temporal trading is feasible or desirable. The dynamics of an ecosystem must be carefully considered. If a firm or country wanted to trade over-harvesting of fish stocks today with reduced yields in the future, there would be many legitimate ecological concerns. Considerations of time play an important role in pollution emissions and natural resource extraction.

Further, if a market for permits was functioning properly, a firm or country should be able to buy permits now and sell credits later to other companies, which is particularly advantageous as prices go up in the future.

Drawbacks of Tradable Permits

Some environmentalists have objected to a company or country being allowed to buy pollution. Some level of pollution or resource extraction is allowed through regulations and standards. Tradable permits are an economically efficient means of allocating whatever pollution levels or resource extraction levels society desires, within the limits it sets. Tradable permit systems will be structured to complement regulations. The political or social question is what level of pollution is appropriate; a market system based on tradable permits determines the most efficient allocation that is permitted within that level.

The U.S.A. has experience with tradable permits through part of the *Clean Air Act* to reduce the precursors of acid rain. Their experience shows that, although the theory of tradable permits is sound, in practice it has both good and bad attributes. On the positive side, estimates suggest large total cost-savings from tradable permits over a command-and-control approach — it is more economically efficient.[18] On the negative side, there has been less trading than originally hoped and companies are holding onto their permits even though they may not need them — in essence, the market has been less efficient than it could be. A number of reasons have been postulated for this:

- Large uncertainty about the future value of permits (perhaps due to a lack of credible and widely accepted rules) causes permits to be hoarded.
- It is often difficult and expensive to ensure that other firms' credits are accurate and legitimate (i.e., audits are often required).
- Some businesses might keep permits off the market in an attempt to prevent new firms from starting up or to limit existing firms' ability to expand.

A final drawback associated with tradable permits is a potential reduction in innovation and improvement in resource efficiency and pollution prevention. Consider the application of tradable permits to the global climate change problem. Under such a system, developed countries would be able to buy reductions of greenhouse gases in less developed countries (LDCs). Greenhouse gas reductions in LDCs would be much less expensive and the tradable permits system would guarantee economic efficiencies in meeting reduction targets. However, there would be little incentive in the short to medium term for developed countries to innovate and find technological and social means for reducing their own greenhouse gases. Without the proper incentives, the technology improvements required would not be developed in the richer countries[19] and these technological gains would not be passed on to the LDCs. This problem is being resolved by allowing countries and companies to reduce only a portion of the emissions through trading, so that they will be forced to find other means to achieve the total reduction required. With continual monitoring, learning, and improvement the use of tradable permits will be a useful environmental management tool.

Deposit-Refund Systems

A deposit-refund system charges a fee at one period in time and then refunds that fee when a desired behavior has occurred. A common example of this is the deposit on beverage containers that many jurisdictions refund, partially or fully, when the container is returned for reuse or recycling. A deposit-refund system can be used to ensure the return of many types of environmentally damaging products such as hazardous material containers, packaging, and household goods. For example, corporations use deposit-refund systems within their firms to link purchasing with waste disposal and waste costs. Environmentally progressive corporations interested in extended product stewardship also recognize that deposit-refund systems are effective ways to encourage customers to trade in outdated products, allowing the company to keep existing customers and demonstrate a commitment to product stewardship by recovering, recycling, or remanufacturing the used product.

A distinct type of deposit-refund system is the use of performance or assurance bonds that are only returned once environmentally acceptable behavior is demonstrated. Performance bonds can be used in court sentencing (e.g., company puts up a bond, bond is returned when sentencing conditions are met) or in licenses for new developments (e.g., as part of license, company puts up a bond that is only returned when reclamation requirements are met at the end of a mine's life). Performance bonds can be important where corporations can profit in circumstances involving risk and then attempt to transfer the risk to others.

Grants, Loans, and Tax Relief

Organizations and governments can provide direct financial incentives to encourage environmentally sound behavior among specific groups or individuals. These subsidies could be used to accelerate changes that could not otherwise be afforded, and would therefore be reduced or eliminated once the necessary changes were accomplished. Financial assistance could take the form of[20]

- grants — non-repayable sums of money given to an individual or group for environmental reasons,
- interest rate reduced loans — the lender loans money for environmental protection at interest rates below market rates (often called soft loans),
- tax relief — tax or charge exemptions, rebates, or accelerated depreciation allowances for environmentally desirable behavior or products.

Some examples of this type of economic instrument might include providing employees with transit passes and accommodating cycling rather than subsidizing parking and vehicle use, developing special capital investment funds for pollution prevention projects within a company, and an energy company giving soft loans to encourage energy-efficient or water-efficient appliances and home renovations (a demand-side management strategy), among many others. A complementary mechanism provides a revolving loan fund whereby homeowners or small companies can get a loan for improving efficiency and repay it from the savings. This is particularly important in developing countries or communities where access to capital is limited.

Environmentally Progressive Organizations Should Work to Remove Environmentally Perverse Subsidies and Taxes

Government and corporate policies often create financial incentives that harm the environment. These subsidies were meant to do specific things, such as stimulate economic development or employment, but because of unintended side effects, create an environmental problem. For instance, a municipality might fund a highway expansion to alleviate traffic congestion. However, this will inevitably increase vehicle traffic and air pollution in the region, and congestion may build again. By choosing to subsidize a highway expansion over expanding public transit services, the municipality is subsidizing drivers at the expense of transit riders.

The International Institute for Sustainable Development estimates that environmentally perverse subsidies total more than Can$1,450 billion dollars per year.[21] Given the size of this amount, it is imperative that we ensure these subsidies are, at the very least, not damaging, and where possible, promoting conservation and environmental protection.

To prevent and mitigate the unintended environmental impacts of financial policies, an environmental impact assessment of policies must be carried out (sometimes referred to as strategic environmental assessments) before major policy changes are put in place (see chapter 14, EIA). Environmental audits are useful for identifying problems with existing financial policies and where corrections can be made (see chapter 8, Environmental Auditing). For instance, at the government level, Canada's Commissioner of the Environment and Sustainable Development has an ongoing audit program evaluating the environmental consequences of federal programs. In particular, this office evaluates federal department sustainable development strategies but its role can also include policies deemed worthy of investigation.[22]

Using Economic Instruments

Economic instruments are not new; however, most governments, industry associations, and companies have been reluctant to use them for removing market imperfections to achieve their environmental goals. This is slowly changing and these instruments will become increasingly important in years to come. For market advocates, the use of economic instruments is essential in order to internalize external environmental costs, a condition that is necessary if the market is to function properly.

Recommended Further Reading

Barron, W.F., R.D. Perlack, and J.J. Boland. *Fundamentals of Economics for Environmental Managers.* Westport, CT: Quorum Books, 1998.

De Andraca, R., and K.F. McCready. *Internalizing Environmental Costs to Promote Eco-efficiency.* Geneva, Switzerland: World Business Council for Sustainable Development, 1994.

OECD (Organisation for Economic Co-operation and Development). *Managing the Environment: The Role of Economic Instruments.* Paris: OECD, 1994.

Rietbergen-McCracken, J., and H. Abaza. *Economic Instruments for Environmental Management: A Worldwide Compendium of Case Studies.* London, U.K.: Earthscan, 2000.

Turner, R.K., D. Pearce, and I. Bateman. *Environmental Economics: An Elementary Introduction.* Baltimore, MD: The John Hopkins University Press, 1993.

PRODUCT
AND TECHNOLOGY
ASSESSMENT

Andrew Higgins, VECO Canada
and Dixon Thompson

P RODUCT AND TECHNOLOGY ASSESSMENT (PATA) is a systematic assessment of primary, secondary, and tertiary impacts of products and technologies with respect to health, safety, environment, and society that covers the life cycle from raw materials to final disposal. PATA is used for designing regulations and guidelines, approving new products and technologies, designing and improving products, and making purchasing decisions.

The Office of Technology Assessment of the U.S. Senate defined technology assessment (TA) as the systematic study of the effects of technology on society that may occur when a technology is introduced, extended, or modified, with emphasis on the impacts that are unintended, indirect, or delayed.[1]

Products and technologies affect our societies and our natural environment in many different ways, both positive and negative. While some of these impacts are easily predictable, identifiable, and avoidable, others may be unanticipated and more subtle. Primary (direct) impacts and secondary impacts (two steps in a cause-and-effect process) are more easily identified than tertiary, more complex cause-and-effect relationships. Because products and technologies have the potential for unanticipated impacts, methods have been established to assess the impacts of specific types of products and technologies. There are many different types of product and technology assessments for specific purposes, but no recognized generic standard exists.

LIFE CYCLE ASSESSMENT (LCA)

LCA is as objective and value-free as highly qualified professionals can make it, using an established standard methodology. The standards have been established so that different qualified professionals would produce the same results if they were to do the same LCA independently. LCA is a major component of PATA. However, PATA uses the results of LCA and other social and cultural information to inform decisions about the roles that products and technologies should be allowed to play in society — the acceptability of impacts or risks relative to the benefits.

For example, an LCA of firearms would produce similar results if done by qualified professionals using a standard methodology, regardless of what country they were in. However, when social, political, and cultural factors are considered, very different conclusions are reached about the role of that technology in society. In the U.S.A., those factors dictate that only limited constraints can be applied.

An LCA of coins and paper currency would also produce the same results in different countries. Color is used to differentiate denominations of paper currency, design is changed frequently, and high-tech anti-counterfeiting technologies are used. High denomination coins reduce costs and facilitate coin-operated vending machines. Again however, social, political, and cultural factors dictate that different countries use technologies differently. In the U.S.A., social, cultural, and political factors dictate, in this case, greater restrictions on the range of applicable technologies, because money must be green and not look like the money of other, generally weaker currencies.

Product and Technology Assessment

Information about product and technology assessment comes from many different sources or perspectives:

- science, engineering, technology
- economics and finance
- political, cultural, and social sources
- ideological and political thought
- religious organizations

Because of the wide and disparate nature of the sources, language and terminology varies and methodologies differ as do the purposes and intents of the assessments. Non-quantitative aspects of PATA are always present, but the more formal, objective assessments have specific purposes, such as

- anticipating and avoiding adverse impacts on health, safety, the environment, or society;
- making comparisons of consumer products (e.g., toasters, cars);
- establishing criteria for, and issuing, eco-labels;
- establishing purchasing guidelines;
- setting regulations for the approval and use of new products and technologies;
- setting standards for safety, energy and water efficiency, and greenhouse gas emissions; (e.g., CSA, ISO);
- providing information to:
  - designers or manufacturers,
  - investors and financial institutions,
  - victims of damages,
  - agencies responsible for health, safety, and environment,
  - people responsible for product recalls; and
- identifying and selecting solutions to problems (e.g., comparison of technological options for dealing with solid waste, providing transportation, treating municipal water supplies, generating electricity, etc.).

Classes of products and technologies that are required to have assessments or for which assessments are published include

- pesticides;
- prescription drugs;
- over-the-counter (OTC) drugs and herbal medicines;
- food and food additives;
- water;
- automobiles and ground transportation systems;
- aircraft and aviation safety;
- children's toys, clothing, and furniture, etc.;
- sports equipment (especially for mountain climbing and scuba diving);
- building materials for fire code;
- energy and water efficiency of appliances and equipment; and
- consumer products.

The justification for conducting product and technology assessment includes the following:

- Technologies have large negative and positive effects on societies and individuals.
- The distribution of costs (adverse impacts) and benefits is often uneven.
- Technological development implicitly reflects conscious choices by some segments of society as to what our society should be like.

- Individuals do not have the time, skills, knowledge, and resources necessary to conduct assessments.
- Market imperfections mean that the market is an inadequate means of control.
- Citizens have the right to participate in choices about the nature of society.

To some extent then, product and technology assessment provides a process and forum for a discussion of the issues about the role(s) of products and technologies in society. While the technical complexities often discourage lay people from entering into the debate, most of the fundamental choices about technologies involve questions about basic human and social values.[2]

PATA is a process that relies on a set of different assessment approaches, in particular, Life Cycle Assessment (chapter 18). PATA differs from LCA by including health, safety, social, and cultural factors and by not having an established methodology. Other tools in the set include: Risk Management (chapter 10), Environmental Impact Assessment (chapter 14), Human Factors (chapter 21), and Environmental Communications (chapter 20).

Before formal processes were developed, assessments were left to the market, under the adage Let the buyer beware.[3] However, experience has shown that "[t]he market alone cannot protect the consumer, as it forms its judgments but slowly and retrospectively, and the cost of learning about a product's quality or fitness for purpose by individual consumers could be very high."[4] (See chapter 16, Economic Instruments.) Furthermore, having individuals trying to do their own assessments is problematic because many of today's products and technologies are too complex to be readily assessed by individual consumers.

It is best to use simple definitions of products and technologies because the categories are not clear. Products are things bought by consumers on the open market or under limited controls. Products often contain technologies and/or are produced by technologies. Technologies are used to produce products or provide services (e. g. communication, energy, and transportation), sometimes through closely linked products (telephones, televisions sets, and automobiles).

There is a wide range of consumer products and services that are assessed to assure the public of their acceptability. Consumers are heavily dependent upon the reliability and integrity of organizations and the professionals who do the assessments. Problems with reliability and credibility are:

- The processes are very technical, not well-known, and not understood, even if the information were publicly available.
- There are restrictions on access to the process, the data, and the criteria for decisions.

- Control and independence of the assessment processes varys.
- When the processes are controlled by government agencies, there are overlaps and conflicts of interest (e.g., determining how to assess and maintain water and food quality involves many government agencies which do not always cooperate and sometimes represent the interests of industry rather than the public).
- In some cases, assessments are carried out by industry, under the guidance or supervision of other agencies, but there is always a conflict of interest between short-term profits and long-term public interests.
- Consumers don't have the time and resources to become involved.
- Ultimately, decisions on safety involve political and economic factors (see chapter 10, Risk Management).

It is clear, therefore, that a wide range of segments of society need assessments of products. There is considerable variability in the processes used for the assessments.

Technology Assessment

In the United States, formal Technology Assessment (TA) began in the late 1960s.[5] Two of the major factors contributing to its development were an increasing awareness of the role and impacts of technology, and a trend towards more public participation in decision making. Political decision-makers needed objective information on increasingly complex technological issues. As a result of these forces, TA was institutionalized in the U.S.A. as the Office of Technology Assessment (OTA), formed in 1972 as a branch of the U.S. Congress.[6] The role of the OTA was to provide an analysis of the predicted impacts of a new technology and feed this information into the political decision-making process. A key aspect of this role was to communicate the findings to politicians who typically have no formal training in science or technology. Technology Assessments of importance at that time concerned supersonic passenger aircraft (the SST and the Concorde), in which the U.S.A. and Britain and France came to different conclusions. An interesting sidelight is that protests against testing of technology, the nuclear test proposed for Amchitka Island, involved a disagreement between John Wayne and Chief Dan George and were part of the formation of Greenpeace.[7]

In Europe, the development of TA has been uneven, reflecting different social views on the role and regulation of technology and the different political structures within which decisions about technologies are made.[8] The European Commission is considering setting up a European Technology Assessment Network, and there are offices for TA in five European nations (Denmark, France, Germany, the Netherlands, and the United Kingdom) and in the European Parliament.

Technology forecasting was a formally defined process 30 years ago.[9] The U.S. Senate Office of Technology Assessment defined TA as "...the systematic study of the effects on society, that may occur when a technology is introduced, extended, or modified, with emphasis on the impacts that are unintended, indirect, or delayed."[10] Another definition makes the effects that TA is attempting to assess more explicit and much broader: "[t]echnology assessment is the activity of describing, analyzing and forecasting the likely effects of a technological change on all spheres of society, be it social, economic, environmental or any other."[11]

Many believe that technological development is not an autonomous process but is shaped by conscious choices of individuals, organizations, and governments. The literature on this topic also emphasizes that technology shapes our society in very significant ways (e.g., nuclear technology, reproductive technology, communications technology, and genetic engineering).[12]

Globalization is the result of communications and transportation technologies that are eliminating borders and reducing the distances between communities. Marshall McLuhan's reference to the "global village" is a virtual reality.[13] However, that has a mixed set of consequences. On the one hand, the cultural impacts are very large, as homogenization takes place. On the other, problems which were isolated and relatively unknown can now get worldwide attention through the Internet and world media, and so governments and corporations can no longer keep undesirable impacts hidden.

The private sector also conducts TA, but with a focus that is different from that of the public sector. To summarize Bridgewater, private sector TA is, not surprisingly, centered on the corporation, and attempts to assess the impacts that a technology might have on the corporation.[14] This is done to support corporate strategic planning and decision making and to avoid liabilities. Typically, public involvement in private sector TA is limited and the findings are proprietary. In contrast, public sector TA is more participative and is directed towards providing objective support on specific technological issues. It is thus more issue-based and has less of a strategic planning function than does private sector TA.

Methods for Technology Assessment

The methods for TA reflect both the specific problem under study and the relevant social, economic, and political systems. Public sector TAs must have input from those who will be directly affected by the proposed technology. It is critical to have a transparent process so that all may see the underlying value judgments that determine what is considered important.[15] With the factors of public involvement and transparency in mind, the following model for TA has been proposed:[16]

- determine the purpose of the proposed technology;
- describe the proposed technology;
- describe alternatives to the proposed technology;
- describe the current state of society and any applicable forecasts or trends;
- identify affected parties and stakeholders;
- based on the state of society and the proposed technology, identify potential impacts in conjunction with affected parties;
- evaluate these potential impacts to determine significant impacts;
- identify the responsibilities, authority, and limitations of relevant decision-makers;
- identify policy options and outcomes; and
- communicate conclusions to decision-makers.

After implementation of the decision, a follow-up and feedback step evaluates the effectiveness of the TA's results in the decision-making process, the quality and accuracy of the predictions, and the success of constraints or management options employed.

Methods employed in TA include literature reviews, stakeholder meetings, key-informant interviews, trend extrapolation, scenarios, backcasting, qualitative and quantitative modeling, checklists, and matrices.[17]

At the heart of TA is an attempt to look into the future — to see what the future might be and how we might shape it.[18] But the ability to make predictions is obviously limited by issues such as our understanding of factors that shape the forecast; limitations on objectivity of even well-qualified professionals; and the nature of forecasting itself, which tends to assume that the future will follow the patterns of the past. Backcasting is a process of establishing a desirable scenario for the future and then determining what has to done to end up there, rather than somewhere else. Therefore, backcasting has the problem of deciding what a desirable future might be but not the problem of predicting the future. Instead, the actions that are necessary to lead society to that future have to be determined.[19] (See chapter 5.)

Because of limited time and resources generally available for an assessment, it is important to conduct an initial screening stage to identify those assessments on which to focus the limited available resources. In such a screening stage, one can use the concept that the risk of the impact is a combination of the magnitude of the impact (scale of the impact) and the probability of the impact occurring. A screening mechanism based on this concept is shown in Figure 17.1.

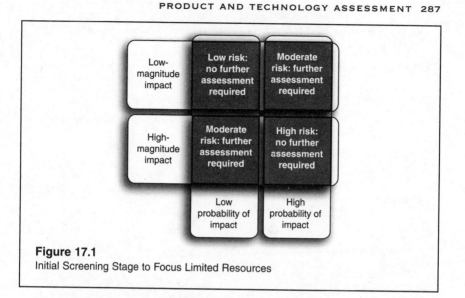

Figure 17.1
Initial Screening Stage to Focus Limited Resources

If the screening-level assessment shows a high probability of a large-scale impact, then the proposed activity could be judged unacceptable without further assessment. The case of a low probability of a small-scale impact would similarly need no further assessment. If the screening indicated a small probability of a large-scale impact, then further assessment would be required. In this case, one would further assess both the potential impact and the probability of its occurrence and the means of reducing both the probability and the scale of the impact (chapter 10, Risk Management). In the case of the technology with a high probability of a small-scale impact, further assessment can identify ways to reduce the magnitude of the impact, because if the use of the technology were to increase, total impact could be significant. When taken cumulatively, a small improvement can have a significant reduction in overall impact.

While this concept of risk is generally applicable, it is more valuable in screening the environmental, health, or safety impacts of a new technology than in screening the social impacts, because the environmental, health, and safety impacts are typically more direct. Social impacts tend to be more indirect and their effects are mediated by our social structures.[20] For this reason, it is more difficult to estimate either the probability or the magnitude of an effect. Predicting such third and fourth order effects at a screening level is very difficult because the behaviors of the individuals in a society adapt in response to the new technology.

Five criticisms have been voiced about TA:[21]

• The assessments do not adequately consider the alternatives to the proposed technology.

- The anticipated demand for the proposed technology is not adequately questioned.
- TA puts an unnecessary burden on those who are developing technologies.
- TA is difficult because of its reliance on trying to predict the future.
- There is too little follow-up and feedback to improve the accuracy of TA.

CELL PHONE EXAMPLE

If assessments were done on cell phones, they would likely have been at the confidential corporate level. If assessments had been done, the adverse impacts that have arisen might have been difficult to predict:

- Cell phones and driving — countries and states have banned the use of cell phones while driving. The B.C. Medical Association states that use of phones, even hands-free, increases the likelihood of accidents by 25 percent, the same as for driving at the legal limit for alcohol.
- Cell phone use is forbidden on aircraft and in hospitals because of possible interference with electronic equipment.
- Cell phone use is so disturbing in restaurants and theaters that management has forbidden their use in some locations. Technology for jamming cell phone technology is now available to keep cell phone users from disturbing others, but it is illegal in some jurisdictions.
- Urban Myths — two urban myths have arisen about cell phones. One is that cell phone use causes cancer of the brain — a myth and a controversy still under investigation, which has led to attempts to sell lead-lined covers for cell phones. The second urban myth, that cell phone use has sparked explosions at service stations, has caused major petroleum companies to ban cell phone use while filling up with gasoline.
- The use of cell phones has been a factor in very fast and fortunate rescues. On the other hand, users are also calling for help when a rescue is not needed because they are tired and lazy.
- Cell phones are now allowing new areas to have phone use without the need for the hard-wired infrastructure.

A Generic Model for Product and Technology Assessments

Society is heavily dependent upon assessments of products and technologies. However, assessments vary in their rigor, thoroughness, transparency, and independence. Assessments of aviation safety (aside, perhaps, from airline food) would score highly on all points. There is rigorous testing of aircraft, navigation systems, airports, pilots, air controllers, and others involved in providing the service. Further, when accidents do occur, there is a detailed investigation to determine the cause and have it corrected. By comparison, automobile safety is more casual. Although new vehicles are tested, older vehicles in many jurisdictions are not. There are standards for highways. However, the testing of drivers is inadequate, because if drivers can drive at city speeds in warm, dry weather in daylight then they are also allowed to drive at high speeds in winter conditions at night. Drivers may also drive any size vehicle in their license class, even if they cannot see properly and/or reach the controls. As stated in chapter 21, human factors is a significant contributor in 90 percent of vehicle accidents, yet control of that factor is very limited — the safety of the system is compromised by failure to put equal weight on all components. The determination of the health, safety, and environmental impacts of prescription drugs and pesticides is controlled by the manufacturers, the processes are not transparent, the data is owned by the proponents, and approvals are provided by bureaucrats, who may not have sufficient independence from political and/or commercial influences. Further, there are limited systems for monitoring the impacts of products, should there have been any errors in identifying and controlling adverse impacts.

All stakeholders must be assured that product and technology assessments are credible and reliable. An independent group, provided with adequate resources by governments and the private sector, should be assigned the task of developing a sound generic model for product and technology assessments. That model could then be used to compare existing processes and provide opportunities for improvements where they are needed. The private sector has a large stake in the generic model because, if it leads to improvements in assessments, overall costs will decrease, although costs for individual products might increase if current systems have weaknesses that need to be improved.

The generic model would have to build on the considerable experience with EIA (chapter 14). The processes should be as independent and transparent as possible. Alternatives must be included in the assessment. The boundary conditions must be set carefully. For example, the assessment of the use of antibiotics in agriculture still tends to ignore the possible impacts of increased antibiotic resistance in pathogens, which can affect human health and health care costs. Pharmaceuticals are only now being recognized as a possible threat to the environment, because they are present at very low levels in sewage effluents. Rigorous assessments of products and technologies, akin to that for aviation safety, are not possible because of politics, economics, or international agreements; therefore, an increased level of scrutiny and monitoring of products approved by less rigorous assessments is required.

Why have no formal processes for product and technology assessment evolved as they have for Environmental Impact Assessment and environmental audits? We could find no formal studies of this but a combination of reasons is likely:

- It has been assumed that the market will be an adequate mechanism for removing unsatisfactory products. However, this is not sufficient if damage is severe (see chapter 16, Economic Instruments).
- The impacts are small, diffuse, and cumulative rather than large and focused, as with the impacts of large construction projects that led to the demands for EIA legislation.
- Industries have managed to convince governments that less control, rather than more control, is essential for economic reasons.
- Assessment methodologies have been developed and applied in separate, isolated agencies and bureaucracies (pesticides, drugs, food additives, automobiles, aircraft, children's toys and equipment, etc.).
- There has been no perceived need to cooperate or surrender bureaucratic control to an improved system.

It would be in the interest of consumers, governments, industry, and other stakeholders to develop and apply an improved generic model for product and technology assessments.

For reasons of health, safety, and protection of environmental and social factors, consumers need better assessments. Improved labeling, using international standards, is one way to provide important information. Improved support for consumers groups and reports on consumer products is another. Where those systems fail, enforcement of regulations and class actions to recover damages from negligent corporations would have to be used to force improvements in product assessments.

Governments at all levels are responsible for the public interest and often bear the costs of products and technologies that have not been adequately assessed. They might also be accountable where less rigorous assessments have led to approvals to put products which subsequently cause damage, on the market.

Industry has the most to gain from an improved assessment process. Clearly the aviation industry recognizes the benefits of rigorous, comprehensive assessments with follow-up. Other industries should follow that example:

- PATA can help industry anticipate and avoid problems, just as EIA (chapter 14) does with construction projects.
- The reputation of industry as a whole, industry sectors, and individual corporations suffer at times as a result of the public's lack of faith in assessments, and PATA is essential for improved reputation management. Better assessments of GMO foods might have avoided the unforgiving labels Frankenfood and Farmageddon[22] and their indelible impact on the debate

about biotechnology. The pharmaceutical industry is finding itself labeled as the villain in novels such as Le Carre's *The Constant Gardener* and the movie *The Fugitive* with Harrison Ford, in which the industry is portrayed as having abused the assessment process with criminal intent. Better assessments would have made that characterization unrealistic and another villain would have had to be found; the industry's reputation would have been less sullied.

- More care with assessments of impacts in other countries might have lead to changes in some unfortunate product exports which did not sell well.
- Improved assessments are important for those corporations using purchasing guidelines (chapter 19) to reduce environmental impacts.
- Improved assessments enhance the credibility and the usefulness of product labels, whether health, safety, eco-labels, water and energy efficiency, or greenhouse gas emissions.
- PATA is important for marketing. Green products, healthy and safe products are now advertised to provide a market advantage. However, with decreasing consumer confidence and increasing skepticism coupled with greater knowledge and access to information (the Internet) telling consumers about the process used, and involving them in it will give an even greater market advantage.
- PATA is essential for excellence in design of products and technologies.
- PATA will be increasingly important because of take-back legislation, even if it only applies in Europe for the time being,
- PATA reduces manufacturers' liabilities for damages due to products and technologies. That is, manufacturers can spend time and money now on improved assessment processes or spend it later in litigation.
- PATA is important for the health, safety, and well-being of employees.
- For corporations committed to product stewardship and customer service, including education and training of customers, PATA is essential.

Failure to assess product names for export markets have led to some humorous mistakes:

- Estee Lauder Country Mist Perfume did not sell well in Germany where mist is manure.
- Cue toothpaste did not sell well in France where Cue is a notorious porno magazine.
- Toyota obviously did not check the fact that Cressida is the name of a woman in Greek mythology best known for being unfaithful.
- Similarly, Reebock did not check out the mythical Incubus before using it as the name for a woman's shoe.

- The Chevy Nova won't go in Spanish.
- Pinto means small male genitals in Brazilian slang, which should have been of interest to Ford exporters.
- Mitsubishi should have checked out the connotations of pajero in Spanish before naming their vehicle.
- Coca Cola had difficulty with the original translation into Chinese.[23]

Other groups have a stake in improved assessments:
- Investors would reduce investment risks.
- Insurers would pay less in damage claims and be better able to evaluate risks.
- Employees would be more confident of their own health and safety and take greater pride in the products and services their provide.
- Consumers would have more confidence in products and services, get better value for the purchasing dollar, and suffer fewer ill effects.
- Consumer groups could provide better services.
- The professionals involved in assessment would be provided support and feel less pressure to reach hasty conclusions or to approve products that had not received a thorough assessment and met appropriate criteria.
- Health and safety agencies could reduce the problems they have to face and the expenditures they have to make.

Profit-driven assessments of products and technologies are a major issue. Until individual corporations, industries, and governments improve the PATA process, those involved in providing goods and services and regulating them where necessary are going to receive increased criticism from consumers and decreasing consumer confidence.

Recommended Further Reading

Consumers Report

Journal of Technology Assessment

La Porte, T. "Technologies, decision making processes, and technology assessment." *Technology: Whose Costs? Whose Benefits?* The International Symposium on Technology and Society 1993. Washington DC: George Washington University, 1993.

Porter, A. L. "Technology Assessment." *Impact Assessment* 13 (1995): pp.135-151.

Porter, A. L., and others. *A Guidebook for Technology Assessment and Impact Analysis.* New York: North Holland, 1980.

Websites:

<www.ota.nap.edu> This site contains information on the OTA, including its structure and purpose. It also contains an archive of OTA publications.

CHAPTER

LIFE CYCLE ASSESSMENT

Andrew Higgins, VECO Canada and Dixon Thompson

I SO 14040 SECTION 3.9 DEFINES LIFE CYCLE ASSESSMENT as a method for assessing the environmental impacts of a product or service over its entire life cycle, and identifying opportunities for reducing these impacts.[1] It assesses resource extraction and processing, product manufacture, marketing, product use, and recycling or disposal, and includes transportation and energy.[2]

Life cycle management is another term used to describe approaches to product stewardship and design and management of issues from cradle to grave (disposal) or cradle to cradle (recycle). A more complete definition would be a method for assessing the biophysical and health impacts and resource consumption of a product over its entire life cycle (from raw materials to final disposal) and identifying opportunities for reducing those impacts.

Life Cycle Assessment is one component of Product and Technology Assessment (PATA) (chapter 17). PATA can be simply defined as a collection of techniques for assessing the impacts of products and technologies and identifying ways of mitigating these impacts, which include health, safety, environmental, cultural, and social impacts. Safety, cultural, and social aspects distinguish product and technology assessment from Life Cycle Assessment.

LCA is a rapidly maturing environmental management tool. Stewart et al review recent examples of LCA and use of LCA in a major component of an EMS.[3] The American Center for Life Cycle Assessment and the SETAC Europe Working Group on LCA and Decision Making are refining and improving LCA.[4] LCA is continually improving its methodology, standards, and software, so readers are urged to seek up-to-date information (refer to the websites and newsletters at the end of the chapter for updates).

Users of LCA

The development and application of LCA has been driven by five groups:

- product designers and product manufacturers who use LCA to evaluate the environmental performance of products and to identify ways of improving products and their performance;

- shareholders, financiers, and insurers who seek to preserve shareholder value by controlling environmental liabilities, improving production processes, and (in some cases) capturing market share based on the company's environmental performance;

- customers who demand information on the environmental performance of a product and the producer's stewardship of that product, including purchasing guidelines (chapter 19);

- environmental and consumer groups, who use LCA as a source of information on the environmental performance of products; and

- regulators who enact and enforce regulations in response to public concerns about the environment or in order to meet international commitments related to environmental performance.

History of LCA

LCA is generally considered to have begun in the 1960s, initially focusing on the energy requirements for the production of chemicals.[5] The first LCA of a product is widely believed to have been a study of beverage containers. The work was an inventory of the quantities of natural resources consumed in production and the quantities of effluents — the effects of these burdens on human health and the environment were not quantified.[6] Approximately 15 such studies were done between 1970 and 1975.[7]

In 1988, growing public concern about solid waste caused renewed interest in LCA.[8] Public concerns were reinforced by regulations from the European Commission that required the monitoring of raw material and energy consumption, and solid waste generation for the life cycle of liquid food containers.[9] Among regulators, there was a recognition that the focus on laws and regulations dealing with only one environmental medium (e.g., air or water) might just shift pollution from one medium to another (e.g., from water to solid waste) without reducing the amount of pollution.[10] In the U.S.A. this meant increased emphasis on pollution prevention and a more holistic view of the fate of pollutants.[11]

The following organizations have been involved in the development of methodologies for LCA: (see web pages listed at the end of the chapter)

- Society for Environmental Toxicology and Chemistry (SETAC)
- United States Environmental Protection Agency (U.S. EPA)
- American Center for LCA
- Nordic Council
- International Standards Organization (ISO)
- Canadian Standards Association (CSA)
- Pembina Institute
- Carnegie Mellon University, and
- The Royal Melbourne Institute of Technology

LCA Methodology

LCA has four phases:

1. initiation,
2. inventory,
3. impact assessment, and
4. improvement assessment.

These phases are not necessarily sequential and may be iterative.[12] LCA efforts may range from a conceptual evaluation through to a qualitative evaluation, and ultimately to a quantitative assessment.[13] For details on definitions, methods, and processes, environmental managers interested in various applications of LCA should refer to the ISO Standards:

- *ISO 14040 Environmental management — Life cycle assessment — Principles and framework;*
- *ISO 14041 Environmental management — Life cycle assessment — Goal and scope definition and inventory analysis;*
- *ISO 14042 Environmental management — Life cycle assessment — Life cycle impact assessment;*
- *ISO 14043 Environmental management — Life cycle assessment — Life cycle interpretation; and*
- *ISO 14049 Environmental management — Life cycle assessment — Examples of application of ISO 14041 to goal and scope definition and inventory analysis.*

Initiation Phase

In the initiation phase, the study goals are defined; the system boundaries, data requirements, study review processes are determined; and a system flow diagram is developed. From the system flow diagram, unit processes (the most basic stages of a product's life cycle) are identified and used to specify the data requirements for the study. Finally, a study review process is developed, based on how the findings will be used.

Inventory Phase

The inventory phase consists of gathering, aggregating, and presenting data on the life cycle environmental loadings, which are defined as the movements of materials or energy between the system under study and its environment. The inventory phase is the largest phase of LCA in terms of the time and resources required. There are a variety of sources for data, including facility-specific information, government databases, other LCAs, and scientific and trade literature. Once all data has been gathered, there is a computational step to normalize the data and to aggregate the resulting normalized data.

Impact Assessment Phase

The impact assessment phase uses the results of the inventory phase to associate the calculated environmental loadings with environmental impacts. The use of the stressor concept provides a means for linking environmental loadings to environmental impacts. The impact assessment phase also attempts to weigh the importance of the various impacts with respect to one another. The valuation stage provides a framework for making decisions about what is better or worse in terms of changes to a product's environmental performance. Such a framework is essential because many changes to a product or process will involve trade-offs.

Improvement Assessment Phase

The final phase of LCA is the improvement assessment phase, in which improvements are identified that will reduce the product's life cycle environmental impacts by identifying design options that would achieve reductions in impacts.

Life Cycle Assessment processes can be illustrated in different ways, as shown in Figures 18.1, 18.2, and 18.3.

As shown in Figure 18.1, LCA includes all the inputs to the phases of the product development and use cycle (or throughput model, if there is no recycling). Therefore, LCA requires knowledge of energy, material, and transportation inputs to the processes that produce, use, and dispose of products, and all the waste outputs.

A complete LCA of an entire industry could be prohibitively expensive and time-consuming. Therefore, a segment of an industry might want to focus on their particular part of the production process, as shown in Figure 18.2.[14] In this

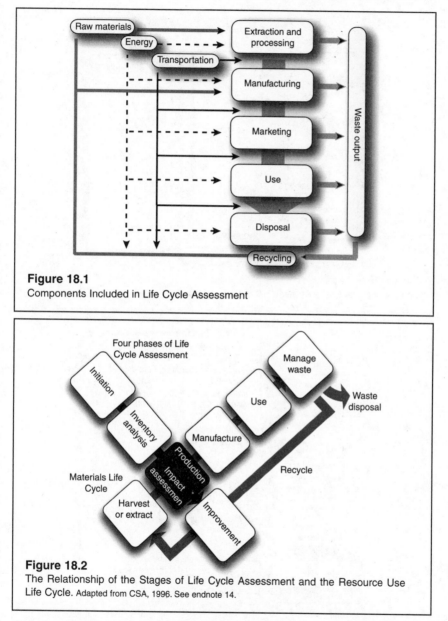

Figure 18.1
Components Included in Life Cycle Assessment

Figure 18.2
The Relationship of the Stages of Life Cycle Assessment and the Resource Use Life Cycle. Adapted from CSA, 1996. See endnote 14.

case, to assist the managers of processing plants, the assessment could focus on the inputs and outputs to processing but leave the LCA of other parts of the process to other studies. This is related to the question of the purpose of the LCA — who is doing it for what purpose. As shown in Figure 18.3, the four phases of an LCA do not change, but the user of the LCA may have a purpose for the

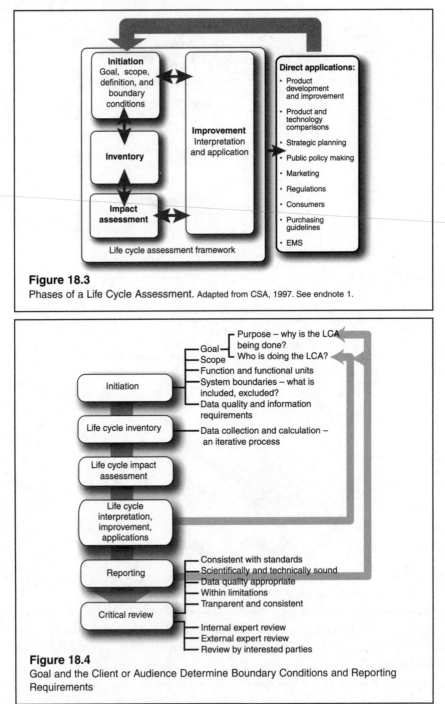

Figure 18.3
Phases of a Life Cycle Assessment. Adapted from CSA, 1997. See endnote 1.

Figure 18.4
Goal and the Client or Audience Determine Boundary Conditions and Reporting Requirements

results, which would mean that focusing on part of the process could produce useful results, without incurring the expense of an entire LCA. Another example might be the use of LCA to help solve problems of municipal solid waste from manufacturing and marketing, in which the focus would be on identifying those components which contributed to municipal solid waste: the product itself, parts or materials used by product users, packaging, and advertising (leaflets, mailing, newspaper inserts).

The goal (purpose) and the client or audience (who is doing the LCA or having it done) will be critical in setting the boundary conditions determining what happens in the interpretation or improvement phase, and what is required for reporting. As shown in Figure 18.4, reporting requirements and a critical review of the LCA report are very important. If an LCA were strictly for internal purposes (e.g., improvement of products or processes), the critical review would be less important. However, if the LCA or its results are to become public for marketing, various comparisons of products or technologies, or for regulations or policy formulation, then a critical review by external experts or reviews by interested parties would be expected.

The amount of data or information required for an LCA depends upon whether it is qualitative or quantitative, and the purpose of the exercise, as shown in Figure 18.5.

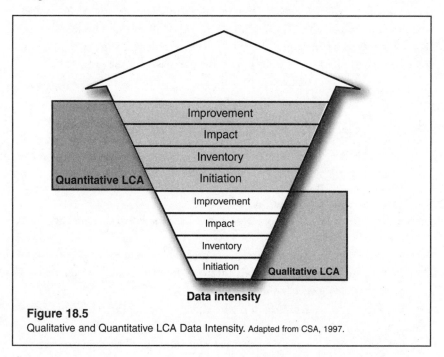

Figure 18.5
Qualitative and Quantitative LCA Data Intensity. Adapted from CSA, 1997.

LCA and Environmental Management

LCA is closely tied to life cycle costing (LCC), in that both tools are evaluating a product or a service throughout its life cycle. In this case, LCC means inclusion of all costs which appear directly on the corporation's accounts — whether directly or in pooled or overhead accounts. LCC is quantitative and would typically include capital costs, operating costs, and recycling or disposal costs, as well as cost-savings and other benefits. (See chapter 15, Environmental Accounting.)

LCA allows a corporation to determine the environmental impact of its products in the same way that an Environmental Impact Assessment allows it to determine the environmental impacts of, for example, a new mine or hydroelectric dam. The data gathered in an LCA might be used to develop an environmental performance indicator (e.g., to state that "the production of this product yields x tonnes of CO_2"). A corporation's environmental policy statement might include a commitment to performing Life Cycle Assessments (for instance, Hewlett-Packard's policy includes a commitment to provide products and services that are life cycles), and its environmental reporting could include information on its progress in this area.[15] When an LCA includes the impact assessment component, it can be used to develop economic instruments for certain products (e.g., a green tax on environmentally unfriendly products, or effluent taxes). For instance, the Norwegian government has used the results of LCAs in setting the environmental taxes on packaging materials.[16] In a similar way, LCA could be used in environmental accounting to generate the full cost of a product, i.e., the cost of the product including the value of environmental impacts that are currently borne by all of society, not just by the purchasers of the product.

An LCA is conducted to

- identify product and manufacturing improvements;
- reduce supply chain (input) costs and impacts;
- demonstrate product stewardship and reduce downstream impacts;
- validate green marketing claims;
- respond to customer demands;
- influence regulatory initiatives;
- meet the requirements of ISO 14001;
- compare products or processes on the basis of impacts, efficiency, or emissions (GHG);
- facilitate purchasing environmentally preferable products; and
- compare technologies available to solve problems (solid waste, transportation, energy generation, etc.).

By doing a life cycle inventory of the energy consumption of laundry detergent, Procter and Gamble learned that from 80 to 90 percent of the total energy consumption was in heating the water used for laundering. The company was then able to target its efforts to develop an effective cold-water detergent.[17] Without this knowledge, they might have targeted improvements only to their manufacturing and distribution systems, thereby missing the potential to reduce the greatest energy consumption factor — the heating of the wash water. If this detergent LCA were combined with an LCA of washing machines to compare the energy, water, and detergent-use efficiency of front-load and top-load machines, designers, manufacturers, and consumers would have essential information for purchases with respect to environmentally preferable products and utility bills.

Canfor Forest Products in British Columbia analyzed the life cycle of its pulp and lumber production from harvesting to reforestation. They learned, to everyone's great surprise, that the largest impact of their activities was the energy usage associated with production and transportation.[18] This information was then used by the company to make the most cost-effective environmental improvements to their production processes. In this way, the LCA complements the available forest codes that deal more explicitly with the biophysical impacts of forestry and reforestation practices.

At Hewlett-Packard, product stewardship represents changing the focus from narrow environmental compliance measures at their manufacturing facilities to considering the environmental performance throughout the product life cycle. This means broadening the responsibilities for environmental performance to include designers, suppliers, purchasers, and product managers.[19]

Regulatory pressures for product stewardship are increasing. For example, in addition to enacting legislation to require manufacturers to take back product packaging, Germany now has legislation that would require manufacturers to take back products that are returned by consumers at the end of the product's useful life. Similarly, in Norway, legislation will require the take-back of electrical and electronic equipment (e.g., home appliances, computers, and telecommunications equipment).[20] Similar legislation is under consideration in at least 23 countries, but not in North America.

The Netherlands Ministry of Housing, Spatial Planning, and the Environment is also incorporating product stewardship into its national environmental policy. The cornerstone of their product policy is that all market actors have access to information on the environmental impacts of products on product labels or dossiers. The expectation is that such information will reflect all the environmental considerations relating to a product in each phase of its life cycle from cradle to the grave.[21]

An example of a market-based initiative that is promoting product stewardship is the U.S. EPA's Energy Star program for printers and computers. By meeting the energy efficiency requirements for the use of the product, a company can use the Energy Star logo in marketing its product. The competitive advantage of meeting the Energy Star criteria became apparent in 1993, when an executive order required U.S. federal agencies to purchase only those computers and printers that were certified by the Energy Star program.[22]

Green marketing provides consumers with information on the environmental performance of products without consumers having to gain the skills, knowledge, and data to do an LCA. Examples of environmental labeling programs (also called eco-labeling) are the Blue Angel program in Germany, the Environmental Choice program in Canada, and the Green Seal program in the U.S.A. LCA is an obvious tool for identifying a product's environmental burdens, making comparisons with other similar products, and validating green marketing claims. An EPA study concluded that the life cycle concept is used by some of the environmental labeling programs.[23]

There has been considerable debate about the use of LCAs in environmental labeling programs, which recognizes the market impact that eco-labeling programs can have, and thereby the responsibility that LCA practitioners have in providing such information. In its Code of Practice, SETAC includes a section on the use of LCAs in eco-labeling programs and for claims about the environmental impacts of products.[24] There are more than 40 eco-labeling programs worldwide and the credibility of the labels depends upon the quality of the LCA on which they are based. Unless the process is independent, transparent, and can be reviewed by interested parties consumers should be cautious. The International Organization for Standardization is in the process of reaching an agreement on a labeling standard, but progress is slow.

Scott Paper (U.K.) committed to understanding the life cycle impacts of its products and incorporating environmental performance standards in its supplier selection process. One measure that Scott developed was the number of kilograms of CO_2 emitted per tonne of pulp produced, which varied by a factor of 17 among their different suppliers. From this and four other measures of environmental performance, Scott calculated an eco-point score for each supplier. As a result, Scott dropped two suppliers because of low eco-point scores.[25]

Hewlett-Packard incorporates environmental performance into their criteria for selecting and retaining their suppliers. The environmental criteria include whether the supplier has a policy committing them to environmental improvement, a plan to measure and track this improvement, and whether the supplier has eliminated the use of ozone-depleting substances.[26]

The information generated by an LCA can be brought into the policy formulation process including new regulations, voluntary government programs, or voluntary industry programs. For instance, an LCA that compares disposable diapers with reusable diapers could be used to help make decisions about a proposed ban on disposable diapers in a landfill, or to redesign them to be compostable. In this case, the LCA would show that both types of diapers have numerous environmental impacts beyond that of their solid wastes. This data would then make both decision-makers and the public realize that a narrow focus on reducing one particular impact (generation of solid waste) may in fact increase the overall environmental impact, because of the energy and water use for laundering cloth diapers, as well as the waste water produced.

In 1993, the French government commissioned an LCA of a draft of the *European Directive on Packaging and Packaging Waste*, which had a requirement to recycle 54 percent of total packaging waste within ten years. It showed that recycling cardboard, compared to virgin cardboard, reduced water effluents and increased air emissions. More importantly, at high rates of recycling, there is a dramatic increase in air emissions because of the increasing amount of transportation needed to gather the cardboard for recycling. The French government used these results to argue successfully against the high recycling targets that were in the draft Directive.[27] The issue of collection of recyclable materials is especially important in countries with low population densities (e.g., Canada).

To become registered under ISO 14001, companies must be audited by independent certified auditors to confirm that their operations are in compliance with ISO 14001 and become registered.[28] A comprehensive approach to ISO 14001 would include LCA. See chapter 2 for further information on ISO 14001.

Barriers to LCA

The following factors are possible barriers to conducting an LCA:
- cost,
- lack of reproducibility and credibility,
- lack of data,
- problems of methodology,
- isolation of LCA within an organization,
- large differences in time and location of impacts (e. g., mining and metal recycling), and
- the consequences of accidents which cause environmental damage are not included in LCA.

A 1993 report stated that a comprehensive LCA typically costs approximately U.S.$100,000,[29] which would make an LCA unsuitable for routine use. However, databases are becoming available, software is being improved, and experience is being gained, so the costs of LCA continue to decrease.

The requirements for an effective and credible LCA are:
- standard methodology, so reviewers know the steps that were taken;
- transparency of the process, so users and critics can understand all steps of the process;

- reproducibility, so that reviewers and critics can redo the LCA and produce similar results; and
- external, independent review and verification.

External review is critical for credibility. However, much of the data that is used in an LCA by a particular company is confidential. Therefore, it is difficult for external reviewers to properly review or reproduce the study findings. When these LCA results are used externally to make product claims, a lack of external review and reproducibility can lead to claims that the LCA is not objective. This can be offset to some extent by having a respected third party conduct the LCA and certify that it is accurate, or by having reviewers sign confidentiality agreements, so that concern about release of sensitive information will be reduced.

The findings of an LCA are dependent on the initial assumptions of the study, particularly boundary conditions. Because of this, LCAs of the same product can lead to conflicting findings. Guinée et al cite three studies on milk packaging: the first demonstrated that the reusable glass milk bottle had the least impacts; the second study found that the milk carton had the least impacts; the third study concluded that the impacts of these two types of packaging were comparable.[30] In another example, Curran cites two LCAs on diapers that were conducted in 1990 and 1991. The first, sponsored by Procter and Gamble, concluded that (for the same number of uses) cloth diapers use three times as much energy over their life cycle than did disposable diapers. The second study, sponsored by the National Association of Diaper Services, concluded that the life cycle energy consumption of disposable diapers was in fact 70 percent higher than cloth diapers.[31] More recently, opposite conclusions on the life cycle impacts of using aluminum and steel for the manufacture of cars were reported by the industries producing those materials. It was this sort of results-directed or market-directed LCA that has lead to the demand for standardization and transparency, especially in LCAs used for marketing.

The lack of accurate data and the cost of gathering data have been identified by Huang and Hunkeler as significant barriers to the practice of LCA, in their 1995 survey of U.S. companies.[32] One estimate is that data collection in the inventory phase can account for as much as 80 percent of the total time it takes to do an LCA.[33] However, this problem is increasingly being overcome by the development of new databases, such as by U.S. EPA and Environment Canada.

While there is broad agreement on the methodology of the inventory component, there is still considerable debate over the impact assessment portion of the methodology. One area of debate is whether emissions should be aggregated throughout the life cycle (e.g., a certain number of tonnes of SO_2), regardless of the location of the release.[34] The methodology problems with the impact assessment phase have received attention.[35]

In a survey of U.S. companies, Huang and Hunkeler identified that the health, safety, and environment discipline was most likely to be involved with life cycle activities.[36] A substantially smaller percentage of companies had design engineers or product teams involved in LCA activities. This indicates that companies may be missing opportunities to use LCAs in design and product improvement programs.

Current Issues in LCA

Some people thought that LCAs would determine unequivocally which products had fewer environmental impacts than others. This has not yet been possible for three reasons:

- Not all types of environmental impacts are included in the assessment (effects on biodiversity, urban infrastructure, transportation, and the landscape).
- It is difficult to make meaningful, quantitative linkages between environmental releases and environmental impacts.
- Valuing and trading-off impacts is inevitably a value-driven process based on a society's values, the range of technological choices, and current scientific knowledge.

Conclusions

LCA offers a means for assessing the environmental impacts of a product or service throughout its life cycle. LCA is also a mode of thinking about environmental problems. As such, it takes a systems approach, meaning that it looks beyond the traditional, narrow product evaluation criteria (e.g., functionality and cost) to include material inputs, energy use, and management of the product at the end of its life. It offers opportunities for reducing environmental impacts and avoid transferring environmental loadings between life cycle stages rather than reducing them.

A qualitative LCA is useful at the initial stages of policy or product design. A quantitative LCA is still expensive but costing less as databases, software, and experience improve. Carnegie Mellon University and the Centre for Design at the Royal Melbourne Institute of Technology in Australia provide on-line information about LCA, and it is expected that such on-line sources will continue to increase in number and improve in quality.[37]

Recommended Further Reading

Curran, M. *Environmental Life-Cycle Assessment*. Toronto, Ontario: McGraw-Hill Ryerson, 1996.

Fava, J., Consoli, R. Denison, K. Dickson, T. Mohin, and B. Vigon. *A Conceptual Framework for Life-Cycle Impact Assessment*. Pensacola, FL: SETAC, 1993.

International Journal of Life Cycle Assessment

Journal of Cleaner Production

SETAC Globe — Section on LCA

Society for Environmental Toxicology and Chemistry News (SETAC) has six publications on LCA for sale on their website <www.setac.org>, including Fava et al above.

Websites

<www.carnegiemelon.edu>

<www.cfd.rmit.edu.au >

<www.ec.gc.ca/ecocycle/issues>

<www.ecosite.co.uk/>

<www.eiolca.net>

<www.iso.ch>

<www.norden.org>

<www.pembina.org>

<www.setac.org/lca.html>

<www.tiac.net/users/tgloria/lca.html>

ENVIRONMENTAL PURCHASING GUIDELINES

Dixon Thompson
with Karla Berg

P RODUCTS AND SERVICES purchased by organizations have a significant impact on how efficiently resources (water, energy, and materials) are used and how much and what kinds of wastes are generated. Therefore, purchasing guidelines are important both to reduce the upstream impacts caused by the purchase of raw materials, products, and services and to reduce the direct environmental impacts of the corporation's own operations.

Purchasers are selecting products that demonstrate environmentally preferred qualities: recycled content; recyclability; durability; fuel, energy and/or water conservation; a non-hazardous nature; waste minimization; and packaging considerations, etc. These guidelines are referred to as environmental purchasing guidelines, environmental procurement policies, or green product guidelines but here we will use the term purchasing guidelines.

Definitions and Driving Forces

Purchasing is defined as "the acquisition of needed goods and services at optimum cost from competent, reliable sources."[1] However, purchasers must be concerned with the best cost, quality, timing, price, operating and maintenance costs, and environmental performance.

Environmental purchasing guidelines are a set of criteria, often targeting a specific product, that evaluate the product based on environmental considerations so that the most appropriate alternative can be selected. Environmental purchasing guidelines provide a useful means of assessing products and services based on environmental criteria and life cycle considerations.[2]

Environmental purchasing guidelines should specify products and services that[3]
• are considered to be more environmentally sound,

- meet environmental specifications,
- examine suppliers environmental management standards,
- build environmental clauses into contracts, and
- rate supplier performance against environmental criteria.

The heavy influence of the purchasing power of governments and major corporations is now being applied and will have major impacts on environmental management of all suppliers. For example, the governments of the U.S.A., Denmark, the Netherlands, the Nordic countries, and Japan have formal requirements for environmentally preferable purchasing.[4] The U.S. EPA publishes a newsletter, *EPP Update: Environmentally Preferable Purchasing*, and a series of purchasing guides.[5] Almost 90 percent of Danish state institutions have a green purchasing policy.[6] Canada is less assertive, but the National Round Table on the Environment and the Economy released a report on green procurement practices and opportunities,[7] while the Canadian Standards Association has published guidelines on environmentally responsible procurement.[8] The purchasing guidelines of large corporations, including Ford, General Motors, Xerox, and IBM, state requirements for their supplies, including ISO 14001 registration in some cases.

Successful development and implementation of environmental purchasing guidelines require an understanding of the forces that drive an organization's environmental actions. Driving forces are discussed in chapter 3. Specific driving forces behind the need for environmental purchasing guidelines include

- government commitment to reduce solid waste,
- increased cost-effectiveness for organizations through reduced waste disposal costs,
- reduced costs through more efficient resource use, (utilities and material inputs)
- corporate policies and industry codes requiring waste minimization and increased efficiency,
- consumer (individual, corporate, and institutional) demand for the provision of more environmentally preferred products, and
- the influence of the German take-back legislation.

Product Stewardship and Purchasing Guidelines

Purchasing guidelines are an effort to reduce upstream environmental impacts (impacts in the supply chain). Product stewardship is the concept of taking responsibility for environmental impacts downstream: responsibility for goods and products that are sold to customers. It would seem that these two responsibilities should have equal importance but this is not always the case. Some manufacturers have started to require suppliers to obtain ISO 14001 registration, but have not yet put equal weight on the impacts of their own goods and products. For example, with the exception of aluminium, the mining and mineral processing industry plays little role in recovery and recycling; the pulp and paper industry has a very low profile in paper recycling, even though they need recycled fiber to meet content rules. In these cases, industry feels that recycling is not part of their industry and therefore is not their responsibility.

Automobile, truck, and SUV manufacturers appear to have a greater concern about upstream (supply chain) environmental impacts than they do about the impacts of their vehicles on fuel efficiency, air quality, and greenhouse gas emissions.

The environmentally responsible position would be for corporations to develop environmental policies that place equal weight on environmental concerns throughout the entire life cycle. That is, policies that balance concerns about upstream (supply chain) impacts and control through purchasing guidelines with equal concern about impacts of goods and services downstream (product stewardship).

Environmental Management Tools in Support of Purchasing Guidelines

Tools which support environmental purchasing guidelines include: Environmental Policy Statements, Product and Technology Assessment, Life Cycle Assessment and Life Cycle Costing, Environmental Audits, Environmental Indicators and Reporting, Environmental Accounting, and Education and Training.

Environmental Policy Statements

One section of the environmental policy should address waste minimization and eco-efficiency and promote the purchase of products and services shown to be less harmful to the environment. The policy should be clearly communicated to employees and suppliers. Specific goals and objectives should be stated in the purchasing guidelines.

Management must have a firm commitment to both the environmental policy and the purchasing guidelines because adequate time and resources must be allocated to meet their objectives.

Product and Technology Assessment

Product and Technology Assessment, chapter 17, is an evaluation process that can aid in comparing and assessing alternative products and technologies, helping to make better informed purchasing decisions.

Life Cycle Assessment and Life Cycle Costing

Life Cycle Assessment (LCA), chapter 18, allows purchasers to compare the life cycle impacts and the life cycle costs of product and technology alternatives.

Environmental Audits

Audits specifically dealing with waste, packaging, water, and energy will aid in establishing baseline information by evaluating current products and purchasing practices. Initial targets for change can then be identified and prioritized. A detailed action plan should be created to respond to issues identified in an audit.

Environmental Indicators and Reporting

The following are examples of environmental purchasing performance indicators that would appear in environmental reports:

- number of purchases made based on environmental criteria;
- percentage of environmentally conscientious suppliers being sourced;
- number of different forms of packaging material entering the workplace;
- percentage of suppliers with an audited EMS or ISO 14001 registration;
- percentage of suppliers taking back packaging, containers, and pallets; and
- trends in solid waste shipped, versus receipts of goods and products.

Environmental Accounting

Environmental accounting determines current costs, revenues, and benefits provided by using purchasing guidelines. A new or revised accounting subsystem may be necessary to link the use of purchasing guidelines with cost savings in raw materials, utilities, and solid and hazardous waste disposal.

Education and Training

Educate employees about what the corporation purchases and how that affects the environment so that they clearly understand their roles and responsibilities. Train purchasing and accounting staff.

Existing Green Procurement Models

Information is available, much of it to be found on the Internet, to guide those corporations interested in developing environmental purchasing guidelines. Five documents present key elements for developing and establishing these guidelines and evaluating products, services, and suppliers.

1. GIPPER (*Governments Incorporation Procurement Policies to Eliminate Refuse*) focuses on factors contributing to waste reduction that should be considered prior to specifying and purchasing materials.[9] A strong emphasis is placed on the 3Rs hierarchy of reduce, reuse, recycle; a primary focus of waste minimization.

2. Transport Canada's *Choose Green Procurement Guide* outlines a hierarchy of Environmentally Preferred (EP) qualities (non-hazardous nature, recycled content, toxicity, and biodegradability), medium-priority qualities

(durability, reusability, upgradability, and fuel, energy, or other resource conservation), and low priority qualities (recyclability and packaging).[10]

3. CSA Guide Z766-95 — *Environmentally Responsible Procurement: Green Procurement* is a workbook of user-completed tables for gathering information and targeting areas for improvement.[11] Organizations are encouraged to evaluate current procurement practices relating to existing and future environmental regulations, customer and shareholder concerns, and employee compliance and initiatives. Establishment of a formal review plan, stakeholder review process, and mechanism for change are recommended.

4. *Buying into the Environment: Guidelines for Integrating the Environment into Purchasing and Supply* presents a framework for adopting environmental purchasing guidelines. Seven principles are outlined with elaboration on the issues stemming from each principle: actions to be taken, further guidance on how to accomplish them, and additional references are provided. With a partnership approach, open and clear communication is necessary so the buyer and supplier can mutually benefit. Essential information on products, processes, supplier history, and the environmental management system should be collected and validated. Finally, through discussion with environmental managers and suppliers, improvement targets and an appropriate time for review can be determined.

5. The NRTEE document *Development of Criteria for Green Procurement* is a summary report examining approaches and criteria for evaluating suppliers, products, and services. Case studies illustrate successful initiatives and approaches, as well as generic criteria, sample procurement policies, product and supplier verification, sample forms, a list of directories, and references.[12]

The Essentials

Purchasing guidelines have four objectives:

- to improve resource use efficiency and to reduce waste, which is generally cost-effective;
- to encourage recycling by helping to create a market for secondary materials;
- to encourage other environmentally desirable practices; and
- to encourage product, packaging, and process redesign.

Table 19.1 presents a list of questions to ask during product selection. An affirmative response would indicate a preference for the product; a negative response would suggest that further investigation into the product itself, as well as possible alternatives, is needed. Questions are grouped according to major consensus (at least four of the six sources mentioned the attribute), significant consensus (either two or three of the sources mentioned the attribute), additional questions (only one source mentioned the attribute). Questions may be placed under the headings: planning, acquisition, packaging, operation-use-maintenance, disposal, and supplier practices, which address issues related to the procurement process and product lifecycle and attributes. Purchasing guidelines might also be organized based on the four objectives stated above, but they are not clearly distinct and mutually exclusive. Other organizational approaches include: by functional unit of the organization; according to who is involved with the product or service; following the life of the product; and according to the purpose of the purchasing guidelines, which is likely one or more of the objectives stated above.

When comparing products and services using the product selection questions in Table 19.1, preference should be given to those products or services having the most positive responses to the questions posed. This approach (whether in question or statement format) raises an interesting dilemma as to whether some criteria are more important than others. This difficulty should be recognized as a limitation — although some effort is still better than none at all.

Table 19.1 Questions To Ask During Product Selection

The Product or Service
- Is the product or service really needed? If so, what features are really needed?
- Can environmentally harmful features be eliminated?
- Is the product size/magnitude necessary?
- Can departmental surpluses be checked to ensure that no comparable product is available internally?
- Has the possibility of using a service rather than buying the product to meet the needs been investigated?
- Has the feasibility of short-term rental or sharing the product been investigated?
- Allowing for future needs, can the product be easily enhanced or upgraded?
- Will the product be used to the end of its useful life/obsolescence? If not, can it be easily reallocated or sold?
- Is the product designed to be durable, repairable, and long-lasting?
- Does the product have clear and comprehensive operating instructions?
- Is the product designed for easy and economical maintenance and repair?
- Is product maintenance and upkeep free from the use of environmentally damaging products?
- What volume and type of wastes are generated during maintenance and repair over the life cycle of the product?
- Are there environmental performance standards relating to this product or service?
- What eco-labeling standard or certification does this product meet?
- Is the product free from banned substances?

- Does the product contain WHMIS-controlled substances that require special training, labeling, handling, and/or waste disposal practices?
- Do any anticipated regulations, which would phase out the use of products or services, apply to this product or service?
- Is the product exempt from special disposal considerations?
- Is the product free of any materials from endangered species?

Efficiency

- Has a Life Cycle Assessment been done on this product or similar ones?
- Is the product designed to minimize waste during normal use?
- Is the product efficient with respect to energy, water, and materials?
- Is the product less polluting during use than competing products on a life cycle basis?

Packaging

- Has the supplier/manufacturer made efforts to reduce the amount of packaging necessary to ship, store, and use the product properly and safely?
- Does the packaging material(s) have post-consumer recycled content?
- Can the product and packaging material(s) be recycled within established and available collection and recycling programs?
- Does the product arrive from the supplier packaged in material(s) that are refillable or reused, e.g., plastic totes, reusable skids/pallets?
- Can the packaging be eliminated?
- Is the product packaged in bulk?
- Can the product, its parts, or its packaging be returned to the supplier for reuse, recycling, or recovery?

Supplier

- Does the supplier/manufacturer have an environmental policy?
- Do the product's manufacturing processes minimize:
    - energy expenditures
    - total atmospheric emissions
    - resource consumption
    - noise
    - fugitive emissions
    - discharges to water bodies
    - habitat destruction
    - workplace hazards?
- Does the supplier conform to all applicable legislation and regulations?
- Can the supplier justify all their environmental claims?
- Does the supplier conduct regular internal environmental audits to legislative and policy standards and the EMS using set procedures? Has the supplier conducted a comprehensive audit for waste, energy, greenhouse gases?
- Does the supplier have waste management programs in place?
- Does the supplier have an Environmental Management System in place?
- Is the supplier certified to a recognized standard (e.g., ISO 14000, EMAS)?
- Does the supplier make available appropriate training to employees having responsibilities and jobs with environmental risks?

The Use of Checklists

In most instances, a checklist will be adequate in assisting procurement officials to purchase environmentally sound products and services. In developing a checklist to suit an organization's needs the following steps should be taken:

1. Determine priorities — establish objectives giving due consideration to both existing and anticipated legislation, and the business environment.
2. Search for existing checklists — review established guides, such as those mentioned in this chapter, especially the EPA.
3. Create your own checklist — where no example of a checklist is available, an organization may have to generate its own. Consider environmentally preferred characteristics and consult local contractors, product suppliers, and product guides to ascertain if such products are available and what alternatives might be recommended.

To create a checklist:

- Use guides to find new products and/or specialty suppliers.
- Ask suppliers to include information in bids, including data on resource consumption, emissions, expected lifespan, power-saving features, service, and special disposal requirements.
- Do performance testing during a week-long trial, for example, or request a demonstration of a product. Assess eco-labeling certification obtained by suppliers for credibility.
- Establish payback periods. Capital costs in one year may be offset by operating savings in another year. It is necessary to do this work in advance and suppliers should be able to do this for an organization.

Whether existing checklists and specifications are to be modified, or new ones generated, it is important to differentiate between prescriptive and performance based requirements. Both types are useful and a combination of the two may be necessary.

"Prescriptive requirements describe specific materials, contents, quantities, etc. that are either prohibited or desired in a good or service. A performance based requirement is ideal when it is difficult to specify the criteria for a product or service. It focuses on the desired result or performance in terms of the environmental impact of the proposed purchase."[13]

Checklists should be revisited periodically to incorporate changes in legislation, new products and services, recent innovations, and concerns. By subscribing to environmental journals, newsletters, and annual product directories or periodically reviewing Internet sites, purchasing personnel will be informed of newly certified products and introduced to new technologies and services. This, in turn, will assist employees to update checklists and ensure that the organization is purchasing the most environmentally appropriate alternatives.

General Principles for Environmental Purchasing Guidelines

A list of general principles for environmental purchasing guidelines is presented in Table 19.2. These will prove useful for procurement officials when developing an environmental purchasing policy for their organizations; and, subsequently, formulating pertinent questions to ask as part of product and supplier selection.

Table 19.2: General Principles for Environmental Purchasing Guidelines

1. **Incorporating environmental concerns into purchasing**
   Environmental considerations should be incorporated into purchasing policies and strategies as a central component of the decision-making process, with an emphasis placed on waste reduction. Purchasing managers must be closely involved with all changes and developments and actively consult with environmental advisors.

2. **The 3Rs hierarchy (reduce, reuse, recycle)**
   Purchasing decisions should be based on the 3Rs hierarchy; trying first to reduce, secondly to reuse, and lastly, to recycle. Application of the life cycle concept should be used to support variances from this principle. Where practicable, specifications should be amended to include environmentally preferred products, with recyclable materials being used wherever possible.

3. **Life Cycle Assessment (LCA)**
   Purchasing decisions require the integration of economic and environmental considerations in decision making. Products should be evaluated on their environmental impact throughout the entire life cycle. Improvements made on a life cycle basis should be considered.

4. **Life Cycle Costing (LCC)**
   Purchasing decisions should not be based on the initial cost of a product, but on a life cycle cost that includes liabilities from production, usage, and disposal. The cost of using the product or service over its entire life cycle should be compared with other similar products or services. Environmental factors should be taken into account to establish life cycle costing criteria to be used in evaluating tenders. Factors that might appear in tenders' terms and conditions include price, economic and environmental impact (such as unnecessary or unsuitable packaging), production processes, energy use, water consumption, maintenance, and disposal requirements.

5. **Claims and their verification**
   A product that is less harmful to the environment must possess an environmentally preferred quality, and the existence of this quality must be verifiable. An accurate verification process employs suitable scientific verification methods and produces unbiased, reliable data regarding environmental claims. All supplier or manufacturer claims should be supported with appropriate documentation on first-time buys, or if any of the original information changes, such as types of material or production processes (toxicology reports, laboratory results, and source of recycled content information). The determination of which products are less environmentally harmful will change constantly as new products and new evaluation standards are introduced. Frequently, choice between products will involve trade-offs.

6. **Reduction of hazardous materials and toxicity**
Whenever possible, hazardous materials and products requiring the use of hazardous chemicals in their production or maintenance should be eliminated or replaced. The use and release of toxic compounds or materials should be reduced throughout the entire life cycle of a product.

7. **Increasing resource use efficiency**
Organizations need to be realistic about resource use. Optimal use should be made of all resources, including energy, water, and other materials used in, or by, products and services.

8. **Adopting a partnership approach with suppliers**
A partnership with suppliers will ensure that they understand the objectives of the purchasing organization and are better able to supply products to the desired specifications. Furthermore, working together can bring mutual benefits. When implementing environmental purchasing practices, it is essential to consider the problems suppliers will face and to make the suppliers understand the reasons for any change in purchasing policy or philosophy.

9. **Supplier commitment**
Purchasers should deal only with suppliers expressing a commitment to protecting the environment — those who have implemented environmental policies and are actively seeking ways to minimize adverse impacts on the environment through their operating practices. A supplier's approach can affect a purchasing organization's credibility. Therefore, purchasers should carefully select suppliers based on environmental performance. An effective environmental audit of suppliers can prevent expensive cleanup in the future.

10. **Demonstration of compliance by suppliers and manufacturers**
Suppliers and manufacturers should demonstrate that they are in full compliance with current legislation. Consumer and customer requirements will change as their knowledge improves and as the development of legislation and standards brings more issues into the public domain.

Relevant points receive less emphasis in the original documents but were considered important as general principles:

- All tender specifications and contracts should be printed double-sided and suppliers should be encouraged to correspond with a minimum of paper waste.
- To ensure quality, suppliers and contractors should be requested to provide representative samples of materials and identify previous users of the product or service.
- Purchasers should evaluate not only the product purchased, but the packaging used by the manufacturer or supplier.
- Purchasing should consider the opportunity costs associated with resource development and the need for quality-of-life considerations

(including the importance of green space and the knowledge that all flora and fauna deserve a place to exist).

- Customers have the power to influence which products will succeed. The law of supply and demand can lead to a product base that is designed to protect the environment.
- Consider what systems already exist such as quality or health and safety in purchasing practices. It may not be necessary to reinvent the wheel to integrate the environment into purchasing decisions.

Implementation of Environmental Purchasing Practices

The Level of Development of the Environmental Management System

Organizations are finding it necessary to address, as appropriate, the environmental effects resulting from the products and services they purchase. The stage of development and sophistication of the corporation's EMS plays a role in developing and implementing environmental purchasing guidelines. If the EMS is well established, purchasing guidelines will fit relatively easily into this system. ISO 14001 requires the corporation to consider the activities of suppliers, which is best done through purchasing guidelines.

When an organization does not have an EMS, or is considering developing one, it is still possible to introduce environmental purchasing guidelines at a modest level, independent of the EMS. Three basic components for such a program would include

- an awareness and training program for those responsible for purchasing and waste disposal (general principles and some training),
- a letter to suppliers outlining intent and requesting cooperation and information on their environmental policies, and
- a start on the development of accounts on waste disposal and utility costs in a way that they can be linked to purchasing decisions.

Commitment from Upper Management

Two major steps must be taken at the executive level in order to support the development and implementation of an environmental purchasing program within an organization:

- recognition of merit (costs and benefits) and
- commitment in the form of additional resources, including funds, personnel, and time.

Environmentally responsible procurement should be based on sound business reasons and an evaluation of costs and benefits. The driving forces should be examined carefully. Costs and benefits need to be quantified where possible and the cost of inaction weighed against the cost of action. Potential costs and benefits are summarized in Table 19.3. Costs may be in the form of additional resources including personnel, time, and funding required to support capital expenditures, training and education, and the hiring of new employees or consultants.

Table 19.3: Potential Costs and Benefits Associated with Environmental Purchasing Guidelines

Costs
- the cost of first improving your organization's performance in order to be credible with suppliers
- the time and resources necessary to assess suppliers' performance
- the cost of systems to monitor suppliers' performance
- the cost incurred in supporting improvements at key suppliers
- the improvement costs incurred by suppliers which may be passed on as increased prices
- the establishment of new accounting (sub)systems (not pooled accounts)

Benefits
- savings realized from conserving water, energy, and fuel resources, and reducing waste disposal costs, material usage, and packaging costs
- savings through avoided costs, such as lower waste management fees, hazardous materials management fees, and pollution prevention expenses
- purchase price reductions as a result of suppliers' environmental improvements
- gaining market share
- having a secure supply chain with no hidden or unexpected costs
- more cost-effective compliance with environmental regulations and demonstration of due diligence
- reduced risk of accidents
- savings from introducing change gradually rather than being forced to react on short notice

Purchasing managers need to work with upper management to gain recognition, and generate awareness, of the purchasing function, its importance, and the services it provides within the organization. A short, clear, concise, and convincing statement addressing the organization's view on the environment is needed as the foundation for further environmental initiatives.

Purchasing management and staff should build on the organization's environmental policy by requesting the writing of a waste minimization and resource conservation policy that includes the use of purchasing guidelines. A succinct statement as to why purchasing guidelines should be developed and implemented within the organization is necessary as part of this request to senior management. Purchasing personnel should prepare a budget for implementation as well as an estimate of the benefits of environmental purchasing.

The Responsibilities of Middle Management

While it is anticipated that eventually day-to-day environmental management responsibilities will be integrated at all levels of management, at this time, they generally lie with those individuals having a technical or general management role. They are frequently the employees who are paying for utilities and waste disposal out of their department budget (pooled or overhead accounts) and, as such, are the people with whom purchasing managers need to work. Middle managers need to understand that they can ask purchasing for advice and assistance in deciding upon what item to purchase, when, from whom, at what price, and to what specification, including environmental criteria.

The Role Played by Employees

Employees will not necessarily have direct interaction with the purchasing department. However, they are frequently the end-users of numerous products. Purchasers must ensure that the environmental benefits of their product choices are realized. Communication is essential. For example, a purchaser may select an environmentally preferred product based on its qualities of recyclability, durability, and returnable packaging. If the shipper-receiver is unaware that the supplier has a packaging take-back program, the packaging might find its way into the garbage bin. If the employee using the product does not know that the product is recyclable, it may be discarded into the solid waste stream. In this instance, a lack of communication, education, and training resulted in increased waste disposal costs, possible lost revenue, and a wasted effort by the purchaser.

It is the responsibility of the purchasing department to convey adequate guidance and instruction to those people using the selected products and services in order to effectively realize the environmental benefits. The consumption habits of products or services can have a significant impact. They may be negative and damage attempts to implement greener purchasing practices or be a positive influence by creating demand for environmental products and services.[14]

Relationship with Suppliers

It is critical to communicate information about purchasing guidelines to suppliers. An organization must inform suppliers of its environmental policy, procurement policy, and the criteria being used to evaluate a product's environmental merit. Seminars or technical bulletins are useful in communicating this information.

Recommended Further Reading

Baily, P. *Purchasing and Supply Management.* London, U.K.: Chapman & Hall, 1987.

Davis, G.A. *The Use of Life Cycle Assessment in Environmental Labelling Programs.* Washington DC: U.S. Environmental Protection Agency, 1993.

EPP Update: *Environmentally Preferable Purchasing*. U.S. EPA:
   <www.epa.gov/opptintr/epp>

Husseini, A., and Kelly, B., eds. "Environmentally Responsible Procurement (Green Procurement)." *Environmental Technology*. Toronto, Ontario: Canadian Standards Association, 1995. Z766-95.

Ibbotson, B., and J.-.D. Pyper, eds. *Environmental Management in Canada*. Whitby, Ontario: McGraw-Hill Ryerson, 1996.

Russel, Trevor, ed. *Greener Purchasing: Opportunities and Innovations*. Sheffield, U.K.: Greenleaf, 1998.

Websites

<http://www.ec.gc.ca/eog-oeg/greener>

<www.econexus.net>

<http://ew-news.eea.eu.int/ManagementConcepts.Greenp>

<http://www.greenmarketplace.com/greenmarket/index >

<http://www.greenontario.org/buygreen/greenp>

ENVIRONMENTAL COMMUNICATIONS

Lynne Kailan
and Dixon Thompson

THIS CHAPTER ADDRESSES TWO CRITICAL ELEMENTS of communication — a corporate communications strategy to provide and receive information about the corporation's environmental performance, and risk communication with stakeholders who have more immediate and direct concerns about existing or potential risks. These elements of communication must be integrated, philosophically compatible, and mutually supportive. The objective of all communications is to build trust; therefore, efforts to cover up, minimize, or disguise faults or failings of the organization would be counterproductive. Given the increased cynicism and skepticism of stakeholders, the hypocrisy of different parts of the system delivering different messages would ultimately defeat the purpose of communications. A third, small but vital, element of the communications strategy is crisis communications.

Three basic environmental communications components are communications strategy, risk communication, and crisis communication.

Communications Strategy

WHO — all stakeholders and identified and potential audiences.

WHAT — long-term, cumulative, with the objective of building trust and relationships using accurate information on environmental, biophysical, social, and economic issues (see chapter 13, Environmental Reporting).

HOW — all communications tools, as required.

Risk Communication

WHO — those stakeholders who are, or may be, at risk because of the organization's activities, or who are concerned about biophysical or social risks.

WHAT — two-way communication on issues of concern to the stakeholders and the organization's response.

HOW — dialogue, participatory processes, other information as appropriate.

Crisis Communication

WHO — those people affected by, or interested in, the crisis and its outcome.

WHAT — determined by the nature, location, and timing of the crisis.

HOW — determined by the nature, location, and timing of the crisis.

Why Communicate?

Without communication, understanding is impossible.
Without understanding, conflicts are probable. — Source unknown

Keeping lines of communication open is important for any organization that wants to maintain its social contract to operate. If the products, processes, or activities of an organization can have an environmental impact on the community in which it operates, or the larger community that it influences, that organization requires a communication strategy and ongoing environmental risk communication. After an environmental crisis occurs, or an organization finds it has a major environmental problem, there will be no time to educate key stakeholders about the quality of the science behind the organization's decision or actions. If a communications strategy has not already built a foundation of public understanding and acceptance, it will be too late to do so. And if there is no existing credibility or trust factor, communications in a crisis will be difficult if not impossible.

Strategic Communications Planning

Mintzberg, Ahlstrand, and Lampel outline four things that any strategy, including communications, must accomplish:[1]

• set direction
• focus efforts
• define the organization
• provide consistency

Templates are readily available that can assist in developing a communications strategy that can be adapted for specific situations or organizations. Generally, templates have the following components:

- a clear statement of communications objectives,
- identification of critical audiences/stakeholders,
- an analysis of existing or previous communications products,
- a situational analysis or environmental scan,
- an overview of strategy needed to achieve communications and other corporate objectives,
- key messages or a positioning statement of 25 words or less,
- a list of communications tools needed to achieve the objectives,
- an action plan complete with timelines and individuals identified for responsibility for each component,
- an evaluation mechanism for measuring success,
- an ability to adjust the strategy based on feedback and evaluation,
- a carefully designed, implemented, and integrated risk communications,
- a plan for crisis communications, and
- a plan for sustaining activities that will continue to build on the momentum.

These components of the communications strategy need clear support and written approval by the organization's top executive to ensure buy-in at all levels. They must be reviewed and updated regularly, as with all effective strategies and policies.

Environmental communication strategy is supported by, and conversely provides support to, the other environmental management tools. ISO 14001 requires that

- environmental policy is communicated to all employees (Section 4.2 e),
- roles, responsibilities, and authorities are to be communicated (Section 4.4.1), and
- an organization must establish and maintain procedures for internal and external communication (Section 4.4.3).

The remaining environmental management tools in the set require communication as part of their operations and/or to provide information as content for the communications strategy. Therefore, people involved in environmental communications must know how to interact with those using the other environmental management tools and how the other tools can help them, especially policy, indicators, auditing, reporting, purchasing guidelines, education, and training. Communication must be managed strategically before it can contribute to organizational effectiveness.

Communications Objectives

Objectives must be specific and measurable and describe what the communications strategy expects to achieve. Legitimate objectives relate to influencing awareness, attitude, or behavior of a target audience. However, awareness itself may not be that useful unless it leads to changes in attitude or behavior.

Developing a vision statement is one way to focus communications objectives (chapter 5, Strategic Environmental Management and chapter 6, Environmental Policy). Communications objectives can also be used after the fact as a reality check on the vision statement. If it becomes clear that you can't get there from here, perhaps some re-thinking is required.

Identification of Critical Stakeholders and Audiences

Stakeholder is a term used to describe individuals, groups, or institutions that could be affected by the organization's services, processes, products, or other activities or that could affect the organization's performance, positively or negatively. Communications programs for general audiences or the public at large might build relationships accidentally with stakeholders, but more often than not they communicate with no one important to the organization. And, in the process of doing nothing, they can cost the organization a great deal of money.[2]

A carefully maintained stakeholder list is a basic communications tool that must be specific and include

- who they are;
- a summary of major stakeholder issues;
- the level of support or opposition (active or passive);
- how to reach them quickly by phone, fax, or e-mail;
- contact names of who needs to be kept informed, how often, and by whom; and
- their preferred method of receiving information (website, newsletters, e-mail, personal contact).

This stakeholder list must be constantly revised and updated to be a major asset.

Audiences (people or organizations) need to be convinced, educated, or informed during the course of an organization's business. Listing general public as an audience is a lot less useful than listing suburban homeowners as an audience distinct from urban environmentalists; these are different groups, with different information needs and expectations, who could provide the organization with different information whether solicited or not.

An organization's employees and their families are an audience that is often overlooked. Internal communications is a concept that has gone out of favor recently due to cutbacks and downsizing. It will be interesting to track the outcome of this omission for the future of organizations in terms of staff loyalty, pride in contributions to the organization's success, or even in a willingness to perform, beyond meeting the basic requirements of the job.

Analysis of Existing Communications

Communication does not happen in a vacuum. If an organization has been in operation for more than six months, there has been communication whether deliberate or not. Every time a phone is answered — or not answered — the organization is communicating with stakeholders or clients, sometimes in ways it might not intend. What is the message to clients if they are never able to speak to a real person when they try to contact an organization? Communications strategy requires monitoring and a mechanism for feedback as well as an ability to fix the situation immediately if the feedback is negative.

To have a significant influence on attitude or behavior, communications efforts must be sustained and coordinated enough to become a consistent, integral part of every facet of the operation. Analysis of existing and previous communications, as well as an objective determination of the reputation or image of the organization, gives the communications professional a base to work from. New communications initiatives must be relatively consistent with what's already in the public domain, or they will cause confusion and create an atmosphere of mistrust. While communications can (and should) be constantly refined and updated, an organization can only reinvent itself so many times before it loses focus in the public's mind. Confusion is rarely a communications objective, but unfortunately, too often an outcome.

It is also essential to ensure two-way communication takes place. Getting information from employees or field operations, for example, is as important as getting it out. Comments from an organization's employees are sometimes the first indication that an issue might be developing. Regular contact with the community in which you operate and with key stakeholders will help to incorporate their concerns into the organization's decision making before they become an issue that needs to be managed. This gives an alert communications professional the opportunity to head off issues before the organization needs to go into full issues management mode (issues management is dealt with elsewhere in the chapter). Issues that develop into crises can use unacceptable amounts of executive time and organizational resources that could better be applied elsewhere.

Situational Analysis

Situational analysis is a description of the environment in which communications will take place – the communications environmental scan. Pearce and Robinson describe the process of balancing the organization's mission — what it is, what it wants to be, and what it wants to do, with what the environment will allow or encourage it to do — as "interactive opportunity analysis."[3]

It should contain research into attitudes of stakeholders, media, and other target audiences and describe people and organizations trying to influence attitudes about the organization or product. It should also clearly outline the geographical scope of the communications strategy.

The situational analysis should identify vulnerabilities that could hamper the success of the project and should try to anticipate things that could inhibit the organization's ability to meet its communication objectives. This will include risk management (chapter 10) and a recommended strategy for managing each risk or vulnerability. It is also a good time to re-examine the organization's stakeholders and update their positions. The situational analysis should also identify opportunities to enhance the organization's ability to meet its communications objectives.

Outline of Communications Tools

Communication plans need a comprehensive description of the tools that will be used to deliver the key messages to the target audiences in ways that achieve the objectives. Many communications strategies have no real strategy and consist solely of tactics or specific activities such as an announcement or event with a news release — maybe a stakeholder briefing thrown in for good measure. This doesn't usually accomplish much.

Table 20.1 List of Options Available to Communications Professionals

People to people directly
Meetings
- face-to-face
- large and small groups
- town hall meetings
- teleconferencing
- video conferencing

Displays
- trade shows
- exhibits
- conferences, malls

Letters
- informational
- invitational

Conferences/Seminars
- workshop speaker
- exhibitor
- program advertising
- sponsorship

Public speaking/speeches

Telephone
- hotlines
- recorded messages
- automated phone trees
- 1-800 numbers

Open houses

Independent third party verification

Third party testimonials

Electronic tools — less personal, but reach a broader audience

- websites
- e-mail
- chat rooms
- videos
- cable TV programming
- electronic bulletin boards

Media/ Publicity

- news releases
- news conferences
- interviews
- letters to the editor
- op-eds
- newsletter/magazine articles
- editorial board meetings
- public service announcements

Print Materials — not everyone has access to the Internet

- newsletters
- direct mail pieces
- newspaper and magazine inserts
- household flyers
- brochures
- fact sheets
- publications
- reports
- envelope stuffers
- annual reports
- information kits
- calendars
- posters
- photography
- pay stub messages

Advertisements
- radio
- TV
- newspaper (daily, weekly, alternative)
- magazine
- bus boards
- bus shelters
- billboards
- facility/building
- Internet

Philanthropy
- sponsorships
- donations of product or services

Research
- exit surveys/interviews
- surveys/questionnaires
- focus groups
- media monitoring

Source: adapted from S. Smith, J. Yates, CommPlan Canada, Strategic Communication Planning Workshop, 1999.

In addition to this list of general communication tools, it is important to note that the right tools must be found to communicate with specific ethnocultural groups. Different cultures may respond differently to commonly used communications tools. Communicating with these audiences requires reliable translation services and an awareness of cultural sensitivities, specific needs, and preferences for receiving information.

Humor, Photographs, and Endorsements

Humor, photographs, and endorsements can be powerful but risky communications tools that should only be used with caution within an environmental communications strategy.

Humor could be useful to lighten up what might be an otherwise negative or overly serious topic. However, it is easy to offend a part of the audience causing the attempt at humor to backfire. This is particularly risky when there are widely divergent opinions on the issues, which all sides take very seriously, as is often the case with environmental issues. Often, by the time something that is funny has been altered so that it will offend no one, it will no longer be humorous. Use only with caution.

Pictures are worth a thousand words. However, the problem is how to balance the pretty pictures that would please an audience and enhance the image of the organization with the requirement for credibility, which requires representation of both the good and bad news. If only pretty pictures are selected, readers might conclude that the data has also been treated selectively.

Endorsements present the same problems as photographs — how to achieve the good news/bad news balance for credibility. If only positive endorsements are included, then readers could justifiably conclude that data was also selected to enhance the image.

Any, but not likely all, of the tools can be chosen to communicate your message. Careful selection of the most effective tool will depend on budget and the needs and level of sophistication of the target audience. The main point is that communication needs to be ongoing, so the choice of communications tools must be sustainable considering the resource constraints. If the advertising budget is limited and would allow only one or two insertions in a newspaper or other publication, perhaps those resources could be better spent on other more effective methods of getting the message out.

Media Relations

Media relations is a topic that deserves special attention. There is a common saying in media relations, attributed to a number of sources, including the master of irony Mark Twain, Never pick a fight with someone who buys ink by the barrel. It is very true, so media relations should only be undertaken with a healthy respect and due care.

Media relations is an area where most organizations will succeed or fail in a very public way. Successful media relations result from building and maintaining personal relationships with key media outlets. It pays to invest the time and do the necessary research.

Most communications professionals will have had media training in order to act as the organization's spokesperson or in order to train a top executive for that role. Each organization needs to have a designated spokesperson and that person needs to be properly trained and rehearsed.

For each contact with the media, there are five key points to keep in mind:

- Have only one or two key points or messages to deliver and stick with them.
- Be positive.
- Keep answers short and to the point.
- Don't speculate or try to explore new ideas.
- Don't let reporters put words in your mouth.

It is advisable to keep logs of media contacts and be prepared to call and correct any misinformation or provide additional background. An organization should have some method of monitoring the major media for articles that mention the organization or key stakeholders. This is often a service that is purchased on contract, because it can be time-consuming and labor-intensive if done in-house.

Action Plan

The action plan is generally in the form of a chart with headings covering: Date, Action, Responsibility, Support Material, Date Required, and Status. This is the road map to ensure that everything is coordinated and nothing is forgotten. The action plan, sometimes called a communications roll-out, must be approved by the senior executive and circulated well in advance, because it is often necessary to assign responsibilities to other members of the organization. Generally, stakeholder briefings are best carried out by executives or managers closest to the issue, so they should be given enough time to prepare to do this effectively. The communications professional then develops and supplies the supporting material such as a script/speaking notes, key messages, potential questions and suggested answers, backgrounders, and follow-up letters that will make the executives' job easier.

Evaluation

It is important to have measurable objectives so you can determine how well they are being met. The most common method of evaluating a communications strategy is media monitoring. But what if some of the target audiences don't use the media that carried the story? What if they don't like or trust the media commentators who covered the story? In order to effectively measure and evaluate a communications program, it is necessary to ensure the evaluation methods relate directly to target audiences, not just to the messengers (the media).

Public opinion research is the clearest evaluation system but by far the most expensive. A popular indication of public interest in an organization is the number of hits on the website and the amount of time spent there.

The evaluation may highlight the need to adjust the message or strategy. It may also point to secondary and unintended impacts of the communications that could have significant consequences. The key to success is an organization's responsiveness — its ability to adapt and change based on feedback, whatever the source.

Issues Management

When things are going well, tell the media everything they want to know. When things are going wrong, tell them even more. — NASA Public Affairs[4]

Each organization needs to define exactly what constitutes an issue for them, but generally an issue is organized action or opinion that could be (or already is) controversial and could undermine the effectiveness and credibility of the organization.[5] Issues management is the organization's participation in that process.

There are basically three types of issues:

- current issues — those that are known, understood, and moving toward resolution;
- emerging issues — those that are evolving; and
- strategic or long-term issues — those that will require longer term planning and monitoring.

In developing an issues management strategy it is important to note that those who define the issue usually win the debate. So, reluctance to engage with critics is generally not a successful strategy. Successful issues management will include the following elements:

- get the facts
- determine ownership
- assess the impact
- focus your position
- respond quickly
- correct errors
- track events

Vibbert maintains that issues enter the public agenda because someone makes an issue out of a problem.[6] When organizations delay communications until the issue stage, rather than beginning at the stakeholder or public relations stage, they usually are forced to develop programs of crisis communications.

Crisis Communication

Crisis communication is a specialized area of communications that deserves careful attention. Like purchasing an insurance policy, the hope and expectation is that it will never be needed. No crisis ever happens exactly when and where predicted, but it is almost guaranteed that eventually an organization will have a major crisis to contend with.

The first few hours of a crisis are critical because this is when confidence in an organization might be restored with the greatest credibility. Confidence and calmness in the face of a crisis will come from the existence of a carefully prepared and approved crisis communications strategy.

The keys to responding in a crisis are to

- anticipate,
- pre-empt, and
- know your vulnerabilities.

As Sun-Tzu, sixth century Chinese warrior and philosopher said, "A victorious army wins its victories before seeking battle."[7]

Both private and public sector organizations can expect the following stages as a crisis unfolds:[8]

- Surprise. There is generally an element of surprise when an issue surfaces, but it can be mitigated with ongoing research, environmental scanning, and situational analysis.
- Confusion. A lack of information at the outset leads to denial and, at worst, paralysis in developing a response. It is imperative that organizations have solid fact-gathering mechanisms in place.
- Information vacuum. A lack of response by an organization produces a public information vacuum where there is a gap between what is perceived to be the situation and what in fact the story may be. It is vital that this gap be closed as quickly as possible.
- Contradiction. A lack of information, combined with intense outside scrutiny and a demand for instant information, can lead to panic and contradictory internal responses unless a clear and systematic strategy has been decided on in advance.
- Self-doubt and second-guessing. Negative reaction to a strategy in the first 24 hours may lead to self-doubt. It is important to stay the course and maintain the strategy once it has been developed.
- Diffusion. It is common for a single issue to become diffused within hours or days. Parallels to other occurrences may be noted and linkages to past events may be made by critics to magnify the original issue. It is vital to be focused in developing a response and not lose that focus.

In most cases, formation of a crisis management team should be part of the strategy. In event of a crisis, the team should be pulled together immediately to manage the situation. The make-up of the team will depend on the nature of the crisis, but at a minimum should include communications; if an issue is technical in nature, there should be a senior technical person, plus a high-level, trained spokesperson for the organization. It is vital that key staff be accessible at all times to those managing the crisis communications.

In 1988, three years after Bhopal, an Ashland Oil refinery experienced a major oil spill in the Monongahela and Ohio Rivers. Ashland's CEO, John R. Hall, was a little slow out of the blocks, but after a day and a half he began to move heaven and earth ... He pledged to clean everything up, he visited news bureaus to explain what the company would do, he answered whatever questions were asked. Within twenty-four hours he had turned the perception from "rotten oil company" to "they are pretty good guys."[9]

The Ashland case demonstrates that it is possible, through sincere, straightforward, and seen-as-right actions by a key company spokesperson, here the CEO, to gain the public's trust and even accolades for what was really a disaster (failed risk management, major environmental damage, subsequent tens of millions of dollars in payouts).[10]

How Capers dealt with a crisis[11]

Capers, a chain of health food stores in western Canada, has a reputation built on the purity of its natural food products and a devotion to healthy eating and living. On March 26, 2002, a Capers food handler tested positive for hepatitis A, a viral illness that can have serious consequences.

Capers manager Michelle Rentke received a call from the health authority Tuesday afternoon. Within minutes, the regional marketing manager and director of corporate communications were brought into the loop. Capers' crisis management plan quickly moved into high gear.

First, Capers determined which products may have come into contact with the infected employee and pulled them off the shelves by Tuesday evening. The following morning, Capers issued a news release, in close cooperation with the health authority to ensure the news release contained no conflicting information, advising anyone who had consumed the products to go to a clinic for a vaccination. Clinic hours and locations were included in the release. The food service manager was appointed primary spokeswoman because of her expertise in food handling.

The next morning, Capers distributed a customer advisory sheet listing the items that may have been in contact with the infected food handler. Capers also brought health workers into the stores to inoculate all of its employees. The story led every local newscast. The flood of media calls after the release was issued prompted Capers to engage a public relations firm to schedule interviews and monitor media coverage.

The company created a special website where customers could obtain information on health clinics, see the list of affected products, find company contacts, and link to sites with more information on hepatitis A. To further ensure customers got the information they needed, Capers set up a toll-free line to disseminate the corporate message and clarify some of the misinformation in the media. Within a week of the health warning, 6,000 people had been vaccinated.

Capers placed advertisements in the major dailies and community news-papers and bought radio spots to do little more than tell customers that the company appreciated their support. Because of the company's prompt response and the trust already established with their loyal customer base, there have been no financial repercussions. The stock has gained more than U.S.$1.30 since the hepatitis scare.

Part of the crisis strategy should include information on the best available resources to support emergency response such as transportation, helicopters, charter planes, boats, along with 24-hour contact numbers and names. The crisis management team would decide whether the technical support people and/or spokesperson should go to the scene immediately. The strategy should also be able to supply up-to-date background information on the organization and its key projects and operations to the media and the public.

Preparation will not prevent a crisis from happening, but it will increase the chances of the organization emerging relatively unscathed and intact. The development of a general crisis communications strategy is the step that leads to the discussion of risk communications.

Risk Communication

The following section is based extensively on the work of Jean Lucas (nee Mulligan) at the Faculty of Environmental Design, University of Calgary.[12]

One of the most sensitive areas of environmental communications is the relatively new field of risk communication. Conflict over environmental risks has increased substantially over the last few decades, along with a corresponding mistrust of the organizations that expose stakeholders to environmental risks. The National Research Council (NRC) defines risk communication as: "an interactive process of exchange of information and opinion among individuals, groups, and institutions. It involves multiple messages about the nature of risk and other messages, not strictly about risk, that express concerns, opinions, or reactions to risk messages or to legal and institutional arrangements for risk management."[13]

This definition recognizes that risk communication involves many parties, multiple messages, and the importance of dialogue. But there is no explicit recognition of the importance of public input into the risk decision-making process, so the first principle of risk communication needs to be added to the NRC definition. This principle states that citizens "have the right to participate in decisions that affect their lives, their property, and the things they value."[14] Risk communication is based on mutual respect, trust, open dialogue, and participation.

Effective risk communication requires the ability to explain complex scientific information to the public. There is abundant advice on how to communicate risk effectively;[15] however, information on incorporating that advice into the day-to-day operation of the organization is limited.

Companies (and governments) often make decisions regarding the acceptability of a risk without adequately consulting with those potentially affected. With the use of environmental risk communication, this is beginning to change. Companies are starting to recognize the importance of community knowledge and social values in the effective management of risk, and the role that trust plays in communicating risk-related issues.

The aim of risk communication is not to avoid all conflict or to diffuse all concerns, but rather to "produce an involved, informed, interested and fair-minded public, so that public opinions and concerns will be (or remain) reasonable, thoughtful, calm, solution-oriented and cooperative."[16]

There are three benefits to companies that undertake effective and timely risk communication. Increased understanding and community involvement will[17]

- likely yield more informed decisions,
- increase public acceptance of risk management activities, and
- provide more enduring solutions.

Effective risk communication can help companies to[18]

- explain technical risks more effectively;
- understand the multidimensionality of risk, and more easily anticipate community response to company activities (reducing expensive surprises);
- respond to citizen concerns and misinformation;
- increase the effectiveness of risk management decisions, by involving concerned community members, and reduce chances that money and resources are wasted;
- improve dialogue and reduce unwarranted tension between communities and companies;
- build a foundation for dialogue and shared problem solving before the inevitable incident happens;
- build and maintain a relationship based on trust and respect;
- reduce future operating costs; and
- improve reputation with regulators and public (which facilitates business elsewhere).

There is no single best mechanism for risk communication. Each must be evaluated in terms of its ability to address the current situation and meet the needs of the community. There are 16 techniques for encouraging public participation, as part of risk communication:

- Advisory committees
- Community visits
- Electronic bulletin boards
- Focus groups
- Negotiation
- Open houses
- Panels
- Polls
- Public hearings
- Public input by phone
- Public Meetings
- Questionnaires and surveys
- Site visits
- Task forces
- Town hall meetings
- Workshops

The effectiveness of each of these techniques in a specific situation can be assessed by the following criteria:

- Range of issues that can be accommodated
- Degree of interaction
- Time commitment to plan and implement
- Cost
- Ability to accommodate different levels of participation

Trust is one of the key factors identified in risk perception research. Public trust in those managing risks is fundamental to the success of risk communication and conflict resolution.

Risk Perception

Much of the difficulty in risk communication lies in the different perceptions of risk by the experts and the public. Experts define risk with quantitative measures, along the lines of probability and consequence, or in terms of toxicity (see chapter 10, Risk Management).[19] The public, on the other hand, uses a much richer and more complex definition of risk which is influenced by an array of psychological, social, institutional, and cultural factors.[20] Effective risk communication requires the recognition of the legitimacy of these factors and the ability to include them in the processes of open dialogue.

Risk Factors

Sandman identifies 12 dominant factors that consistently appear to affect people's judgment of risk that can amplify risk controversies:[21]

1. Voluntary versus Involuntary. A voluntary risk (e.g., smoking) is judged as less serious than an involuntary risk (e.g., siting an industrial plant without consulting the community).
2. Natural versus Industrial. A natural risk (e.g., lightening strike) is judged as less serious than an industrial risk (e.g., nuclear power accident).
3. Familiar versus Exotic. A familiar risk (e.g., household cleaner) is judged as less serious than an exotic risk (e.g., biotechnology).
4. Not Memorable versus Memorable. September 11, 2001 versus 100 children a day dying of malnutrition.
5. Not Dreaded versus Dreaded. Being attacked by killer bees versus dying at home in your sleep.
6. Chronic versus Catastrophic. A chronic risk, one that is diffuse in time and space (e.g., car accidents), is judged as less serious than a catastrophic risk (e.g., airplane crashes).
7. Knowable versus Not Knowable. A knowable risk (i.e., risks with attributes of low uncertainty, high expert agreement, and high detectability) is judged as less serious than a risk that is not knowable.
8. Controlled by Individual versus Controlled by Others. "Control is related to voluntariness, but it is different. Voluntariness is who decides. Control is who implements."[22]
9. Fair versus Unfair. Equitable distribution of risk and benefits.
10. Morally Irrelevant versus Morally Relevant. For example, pollution is viewed as wrong and unethical.
11. Trust versus No Trust.
12. Responsive Process versus Unresponsive Process. If the communication process is responsive (i.e., attributes of openness, apology, courtesy, sharing, and compassion) the risk is judged as less serious than if the process is unresponsive (i.e., attributes of secrecy, stonewalling, discourtesy, confronting community values, and dispassion).

Driving Forces and Barriers

Despite two decades of discussion, research, and practice, risk communication strategies remain at the periphery of corporate management. Generally, risk communication is not always effective or consistent. Practices vary along a continuum from reactive and advisory to proactive and participatory.

There are five main forces motivating companies to initiate risk communication with stakeholders:

- Concerned public. The public has become more informed and concerned, demanding companies open up their practices to public review and input.

- Communication crises. Examples of a lack of communication that led to distrust and delays, which have opened the eyes of some companies.
- Regulatory requirements. Regulations requiring more openness in information disclosure and public consultation or involvement in decision making.
- Cost avoidance. The economic implications of poor communication are being realized, as evidenced in the financial implications of delays in approvals and production, public hearings, and/or employee time taken to deal reactively with risk communication issues.
- Codes of conduct. Some codes address risk communication directly (e.g., Canadian Chemical Producers Association) while others address the concept indirectly through guidelines and principles related to information disclosure, open dialogue, and community involvement.

There are still obstacles that can prevent companies from being proactive and effective in their risk communication initiatives, including

- lack of corporate commitment,
- perception that only limited resources are available,
- corporate confidence or certainty in their knowledge and expertise,
- fear of losing control,
- fear of creating conflicts,
- fear of causing alarm,
- fear of exposure to legal liability,
- reactive approach,
- underestimation of benefits, and
- perception that risk communication is outside the core business.

Integrating Risk Communication with Environmental Management

There are six fundamental links between environmental risk communication and corporate environmental management:

1. Risk communication must not be designed to cover up or gloss over mistakes and poor management but rather to enable companies and communities to work together to resolve problems. Open, honest dialogue and the resolution of concerns are unlikely if the management of environmental risks is poor.

2. Communication, in which listening and responding occur along with talking, results in changes in the ideas, attitudes, and behaviors of both the organization and the public. For example, local expertise can improve scientific assessments, and some community concerns can be addressed through operational changes and/or improved environmental management practices in response to community concerns. This

will be the case if risk communication is an integral part of a company's environmental strategy, rather than merely a mouthpiece for it.

3. Risk communication must become a routine part of business for those aspects of operations that put the community at risk. The need to integrate environmental factors into strategies, plans, and decisions at all levels is necessary for both environmental management and risk communication.[23]

4. Communication with community members about risks and associated concerns needs to be explicitly addressed in the corporate environmental policy (chapter 6). Wording should demonstrate recognition that people affected by risks have the right to be informed about and have an opportunity to participate in decision-making processes on those risks.

5. A commitment in the environmental policy to regular audits (chapter 8) and public reporting with credible indicators (chapters 12 and 13) will demonstrate that accountability to the public is a corporate priority. At the same time it shows that the organization is interested in identifying and effectively managing its environmental risks. External verification gives the public added assurance that an audit is credible. The periodic environmental audit should include an assessment of the company's conformance to its risk communication policy, because this (ideally) is a component of the environmental policy statement. This part of the audit would examine the management and performance of the risk communication at both corporate and facility levels.

6. A goal of effective risk communication is to provide effective means for members of the communities at risk to understand and participate in dialogue about environmental management and risk management to improve decision making. After considering the social, environmental, and economic costs, benefits, impacts, judgments, and values, a decision regarding the acceptability of the estimated risk must be made. The determination of acceptability cannot take place without the participation of stakeholders. (See chapter 10, Risk Management.)

Risk communication is closely linked to an organization's financial well-being. Failures in risk communication can translate directly into financial payouts through fines, penalties, litigation costs, settlements, and judgments, increased (or cancelled) insurance premiums, and avoidance by investors and customers. Most companies accept that investors, the public at large, and regulators and politicians are seeking to distinguish between environmental "bad guys" and "good guys" in their investment and penalty decisions. Risk management and risk communication closely relate to the core business financial functions, for without positive finance no company can survive.[24]

Conclusion

The three basic elements of strategy, risk, and crisis communications must be carefully developed, documented, integrated, and implemented. Regular reviews and evaluations are important, as are credible indicators of success in reaching goals and objectives. Adequate resources must be allocated and appropriate education and training provided by the organization. The strategy and its implementation must be ongoing and consistent. It is critical to gain senior management support for the communications strategy to resist pressures to use environmental communications for emphasizing the positive in order to enhance corporate image. There is often a tendency at the operational levels of an organization to attempt to censor communications that might admit weaknesses and mistakes. Given the growing cynicism of the public as investors and consumers and, increasingly, government regulators, an effective environmental communications strategy can play a critical role in corporate reputation, financial success, and in retaining the "social licence to operate."

Recommended Further Reading

Crognale G., ed. *Environmental Management Strategies: The 21st Century Perspective.* New Jersey: Prentice Hall, 1999. Chapter 11, Effective Risk Management and Communication: Tips on Working with the Public.

Grunig J.E., ed. *Excellence in Public Relations and Communication Management.* New Jersey: Lawrence Erlraum Associates, 1992.

Powell D., and W. Leiss. *Mad Cows and Mother's Milk: The Perils of Poor Risk Communication.* Montreal, Quebec: McGill-Queen's University Press, 1997.

C H A P T E R

HUMAN FACTORS AS AN ENVIRONMENTAL MANAGEMENT TOOL

Linda Miller, Ergoworks
Edie Adams, Microsoft and
Ron Wardell, Faculty of Environmental Design,
University of Calgary

HUMAN FACTORS (HF), or ergonomics, can help achieve overall corporate goals of increasing efficiency and therefore profitability, reducing risk, and improving productivity and the quality of the workplace. Human factors can help achieve the goals of the Environmental Management System by anticipating and avoiding problems of safety and waste reduction, reducing the risk and costs of accidents and spills, decreasing waste by reducing mistakes in production and manufacturing, and improving the quality of the workplace.

For example, if an assembly line's design requires the employee to get up and walk around the equipment to push a button that stops an assembly process when errors are occurring, then the individual may delay shutting off a process. During the delay, a large amount of waste product would accumulate. This waste reduces efficiency and must be removed and disposed of in an appropriate manner. The redesign of the control placement would allow for easier access to the stop button, reducing the delay in shutting off the equipment, therefore reducing the overall accumulation of waste and improving efficiency. The redesign could also reduce worker frustration.

Human factors should be considered as a strategy to enhance environmental management because it produces direct and indirect improvements when used in the design of products, work processes, and systems.

Definition

In Canada and Europe, human factors and ergonomics are seen as synonymous, and the terms are used interchangeably. In the United States, human factors tends to focus on the cognitive sciences related to human beings in the workplace, while ergonomics focuses on the physical sciences.

Human factors or ergonomics is a recently evolved science that focuses on individuals and how the design of things affects them,[1] to improve human performance and well-being in relation the environment, buildings, jobs, and equipment. Human factors is not a science of its own but is based on a number of sciences: psychology, engineering, physiology, biomechanics, kinesology, and anthropometry.

The National Research Council of Canada defines ergonomics as the application of scientific knowledge to the workplace in order to improve the well-being and efficiency of both the individual and the organization.[2]

The Center for Chemical Process Safety says, "Human factors, or ergonomics, refers to technical systems and equipment so designed that they can be used safely and efficiently by humans."[3]

Human Factors as an Environmental Management Tool

When well-qualified practitioners apply human factors as an environmental management tool the following benefits can be obtained:

- enhanced effectiveness and efficiency in employees' activities by improving productivity, reducing errors (reducing overall waste and energy consumption), and improving convenience of use of equipment and processes;
- enhanced human values such as improved safety, reduced fatigue and stress, and an overall improved quality of the workplace;
- reduced risk to the environment from accidents, spills, and accidental releases of product or waste; and
- design of improved products that are safer, reduce energy consumption, are easier to use, and have a longer lifetime and therefore also provide the corporation with a competitive advantage in the marketplace.

Human factors is one of those environmental management tools that provides limited opportunities for the environmental manager without formal training to make significant improvements without the assistance of a well-qualified human factors professional. Managers could use the list of benefits to look for indications that a human factors analysis is required:

- repeated production errors and complaints from employees about inconvenience;
- problems with safety, stress and fatigue, repetitive stress injuries, observations by those with responsibilities for health and safety;
- repeated accidents, spills, or releases of products or waste;
- a major accident where the cause is not understood; and

- complaints from consumers about product inconvenience or problems with use.

Environmental managers must first understand how human factors can be advantageous in solving problems. If problems are observed that might be improved with the aid of an HF specialist, then a qualified specialist must be hired. As with the other environmental management tools, in order to benefit from human factors, environmental managers must

- understand the basics of the tool and what it can accomplish,
- make a commitment to use it effectively,
- hire well-qualified practitioners and understand their qualifications, and
- provide the resources to carry out the necessary human factors work and to implement the recommendations.

Achieving all of the above objectives would seem to be an impossible task for anyone, but in fact a human factors specialist will only select a subset of these objectives to act on or will focus on a particular problem. In many cases the objectives are correlated.[4] For example, if a piece of equipment is fabricated so an individual can use it more comfortably it is likely that an increase in productivity and minimization of errors will result from applying human factors principles to the design.

In the past, we improved the design of equipment, tools, and activities mostly through trial and error. Today, the systems and products that we utilize are so complex that it is impractical to make changes after the installation of a system or introduction of a product. The cost of retrofitting is often extremely expensive and hence delayed or avoided, thus limiting the effectiveness and acceptance of the system or product. Therefore, whenever possible, it is critical that, prior to implementation or production, both the functionality of the product or system and the interface between the individual and the product, system, or environment are considered. The improvement of the human, environment, and machine interaction is the function of a human factors specialist, including the optimization of

- an employee's activities considering environmental conditions such as snow and ice, humidity, poor lighting, and air quality;
- an employee's response or interaction to job demands such as excessive work pace, emergency situations, shift work, overtime, decision making and work relationships; and
- an employee's use of, or response to, a piece of equipment, tool, office furniture, vehicle, etc.

Ignoring the application of the principles of human factors within the workplace or in everyday life can result in the mismatch between the capabilities and limitations of the individual and the work environment, resulting in a decreased quality of workplace or life for the individual and increased stress on the environment. Stress on the environment can arise in the form of damaged or wasted product, chemical spills, and even environmental disasters.

The rest of this chapter will introduce environmental managers to human factors including

- reviewing the history of human factors,
- identifying methods to apply human factors to improve environmental management,
- describing the professional qualifications of those who practice in the field of human factors, and
- providing key resources to assist the environmental specialist when applying human factors.

History

The origins of human factors came with technological advancement. Many of the first records of the application of human factors are from the late 1800s and early 1900s. For example, in the early 1900s, Frank and Lillian Gilbreth began their work on time and motion studies and shop management techniques, which can be considered the forerunners to human factors. Their work included evaluation of skilled performance and fatigue and the design of workstations and equipment.

The next major documentation of human factors was in World War II with the use of tests for selecting the proper people for the job (fitting the people to the job) and improved training techniques. It soon became clear that, even with selection, some of the complex equipment exceeded the capabilities of the people who had to operate the equipment. It was at this time that the focus started to change to fitting the equipment to the person.

The Birth of the Profession: 1945 to 1960

After World War II, a number of military and civilian laboratories were established to focus on the application of human factors. At the same time, a number of scientific societies were formed in both Britain and the United States. In 1959, the International Ergonomics Association was founded to link several of the societies.

Growth of the Discipline: 1960 to 1980

Prior to the 1960s, most of the work in human factors focused on military applications, then companies started to employ specialists to help optimize human factors in both the design of products and within the workplace. Industries that employed human factor specialists included pharmaceuticals, computers, automotives, and other groups producing consumer products.[5]

Disasters and the Computer Industry: 1980 to 1990

Meshkati analyzed a number of disasters and concluded that inadequate attention to human factors considerations played a significant role in contributing to these disasters.[6] For example, the incident at the Three Mile Island nuclear power plant in 1979 could have had substantial impact on human life if it had not been controlled. Another incident with more tragic results occurred on December 4, 1984. A leak of methylisocyanate at the Union Carbide facility in Bhopal, India, resulted in the deaths of nearly 4000 people and injuries to 200,000. The health problems of the victims are still an issue today. In 1986, the incident at the Chernobyl nuclear power station resulted in more than 300 deaths and widespread human and environmental exposure to harmful levels of radiation. The problems with radiation exposure and the disabled reactor continue.

Why should human factors be used by environmental managers?[7]

Human error caused
- 90 percent of auto accidents,
- 86 percent of hazardous material spills in 1986,
- 80-90 percent of chemical industry accidents, and
- 80 percent of offshore oil accidents over the last decade

Examples of major accidents caused by human error:
- Three Mile Island nuclear power plant loss of coolant, 1979. No lives lost, property damage confined to reactor building, core melting occurred which came close to breaching containment vessel.
- Ocean Ranger, Newfoundland, 1982. Ocean drilling platform capsized — vessel lost with all crew.
- Union Carbide, Bhopal, India, 1984. Methylisocyanate leak at pesticide plant, 4000 died, 200,000 injured, victims still suffering.
- Chernobyl, Ukraine, 1986. Explosion and fire in nuclear power plant. Three hundred dead, initially many rescue workers and volunteers who worked on controlling and containing radiation received doses of radiation that were eventually fatal. Widespread exposure to radiation. Millions of hectares contaminated with radioactive material.
- Occidental Petroleum, Piper Alpha, 1988. Offshore oil platform explosion equivalent to 10 tons of TNT — 167 died. Causes not related to mechanical failure.
- Phillips Petroleum, Pasadena, California, 1989. Explosion and fire, 23 died, 100 injured, largest single business loss in U.S. history (U.S.$1.5 billion).
- Hinton, Alberta, 1986, railway collision — 23 died, 71 injured, cost to railway estimated Can$35 million, judicial inquiry identified the cause as human error.

Human Factors and Computers

The computer revolution brought human factors to the attention of the public. Human factors is applied to the design of control devices, screen presentation of information, and office workplaces.

Human Factors To Date

Human factors will continue to grow as a science and profession. The application of human factors is expected to expand its influence in computer technology, transportation systems, product design, and the occupational environment. Application of human factors to environmental management may come in the form of new product design, set-up and operation of the workplace, and within Environmental Management Systems.

System — A Concept in Human Factors

System

In order to understand how human factors can play an active role in environmental management, it is important to consider that the system is a fundamental concept in human factors. A system is an entity comprised of humans, machines, and other items that come together in order to achieve some purpose or goal[8] Thinking in terms of a system provides a structure to approach development, analysis, and evaluation of complex collections of humans and machines. Bailey states, "The concept of a system implies that we recognize a purpose; we carefully analyze the purpose; we understand what is required to achieve the purpose; we design the system's parts to accomplish the requirements; and we fashion a well-coordinated system that effectively meets our purpose."[9]

In order to apply human factors principles to improve environmental management, the environmental manager, with the aid of an HF specialist, examines the environment as a system rather than a set of separate entities to accurately identify the key factors of an activity or an event.

Human-Machine Systems

A human-machine system is comprised of one or more humans and one or more physical components interacting to bring about a desired output.[10] The term machine is somewhat restrictive since in the phrase human-machine system the machine can represent any type of physical object, device, equipment, facility, or thing the person will use on the job. In a simple system, the human-machine system can be a person working with a shovel. More complex systems can include the operation of a control room in a nuclear power plant, an aircraft, or an oil refinery.

The amount and type of human interaction with the system will vary with the level of manual versus machine control. For example, a manual system will often be comprised of hand tools and other aids for the operators to control the operation. In this type of system, the operators utilize their own physical energy to power the system. In a fully automated system human interaction is minimal to operate the system. In fact, there is human interaction with the system but the interaction is in another form such as installation, programming, maintenance, and monitoring of the system. In order to fully maximize the human-machine interface or interaction, it is important to understand the purpose of the system, components of the system, and the type of interactions that will occur within the human-machine system. In order to optimize the human interaction a number of key criteria should be used to guide good design of products, systems, facilities, and work tasks.

Applying Human Factors to Improve Environmental Management

In order to capitalize on the human interaction that takes place in a human-machine system it is important to consider eleven key design criteria. These criteria are not unique to human factors; they are essential to good design. The following section is an overview of each of these criteria with examples illustrating their impact on environmental management.

Compatible with Business Goals

Design that is compatible with business goals has a clear purpose and is consistent with the organization's business goals and mission statement.[11] This means that the activities or output intended by the design of the product, facility, work task, or system are well-defined and achievable, and the groups that are intended to interact with the design are considered and accommodated in the design. For example, if a new computer software package is purchased to alert operators in a chemical plant that chemicals are approaching toxic levels in the water systems or soils, the software should achieve such goals. In one instance, a software package frequently provided false alarms associated with a potential environmental concern. Over time, experience with the system gave operators little confidence in the software package, and eventually they ignored all the alarms or indicators. Operators were frustrated and believed that the software was something to ignore. As a result, field staff were often the first to intervene on a toxic spill and by that time spills were substantial, resulting in massive cleanup efforts, costs, and risk of prosecution for noncompliance with regulations. To remedy the situation, a human factors specialist, along with the software and facility engineers, redesigned the system so that alarms and indicators truly reflected the physical environment. Education and training was also provided to operators to help improve confidence levels with the system thus resulting in early detection of toxic chemical levels within the environment. The result of the re-engineering allowed for early detection of toxic spills and intervention to occur, minimizing the impact to the environment, cleanup costs, and risk of prosecution.

Ashely identified ten criteria for good design: appropriate, clear, simple, learnable, discoverable, comfortable, adaptable, natural, invisible, and consistent.[12]

Appropriate

Good design of an item, system, or environment is appropriate to the user. The design should be practical and feasible taking into account social, cultural, economic, environmental, and technical factors.

Clear

Design should allow the user to see the primary purpose clearly and the main concept of what is intended by the design or process. If a product or process is difficult to interpret, a user may disregard the product or not use the product to its fullest. For example, if a product is difficult to set up and operate the user may choose to discard the object and purchase one that is easier to operate, therefore adding an unwanted product to the accumulation of waste.

Simple

The design should be simple and familiar. If a system is difficult to learn or requires a large investment of time and effort, this may limit user acceptance and usability. For example, a control room of a nuclear power plant may utilize a computer display layout to represent a system. If a display is too complex, the user may have difficulty using the software, thus limiting success and acceptance. The complexity may result from the design of system symbols, color layout, and the size of the fonts. Inappropriate design of a layout may limit the users' ability to understand the information, or it may be very time consuming to retrieve the necessary information and then interact with the system. The lack of usability perceived by the operator may result in the misreading of pertinent information and making a wrong decision on interaction, or cause user frustration or discomfort. In order to improve the usability in that example, the selection of symbols should be compatible with the users' experience; color and font style should be maximized for the screen layout, and information presented on the screen should be compatible with user capabilities and limitations.

Another example of simplicity that was a direct interaction within the human-machine system occurred after an aircraft full of passengers and cargo had taken off. A cargo door was not secured and the aircraft was forced to land after dumping thousands of gallons of fuel. The investigation noted that the cargo door was not secured correctly and may have been a result of operator error, since there was no indicator to the cargo crew that the door was fully engaged and ready for flight. In this incident, no lives were lost, but the environment was affected by the massive discharge of fuel. Installation of a system to show that cargo doors were properly secured was necessary.

Learnable

The design of the system should allow the individual to feel confident about mastering the design and be successful when using the product or system or when performing an activity. The goal of good design is that the user should be able to do the necessary work or at least learn how to do it. For example, if a new computer software package hinders the users from completing a work task or if they must relearn each step each time they use the software package, the users may choose not to use it to complete the work task. In this case, the software designer must be aware of the basic human capabilities and limitations related to information processing.

Discoverable

The design of a product, system, or activity should be discoverable, understandable, and enjoyable. An individual's ability to discover how to use a product or accomplish a task will encourage learnability.

Comfortable

Ideally, an object, piece of equipment, or system should be designed so that when it is used the operation is within the user's comfort zone. The activity should build on the user's knowledge but not require the individual to move dramatically away from what's familiar. For example, if an oil refinery requires that all operations change from a manual or mechanical environment to a totally automated environment, the unfamiliarity with the new system can cause stress on the operator. If engineering and training does not bridge the movement from a mechanical to an automated environment through education, training programs, and a step-by-step installation of a system, the operator will not trust the new system. In many environments, the transition is too drastic and affects the operator's trust levels with the new system. The operator will often second-guess the information presented on a display and, in some cases, discount the information and decide to leave the control room to check the environment to confirm or discredit results. If this occurs over an extended period of time, efficiency and productivity are often affected and may even lead into an incorrect decision resulting in environmental risk.

Adaptable

The design of the product or system should be adaptable for a variety of users and user scenarios. For example, when a number of operators are required to operate a piece of heavy equipment, some cab features should be adjustable to accommodate varying operator size and operating styles. If visibility is only optimized for tall individuals then the shorter operators may find it difficult to see outside. To compensate for the mismatch, the individuals may either alter their posture causing discomfort and possible injury, or they may miss a pertinent part of the environment resulting in poor decisions that may result in an accident and/or environmental damage. Therefore, the design of a product, facility, or piece of equipment must consider individual variations in size, stature, and physical and mental capability.

Natural

The product or object should be designed so that it feels right to the user. For example, if the object is designed to be operated by hand but does not fit the hand properly or requires awkward motions to operate it, use of the object may feel unnatural.

Invisible

Ideally, the design of an object should allow the individual to feel that the object is not getting in the way of performing the desired task. The object or system should allow users to achieve the desired goal or purpose effortlessly without having to stop and think a lot about their actions. For example, in a control room setting the operators should not have to focus on the computer or the software. Instead, their attention should be focused on trying to solve an operational problem or monitor a system.

Consistent

A product or system should be consistent, allowing users to understand the intended operation or goal. If the object or system is inconsistent in its presentation or operation, people will often find it difficult and frustrating to work with. For example, if a control room is represented by different visual symbols as the operator moves from one application to the next, it may be very difficult to use since the operator may have to continually relearn each symbol, and predictability is lost. This may result in lost productivity and efficiency and possibly incorrect interpretation of information which could cause an accident.

Human Factors Analysis

Figure 21.1 outlines the general steps in a human factors analysis or investigation.

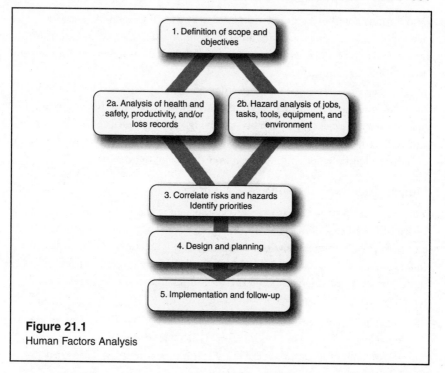

Figure 21.1
Human Factors Analysis

The process starts by setting objectives and defining the scope of the project or program. This would include defining the system's boundary conditions which identify the aspects of the problem to be addressed and the scope of potential interventions.

A concurrent and mutually supporting analysis of risks and hazards are performed. The analysis of effects or consequences of the current situation can be based on existing records or new data, such as symptom surveys, and can use techniques for incident and trend analysis such as scenario analysis or fault trees. The analysis of existing potential loss conditions can use techniques, such as walkthroughs, hazard analysis, or job demands analysis.

The identified potential loss conditions are compared to the documented evidence of negative outcomes to determine priorities and build a case for intervention. Where these are mutually consistent, a strong argument can be made for the existence of the risk and the need to mitigate the hazard. If hazard conditions were not initially identified that might account for a documented type of incident, then further data collection on hazards for that type of incident may be needed. If a hazard is identified that has not resulted in negative outcomes included in existing records, then the records might need validation or the hazard may need to be reassessed for the possible outcome and probabilities.

Solutions for the identified risks and hazards are generated, evaluated, and developed. The business case for interventions is made. Implementation of the interventions is planned with the operating and capital commitments and organizational involvement.

The measures to mitigate risks and hazards are implemented according to the corporate process for participation and buy-in. Mechanisms for evaluating the success are implemented, preferably following the methods used earlier for risk and hazard identification. Continual improvement of the intervention may be built into the implementation process over the longer term.

Human Factors Professionals

There is a certification board for professional practitioners of ergonomics, the Board of Certification in Professional Ergonomics (BCPE).[13] The Board regards ergonomics as synonymous with human factors engineering, and qualified applicants may choose to be certified either as a Certified Professional Ergonomist (CPE) or as a Certified Human Factors Professional (CHFP). Qualifications include:

- Academic requirement: a masters degree, or equivalent, in one of the correlative fields of ergonomics, such as biomechanics, human factors/ergonomics, industrial engineering, industrial hygiene, kinesiology, psychology, or systems engineering.

- Work experience: four years of demonstrable experience in the practice of ergonomics.

- Work product: contribution to ergonomic design of a system, product, or work environment.

- Examination: exam topics include Methods and Techniques, Design of Human-Machine Interface, Human Capabilities/Limitations, Systems Design and Organization, and Professional Practice.

Recommended Further Reading

Baecker, R.M., J. Grudin, W.A.S. Buxton, and S. Greenberg, eds. *Readings in Human Computer Interaction: Toward the Year 2000.* 2nd ed. San Francisco, CA: Morgan Kaufman Publishers, Inc., 1995.

Cushman, W.H., and D.J. Rosenberg. *Human Factors in Product Design.* Amsterdam: Elsevier Science Publishing Company, 1991.

Marras, W.S., W. Karkowski, J.L. Smith, and L. Pacholski, eds. *The Ergonomics of Manual Work.* London, U.K.: Taylor and Francis, 1993.

Noro, K., and A. Imada, eds. *Participatory Ergonomics.* London, U.K.: Taylor and Francis, 1991.

Perlman, G., G. Green, and M. Wolgalter, eds. *Human Factors Perspectives on Human Computer Interaction.* Santa Monica, CA: Human Factors and Ergonomics Society, 1995.

Sanders, M.S., and E.J. McCormick. *Human Factors in Engineering and Design.* 7th ed. New York: McGraw-Hill, 1993.

Tilley, Alvin R. *The Measure of Man and Woman: Human Factors in Design.* New York: The Whitney Library of Design, 1993.

Wilson, J.R., and E.N. Corlett. *Evaluation of Human Work: A Practical Ergonomics Methodology.* 2nd ed. London, U.K.: Taylor and Francis, 1995.

Websites

Association of Canadian Ergonomists: <http://www.ergonomist.ca>

Board of Certification of Professional Ergonomics: <http://www.bcpe.org>

Ergonomic Committee of the American Industrial Hygiene Association: <http://www.aiha.org/>

Human Factors and Ergonomics Society: <http://hfes.org>

Human Factors Research Web Sites: <http://www.apa.org/ppo/issues/shumfac.html>

Industrial Ergonomics Technical Group of the Human Factors and Ergonomics Society: <http://www.dint.com/ietg/>

International Ergonomics Association: <www.iea.cc>

Safety Technical Group of the American Human Factors and Ergonomics Society: <www.hfes.org>

Special Interest Group Computer Human Interaction of American Computing Machinery: <http://www.acm.org/sigs/sigchi>

CLEAN DEVELOPMENT MECHANISM AND JOINT IMPLEMENTATION

Maureen Hill, Highwood Environmental Management and Dixon Thompson

D URING THE LAST DECADE, the issue of global warming has received international political attention and become a priority on national and corporate agendas throughout the world. Scientific reports conclude that human-induced climate change could seriously affect our global environment, economy, and society. Recognizing the threat that climate change poses, 170 countries negotiated agreements to reduce their greenhouse gas (GHG) emissions and therefore reduce global warming. The agreements will be binding when ratified.

The Kyoto Protocol, one of the international agreements, recognizes that some countries might have difficulty reaching emission reduction targets and provides options for achieving the most economically efficient reductions possible. The international community created three flexibility mechanisms under the Kyoto Protocol to help reach GHG emission reduction targets: Joint Implementation (JI), Clean Development Mechanism (CDM), and emissions trading (Articles 6, 12, and 17 under the Kyoto Protocol). These flexibility mechanisms are market-based, cost-effective tools that provide alternatives to domestic GHG emissions reduction projects.[1]

In theory, the use of these tools can be less expensive per tonne of carbon reduced or sequestered than domestic projects.[2] In addition, the CDM has the potential to provide benefits far beyond climate change mitigation, by providing less developed countries with solutions to environmental problems, improved resource efficiency, access to technology and knowledge that might not otherwise be available, and financing for projects.[3]

FLEXIBILITY MECHANISMS IN THE KYOTO AGREEMENT

JI — allows an Annex I country or corporation to receive emissions reduction credits when it helps finance projects that reduce net emissions in another industrialized country, including those with economies in transition. Only emission reductions accruing during the period 2008-2012 are eligible.

CDM — allows governments or private entities in 34 countries with GHG emission targets (Annex I) to fund GHG emissions reduction projects in countries without targets (Non-annex I) and receive credit in the form of tradable certified emissions reductions. Technology and some sink activities (such as afforestation and reforestation) are included but nuclear power is not.

Emissions Trading — allows companies to trade certified emission reduction credits to fulfill their commitments. Trading must be supplemental to domestic actions for the purpose of meeting quantified emission limitation and reduction commitments. In other words, countries are limited in how much reduction can be achieved through trading.

Four Reasons Why Environmental Managers Would be Interested in CDM and JI as Management Tools

1. CDM and JI provide important options for meeting GHG reduction requirements, so managers responsible for this aspect of corporate obligations must understand them, even if details are still under negotiation. Corporations that can assess possibilities and act on viable opportunities could be at a significant competitive advantage.

2. Involvement in successful CDM and JI projects will allow corporations to gain important international skills, knowledge and experience, and the contacts necessary to form productive international partnerships.

3. Current trading, although unofficial, may be much less expensive than once an official market is established.

4. If companies can prove that voluntary measures will work, more drastic legislation might be avoided.

The Clean Development Mechanism and Joint Implementation are similar, but the details are under negotiation and will likely differ somewhat. For the purposes of this chapter, we pay more attention to CDM, because of its importance for development and the particular requirements of agreements between developed and developing countries. This chapter will not provide the specific information required to carry out a CDM or JI project. Readers should obtain detailed, up-to-date information from authoritative sources if considering participation in such projects.

History

The basic science of the greenhouse effect is well understood and widely accepted.[4] Visible light from the sun passes through the earth's atmosphere. Some of the light is absorbed by the earth's surface, increasing its temperature. A portion of the earth's heat is re-radiated at a lower energy, or longer wavelength. Greenhouse gases such as carbon dioxide, methane, and nitrous oxides absorb this longer wavelength. That absorbed radiation is itself re-emitted and some returns to the earth's surface, creating the greenhouse effect. (See Figure 22.1) Few, if any, scientists disagree with this explanation of why the earth's average global air

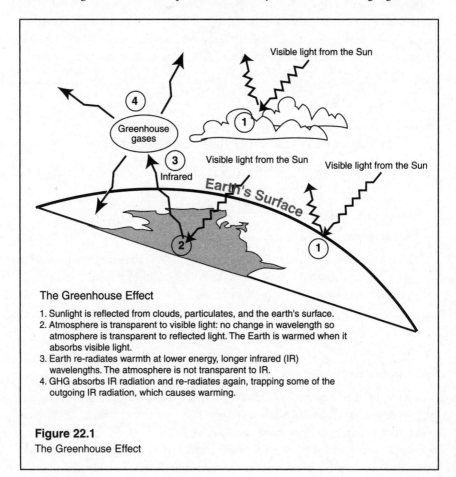

The Greenhouse Effect

1. Sunlight is reflected from clouds, particulates, and the earth's surface.
2. Atmosphere is transparent to visible light: no change in wavelength so atmosphere is transparent to reflected light. The Earth is warmed when it absorbs visible light.
3. Earth re-radiates warmth at lower energy, longer infrared (IR) wavelengths. The atmosphere is not transparent to IR.
4. GHG absorbs IR radiation and re-radiates again, trapping some of the outgoing IR radiation, which causes warming.

Figure 22.1
The Greenhouse Effect

temperature is about 30 degrees Celsius warmer than it would be without the greenhouse effect.

Controversy arises when predictions are made regarding the effect of increased levels of CO_2 on the greenhouse effect. Scientists predict that this increase in atmospheric CO_2 may result in increased global temperatures, or global warming.[5] While there are still some unresolved scientific questions concerning the impacts associated with global warming, the science behind this phenomenon is gaining credibility. There is a general consensus in the international scientific community that an increase in anthropogenic GHGs in the atmosphere could significantly affect global weather patterns, ecosystems, and economic activity. How it will affect these things is still unclear. The 1992 United Nations Framework on Climate Change (UNFCCC or FCCC) defined climate change as a change of climate caused directly or indirectly by human activity that alters the composition of the global atmosphere and which is more than natural climate variability.[6]

Climate change forecasts are difficult to make because of the number of complex subsystems involved (atmosphere, precipitation patterns, oceans, and ocean currents, etc.) and the complexity of the feedback mechanisms within and between subsystems.[7] Predicting changes in climate with confidence is difficult, but predicting that some changes will occur is not.

Even though there are uncertainties in predicting the climates of the future, political momentum and public opinion are motivating action to reduce GHG emissions. The international community is adopting the precautionary principle under which activities that have the potential for serious or irreversible damage can be restricted or prohibited before there is certainty about their effects.[8] Politically, they are moving forward with initiatives to combat global warming at the global level.

CDM and JI provide corporations in Annex I countries with business opportunities that should be given serious consideration in business plans. From a less developed country's perspective, CDM projects could provide significant long-term benefits, provided fair and equitable terms are negotiated at the outset.

Political Context

International Initiatives

International conferences were hosted by the World Meteorological Organization (WMO) to discuss the climate change and variability in the 1970s. Since then, climate change has moved into the forefront of international political negotiations. Table 22.1 summarizes the history of international political events dealing with climate change.

Table 22.1 Summary of Greenhouse Gas Initiatives

Initiative	Date	Description
Intergovernmental Panel on Climate Change (IPCC) two assessment reports	1990, 1995	Confirmed that human activities affect climate and contribute to global warming.
Intergovernmental Negotiating Committee (INC) for a Framework Convention on Climate Change	In session from 1990 to 1995	Committee that negotiated the FCCC for the Earth Summit. The INC had a total of 11 sessions after which the COP (see below) became the presiding body of the FCCC.
United Nations Framework Convention on Climate Change (UNFCCC, FCCC or Convention)	Came into force March 21, 1994	Set up by the INC; signed by 170 countries at the Earth Summit in Rio de Janeiro in 1992. A general treaty that sets the framework for GHG reductions, but doesn't address strict targets.
Conference of the Parties (COP)	1995-present	The supreme body of the FCCC has met eight times, although not all meetings have produced agreements.
Berlin Mandate	1995	Outcome of COP 1. Began a negotiating process that researched and elaborated policies and set quantifiable emission reduction objectives for discussion at COP 3.
Kyoto Protocol	December 1997	Protocol to the FCCC; signed at COP 3 in Kyoto, Japan. Requires specific emissions reductions below 1990 levels by the period 2008-2012. Created the three flexibility mechanisms: CDM, JI and emission trading.
Buenos Aires Plan of Action	November 1998	Created at COP 4 in Buenos Aires. Includes a work program with priority on determining modalities and procedures for CDM and JI.
Bonn Agreements on the Implementation of the Buenos Aires Plan of Action	November 2000, July 2001	COP 6, Part I met in The Hague, the Netherlands. No agreements were reached. COP 6, Part II was held in Bonn, Germany. Political agreement was reached on key issues under the Buenos Aires Plan of Action.
Marrakesh Accords	November 2001	Developed at COP 7 in Morocco, they provide the operational details of the Kyoto Protocol, including CDM and JI. Members of the executive board of the CDM elected.

The Intergovernmental Panel on Climate Change (IPCC)

In 1988, the Intergovernmental Panel on Climate Change (IPCC) was established in response to growing international concern about the possibility of global warming. The IPCC is an international scientific panel charged specifically with the following three tasks:

1. to assess scientific information related to the various aspects of climate change,

2. to evaluate environmental and socioeconomic impacts arising from climate change, and

3. to formulate realistic response strategies for the management of the greenhouse gas issue.[9]

The IPCC assessment reports of 1990 and 1995 confirm the scientific basis for climate change and conclude that there is a "discernible human influence on the global climate" which destabilizes the globe's ecosystem but did not resolve all uncertainties with regard to climate change science. In 2001, the IPCC issued two major reports on global warming. One confirms that emissions from human activities continue to alter the atmosphere, that global warming had been observed, and that most of it is due to human activities. The second discusses the impacts of increased global temperatures: changes in weather patterns, extreme climate events, the cycling of the seasons, water resources, and ecosystems. The two reports, each over 1000 pages (available in pdf from the IPCC website), had been peer-reviewed by experts, were scrutinized line by line by the IPPC and eventually were accepted unanimously by IPPC delegates.

The IPCC is open to all members of the World Meteorological Organization and the United Nations Environment Programme (UNEP). It has involved large numbers of scientists from all over the world who worked hard to keep the processes transparent and to report widely on the issues, even when it meant that the discussion of uncertainties fuelled the arguments of the critics. It has been put forth as a model for dealing with other global issues involving scientific research and uncertainties.

The Framework Convention on Climate Change (FCCC)

One key philosophy of the United Nations Framework Convention on Climate Change is the use of the precautionary principle, where lack of scientific certainty cannot be used to postpone cost-effective measures to prevent serious or irreversible environmental damage.[10]

The Convention gained widespread international recognition in 1992 when it was signed by 170 countries at the United Nations Conference on the Environment and Development in Rio de Janeiro. It received its 50th ratification and entered into force in 1994. China and India are not part of the agreement and when further agreement was reached in Bonn in July 2001, the U.S.A. dropped out of the negotiations. Therefore, three of the largest emitters of GHGs are not included.

The Kyoto Protocol

After negotiations in Kyoto (COP 3, December 1997), Annex I countries made commitments to reductions in GHG emissions. The Protocol was signed by 84 countries and, when ratified, will be legally binding. To come into force, it must be ratified by at least six countries representing more than 55 percent of the total 1990 emissions from industrialized countries.[11] Collectively, the industrialized nations have agreed to reduce their emissions for 2008 to 2012 by 5.2 percent, and demonstrate significant progress by 2005. In reality, the agreement represents a 30 percent reduction if compared to the total GHG emissions expected in 2010.

The agreement reached in Kyoto includes six GHGs: carbon dioxide, methane, nitrous oxide, hydrofluorocarbons, perfluorocarbons, and sulphur hexafluoride.

NATIONAL EMISSION REDUCTION COMMITMENTS	
COUNTRY	NATIONAL COMMITMENT (compared to 1990 levels)
Canada	-6%
United States	-7%*
Switzerland, European Union, many Central and East European states	-8%
Hungary, Poland, and Japan	Stabilize emissions
Norway	+1%
Australia	+8%
Iceland	+10%

*The United States, under President George W. Bush's Administration, pulled out of the Kyoto Protocol in 2001.

While the Protocol provides strict reduction targets for each country, it also provides the tools and flexibility mechanisms to reach those targets, including emissions trading, the CDM, and JI. After much negotiation, the operational details of the Kyoto Protocol were developed in Morocco in November 2001 with the creation of the Marrakesh Accords. The Bush Administration in the U.S.A. has withdrawn from the negotiations.

The Box below illustrates an example of a company that has already started using the CDM.

SUNCOR ENERGY

Suncor Energy Inc. is an international, integrated energy company operating an oil sands plant in Fort McMurray, Alberta; a conventional exploration and production business in western Canada; and a refining and marketing operation in Ontario. Under Canada's Volunteer Challenge and Registry, Suncor has completed a greenhouse gas action plan that details how it will decrease and avoid emissions, domestically and internationally. It includes managing the company's own GHG emissions and their impact; developing renewable sources of energy; supporting environmental and economic research; pursuing domestic offsets; providing constructive public policy input; educating and engaging stakeholders; measuring and reporting on the company's progress; and investing in an international offset project in Belize under the CDM. The project is a carbon sequestration project in the Rio Bravo that is expected to remove at least 400,000 tonnes of CO_2 from the atmosphere — the equivalent of the annual greenhouse gas emissions from about 80,000 cars.[12]

Types of CDM and JI Projects

Sources versus Sinks

Sink projects are land use, land use change, and forestry initiatives (afforestation and reforestation) that sequester or incorporate carbon into plant biomass in soils or terrestrial plants (the sinks). There are some methodological problems related to determining baseline conditions and confirming the amount of CO_2 sequestered. CDM projects are limited to afforestation and reforestation.

Source projects refer to energy projects that decrease CO_2 emissions arising from the use of carbon-based fuels.[13] Projects of this nature include the transfer of technology or improved infrastructure. The partners in these projects may find it easier to establish baselines, confirm CO_2 emission reductions, and meet the additionality criterion discussed below.

The sources versus sinks classification is based on the carbon cycle. The living systems, such as plants, soils, and oceans, are sinks when they absorb CO_2 and sources when they release it. Anthropogenic emissions from human activities, such as fossil fuel use, add carbon to the atmosphere that is in addition to natural processes.[14]

Standards and Criteria

The Marrakesh Accords, developed during COP 7 in Morocco, create modalities and procedures for the flexibility mechanisms. In June 1999, ISO's Technical Committee on Environment Management (TC 207) passed a resolution stating their interest in developing internationally accepted standards. Principles that will help define the scope of the international standards include criteria for project eligibility (measurability, additionality, acceptability, co-benefits, and capacity) and principles for certification.

Project Eligibility

The Kyoto Protocol and the Marrakesh Accords outline criteria to determine which projects are acceptable under the CDM:[15]

- measurability
- additionality
- acceptability
- co-benefits
- capacity

Measurability

Article 12.5(b) of the Kyoto Protocol stipulates that CDM projects must be real, measurable, and have long-term benefits related to the mitigation of climate change. This ensures that the project is combating climate change, and that the carbon credits can be verified and certified. All projects must include a monitoring plan.

Additionality

Article 12.5(c) of the Protocol states that CDM projects shall provide emission reductions that are additional to any that would otherwise have occurred through business as usual. The emissions without the project are termed the baseline scenario. The certified emission reduction (CER) credit is the difference between the baseline scenario and the CDM project emission levels.[16] The Protocol also states that projects must be funded outside the Official Development Agency, sometimes referred to as financial additionality.

Acceptability

Both the host country and the investor must voluntarily accept the project according to Article 12.5(a) and reaffirmed in the Marrakesh Accords. Each participant should decide if the project meets national and corporate objectives, using tools such as Environmental Impact Assessment and risk assessment.

Co-benefits

The CDM is being promoted as a win-win scenario. In addition to emissions reduction or sequestration, projects should benefit the host country in other areas, such as maintaining biodiversity, decreasing local pollution, building infrastructure, training in skills, creating jobs, and providing access to advanced technologies. Social and environmental indicators and Environmental Impact Assessment can be used to ensure that projects comply with local legislation, provide co-benefits, and do not cause detrimental impacts.[17] Assessing co-benefits also guarantees that emissions are not simply being displaced to another area (leakage), thereby resulting in no net decrease of carbon. For example, logging stopped in one location can result in deforestation of another area.[18]

Capacity

The capacity of a CDM project indicates the level of capabilities the stakeholders have to complete the project. Ascertaining the technical and management skills of those who will undertake the project, the financial resources, the level of infrastructure and technology available, the need for education and training, and the ability to demonstrate emission reductions can determine if the project will succeed.[19]

Validation and Certification

Validation is the independent evaluation of a project by a designated entity to ensure it meets CDM requirements. Once it is validated, a project can be registered with the CDM Executive Board. Registration is required before a project can be verified and certified, and certified emission reductions can be issued. The Marrakesh Accords stipulate the requirements for validation of a project, including approval of a project design document that outlines baseline methodology, additionality, environmental impacts, stakeholder comments, and monitoring plans. The validation report is then submitted to the Executive Board for additional comment, approval, and registration.

Certification of the project occurs after the project has been registered. A designated operational entity verifies the monitored emission reductions from the project. To be an effective environmental management tool, certification of emission reductions must be standardized and harmonized. To maintain credibility, annual progress reports, based on monitoring programs that include the quantification of emissions as well as the environmental, social, and economic effects of the project, should also be submitted to the Executive Board. Stringent certification, monitoring, and verification will ensure limited liability for the investor and host in a project.[20]

Incentives and Benefits

Annex I (industrialized) countries, or organizations within those countries, may choose to invest in CDM/JI for many reasons:[21]

- to gain economic benefits,
- to receive early credit against other countries,
- to prevent the predicted environmental impacts of global warming,
- to prevent potential negative economic consequences of global warming,
- to demonstrate that voluntary programs to reduce GHG emissions are viable,

- to reduce a greater volume of CO_2 per dollar invested than domestic projects could achieve,
- to assist with corporate reputation, and
- to fulfill a moral obligation.

Without binding targets, non-Annex I (developing) countries may find less incentive than Annex I countries to participate in projects. Some countries, such as those that may be most adversely affected by global warming (e.g., coastal and small, island states) have a large direct incentive to participate in climate change initiatives.[22] Most developing countries, however, are more concerned with "feeding their children, than with protecting their grandchildren from potential global warming."[23] Sensitive, properly planned and implemented projects offer benefits in addition to climate change mitigation that may appeal to the host country. Potential co-benefits are perhaps the greatest incentive for host countries to participate.

Table 22.2 CDM Potential Co-Benefits for Developing Countries

Environmental
- reduce air pollution caused by old technologies
- transfer of clean technologies that leapfrog the inefficient phase of industrialization
- reduce water pollution and soil erosion caused by deforestation and unsustainable forestry or agriculture practices
- restore degraded lands
- conserve biodiversity
- improve waste management
- support country's goals of sustainable development

Economic
- attract foreign direct investment in priority sectors of host country's economy
- transfer of clean, cost-effective, state-of-the-art technologies and know-how
- improve energy efficiency
- create additional jobs and expertise (capacity building)

Social
- improve access to more efficient technologies
- support community-based livelihoods through CDM power and forestry projects
- improve health through cleaner air
- build capacity in universities and technical schools
- gain access to advanced technologies and related skills and knowledge

Political
- participate meaningfully in emissions reductions
- advance national goals
- improve trade opportunities
- satisfy international commitments

Source: adapted from Trexler and Kosloff, 1998.

THREE DEVELOPMENT STRATEGIES

1. Buy old, dirty, and inefficient technology that has low capital costs but high operation and maintenance costs. Older technologies also have high environmental and social costs and high cleanup costs in the future. Therefore, they often would not meet the goals of sustainable development or pass an Environmental Impact Assessment and would be unlikely to meet conditions to qualify for emission reduction credits.

2. Buy current technology that has moderate costs and is reliable. These technologies have reasonable efficiencies but do have some long-term environmental and social impacts and related cleanup costs. However, they might not meet the additionality criterion for emission reduction credits.

3. Use CDM to gain access to advanced technologies that would not otherwise be available. Advanced technologies would have superior efficiencies and low environmental and social impacts. This would be a superior development strategy and would meet the additionality criterion for emission reduction credits.

Barriers Facing CDM/JI as Environmental Management Tools

CDM/JI are gaining momentum as a pair of emerging environmental management tools, but there are still barriers to success including[24]

- political uncertainty,
- moral and ethical opposition,
- uncertainty on credit for early action,
- uncertainty about future value of emission reduction credits and operation of the market,
- reduced pressure for research and development,
- lack of binding targets for developing countries,
- technical issues (e.g., baseline, quantification of sinks),
- lack of clarity regarding sustainable development objectives,
- poor portrayal and description of CDM to non-Annex I countries,
- lack of skills and knowledge in host countries,
- lack of skills and knowledge in Annex I countries, and
- opposition by some countries and corporations to any action on global warming.

Political Uncertainty

Like any new international environmental initiative, CMD/JI face uncertainty and opposition. The detailed methodologies for determination of baseline emission levels and quantification of emission reductions have yet to be agreed upon. The qualifications for, and training of, those measuring and auditing emission reductions must be established. Ratification of the protocol is in question if the countries with the largest emissions refuse to be parties to it. To be effective, capacity building in all countries is essential. Uncertainty and opposition, however, have not stopped some organizations from being proactive and investing in projects, including trading of emission credits in experimental markets, in anticipation of receiving credit toward their emission reduction targets when those are finally established.

Moral and Ethical Opposition

Philosophically, there is concern that CDM/JI could become tools for maintaining the unsustainable lifestyles of affluent societies at the expense of other countries. CDM projects could enable the North to continue using three times its share of the atmosphere. CDM could allow industrialized countries to buy their way out of their responsibilities for emissions reduction by exploiting the cheap resources of developing countries.[25]

Reduced Pressure for Research and Development

There is a concern that CDM/JI projects could stop the adoption of needed domestic improvements in the energy efficiency of industrialized countries by reducing pressure to invest in research and development. If fast and inexpensive offsets are available in other countries, there is less need to develop solutions at home. This concern has been reduced by limiting the amount of emission reduction that can be obtained through CDM/JI, and by stressing that these projects must be supplemental to domestic action.

Lack of Binding Targets

The lack of binding emission reduction targets for non-Annex I countries imposes another barrier on the success of CDM, both as a management tool and as an effective initiative to reduce global greenhouse gas emissions. Annex I countries that have binding targets could be at an economic disadvantage in the long-term. Industries that rely heavily on carbon-emitting technology or substantial energy will become more expensive and less competitive in Annex I countries. As developing countries advance, develop, and participate in CDM projects, they have a temporary competitive advantage. In the future, host countries may be reluctant to accept GHG reduction targets if that would threaten the CDM projects.

Technical Issues

Technical issues currently plague CDM/JI projects, for example, quantification of the baseline scenarios and sinks; however, they are slowly being resolved.[26]

Lack of Clarity Regarding Sustainable Development Objectives

The Kyoto Protocol stipulates that CDM projects shall assist developing countries in achieving sustainable development. This is a vague objective that is open to interpretation.

Poor Portrayal of CDM to Non-Annex I Countries

Host countries need clarification of the benefits CDM/JI projects. In the case of CDM, this is especially true regarding the promise of sustainable development. The Chair of G-77/China, Ambassador Arizal Effendi, has stated that sustainable development needs to be spelled out in dollars and cents, in terms of "poverty alleviation and job creation."[27]

Links to Other Tools

To be successful as environmental management tools, CDM/JI require the use of other tools to aid in implementation and operation.

Environmental Impact Assessment

The Marrakesh Accords stipulate that project participants must submit documentation of the environmental impacts of the project activity, including transboundary effects. If any impacts are considered significant, then an Environmental Impact Assessment must be conducted in accordance with host country procedures. The EIA will assure the partners of the benefits of the projects and that direct and indirect costs will be acceptable.

Strategic Planning and Management

Corporations must track the development of CDM/JI and develop the skills and knowledge necessary to make strategic decisions about when, where, and how to become involved.

Environmental Accounting and Environmental Auditing

Accounting and auditing must be used to calculate and verify the baseline and CO_2 emissions, costs and benefits, and provide feedback on success or failure.

Environmental Reporting

Environmental Reporting on CO_2 emission reduction and other benefits and costs must be used to inform the partners on the project's progress, or lack thereof. Reports must be used in the independent verification process and be submitted to the Secretariat of the Executive Board of COP.

CDM/JI are evolving and have the potential to be effective mechanisms for managing greenhouse gas emissions, but not in the current form. Several logistical

issues must be resolved for CDM/JI to become practical and mutually beneficial environmental management tools, including
- an effective emissions trading system,
- transparent and cost-effective carbon quantification models, and
- training and certification of auditors and other professionals.

Decisions on these issues will largely determine the effectiveness of CDM/JI as tools to manage greenhouse gas emissions and support sustainable development. Conceivably, CDM/JI could produce a huge bureaucracy and plenty of red tape but fail to reduce emissions significantly. Not only would the creation of a bureaucracy be costly, it would deter corporations and other organizations from investing in projects.

Non-Annex I (Developing) Countries

As negotiations on flexibility mechanisms proceed, developing countries have two tasks that are of paramount importance: negotiating the agreements so that they gain acceptable advantages, and developing the capacity to enter into and implement partnerships. Developing countries must consider five factors during negotiations on CDM projects:

1. Will an EIA properly demonstrate that the benefits are significant and that the negative impacts are acceptable?

2. Will partners and participating governments ensure access to financing and advanced technologies consistent with sophisticated development strategies?

3. Will the partnership facilitate development of infrastructure and capacity for essential education and training so that developing country partners can meet their obligations?

4. Employees responsible for running CDM projects, who have gained the required skills, knowledge, and experience, will have career opportunities that could lead to high employee turnover. Therefore, the developing country partner must build the educational capacity to fill those positions with new, qualified individuals.

5. Developing countries may eventually be required to meet emissions reduction requirements. If all the easy and profitable reductions have been taken by CDM projects, how could this affect the ability to meet obligations in the longer term?

Environmental managers must keep abreast of negotiations on flexibility mechanisms, so that they can assess opportunities for cost-effective ways to meet emission reductions and develop productive partnerships in developing countries. As negotiations lead to more concrete agreements on technical issues, managers must be informed and prepared to decide when and where to get involved.

Some corporations have already made strategic decisions to start projects in anticipation of the advantages. When such strategic decisions have been made and early action taken, managers must clearly understand the requirements of their partners, and be prepared to work hard, often under challenging conditions, to make the partnerships successful.

Recommended Further Reading

Baumert, K., N. Kete, and C. Figueres. "Designing the Clean Development Mechanism to Meet the Needs of a Broad Range of Interests." *World Resources Institute Climate Notes* August (2000).

Intergovernmental Panel on Climate Change (IPCC). *Scientific Assessment of Climate Change: The Policymaker's Summary of the Report of Working Group I of the Intergovernmental Panel on Climate Change.* Geneva: World Meteorological Organization/United Nations Environment Programme, 1990.

López, Ramón. *Incorporating Developing Countries into Global Efforts for Greenhouse Gas Reduction.* RFF Climate Issue Brief #16. Washington DC: Resources for the Future, January, 1999.

The Marrakesh Accords and the Marrakesh Declaration, 2001, available on the UNFCCC website: <www.unfccc.int>

Stewart, R., D. Anderson, M. Amin Aslam, C. Eyre, G. Jones, P. Sands, M. Stuart, and F. Yamin. *Building International Public-Private Partnerships under the Kyoto Protocol: Technical, Financial and Institutional Issues.* UNCTAD/GDS/GFSB/Misc., 7. New York: United Nations, 2000.

Trexler, M.C., and L. Kosloff. "The 1997 Kyoto Protocol: What Does It Mean for Project-based Climate Change Mitigation?" *Mitigation and Adaptation Strategies for Global Change* 3 (1998): pp.1-58.

Websites

Center for International Climate and Environmental Research: <http://www.cicero.uio.no/index_e.asp>

Government of Canada's climate change site: <http://climatechange.gc.ca>

International Institute for Sustainable Development: <www.iisd.ca>

IPCC website: <www.ipcc.ch>

Pembina Institute for Appropriate Development: <www.pembina.org>

Tiempo Climate Cyberlibrary: <www.cru.uea.ac.uk/tiempo/>

United Nations Framework Convention on Climate Change: <www.unfccc.int>

Voluntary Challenge & Registry Inc. <www.vcr-mvr.ca>

World Business Council for Sustainable Development: <www.wbcsd.org>

CHAPTER

ECOSYSTEM-BASED MANAGEMENT

Michael S. Quinn, University of Calgary

"[T]he future of much of the biosphere will depend on managing large
areas using an integrated approach that recognizes human populations
as having a keen interest in ensuring the continuing productivity of the
ecosystems within which they live. Such an approach will have to meet
local needs, maintain or restore ecosystem integrity and conserve biodiversity, simultaneously." [1]

Introduction

Ecosystem-Based Management (EBM) is a dominant emerging philosophy for
natural resource management.[2] It is born of the recognition that reductionist
approaches to natural resource management have largely failed. An ecosystem
approach entails a more holistic view of natural and social systems and calls for an
integration of traditionally disparate fields of study. A significant characteristic of
EBM is the focus on the long-term sustainability of systems (ecological, economic, social) rather than outputs. Furthermore, EBM approaches are bounded by
these (eco)systems and not by existing administrative boundaries. EBM recognizes
that ecosystems are both biophysical systems and sociocultural systems. The successful implementation of EBM will depend on the management of social,
economic, and institutional factors. In the context of this book, Ecosystem-Based
Management is less of an emerging environmental management tool and more of
a context or framework in which Environmental Management Systems (EMSs)
will be required to operate. It is expected, for example, that an organization pursuing an EBM approach is also likely to have (or be developing) an EMS.

Ecosystem-Based Management is an evolving set of constructs. The main purpose here is to provide some discussion of the range of thought and activity that
circumscribes this dynamic, evolving field of theory and practice. The first section will provide the historical context and the theoretical roots of ecosystem

management. Next, the primary schools of thought and common themes of EBM will be identified and discussed. Finally, some issues and challenges arising from current EBM implementation will be presented.

> Definition: Ecosystem-Based Management is an approach to guiding human activity using collaborative, interdisciplinary, and adaptive methods with the long-term goal of sustaining desired future conditions of ecologically bounded areas that, in turn, support healthy, sustainable communities.

Historical Roots of Ecosystem-Based Management

The modern conception of an ecosystem approach is often attributed to Aldo Leopold. Much of his philosophy is espoused in two short, but poignant, essays, "Round River" and "The Land Ethic."[3] Leopold calls for an ethic that treats the land as an organism and humans as an integral part of the biotic community. "In short, a land ethic changes the role of *Homo sapiens* from conqueror of the land-community to plain member and citizen of it."[4] Leopold goes on to stress that our relationship to the land implies not only privileges, but also obligations. The obligations included maintaining intact ecosystems. In Leopold's words, "To keep every cog and wheel is the first rule of intelligent tinkering."[5] Leopold's call for citizens to "think like a mountain" may have planted the seeds of an ecosystem approach, but it would be nearly half a century until anything approaching Leopold's vision was operationalized.

One of the earliest attempts to explicitly employ EBM occurred in the Great Lakes region of North America. The Great Lakes Research Advisory Board advocats an ecosystem-based approach to ecological management in a 1978 special report to the International Joint Commission. The ensuing Great Lakes Water Quality Agreement entrenches the idea of the ecosystem approach in managing the Great Lakes environs.[6] Globally, the World Conservation Strategy[7] implicitly identifies the need for EBM and, subsequently, Agenda 21[8] explicitly recognizes the requirement for EBM within an overall approach to sustainable development and the maintenance of biological diversity.

The emergence of conservation biology as a new meta-discipline[9] and the growth of landscape ecology in North America[10] have been significant catalysts in the development of EBM. Both of these fields arose in response to the recognition that environmental problems were multidimensional, multi-scalar, and required novel integrated approaches to work towards resolution.

Agee and Johnson crystallize much of the ensuing discussion arising from managers, planners, policy-makers, and scientists in the first book-length treatment of ecosystem management.[11] In *Ecosystem Management for Parks and*

Wilderness, the proceedings of one of the first conferences to be held under the banner of EBM, the authors effectively combine a dynamic pattern-and-process view of nature with the complex social milieu that provides the context for resource management. Their work marks the beginning of a flood of EBM books, papers, and studies. Ecosystem-Based Management has now been legislated or adopted in formal policy by a broad suite of government agencies and private corporations around the world.[12]

A Spectrum of Views on an Emerging Approach

Defining Ecosystem-Based Management

Published attempts to define and describe Ecosystem-Based Management circumscribe a wide spectrum of thought. Grumbine suggests four reasons why a simple definition is not currently possible:[13]

- Defining any term is a political act, an act of power that requires negotiation of political questions.
- Ecosystem-Based Management challenges societal myths and assumptions because it changes the management focus from resource extraction to ecosystem protection.
- New ways of thinking are challenging and difficult and thus take time.
- It is difficult to define complex problems.

Furthermore, resource allocation decisions are strongly value-laden. Therefore, most attempts to provide a definition for ecosystem management are considered fuzzy or incomplete. The following are some working definitions of ecosystem management:

- involves regulating internal ecosystem structure and function, plus inputs and outputs, to achieve socially desirable conditions;[14]
- integrating scientific knowledge of ecological relationships within a complex sociopolitical and values framework toward the general goal of protecting native ecosystem integrity over the long term;[15]
- management driven by explicit goals, executed by policies, protocols, and practices, and made adaptable by monitoring and research based on our best understanding of the ecological interactions and processes necessary to sustain ecosystem composition, structure, and function;[16]
- Ecosystem-Based Management attempts to regulate our use of ecosystems so that we can benefit from them while at the same time modifying our impacts on them so that basic ecosystem functions are preserved;[17]
- the maintenance of sustainable ecosystems while providing for a wider array of uses, values, products, and services from the land to an increasingly diverse public;[18]

- skillful manipulation of ecosystems to satisfy specified societal goals;[19]
- a goal-driven approach to environmental management that is at a scale compatible with natural processes; is cognizant of nature's time frames; recognizes social and economic viability within functioning ecosystems; and is realized through effective partnerships among private, local, state, tribal, and federal interests. Ecology is the supporting science for EM. EM considers the environment as a complex system functioning as a whole, not as a collection of parts, and it recognizes that people and their social and economic needs are part of the whole. EM therefore draws on a collaboratively developed vision of desired future conditions that integrates ecological, economic, and social factors. The overall goal of EM is to maintain and improve the sustainability and native biological diversity of terrestrial and aquatic, including marine, ecosystems while supporting human needs.[20]

Notwithstanding the definitional difficulties, surveys of the EBM literature have identified common threads. Grumbine was the first to identify a suite of elements or themes characterizing EBM (see Table 23.1).[21]

Table 23.1 Ten Dominant Themes of Ecosystem Management

Hierarchical context: The need for system focus at multiple scales. This is part of systems, contextual, or big-picture thinking.
Ecological boundaries: Management at ecologically appropriate scales that utilize ecosystem rather than political boundaries. This has also been called a place-based approach.
Ecological integrity: Maintaining viable populations of native species, ecosystem representation, maintenance of ecological processes, long-term management, and human use with constraints.
Data collection: More research and better organization and use of existing data.
Monitoring: Tracking and assessing results of management activities in an ongoing feedback loop.
Adaptive management: Scientific information is provisional and incomplete — need for a commitment to a learning process for flexibility in the face of uncertainty.
Inter-agency cooperation: Cooperation of agencies and individuals involved is required.
Organizational change: The structure of land management agencies requires change to work with ecosystem boundaries and ideas.
Humans embedded in nature: Humans are both agents of ecological change and participants in the effects of change. Humans are part of the ecosystem.
Values: Human values play a significant role in ecosystem management goals.
Source: adapted from Grumbine, 1994.

A subsequent paper based on feedback and re-evaluation of the initial themes led Grumbine to conclude that the ten themes he proposes were generally accepted by academics and practitioners in the field.[22]

A comprehensive review of Ecosystem-Based Management prepared by the Ecological Society of America resulted in the identification of eight characteristic elements (see Table 23.2).[23]

Table 23.2. Elements of Ecosystem Management

Sustainability: Intergenerational sustainability as a precondition, rather than focus on deliverables.
Goals: Specific future processes and outcome goals for sustainability.
Sound ecological models and understanding: Founded upon ecological research at all levels of organization.
Complexity and connectedness: Recognition that biodiversity and system complexity contribute to resistance, resilience, and adaptability.
The dynamic character of ecosystems: Change and evolution are necessary.
Context and scale: Management requires attention to multiple temporal and spatial scales.
Humans as ecosystem components: Active role of humans in achieving sustainability.
Adaptability and accountability: Ecosystem management is an experimental approach that requires research, monitoring, and adaptation.
Source: adapted from Christensen et al, 1996.

A comparison of the themes and elements in Table 23.1 and Table 23.2 shows considerable correspondence of ideas. For the purposes of this chapter, the elements that distinguish EBM from other approaches to natural resource management can be distilled into four primary characteristics:

• ecosystem boundaries,
• ecosystem sustainability,
• adaptive management, and
• human dimensions.

Ecosystem Boundaries

"Ecosystems (classifications) are human constructs that only have value if they assist us in understanding complex biological-socioeconomic systems and aid us in conserving our resource base while meeting societal expectations."[24]

The ecosystem concept has existed and evolved within the field of ecology since Sir Arthur Tansley first employed the term is 1935.[25] Ecosystems are defined as open systems comprising living and non-living components and the physical, chemical, and biological processes that take place between them.[26] By definition, this is a holistic concept that requires an interdisciplinary approach to understanding. The ecosystem concept can be applied to demarcate naturally occurring thresholds or boundaries between physical areas. For the purposes of natural resource management, ecosystems are most often described as landscape-scale functional units with somewhat arbitrary, but defensible, boundaries (e.g. watersheds). Bounding the system of concern defines the kinds of management approaches that are possible. The significant change in pursuing an EBM approach is the transcendence of administrative boundaries that rarely have any correspondence to ecological reality. The upshot is that an EBM approach will necessarily require inter-jurisdictional collaboration at many levels.

Ecosystem Sustainability

Perhaps the most important central idea of EBM is sustainability. What makes an ecosystem approach significantly different from single and multiple-use approaches to resource management is the emphasis on exactly what is to be sustained. Rather than focus on the sustained yield of some output, EBM aims at long-term sustainability of the ecological system that produced those products or services. Sustainability that is premised on maintaining both composition and process must recognize the need to embrace the dynamic nature of ecosystems.[27] Ecosystems are characterized by constant change, but within a natural range of variation. The term ecological integrity has been used to describe the properties of an ecosystem that maintains its organizational structure and function in the face of perturbations.[28] The aim of EBM is to manage human use of ecosystems so as not to impair ecological integrity, thus ensuring the perpetual capacity of the system to sustain human use. Finally, sustainability requires not only the anthropocentric consideration of ecosystem goods and services necessary for intergenerational human requirements[29] but also a view of nature for its own sake.[30]

Adaptive Management: Management in the Face of Uncertainty

Ecosystem-Based Management is fraught with uncertainty. Humility and a commitment to learning are the hallmarks of an EBM approach. Egler suggested that ecosystems are not only more complicated than we understand, they are more complicated than we can ever understand.[31] Therefore, humility dictates the application of the precautionary principle which states that it is better to be safe than sorry. In an EBM context, this means not subjecting the entire landscape to one kind of management, but maintaining control areas such as protected areas and biosphere reserves. However, it will always be necessary to take some management action with limited information. The approach to dealing with uncertainty in EBM is known as adaptive environmental management, or simply adaptive management.[32]

Adaptive management is an approach that is best characterized as learning by doing. It entails

- explicitly recognizing that there is uncertainty about the outcome of management activities;
- deliberately designing management policies or plans to increase understanding about the system and reveal the best way of meeting objectives;
- carefully implementing the policy or plan;
- monitoring the response of indicators;
- analyzing the outcomes, considering the objectives and predictions; and
- incorporating results into future decisions.[33]

Adaptive management is a commitment to continuous improvement. In the words of one EBM analyst, "the best way to implement ecosystem management may be to learn from past mistakes and also systematically make some new but different ones."[34]

Human Dimensions

At the core of EBM is the realization that humans are members, not just spectators, in ecosystems. Humans both influence and are influenced by ecosystem processes. Williams points out "ecosystem management, whether it is understood by biologists or social scientists, is really about contextually sensitive (spatial and temporal) management of a bio-social system."[35] The inclusion of human dimensions calls for a reconsideration of institutional frameworks. Successful EBM is predicated on cooperation across administrative and disciplinary boundaries. This may be one of the greatest challenges to the ecosystem approach because it requires learning new skills, adopting more inclusive policies, and may necessitate reforming existing management agencies and academic frameworks. At a minimum, it calls for a shift of attention from inward to outward and across rigid boundaries.

If Ecosystem-Based Management is to be part of a transition to a new paradigm, then central to our understanding must be the notion that our focus should be the management of human actions in an ecosystem context. In other words, it is not ecosystems that require management, but people. Hence, ecosystem management, the term most often used in the literature, is really a misnomer because it obfuscates this distinction. The author of this chapter chooses to use the term Ecosystem-Based Management in an attempt to make the management intent explicit. As Orr explains:

> "...it is humans that need managing, not the planet. This is more than
> semantic hairsplitting. Planetary [ecosystem] management has a nice
> ring to it. It places the blame on the planet, not on human stupidity,

arrogance, and ecological malfeasance, which do not have a nice ring... Management is mechanical not organic, and we like mechanical things: they reinforce our belief that we are in control.... It is a mistake to believe that we face only problems solvable by painless market adjustments and better gadgets, not dilemmas that will require wisdom, goodness, and a rationality of a higher sort."[36]

Philosophies and Values

Although there is consensus on the broad principles of EBM, there are differences in how the principles are operationalized. These differences are indicative of significantly different philosophical underpinnings and values. Grumbine is representative of a biocentric to ecocentric philosophy that views the goal of maintaining natural functional ecosystems (ecological integrity) as paramount.[37] This perspective sees humans as a part of ecosystems and dependent on the maintenance of those systems. Christensen et al portray a more anthropocentric view that maintains the primacy of maximizing human resource use within a set of ecological constraints and wider social considerations.[38] Grumbine's view is consonant with a significant paradigm shift or revolution in natural resource management. The latter is akin to an evolution of the existing paradigm towards more enlightened multiple-use management and construes ecosystem management as more of a "magical theory"[39] that promises what Stanley suggests is impossible — that we can have our cake and eat it too.[40]

These differences explain how EBM has been accepted in principle by such a wide array of interests. For example, it has been suggested that when environmental groups hear the term ecosystem management, they hear ecosystem; when development and commodity interests hear the term, they hear management.[41] Rather than viewing these perspectives as polar opposites, they are better understood as a continuum of ideas and approaches to EBM that is shifting management in a positive direction. In an articulate explication of this continuum, Yaffee provides a typology of EBM approaches and concludes, "the term itself (ecosystem management) is not sacrosanct, but the direction it implies is. We need to move management toward more sustainable and ecologically sensitive approaches, and that will come from shifting management practice across the multiple faces of ecosystem management."[42] Hence, EBM must be understood as a stage in the continuing development of societal values and priorities and not an end in itself.[43]

Such a shift in the way we have practiced management will require the development of new interdisciplinary theory. Part of the challenge is in a more integrated approach to problem solving that brings together social and natural scientists around common themes.[44] It remains to be seen whether or not

Ecosystem-Based Management can develop into a truly different way of interacting with the rest of the natural world. In the meantime, practitioners continue to implement programs using ecosystem-based concepts, and evidence suggests that they are achieving some level of success.[45] An examination of these efforts illustrates the emergence of a consistent set of general characteristics and the emergence of an EBM process. The following section highlights this process and the lessons learned from EBM efforts to date.

Ecosystem-Based Management in Practice

A Model for Ecosystem-Based Management

Ecosystem-Based Management can be implemented through a sequential series of management steps with several feedback loops for adjustment and improvement. Figure 23.1 provides a simplified model of this process.

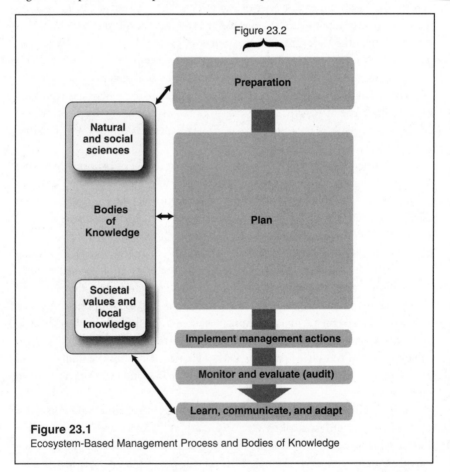

Figure 23.1
Ecosystem-Based Management Process and Bodies of Knowledge

Figure 23.2 provides further details of the Ecosystem-Based Management process.

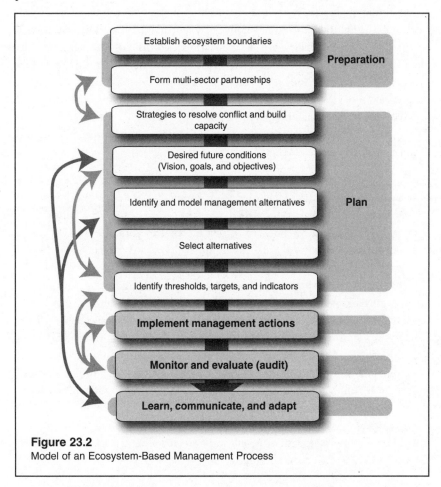

Figure 23.2
Model of an Ecosystem-Based Management Process

A key element of the process is the continuous inclusion of both scientific information and public values and knowledge. It begins with a determination of ecosystem boundaries then the formation of partnerships from the agencies and stakeholders that occur within the boundaries. The success of such partnerships relies on ongoing attention to building capacity and striving to resolve conflict. These collaborative unions will finalize the ecosystem boundaries and then take on the onerous foundational effort of expressing a vision for desired future ecosystem conditions. This may be the most difficult stage in an EBM process and adequate time must be devoted to achieving some level of comfort among all the participants. The desired future conditions should be an articulation of societal needs and wants balanced against the long-term capacity of the ecosystem to maintain ecological integrity.

Attaining the desired types and intensities of human use can then be facilitated by modeling and developing of management alternatives. The selection of alternatives must be made with a set of criteria consistent with achieving the desired future conditions. The next step is the identification of objective measures (thresholds, targets, and indicators) to evaluate management outcomes. Implementation of actions is then initiated along with careful monitoring and feedback programs. Evaluation of the monitoring data should drive a continuous learning and improvement process. Communication of outcomes and lessons learned must take place among all participating parties.

Ecosystem-Based Management and Environmental Management Systems have a great deal to learn from each other. EBM originated in the study of ecosystems affected by industrial activities, whereas corporate EMS arose from the need to comply with environmental laws and regulations and to improve economic efficiency by increasing the efficiency of resource use. The different origins and evolutionary processes produced complementary strengths and weaknesses. The strengths of EMS are the standards such as ISO 14001 or GEMI and the feedback mechanisms on the success or failure of achieving goals and objectives, which lead to continual improvement. Feedback is provided through a standardized process of environmental audits, including specific qualifications for the professionals doing the audits. EMS weaknesses are the failure to deal at all with natural areas controlled by organizations and weak stakeholder involvement. EBM is very strong on understanding and protecting ecosystem integrity and in stakeholder involvement but is very weak on credible standardized processes and feedback on goals and objectives.

EMSs have evolved from a single bottom line preoccupation with costs and compliance to a triple bottom line approach and corporate social responsibility. Continued evolution could be based upon learning from EBM how to manage natural areas and green spaces.

EBM's focus on ecology has evolved to include stakeholder involvement in setting goals and objectives and institutional change. EBM can improve by learning how to develop a credible but flexible standardized approach with specific requirements for feedback, especially by replacing informal monitoring with a formal, standardized auditing system.

Projects espousing the ideas of EBM have existed for over a decade. A growing number of books and papers document the successes and challenges of these projects through interviews with EBM practitioners and participants as well as through detailed case study analyses (see for example: Brush et al.,[46] Pirot et al.,[47] Quinn and Theberge,[48] SNEP Science Team 1996,[49] Yaffee et al.[50]). An examination of these reviews allows for some general conclusions to be drawn about this dynamic, evolving field.

What Have We Learned From Implementation?

Evaluations of Ecosystem-Based Management invariably mention the importance of collaboration and inter-agency cooperation. Successful initiatives devote a significant amount of time and resources to establishing partnerships at the outset. Such partnerships include not only management professionals, but also the general public and stakeholder groups. The participation of the public and/or communities is essential to making an EBM approach place-based. This collaborative and participatory emphasis facilitates the development of common goals. The presence of a key group of individuals or champions to drive the EBM process within collaborative approaches is also frequently cited as essential for success. Whereas natural resource management has historically relied more on (natural) scientific and economic information to drive decision making, experience in EBM suggests that sociocultural, value-based input is at least (and perhaps more) important to effective management. There is a need for more research into the human dimensions of EBM.

Research into human dimensions of EBM is not the only topic requiring more research. Other topics include: understanding the dynamics of large ecosystems over long periods of time, development of effective indicators, and better implementation of EBM.

Some of the barriers that are most commonly mentioned in evaluating EBM initiatives include

- lack of required resources (money, time, personnel),
- lack of common vision and goals,
- inter-agency conflict,
- organized opposition,
- lack of data, and
- lack of long-term political commitment and pressure for development.

Not surprisingly, many of the impediments to progress identified by EBM practitioners could be lessened through greater attention to involving stakeholders and developing a strong support constituency.

Conclusion

Ecosystem-Based Management is a long-term process involving goal setting, decision making and action directed towards the long-term sustainability and ecological health of the land and all its communities. Ecosystem-Based Management is not currently a prescription or single set of principles. It is a set of constructs that has been evolving over the last decade, but has its roots in earlier notions of stewardship and a land ethic. Because ecosystem management is in a nascent stage of development, there is no general agreement on one operational definition. The value in a currently fuzzy definition is that it is broad enough to provide an umbrella for multiple interests with overlapping objectives across the landscape. Success is dependent on dedication to an adaptive approach and more comprehensive theoretical development. It may not be perfect, but the evolving realm of Ecosystem-Based Management may be the best hope for ecological management, now and in the future.

Recommended Further Reading

Christensen, N. L., A. M. Bartuska, J. H. Brown, S. Carpenter, C. D'Antonio, R. Francis, J. F. Franklin, J. A. MacMahon, R. F. Noss, D. J. Parsons, C. H. Peterson, M. G. Turner, R. G. Woodmansee. "The Report of the Ecological Society of America Committee on the Scientific Basis for Ecosystem Management." *Ecological Applications* 6, no.3 (1996): pp. 665-691.

Grumbine, R. E. "What is Ecosystem Management?" *Conservation Biology* 8 (1994): pp. 27-38.

Grumbine, R. E. "Reflections on 'what is ecosystem management?'" *Conservation Biology* 11, no.1 (1997): pp. 41-47.

Lackey, R.T. "Seven Pillars of Ecosystem Management." *Landscape and Urban Planning* 40 (1998): pp. 21-30.

Pirot, J.-Y., P. J. Meynell, and D. Elder., eds. *Ecosystem Management: Lessons from Around the World*. Gland, Switzerland: International Union for Conservation of Nature and Natural Resources, 2000: p.viii.

Yaffee, S.L. "Three Faces of Ecosystem Management." *Conservation Biology* 13, no.4 (1999): pp. 724-727.

Yaffee, S. L., A. F. Phillips, I. C. Frentz, P. W. Hardy, S. M. Maleki, B. E. Thorpe, *Ecosystem Management in the United States: An Assessment of Current Experience*, Washington DC: Island Press, 1996.

Websites

Applegate Partnership: <http://www.mind.net/app/ghome.htm>

Cascade Center for Ecosystem Management: <http://sequoia.fsl.orst.edu/ccem/home.html>

Ecosystem Management in the Great Lakes Region: <http://www.great-lakes.net/envt/air-land/ecomanag.html>

Parks Canada – Ecosystem Management:
    <http://parkscanada.pch.gc.ca/natress/env_con/eco_man/eco_mane.htm>

People's Glossary of Ecosystem Management Terms: <http://www.fs.fed.us/land/emterms.html>

Saskatchewan Environment and Resource Management: <http://www.serm.gov.sk.ca/ecosystem/>

University of Michigan, School of Natural Resources and Environment:
    <http://www.snre.umich.edu/emi>

World Conservation Union (IUCN) Commission on Ecosystem Management:
    <http://www.iucn.org/themes/cem/>

CHAPTER 24

THE NATURAL STEP

Sherry Sian, Inuvialuit Environmental and Geotechnical
and Dixon Thompson

THE NATURAL STEP (TNS) is a Swedish non-profit environmental organization that developed and disseminated The Natural Step framework to foster the coordinated implementation of environmental management tools and systems. The TNS framework leads to sustainable development by coupling resource efficiency with increased profits to diminish environmental degradation by transforming sustainable development from a soft idea into an achievable outcome.

Over the past decade, TNS has expanded into an international network devoted to sustainable development education, dialogue, and continual learning. TNS chapters have been, or are being, established in the U.S.A., the U.K., New Zealand, Australia, France, Brazil, the Netherlands, and Canada. In our discussion, references to The Natural Step indicate the Swedish organization unless otherwise stated.

Brian Nattrass and Mary Altomare provide comprehensive information in *The Natural Step for Business*,[1] which can be augmented through the websites listed at the end of this chapter. Two new books on TNS are now available, published in 2002.[2]

> The Natural Step is a framework for integrating environmental issues into the frame of business to move the company towards sustainable development through backcasting principles of sustainability and a strategic step-by-step process.[3]

Environmental managers should learn about TNS as a framework for the following reasons:

- For organizations interested or committed to the concept of sustainable development, the TNS framework helps sustainable development become more concrete.
- There is a broadly based agreement on the scientific basis for the Four System Conditions and the strong link they provide between environmental science and environmental management.
- The Natural Step is a management framework which is growing in profile and popularity, so environmental managers will have to be able to discuss it and assess it as an option for their company.
- Leading-edge companies are now using The Natural Step framework to structure policies, educational programs, and their Environmental Management System.
- TNS framework may be a criterion during benchmarking excercises.

Environmental managers should learrn about TNS as an organization because:

- The Natural Step has a strong business orientation: it is not an academic organization nor is it involved with governments.
- Corporations are joining and supporting national TNS chapters.

Background and History

Karl-Henrik Robèrt, a pediatric oncologist, founded The Natural Step in Sweden in 1989. Dr. Robèrt witnessed first-hand the connection between human illness and toxins. Aware of the limits for proper cellular function, he was concerned that too much of the environmental debate focused on downstream issues rather than the systemic causes of problems.[4] The systems focus is a point of departure for sustainable development, based on first-order principles for ecological, economic, and social sustainability.

In 1988, Dr. Robèrt wrote a paper describing the prerequisites for a sustainable society and invited 50 Swedish scientists to review it.[5] The report was circulated for comments and after 21 iterations, a consensus report emerged. The report describes the biosphere's functions to show how humans alter natural systems and threaten themselves by deteriorating natural functions — the only solution being a society based upon the principle of sustainable development.

In the early 1990s, Dr. Robèrt collaborated with Swedish physicist John Holmberg to define four System Conditions for sustainability based on the laws of thermodynamics and natural cycles. (According to the laws of thermodynamics, matter cannot be created nor destroyed: it can only change forms. Energy tends to disperse although the mass of reactants equals the mass of products.) The ideas behind the report and the System Conditions for the equitable and sustainable use of ecosystem resources are the foundation for The Natural Step framework. The scientific premises of the framework have yet to be discredited.

THE NATURAL STEP'S FOUR SYSTEM CONDITIONS[6]

1. Substances from the Earth's crust must not systematically increase in the ecosphere.

2. Substances produced by society must not systematically increase in the ecosphere.

3. The physical basis for productivity and diversity of nature must not systematically be diminished.

4. There must be fair and efficient use of resources with respect to meeting human needs.

Dr. Robèrt invited others into a dialogue about sustainability. Joining efforts with artists and scientists, he launched a campaign to share the sustainability principles. This comprehensive education program captured the public's interest.

The endorsement by King Carl Gustaf of Sweden added to the credibility and popularity of the framework and provided legitimacy to The Natural Step as a non-commercial, apolitical and non-religious entity.[7] This attracted the attention of political and business leaders.

GETTING THE WORD OUT

TNS used a multi-pronged approach to share their findings about the requirements for sustainability, including

- mailings of 4.3 million copies of The Natural Step report to Swedish homes and schools;
- concerts and cabarets;
- seminars for business organizations and parliament;
- annual youth parliaments featuring environmental activities in schools;
- mobile exhibitions, including environmental displays at provincial museums;
- training in ecological systems thinking for businesses and local authorities through The Natural Step Environmental Institute;
- the *Swedish National Environmental Encyclopaedia* was written by The Natural Step's scientists and experts;
- annual seminars on the role of business and industry; and
- four annual environmental awards to companies for bold and visionary decisions.

The Natural Step changed how Swedish individuals, schools, communities, and businesses thought about the natural world and sustainability. Municipalities and corporations throughout Sweden are using the framework to modify business practices. IKEA, ICA, Electrolux, Sweden McDonalds, Scandic Hotels, and OK Petroleum championed the use of the framework. North America now boasts its own suite of companies that use the framework, including Interface Inc., Nike, DuPont, and Collins Pine Company.

In Sweden, 20 independent, professional networks for the environment, such as Scientists for the Environment, Doctors for the Environment, and Farmers for the Environment, were initiated and supported by TNS to build consensus on a systematic approach to sustainable development.

TAKING THE NATURAL STEP AROUND THE WORLD

Electrolux

This Swedish-based appliance manufacturer uses the framework as the basis for its environmental vision and policies.[8] Corporate policy states that although environmental performance is important, as an industrial company their goal is to produce and sell products at a profit. The Electrolux strategy is to make environmentally sound products to stimulate the demand for green products to make their enterprise profitable.[9] Electrolux has begun to satisfy System Conditions by recycling 70 per cent of steel recovered during production, reducing hazardous wastes, developing CFC-free refrigerators, reducing water consumption by 30 percent, reducing packaging, and making products from recycled materials.

Interface Inc.

This leading carpet tile manufacturer became the first American company to apply The Natural Step framework. It is committed to a sweeping environmental vision that aims to make Interface the leading name in industrial ecology worldwide, through substance, not words. A systems view of its relationships with suppliers, customers, the market, ecosystems, and the community revealed a heavy reliance on petroleum products in their carpet manufacturing processes. The Evergreen lease agreement was developed to comply with the System Conditions. This agreement ensures that Interface retains ownership of the carpet tile for the duration of its use. When a tile is worn Interface replaces the old tile and recycles it to reduce petroleum use. In effect, Interface is becoming more service-oriented through eco-efficient design.

The sustainability approach has already provided a significant competitive advantage with tangible benefits. Interface enacted their sustainability vision in 1994, after four years of flat growth, and by 1997 showed a 25 percent increase in revenues (from U.S.$800 million to over U.S.$1 billion in sales) and doubled their stock price.

DuPont

This American chemical producer has been using the framework since the 1990s when CEO Edgar Woolard challenged employees to develop cleaner processes to make new products environmentally safer.[10] In the intervening years, DuPont has reduced wastes and emissions. Total releases to air, land, water, and underground injection wells declined by 80 percent between 1987 and 1996.[11] Engineers also established a zero-waste goal for their Chattanooga Plant. This has largely been realized going from 8 percent waste to 0.2 percent with savings of U.S.$250,000 in annual operating costs.[12]

Standards and Legislation

The Natural Step framework is loosely controlled by TNS International, the umbrella organization that oversees international partnerships. Contractual arrangements between national organizations and TNS International define user rights for copyrighted material and duties as a licensee. In order to secure a formal agreement, candidate national organizations must show

- sufficient human resources to develop the concept;
- adequate financial backing (i.e., seed funding to finance initial activities);
- a cost-effective and efficient corporate structure;
- realistic business, marketing, and action plans describing plausible long- and short-term objectives and methods to achieve them; and
- a realistic budget for first year's activities with a balance between income and outflow, in addition to a long-term budget.

Governments have not passed legislation to guide the implementation of the framework. However, recent legislation passed in Connecticut could foster tangible improvements in environmental management in exchange for meaningful business incentives. Streamlined permit processes and possible savings in fees offer a reward for a demonstrated commitment to sustainable development principles.

CONNECTICUT LEGISLATION OFFERS INCENTIVES FOR SUSTAINABLE PRACTICES

In 1999, the General Assembly of the State of Connecticut passed a bill to reward companies showing "an exemplary record of compliance with environmental laws" by adopting ISO 14001 Environmental Management Systems Standards and internationally recognized principles for sustainability (e.g., The Natural Step framework). Businesses apply for program benefits once they are certified in ISO 14001 and have demonstrated the adoption of sustainability principles. Program benefits are system-wide permits, an acceleration of the permit process, and the possibility of waiving certain fees. The *Act Concerning Exemplary Environmental Management Systems* was the first of its kind in the United States and shows how policymakers can accelerate sustainable development.[13]

Certification and Professional Organizations

TNS framework is designed for simplicity and accessibility, not to replace existing certification and professional organizations. Instead, the framework adds value to existing structures by showing employees how they can achieve personal sustainability goals by helping their companies to achieve a sustainable future. The framework elevates the role of certification in environmental compliance above "box-checking for form's sake" to make tangible improvements in the environment for the benefit of society.[14]

Existing professional organizations also can form networks in issue-specific areas. These may or may not be part of, or affiliated with, existing professional organizations. Some professional networks in Sweden have incorporated the sustainability ethic implicit with each of the four System Conditions into existing codes of ethics. Whether or not this will occur in North America remains to be seen.

Established Methodology

Key Concepts

Originally developed for education and training about sustainability, the framework has evolved into a tool that promotes organizational learning to achieve systemic change.[15] The conceptual underpinnings of the framework reflect the key characteristics of learning organizations developed by Peter Senge.[16] The System Conditions, backcasting, and consensus building are embedded in systems thinking, personal mastery, shared vision, mental models, and team learning in organizations in which people at all levels, individually and collectively, are continually increasing capacity to produce results they really care about. These linkages facilitate the adaptation of scientific principles to business management, making it easier to identify the steps required for successful implementation. This evolution, still in its infancy, is appropriately called "sustainable organizational learning."[17]

SENGE'S FIVE DISCIPLINES[18]

- Systems Thinking: a conceptual framework, a body of knowledge, and tools that have developed to make the full patterns clearer
- Personal Mastery: the capacity of individuals to consistently realize the results that matter most deeply to them such that they approach their life as an artist would approach a work of art and are committed to lifelong learning
- Shared Vision: view of the desired future held by all individuals involved in implementing it
- Mental Models: deeply ingrained assumptions and perspectives that inform the way we see our world and take action
- Team Learning: the dialogical process used by a team, whereby team members suspend individual assumptions and enter into a genuine thinking together

Four System Conditions

The central feature of The Natural Step framework is systems thinking that is encapsulated in the four System Conditions. Mastery of the System Conditions enables employees to address the details of environmental problems related to operations without losing sight of the big picture.

Table 24.1 The Natural Step System Conditions

System Condition	Meaning	Rationale
Stored Deposits: Substances from the Earth's crust must not systematically increase in the ecosphere.	In the long-term, fossil fuels, metals, and other minerals must not be released at a faster pace than their slow redeposit and reintegration into the Earth's crust.	If this condition is not met, the concentrations of substances within the ecosphere will increase and eventually exceed limits, often unknown, beyond which irreversible changes occur.
Synthetic Compounds and Other Societally Produced Material: Substances produced by society must not systematically increase in the ecosphere.	Substances must not be released at a faster rate than that at which they can be broken down and integrated into cycles of nature or re-deposited into the Earth's crust.	If this condition is not met, the concentrations of substances in the ecosphere will eventually exceed limits, often unknown, beyond which irreversible changes occur.

Ecosystem Manipulation: The physical basis for productivity and diversity of nature must not systematically be diminished.	We cannot harvest or manipulate ecosystems in such a way that productive capacity, ecosystem services (natural capital), and diversity systematically diminish.	Our health and prosperity depend on the capacity of nature (natural capital) to regenerate resources through the natural cycles of water, energy, nutrients, and the geological processes.
Socioeconomics: There must be fair and efficient use of resources with respect to meeting human needs.	Basic human needs must be met with the most resource-efficient methods possible.	Unless basic human needs are met worldwide through fair and efficient use of resources, it will be difficult to meet conditions 1-3 on a global scale and ensure peace and security.
Source: adapted from Nattrass and Altomare, 1999.		

Personal Mastery

Success for organizations adopting the System Conditions depends on the personal and professional development of employees. Personal mastery requires lifelong learning in areas related to the product or service of the organization, as well as the enhancement of interpersonal competence, personal awareness, emotional maturity, and understanding the ethical dimensions of organizational life.

Personal mastery manifests itself in community outreach, often under the purview of corporate social responsibility, to build stronger relationships with the communities where the company resides. For example, Nike offered a series of training courses in Asian factories on a range of subjects including pollution prevention, materials substitution, environmental management, and innovative technologies.[19]

Mental Models

Companies adopting the TNS framework promote ingenuity in decision making and design by using the System Conditions to filter mental models. Some of these limiting assumptions must be adjusted to avoid slipping into the habit of using only immediately available or well-known tools that hinder a more self-reflective appraisal. The mental models that prove most useful reinforce systems thinking to improve risk management.

Table 24.2 Making the Shift to Sustainable Mental Models

Unsustainable	Sustainable
The economic system is the entire system.	The Earth is the source of all profits with three interacting systems: social, biophysical, and economic.
Industrial processes are linear.	Product development, use, and disposal is a cyclical process.
There are infinite resources for the production of goods so we can be inefficient.	We do not have unlimited supplies of energy and raw materials.
Source: adapted from Schley and Laur, 1998.	

The re-framing of unsustainable mental models occurs as consensus-based decisions draw from a scientific dialogical method called "simplicity without reduction" that aims to understand the ecological connections without reducing the whole into a collection of details.[20]

Backcasting, often married to strategic planning, allows employees to avoid using unsustainable mental models altogether. Backcasting is the creative process of identifying a desired outcome and determining short-term decisions and investments needed to achieve that future. The System Conditions can be used to define a desired situation in the future.[21] Scenarios are then developed to connect the company's status with the desired future.

Shared Vision

A corporate ethic embracing the System Conditions is critical. Goals, values, and a mission have the most impact on behavior if they are widely shared by all employees and entrenched in corporate culture. The process of discovering the System Conditions makes environmental and social concerns personally relevant and prompts a sustained commitment by creating a shared vision. Paul Hawken describes this as an easy shift whereby The Natural Step's educational programming creates the milieu for the learner to have their own *aha* experience of sudden understanding that is hard to lose.[22] A corporate ethic embracing the System Conditions is critical to support this change in thinking, once it occurs.

INCORPORATING SUSTAINABILITY PRINCIPLES INTO CORPORATE POLICY

The incorporation of The Natural Step's sustainability principles into the corporate policy statement would include the following:

- start the process of eliminating the release of substances from the Earth's crust that could accumulate,
- start the process of eliminating the release of persistent synthetic chemicals,
- identify and reduce activities that could adversely affect natural productivity and/or biodiversity, and
- improve the efficiency of resource use and work toward fairer distribution of wealth.

Team Learning

Teams are the fundamental unit for implementing the change required to comply with the four System Conditions. Team learning improves the effectiveness of the team by preventing it from getting caught in a rut. This process reinforces the shared vision of the System Conditions. Feedback loops increase the skills and expertise of all employees in cross-functional teams, leading to greater efficiency in achieving consensus.

Framework in Action

The Natural Step framework provides a scientific and ethical justification for corporations to improve environmental management practices. Using the framework is economically justified through efficiency improvements and strategic positioning for emergent markets created by adopting sustainability principles. Progress is incremental and motivated by self-interest in increasing competitive advantage and achieving long-term viability.

Environmental and Social Trends and Resulting Corporate Strategies

Constrained by rising societal demands and declining resources to meet those demands, businesses have fewer, more expensive strategies for survival. Corporations are at a critical juncture, either choosing to make necessary changes or being forced to change when the inefficient use of resources and environmental deterioration ceases to be overlooked.

The options for companies facing constraints due to increasing demands and decreasing resources depend on corporate culture:

- Inert organizations, not attuned to their operational environment, do not last.
- Reactive organizations respond only to definite environmental signals and are eventually forced to implement expensive, risky options to address threats with uncertain results.
- Anticipatory organizations predict the future from unsustainable past trends and require quick, costly relief from unexpected market changes.

- Sustainable organizations are strategic and proactive, ensuring that the corporate vision and operations address the System Conditions.

Implementation of The Natural Step Framework

Implementation of The Natural Step framework is flexible so it can be applied at different scales in various organizational settings. This informality allows organizations to determine the best ways to apply sustainability principles using their understanding of their operations. Although the application of the framework varies, there are common elements intended to transform organizations into strategic, learning entities. The critical steps are

- to identify leaders to oversee the implementation of the framework, starting with the highest executive levels or a specific branch of operations;
- to formalize the commitment to environmental excellence and sustainability in the corporate vision and strategy;
- to educate employees about sustainability and to offer specialized training, and coaching for employees to reinforce the System Conditions in the corporate culture;
- to encourage employee participation through leadership development, team building, and scenario games that test abilities to reduce waste and resources use, inter-divisional competitions to achieve specific sustainability goals, advanced training workshops, and celebrations;
- to apply the framework in a practical way, focusing on easy options and changed practices that offer a platform for maximal flexibility for later investment;
- to provide feedback and measurement to validate suggested approaches or to explain the reasons behind rejecting the unsustainable proposals, document and learn from successes and failures, measure and share results, and reward innovators;
- to influence employees, suppliers, customers, competitors, shareholders, communities, and stakeholders through targeted actions that increase awareness of the company's environmental commitments to increase the market for green products or services; and
- to fully integrate the framework with business functions by incorporating sustainability considerations into business meetings and performance evaluation through the use of other environmental management tools (life cycle assessment for all products, environmental purchasing) and systems (ISO 14001).

The Natural Step framework must be integrated throughout the corporation's EMS using the steps illustrated in Figure 24.1.

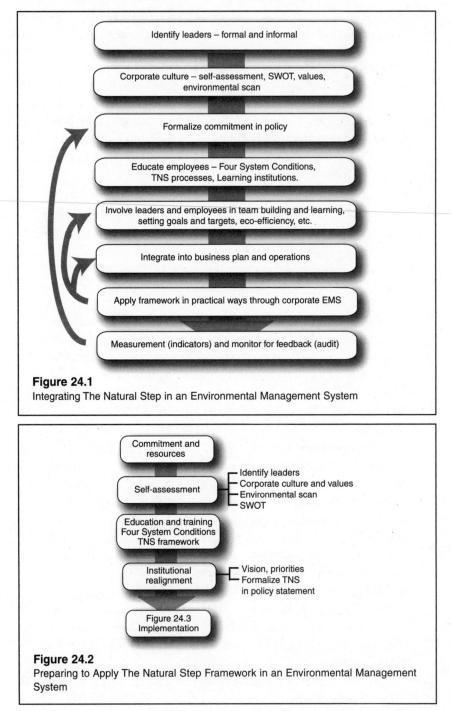

Figure 24.1
Integrating The Natural Step in an Environmental Management System

Figure 24.2
Preparing to Apply The Natural Step Framework in an Environmental Management System

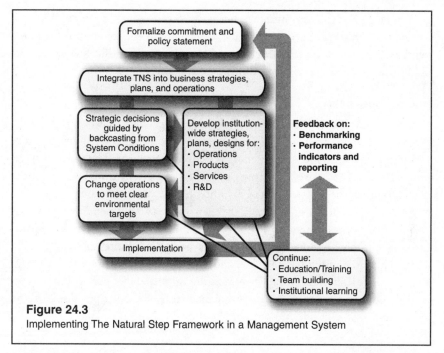

Figure 24.3
Implementing The Natural Step Framework in a Management System

The processes of applying TNS principles and System Conditions in the organization is illustrated in Figures 24.2 and 24.3.

The Natural Step framework helps organizations to "do well by doing good."[23] The framework makes them aware that optimization is not complete until all conditions are satisfied, so that, rather than abandon the journey, businesses continue to improve. The framework engages employees' ingenuity to develop completely new ways to achieve ecological conditions and create new, profitable opportunities.

Ways The Framework Enhances an Environmental Management System

The framework improves the Environmental Management System by
  • forcing the corporation to examine the long-term consequences of impacts that appear to be insignificant in the short term,
  • requiring education of employees and team learning,
  • obtaining corporate and employee commitment, and
  • changing corporate culture so that it enhances sustainable development.

Actors, Participants, and Stakeholders

There is an assortment of actors, participants, and stakeholders that influence organizations, both externally and internally. The Natural Step framework is useful because its pedagogy was designed for others besides business, including governments, academic institutions, non-profit organizations, communities, and individuals. This broad accessibility and availability of the framework for independent use, especially in Sweden, has improved the scientific literacy of the public, thereby raising expectations of acceptable business practices.

Internal Motivation

Employee concerns and personal values can change corporate or institutional behaviour. The constraints on this behavioural response are the employee's place within the organizational structure and the corporate culture. The main leverage points are senior executives, managers, and informal leaders. Senior executives and managers are in the best position to institute the process or design changes needed to fulfill the System Conditions, if they can inspire commitment to innovation.

Informal leaders, often trusted advisors within the organization, can make management more responsive to new approaches by motivating their colleagues. They demonstrate multiple, tangible, and quantifiable benefits of eco-efficiency. Resource efficiency and waste minimization improve the public image and increase profits by reducing the environmental costs of existing practices. This is an enticing argument likely to prompt institutional change.

External Pressure

Stakeholders outside the company change what is viewed as acceptable from a sustainable development standpoint by becoming, or using, driving forces. The following examples illustrate this:

- Non-governmental organizations lobby for more or improved environmental legislation and act as watchdogs for environmental infractions.
- Consumers change purchasing practices and invest in green companies.
- Banks examine their clients' eco-efficiency records to ensure that they are not liable for corporations with poor environmental compliance.
- Insurance companies that have paid for previous pollution damage give preferential treatment to companies that demonstrate a verifiable commitment to effective risk management.
- Governments provide opportunities for business to avoid costly, bureaucratic red tape and impediments by encouraging self-regulation.
- The best and brightest young professionals are more selective about their employers, seeking a personally and professionally rewarding work environment.

Benefits and Incentives

The Natural Step framework creates opportunities to implement easily accessible options and to invest in process improvements that help to identify design issues to be addressed by new businesses.[24] This means a change from cradle-to-grave systems requiring end-of-pipe treatment technologies to cradle-to-cradle (recycling) systems. Enhanced profits from resource efficiency and waste reduction make further innovation economically feasible, thus stimulating expansion. New business opportunities emerge to fulfill the continuing need for value-added products and services.[25] This in turn increases market share.

The Natural Step framework provides employees with a common language that makes consensus building easier. Employees gain a sense of achievement by seeing how their actions contribute to reducing environmental impacts and understanding their role in the shift to sustainability.

BENEFITS AT A GLANCE

- Improved competitiveness
- Lowered costs
- Enhanced profits
- Greater resource efficiency
- Enhanced product innovation
- Improved staff morale
- Reduced staff turnover
- Lower environmental impact
- Greater market share

Problems and Barriers

CHALLENGES AT A GLANCE

- No guarantee
- Vague, broad System Conditions
- System Conditions too limiting
- Lengthy transition to innocuous materials
- Inadequate sharing of information
- System Condition 4 is an ethic
- "Movement" image
- Government subsidies for resource use

The framework, when used as a guide, offers no guarantee.[26] Employees receive framework training but must decide how to apply it. This is a challenge because many companies are still trying to clarify linkages between scientific System Conditions and business practices. Innovative companies that already tested the standards grasp the practical challenges to implementing the framework. These lessons in implementation are not widely shared. Many national organizations remedy this through large training workshops targeting several companies. The information age has hastened the learning process through on-line discussion groups to share experience and get advice.

Beyond communication issues, the System Conditions are problematic. The long-term implications of System Conditions 1 and 2 are intimidating and will take a very long time to achieve. Nonetheless, starting the process to stop the buildup of pollutants in the environment has to begin some time. System Condition 3 addresses the maintenance of ecological function and is thought by some to be too vague, broad, and impossible to measure because it involves so many subtopics. The revision to existing practices may require drastic restructuring and expansion into entirely new markets. For example, oil and gas companies may have to change from being fossil fuel companies to energy companies with a broader resource base by developing clean and green technologies. Some industries are intimidated by the framework and consequently are not easily converted to principles of sustainability. In the late 1980s, the Swedish pulp and paper industry met with pressure to stop using chlorine in its manufacturing process. Later, they learned they could prosper from converting to non-chlorine processes.[27]

Companies also have reservations about System Condition 4, because it involves ethical issues of equity and fairness. However, resource efficiency and the distribution of wealth within and between nations can be measured. Nike views this System Condition as critical to success. Other less innovative companies, or those that do not understand the ramifications of distributional inequities, view this condition as imposing an uncertain future on profitability.

The System Conditions are also deemed too limiting because they cannot deal effectively with emergent contentious issues such as genetic engineering. Consequently, individuals concerned with issues peripheral to the System Conditions drop out of the collaborative process, uncertain as to where their views fit.

Governments continue to subsidize the consumption of undervalued resources (perverse subsidies) and the market continues to give false signals because of externalities which mean that prices do not include all costs.

TNS is perceived by some as a movement with its own jargon rituals and adherents that urge others to join. This could have serious consequences: movements become fads and then fade, and some managers may be reclutant to join what they think is a movement.

Keeping Current

The Natural Step websites listed at the end of this chapter, particularly the U.S. websites, are good sources for getting an introduction to the framework; identifying key literature; offering links to other countries; and keeping informed of upcoming training sessions, and video and cassettes tapes of speakers at major national conferences. Brian Nattress and Mary Altomare's *The Natural Step for Business: Wealth Ecology and the Evolutionary Corporation* and the two forthcoming books from New Society Publishers[28] present the value of the framework for organizational persistence in innovative corporations by linking the framework to effective management through case studies.

Recommended Further Reading

Nattrass, B., and M. Altomare. *Dancing with the Tiger: Learning Sustainability Step by Natural Step*. Gabriola Island, B.C.: New Society Publishers, 2002.

Nattrass, B., and M. Altomare. *The Natural Step for Business: Wealth, Ecology and the Evolutionary Corporation*. Gabriola Island, B.C.: New Society Publishers, 1999.

Robèrt, K.-H. *The Natural Step: A Framework for Achieving Sustainability in Our Organizations*. Cambridge, Massachusetts: Pegasus Communications, 1997.

Robèrt, K.-H. *The Natural Step Story: Seeding a Quiet Revolution*. Gabriola Island, B.C.: New Society Publishers, 2002.

Schley, S., and J. Laur. *Creating Sustainable Organizations: Meeting the Economic, Ecological, and Social Challenges of the 21st Century*. Cambridge, Massachusetts: Pegasus Communications, 1998.

Newsletters

BWZ

Developing Ideas

In Context

Living Gently Quarterly

The Natural Step News

The Newsletter of The Natural Step (U.S.)

The Natural Step International Newsletter

Websites

The Natural Step, Canada: <www.naturalstep.ca>

The Natural Step Environmental Institute Australia Limited: <www.ozemail.com.au/~natstep>

The Natural Step, Japan: <www.tnsj.org>

The Natural Step, New Zealand: <www.naturalstep.org.nz>

The Natural Step, Sweden: <www.detnaturligasteget.se>

The Natural Step, U.K.: <www.naturalstep.org.uk>

The Natural Step, U.S.: <www.naturalstep.org>

CHAPTER

WHERE DO WE GO FROM HERE?

Dixon Thompson

T HIS CONCLUDING CHAPTER is divided into four sections. The first deals with general improvements to the Environmental Management Systems (EMSs), the tool set, and individual tools.

The second discusses what national governments must do to facilitate the use of EMSs and the tools and improvements to them, to improve government environmental performance, and to change the economic and regulatory framework within which corporations operate. Those changes will make it easier and more profitable to be a socially and environmentally responsible corporation. Governments and organizations outside the corporate world must recognize the value of the EMSs and tools and apply them appropriately.

The third section deals with what I call the sustainable development gap. If the best available technology were applied universally, it is estimated that we would achieve an increase in energy and material efficiency by a factor of four (400 percent).[1] Much more is required — perhaps as much as a factor of ten (1000 percent).[2] Therefore, actions by national governments and international agreements have to start making it possible to move on from factor four to factor ten in improvements in material and energy efficiency. It will also be essential to develop effective means to protect the global commons, the environment outside national boundaries — the oceans, atmosphere, and space.

The final section argues that pollution and abuse of resources may be due not only to technology and industrial development, but to the very nature of human organizations and society. If that is the case, then we have further to go than we thought; EMSs, the environmental management tools, and the recommended changes to the economic and political frameworks may not be sufficient to solve the fundamental problem.

Improvements to EMSs, the Tool Set, and the Tools

Environmental Management Systems

EMAS II, the revised version of EMAS, has been published. The first draft revision of ISO 14001 EMS should be available in 2002. Use of those two international standards is increasing rapidly. BSI's (British Standards Institute) SIGMA project[3] will deliver the next generation of EMSs for those organizations that want a more advanced and effective EMS.

These three EMS standards would all be improved if a more explicit description of the environmental management tool set were incorporated into them or if their guidance documents provided advice on the broader environmental management context.

ISO 14001 has four areas where major changes are needed: social aspects and impacts and how to control them; effective management and protection of green spaces and natural areas; linkage to a set of widely recognized and accepted environmental performance principles, such as The Natural Step that could serve as an overall moral compass for the ISO 14001-based organizations; and reporting of environmental performance information to external stakeholders and decision-makers.

Definitions of the environment do not limit it to biophysical components; it includes social, cultural, and economic factors. This concept is consistent with the triple bottom line, corporate social responsibility, the global reporting initiative, and sustainable development which all include those factors. However, most of the work on aspects and impacts in ISO 14001 EMS deals with factors that cause (or could cause) changes in the biophysical environment. That has to change so that corporations using ISO 14001 and other EMSs will recognize that their products and activities produce, or could produce, undesirable social and cultural impacts. The most obvious examples are those situations in which corporations provide services to employees and their families that are not available to others in the community (e.g., health services, transportation, education and training, computer literacy, and access to the Internet). The differences in the availability of services could create tensions in the community, which would be an undesirable social impact. When corporations expand into communities and change transportation and communication systems, there will be impacts due to global influences. Where those cultural changes have been identified in different locations, concerns, if not outright protests, have been the result. Identifying and controlling those undesirable social and cultural impacts is a new and difficult area, but one which companies at the leading edge cannot avoid.

Current EMSs also have a difficult time dealing with the management of green spaces and natural areas. In this case, the skills, knowledge, and experience of those working on Ecosystem-Based Management (chapter 23) will be valuable.

When applying ISO 14001, aspects and impacts are most easily identified for normal conditions for processes, activities, products, and services. Under upset conditions, during spills and accidents or other abnormal situations, aspects and impacts are different, and it is more difficult to identify them and estimate their significance. Risk management (chapter 10) is designed to identify and reduce the likelihood of accidents during upset or abnormal conditions, and other risks. That is, risk management is the process of identifying and dealing with aspects and impacts when conditions are not normal and should be used to improve the identification and estimation of significance of aspects and impacts.

The Roles of Governments

Governments can benefit by encouraging and facilitating the use of EMSs by corporations — and some have done so through reduced regulatory scrutiny. Further efforts by governments should include working with academics and industry to build the business case for improved social and environmental performance. We currently understand the direct costs and have anecdotal evidence of some of the benefits, but a robust business case needs a good deal of work so that both governments and corporations will be persuaded of the benefits.

Governments must examine the benefits of backdrop legislation — legislation designed to make a widely accepted voluntary practice into a legal requirement — for EMSs and some of the tools, especially environmental audits and reporting, and be prepared to introduce it when consensus about their usefulness is reached.

Governments must help to ensure credibility of the EMSs and the environmental management tools by working with NGOs and professional organizations to guarantee quality control of practitioners and registrations. Very few of the registrations of EMSs to ISO 14001 or EMAS standards or certification of auditors have been revoked, so either the quality control system is working extremely well or it has to be improved. There are cases where the environmental performance of companies with a registered EMS has been very poor and there have been no revocation of registrations. It is rumored that, in some countries, certification as an auditor can be purchased with little education or experience and no commitment to a code of ethics, so the resulting audits are not credible.

Governments also have a critical role in working with professional organizations and universities at building capacity, to ensure that the well-qualified professionals who are needed will be available.

The Set of Tools

This book defines the set of tools available to environmental management professionals. The concept of using the tools as a set, rather than individually, is an important one. It also helps to define what environmental management is and helps environmental managers gain a better grasp of what is possible.

Our knowledge and experience has limited our selection of tools for this book; other tools, like eco-efficiency and ecological footprint, could be added to the set. Some of the tools for strategic environmental management could also be better defined, described, and added to the set.

The next phase of development of the tool set would be broader, more official recognition of a set of tools by environmental professional societies (SETAC, IAIA, AWMA, ONE of the Academy of Management) and other organizations (ISO and the national standards organizations in each country, the OECD, UNEP). We can anticipate prolonged discussions, if not heated debates, about which tools are included and which ones should be included in the set. However, if that discussion starts with the definition of what an environmental management tool is, as opposed to a scientific methodology, techniques for gathering or assessing data, etc., then progress should be possible.

Improvements to Individual Tools

There are obvious, cost-effective improvements that can be made and are being made to all of the tools in the set. The initial focus should be on improving their effectiveness and credibility at conserving resources and protecting the environment within nations and the global commons. Later efforts for improvements in more mature tools should focus on making the tool more efficient. As stated in the introduction, there are entire books on most of the tools, and where there are not, there should be. Therefore, only a very brief description of some of the obvious changes that could be carried out in the near future can be presented here.

Analysis of Driving Forces

The driving forces are relatively well known, but the use of the generic list as a tool is not well-developed. The driving forces have been identified, but most organizations do not use a systematic method to identify the ones that are pertinent in their case, understand them, and respond appropriately. Because the driving forces are so important as a tool for improving environmental management, more work is required to help structure and formalize the tool and its applications. Regulators and investors have a particular interest in the set of driving forces and could contribute to their further development and refinement.

Analysis of Barriers

As with driving forces, this tool has to be structured and formalized. There should be more analysis of many of the barriers, particularly those related to cultural factors. One major barrier is the education of MBAs, who according to a recent study do not receive sufficient exposure to environmental issues.[4] Because business school graduates become managers and executives, they play strong roles in directing corporate activities and establishing corporate culture, so their lack of awareness and knowledge is a significant barrier. The point is not to try to dismantle existing MBA curricula but to instill an appreciation of the role of environmental issues in business decisions. This might include, for instance, using a clear presentation of the business case for improved environmental performance to show profit-oriented managers that it offers a competitive advantage.

Strategic Environmental Management

Benchmarking, environmental scanning, forecasting and backcasting, and policy EIAs to remove conflicts in policy within corporations are all areas needing improvement. Including environmental issues in the reform of corporate governance is essential.

Environmental Policy

Benchmarking will improve policy development. As indicators are improved, feedback on success or failure of policies and their implementation will improve, and continual improvement will be enhanced. Auditing of policy issues and reporting on the results will also create significant benefits.

Environmental Management Structures

Significant improvements in organizational structures could be achieved by facilitating and encouraging interdisciplinary teams working to solve environmental problems. This will be particularly important for governments where a silo mentality, as defined by departments or agency mandates established by turf wars decades ago, has impeded the creation and adoption of coherent environmental management.

Environmental Audits

Environmental auditing is one of the well-defined tools, but improvements are required in the qualifications required for practitioners, control of quality at the national and international levels (better application of the ISO 19000 auditing guidelines), and integration with financial auditing. As with financial auditing, the credibility of the system is at stake when evidence of lack of integrity comes to light. Improved reporting of audit results, including third party verification, can be expected. Given the justifiably increased skepticism of consumers and investors, leading-edge corporations should be able to achieve an advantage by improving reputation and credibility through effective reporting of audit results.

Education and Training

Cooperation among professional organizations, universities, corporations, and governments will be essential to build capacity to produce the well-qualified professionals we need. That cooperation will have to include definitions of qualifications required, systems for accreditation of educational and training institutions, assistance to developing countries to help meet their needs without contributing to the brain drain, and quality control.

Risk Management

Better examples of the total costs of failures are needed. The perception of the penalties and other costs for accidents do not seem to have always been sufficient to convince corporations and governments to implement the institutional and technical options available to reduce risk. Better understanding of the relationships of risk assessments, risk perception, and the definitions of acceptable risk and "safe" would reduce conflicts and controversies.

Site Assessment

Site assessment is another well-established tool that will be formalized in an ISO standard to be released soon. The big issue here will be applying the site assessment processes to orphan sites and deciding how the cleanup costs should be apportioned. There is a need to integrate site assessment processes and results with other management tools. As concern about audits and liabilities increases, the quality and credibility of site assessments will need to improve.

Indicators

Clearly defined criteria are needed for selection and development of indicators and then standards for those indicators, probably based upon the Pressure State Response model. Linking indictors to other tools such as policy, auditing, and reporting will be essential. It is unlikely that amalgamation of indictors will produce a single indicator that would not suffer from the same problems as Gross Domestic Product does as a single, over-simplified measure of economic progress. One area where there might be grounds for optimism would be the adaptation of the ecological footprint concept for corporations as a means of showing the trends in their environmental performances.

Reporting

With the increasing profile of the accountability issue, excellence in issuing verified reports on corporate environmental and social performance will become more important. Markets, regulators, and investors will be paying more attention to those corporations who prove superior social and environmental performance. The Global

Reporting Initiative (GRI) has set the standard for reporting. At this stage, governments should encourage reporting with verification and should start the process of preparing backdrop legislation to bring all corporations up to a minimum reporting requirement. In the U.S.A., Canada, and EEC, governments have started to require their departments and agencies to prepare environmental reports. Canada has a good record of government reporting[5] but the Environment Commissioner has stated that a great deal of improvement is needed.[6] Governments that expect more of corporations but do not meet the same standards themselves do not have much credibility.

Environmental Impact Assessment

EIA is a mature methodology but several areas are being improved. Cumulative impact assessment is improving. Social and cultural impacts, particularly in developing countries, can still be problematic. For both governments and corporations, the lack of coherence of policies (the existence of conflicts) could be addressed with improved strategic environmental assessments (assessments of policies).

Accounting

Accounting, policy, auditing, indicators, and reporting are linked. Significant improvements are needed in the ability of environmental accounting to produce a balanced report of costs and benefits. A method to identify and describe contingent costs and the benefits of reducing risks would be of great assistance to environmental managers. To date there has been too much emphasis on costs alone. Standardization of terminology and methods is required. If better estimates of costs and benefits are available, it will be easier to make the business case for improved performance which is essential for both corporations and governments.

Economic Instruments

Corporations could make more use of economic instruments to encourage environmentally responsible behavior in employees, suppliers, and customers. Corporations will be affected as governments work to correct market imperfections and apply green taxes. Corporate philosophies often endorse the market as one means, if not the preferred means, of controlling adverse environmental impacts, so their support for action to correct market imperfections should be expected.

Product and Technology Assessment and Life Cycle Assessment

Consumer skepticism and lack of confidence may drive governments and corporations to make better use of PATA and LCA. However, the driving forces that would lead governments to establish a sound generic model for PATA and then use it to improve testing of products and technologies are probably too weak to bring about any change in the immediate future. Profit-driven assessments might eventually push governments and consumers to insist on reform. In the meantime, those corporations that believe that their products are superior could obtain a competitive advantage by establishing a model process for assessing their products and making the details of the process, the data, and the results available to the public (improving transparency).

The improvements being made in LCA, especially labeling, will make it easier for corporations and consumers to apply LCA and have confidence in the results.

Purchasing Guidelines

Purchasing guidelines are becoming a major driving force as they are adopted by corporations, governments, and consumer groups. With improvements in ISO 14001 registrations and labeling, especially the ISO 14040 series of standards, the requirements for purchasing guidelines will be simplified.

Environmental Communications

For many organizations there is likely room for improvement in integrating environmental communications and risk communications strategy with environmental management strategy and overall corporate strategy. This is being forced by reporting on corporate social responsibility and sustainable development, but the integration could be undertaken more directly. As the business case for improved environmental performance is developed, environmental communications will increase to include more than image and keeping out of trouble with stakeholders and become a key factor in gaining competitive advantage. Environmental communications could make better use of the credibility provided by environmental management systems and tools and inform stakeholders about the tools and how their organization uses them.

Human Factors

The biggest issue with human factors (HF) is demonstrating that it has a critical role to play. The contributions that HF can make in reducing risks and costs and improving performance of employees and products are known to too few people. HF faces the same problems as preventive medicine — how do you prove the benefits when they are intangible and difficult to measure? The benefits are from something that didn't happen, or from happy employees. Here, the links to other tools such as risk management and education and training could be significant.

Clean Development Mechanism and Joint Implementation

The details of these two mechanisms for reducing greenhouse gas emissions are being defined by international negotiations. Independent of the details, corporate and host country stakeholders have a great deal to gain from their application.

Ecosystem-Based Management

EBM has a great deal to offer the industry-oriented EMSs (EMAS and ISO 14001) because they are weak on the ability to provide effective management of green spaces and natural areas. On the other hand, EBM can learn a great deal about indicators, reporting, auditing, and feedback from formal EMSs.

The Natural Step

Just as the concept of sustainable development was resisted by many organizations until the concept became familiar, it will take time before TNS is accepted as the next generation of frameworks for introducing sustainable development concepts into corporate strategies and policies.

Areas Requiring New Tools

There is no formal environmental management tool that can be applied to implement product stewardship. Purchasing guidelines direct the upstream side of product manufacturing and purchasing; Life Cycle Assessment identifies and reduces the impact of products and hazardous materials. Take-back legislation in Europe that changed the legal requirements for product stewardship will eventually become a reality in North America. Some products are now registered to facilitate warrantees and upgrades. Deposit/return systems for beverage containers are one form of product stewardship. These examples show that the concept of tracing products has had limited applications. What we need now is a formal, standardized environmental management tool that manufacturers and marketers could apply to minimize the environmental impacts of their products. A credible managment tool for product stewardship would provide a competitive advantage in the marketplace.

Pressure on corporations for product stewardship of chemicals arises from the United Nations' *Stockholm Convention on Persistent Organic Pollutants*,[7] the Centers for Disease Control and Prevention's *National Report on Human Exposure to Environmental Chemicals*,[8] The Commission for Environmental Cooperation's initiatives on sound management of chemicals,[9] and studies raising concern about chemicals in sewage effluents, fish, and wildlife.[10] This is a very serious set of problems, yet the current environmental management tools cannot effectively address the potential threats posed by chemicals in the environment, our food, and our bodies.

Because of legislation protecting employees, corporations must have programs to ensure the safety of employees and to meet increasingly stringent regulations about exposure to toxic chemicals. However, promoting health involves more than providing a safe, clean environment. Leading-edge corporations have recognized that promoting wellness (health, fitness, sleep and rest habits, etc.) for employees provides advantages, but the practice is still in the early development stages.

A Bias for Action and Continual Improvement

Because of their roots in science, study and research are often the activities favored by environmental scientists when confronted by a problem. That propensity is strengthened by politicians and bureaucrats who want to appear to be doing something but are reluctant to attack the problem directly. Continual improvement (see Figure 1.3 in chapter 1 and Figure 2.4 in chapter 2) is critical for getting out of the research and study mode because research should never stop — continual improvement requires implementation of new, appropriate ideas as they are discovered. It is also critical for those who are eager to get started without doing much research — Peters and Waterman's bias for action:[11] ready, fire, aim. Get started and improve your aim as you go.

Is the Glass Half Full or Half Empty?

It could be easy to be optimistic about environmental management, given

- the potential of EMSs and the set of environmental management tools to improve the environmental performance of corporations;
- the pace of their development and improvement;
- the volume and quality of information about environmental management published in *Business Strategy and the Environment, Greener Management International,* and many other journals, by academics from all over the world;
- the work and publications of professional organizations such as Organizations and the Natural Environment (ONE) of the Academy of Management, Air and Waste Management Association, and Society of Environmental Toxicology and Chemistry;
- the work and publications of business-oriented organizations such as the Global Environmental Management Initiative, World Business Council for Sustainable Development, Coalition for Environmentally Responsible Economies, and the Global Reporting Initiative; and
- the progress made by leading-edge corporations.

The unfortunate reality is that the overwhelming driving force for most corporations and executives is profit, and the environment and the triple bottom line place a poor second, if they rank at all. The measures of success that overshadow everything else are profits and productivity for corporations and productivity and GDP for nations. *The Economist* observes that there has been a vehement reaction against business leaders, in part, due to the extent of their personal greed.[12] Corporations at the leading edge of environmental management have demonstrated that it can be good for business to improve environmental performance and report publicly about it. To ensure that all corporations improve their environmental performance, governments have critical roles to play in passing and enforcing legislation and applying incentives and disincentives. It is clear that voluntary measures will not be sufficient.

The heavy focus of some North American political leaders on short-term economic gain and their strong opposition to measures to solve environmental problems because they think that they might hurt the economy is based on the belief that economic growth is the only thing that matters. This could lead to pessimism about governments' willingness to take a proactive role, especially in North America. It makes it that much more important to make the business case for both corporations and governments to improve environmental performance.

The Roles for Government in Improved Environmental Performance

The most forward-thinking corporations, in terms of corporate social responsibility, the triple bottom line, and sustainable development, can only go so far with these concepts before they reach the boundaries of the social, political, and economic frameworks within which they must operate. Therefore, the only way for those leaders to go further is for the frameworks' constraints to be moved, so that rewards and punishments, incentives and disincentives will encourage them to advance their leadership roles and others to follow.

Figure 25.1 shows four areas where actions by governments are needed to make progress toward sustainable development. One set of actions is needed within the current economic, legal, and political framework. A second set is required to change the boundaries of the frameworks within which corporations operate. A third set of activities is required to fix the damage that has already been done. A fourth set involves building the institutional capacity and skills and knowledge, in all countries, that are essential if the above changes are to be made.

Government strategies can be improved in eight areas: legislation, policy coherence, EMSs for government departments and agencies, development of the business case for improved environmental performance, reduction of market imperfections, green taxes and other economic instruments, better measures of progress and well-being to augment the GDP, and more support for improved international environmental standards and practices.

1. Backdrop legislation is used to bring all corporations up to the same minimum performance standard. It does not penalize those who have adopted current practice: it sets minimum standards for all. If the business case for improved environmental performance is established, then opposition would be based upon the ideology that fewer government interventions are required and voluntary initiatives are sufficient. Backdrop legislation in the areas of auditing, reporting, and labeling should be prepared for implementation. Although there is significant

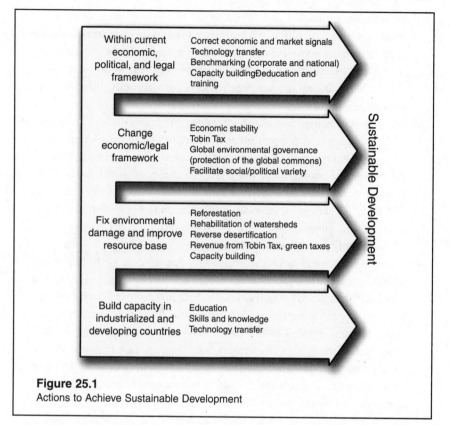

Figure 25.1
Actions to Achieve Sustainable Development

resistance in North America, strategies to introduce the European model of take-back legislation, to move the burden for solid waste from consumer and municipalities to manufacturers, should be developed. This should not be a problem for those who want to trade into the European market and for those who seek a market advantage through their products and their reputation.

2. Government policies affecting the environment and conservation of resources are not coherent — that is, there are significant contradictions and conflicts. Sport-utility vehicles and light trucks do not have to meet the same energy efficiency and air quality standards that have been imposed on cars. Fuel taxes on rail transportation do not benefit the railway companies the way they do the trucking competition where public funds build and maintain the transportation infrastructure for truckers. Efforts at water conservation are frustrated by policies that provide water as a free good delivered through heavily subsidized systems. The medical community is seriously concerned about the growing resistance of bacteria

to antibiotics, and yet the use of antibiotics is still permitted, if not encouraged, in agriculture and consumer products. Governments should apply strategic environmental assessments to reduce policy incoherence (conflicts). Governments should also review and remove perverse subsidies, which discourage environmentally conscientious behavior and encourage waste.

3. Many governments have stated intentions to require their departments and agencies to improve performance by adopting the practices of industry — Environmental Management Systems and the use of the 22 environmental management tools. Improvements in efforts to meet this commitment would give governments a better understanding of what EMSs can do, set a good example, reduce the impact of government activities on the environment, and improve government performance as manager, policy maker, and regulator.

4. Governments must find the means of cooperating with businesses, ENGOs, industry organizations, academics, banks and investors, and other stakeholders to make the business case for improved environmental performance. Having the evidence that improved performance makes good business sense would make it easier to introduce the changes described in the rest of this section. The business case is important for industry and for governments that want to introduce change. But it is also important for governments who consider environmental issues as a constraint on economic growth and on the engines of the economy. Just as improved environmental performance provides corporations with a competitive advantage, so too it would provide the advantages to nations in international markets and international affairs. When governments think that imposing improvements in corporate environmental performance will hinder economic performance, they are out of date and do not understand current economic reality well enough to take full advantage of the opportunities that improved environmental performance offers.

5. Market imperfections are a significant problem because the market cannot deliver the benefits it should. This should be troubling for those who advocate the market as the best means of guiding behavior and should mean that governments would have overwhelming support from industry for measures to remove market imperfections. Unfortunately this is not always the case because corporations often have a vested interest in the status quo due to the benefits (subsidies) they receive as a result of market imperfections — their prices and costs do not reflect the full cost. Correcting imperfections is essential if the market is to play its critical role. Subsidizing undesirable behavior by permitting industry to price

their goods and services at less than the full cost should be opposed by both the left and right of the political spectrum.

6. Green taxes, especially when revenue neutral, should receive support from corporations. Tax what you don't want and don't tax what you do want should fit well with the dominant economic philosophy of using economic means (the market) rather than regulation. In this way, rather than using tax lawyers and accountants as the only sources of ideas and information on how to reduce taxes, environmental managers would be handed a significant role. That is, green taxes are charged based upon use of, or adverse impacts on, the environment. They are designed to be avoidable by implementing effective means of reducing emissions and adverse impacts and proving success at doing so. Therefore, environmental managers who can reduce emissions and adverse impacts that are taxed can provide benefits by reducing green taxes imposed on the corporation.

7. Just as it is essential that the market provide accurate signals to guide the behavior of consumers and producers, so governments need improved signals to guide behavior. In this respect, the Gross Domestic Product, the measure of economic progress, is widely recognized as imperfect because of the way it is calculated and because it does not measure social well-being. Improving and applying more sophisticated measures such as the index of quality of life and the environment being developed by Robert Prescot-Allen[13] and an adjusted GDP[14] should receive priority. It is clear that industry needs a sophisticated set of economic, environmental, and social indicators to make decisions, especially for those corporations committed to corporate social responsibility, the triple bottom line, and sustainable development. Governments have similar but much stronger and compelling needs to meet their commitments and obligations.

8. Governments could help improve protection of the environment and resource conservation by providing assistance to the organizations responsible for national and international environmental standards and practices and to the organizations that govern the professions that apply the standards and carry out the practices. To the extent that the ISO and designated national bodies can improve their capabilities, so will the national and international standards and their applications improve. Similarly, government support for national and international professional organizations (IAIA, SETAC, AWMA, ONE of the Academy of Management, etc.) is a means of improving environmental performances in all sectors by non-regulatory means that do not require increasing the size of government — they complement regulations and the market.

These eight areas for development and implementation of strategies for governments are well understood and not really controversial, even though there will be opposition from those who want to protect their vested interests in the status quo. A cabinet that would set aside turf wars and outdated economic ideology could forge an economic and environmental strategy that corporations have already proved makes good sense.

There are innovative ways for governments to exhibit leadership and apply existing skills and knowledge.

Recession as an Opportunity, Not a Threat

Governments are afraid to use, or even hear, the word recession because of the possible economic repercussions. When threats of a recession arise, governments try to stimulate segments of the consumption-oriented economy — cars, appliances, etc. — all of which are energy and material intensive, with the accompanying environmental impacts. Instead, governments could take a recession as an opportunity to restructure the economy by encouraging activity in the knowledge-based economy and the environment industry: moving from a consumer society to a conserver society.[15] To fight the possible recession, governments could explicitly focus stimulation of activity on education and training, energy and material efficiency improvements, and incentives to put the results of R and D onto the market. As well, policies that promote health and wellness, continuing education, culture, and the arts would improve the quality of life without increasing the economic burden of economic growth. This would be the opposite of fighting a recession by accelerating the consumption of energy and resources. Policies that encourage health promotion, continuing education, community development, culture, and the arts would improve the quality of life without increasing the burden of economic growth as much as conventional efforts to stimulate the economy. These policies would reward those who are efficient and have improved environmental performance and only penalize those who are not and have not.

The business community knows that during an economic downturn care must be taken to avoid spending time and effort on unprofitable activities. Time and money spent on trying to go back to the good old days will likely be wasted. Of course, this would require courage and conviction on the part of governments. But that has not been in short supply when it comes to cutting health, education, and social services. Perhaps a refocusing or balancing of the two approaches would produce better results and achieve more than one set of objectives.

At the other end of the economic spectrum of problems is government fear of inflation. In this case, manipulation of interest rates is used to slow the economy. However, one objection to actions to protect the environment and conserve resources is that they, too, slow down the economy. Perhaps governments should expand their thinking on the set of policies they have to control inflation and again develop a set of strategies, such as green taxes, that would have a wider range of benefits.

International Issues Affecting Environmental Management

Sustainable development cannot be achieved and environments and resources cannot be protected if the global commons cannot be protected. The atmosphere, the oceans, and space, beyond national boundaries or limits of economic influence (200-mile limit), is owned by no one, and controls on use and abuse are limited to voluntary international agreements — they are resources owned by everyone, the global commons.

The issues of globalization, homogenization of global society and global governance, must be resolved so corporations can advance their commitments to being socially responsible. As stated previously, the business case for improved environmental performance becomes essential. Nations are prepared to work hard for several years to be admitted to the WTO. They surrender some sovereignty to do so. When we can make the business case for improved environmental performance, nations will be able to see that it is also in their economic interest to form an organization for environmental protection similar to the WTO.

Maurice Strong has presented the issues of global environmental governance in *Where on Earth Are We Going?*[16] The difficulties of international negotiations are clear. Corporate influence is significant, whether for the good or not. Those corporations publicly proclaiming their commitments to social responsibility and sustainable development have to make their influence more strongly felt.

The set of strategy options is narrower and more difficult at the international level. Nonetheless, controversial initiatives such as the Tobin tax and green taxes or fees for use of the global commons have to be addressed. These two initiatives could provide financing for protection of the global environment.

Civil society and concerned NGOs proved their strength when they caused the defeat of the proposed Multinational Agreement on Investment (MAI).[17] The MAI was drafted to encourage economic growth by protecting foreign investors; however, the public was concerned about the repercussions of providing that protection. Rachel McCormick has proposed a Reverse MAI.[18] A set of criteria for meeting corporate social responsibilities and a means of proving compliance (regular audits and reports) would be established. Those corporations who proved that they met the conditions would then be provided with protection of their investments — with due consideration of sovereignty issues, etc. The Reverse MAI would have components of existing codes (CERES, ICC,

WBCSD, UNEP's global covenant) and, therefore, build on established criteria for performance. It would incorporate the use of established environmental management tools to improve performance and prove compliance with the code, and would provide investment protection as a strong incentive to corporations who subscribed.

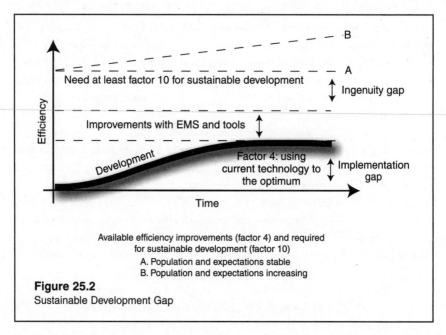

Available efficiency improvements (factor 4) and required
for sustainable development (factor 10)
A. Population and expectations stable
B. Population and expectations increasing

Figure 25.2
Sustainable Development Gap

It has been estimated that wide application of current best-practice and technology could improve energy and material efficiency by a factor of four.[19] But it has also been estimated that an efficiency improvement of a factor of ten is needed to reduce the environmental burden to a sustainable level and address poverty and equity issues in the developing world.[20] That leaves a sustainable development gap of a factor of six. (See Figure 25.2). That is, *business as usual only much better* will likely take us about halfway to sustainable development, if we get some synergy from positive feedback between improved environmental management systems and tools and technology; and improved capacity, especially in developing countries, is also needed. We can expect some technological advances, if not breakthroughs, but cannot rely on them. So we have a long way to go. Effective utilization of currently available techniques and technologies to achieve an improvement of a factor of four will bridge the implementation gap. That problem is not one of lack of knowledge or technology but implementation. Getting beyond that to a factor of ten improvement in efficiency is the ingenuity gap.[21]

Sustainable Development, Global Security, and Distribution of Wealth

Alleviation of poverty to provide the world's population with a reasonable minimum standard of living is a basic tenet of sustainable development and, more explicitly, The Natural Step (chapter 24). Christopher Flavin "speculates that the events of Sept. 11 would not have occurred if the goals of the Rio Earth Summit had been achieved."[22] United Nations Secretary General Kofi Annan observed that there has to be a focus on alleviating the poverty of the one billion people who live on less than U.S.$1 per day, or global instability will result.[23] Thomas Homer-Dixon, Director of the Centre for the Study of Peace and Conflict, has also stated that getting at poverty as a root cause of terrorism is not disloyal or naïve — it's prudent.[24]

Recently, governments have been relying heavily on the trickle-down theory of distribution of wealth to deliver the benefits of economic growth to the poor. However, there is growing evidence that it does not work. Naomi Klein believes that Kenneth Galbraith's ideas are catching on again. "He ridiculed the Reaganite trickle-down theory of wealth distribution, preferring the earthier phrase 'the horse-and-sparrow-theory' — 'If you feed the horse enough oats, some will pass through to the road for the sparrows.' He welcomes the progress by which most Americans can enjoy decent lives but points out that this 'culture of contentment' replaces the old dialectic of capital versus labor with a new one — now it is the rich and comfortable versus the concerned and the poor..."[25]

A critical aspect of the problem of improving global stability by solving the problems of wealth distribution is implementing effective means of providing economic stability to developing countries. Corporations have been provided with mechanisms to protect themselves during times of economic stress — various forms of bankruptcy protection. Banks stop allowing depositors to withdraw their money, when economic instability and heavy withdrawals threaten the banks' stability. Stock exchanges have mechanisms to slow or stop trading under certain circumstances. Similar mechanisms are needed for developing countries to achieve sustainable development and the kind of economic conditions in which environmental protection and conservation of resources is easier. Therefore countries need the equivalent of corporate bankruptcy protection. They need the means to stop the flow of currency out of the country in times of financial stress, just as banks do. The Tobin tax (see chapter 16, Economic Instruments) would assist in maintaining currency stability by discouraging speculation.

Corporations, especially those subscribing to The Natural Step, can only play a limited role in solving the problems of distribution of wealth. It is governments and the international community who must solve that problem.

The nature of the debate about protection of the environment and conservation of resources has changed radically over the decades that I have been involved in it, from a fight over whether there was any problem at all to the current discussion about what we do to solve the problems. Two major changes that go beyond improvements to the EMSs and the set of tools and seem to me to be fundamentally important are correcting market imperfections and making the business case for improved environmental performance. Those two changes would allow the market to play its role more effectively and prompt corporations and governments to protect the environment and conserve resources as part of their own self-interest. Getting those factors into play as part of the solution and largely out of the way as part of the problem will let us see more clearly the next step of dealing with human elements and society.

What are the Dimensions of the Problem?

Adverse environmental impacts have been caused by technologies at all levels of technological development, not just modern. If we examine how the use of technology has affected the environment and the resource base upon which different societies have depended, we find that no particular level of technological development causes problems. Every technological age has systematically damaged its resource base although the scale has increased dramatically.

- Hunters and gatherers on different continents, using primitive tools, contributed to, if not caused, the extinction of species.
- Agriculture, forestry, and fisheries have caused problems of over-harvesting, soil erosion and salinization, water pollution, and watershed damage from earliest times to the present. Societies using relatively primitive technologies today cause damage to their agricultural land, forests, and fisheries just as those using modern technologies do. The kind of technology did not reduce the propensity for damage, nor did widespread knowledge about the damage lead to a stop.
- Industrial age pollution of air, water, and soil, and the biosphere (including humans) is well documented. Damage from the use of energy and materials is controllable and control is being applied, but there is still a fierce debate about how much control we should exercise over technology and how much damage we can tolerate in the interests of protecting the environment.
- The information age has a resource base of information technology and the information it stores, moves, or processes. Viruses, hacking, spam (junk e-mail), junk mail, junk faxes, phone calls soliciting funds or selling stuff, and telephone/fax/e-mail fraud damage the resource base of the information age. In addition, there is the problem of lack of quality control of information. On the one hand, the information age provides more information in a greater variety of ways than ever before. On the other hand, lack of quality control over what enters the

information systems creates problems. Information overload, especially when it is poor quality, can be a greater problem than too little information. Contaminating high quality information is just like contaminating high quality water, air, or soil and just as hard and expensive to fix.

- The space age is exploiting the new frontier of earth's orbit and we're polluting that resource base too. It has been predicted that eventually there will be so much space junk in orbit that it will not be safe for humans. Space junk will threaten communications, remote sensing, and global positioning system technologies and inhibit our ability to repair them when damage occurs.

So we can conclude that it is not a particular level of technological development that is responsible for damage to the environment and waste of resources. We can also conclude that going back to the good old days is not the way to solve the problems.

Another informative historical perspective is an examination of the factors that have contributed to the collapse of societies at different times and places. Societies in Mesopotamia, Egypt, the Indus Valley, and on Easter Island collapsed as did the Khmer in Cambodia, the Anasazi, the Classic Maya, and others. Archeologists and anthropologists still argue about *the* cause of collapse but it is likely that it was a combination of factors, including destruction of the resource base, water pollution and destruction of water sheds, deforestation, soil erosion and salinization, overharvesting of renewable resources, population growth, and disease.

From this we can conclude that damage to the environment and the resource base upon which societies depend is not confined to modern North American and European societies. Societies in different ages, races, and religions probably contributed to their own collapse by harming the environment and failing to learn about damage and respond to it quickly enough.

Therefore, we are dealing with a very fundamental characteristic of human societies, not just with the products and technologies of particular levels of development. The issues are clearly not just related to technology, but are deeply rooted in society and our philosophies, cultures, and traditions. Our technology and industrial development are not separate from our culture but are a necessary expression of it. Therefore we must further examine, understand, and change the societal underpinnings that created the propensity to abuse the resources upon which we are so dependent. Failure to do so is simply treating the symptoms.

NOTES

Chapter 1. Introduction: The Environmental Manager's Toolbox

1. Musashi Miyamoto, *The Book of Five Rings*, trans. Thomas Cleary, Shambhala, Boston and London, 1993, p. 11.

2. Ibid., p. 13.

3. Brian Nattrass and Mary Altomare, *The Natural Step for Business*, New Society Publishers, Gabriola Island, B.C., 1999.

4. John Elkington, *Cannibals with Forks: The Triple Bottom Line of 21st Century Business*, New Society Publishers, Gabriola Island, B.C., 1998.

5. M. Wackernagel and W. Rees, *Our Ecological Footprint: Reducing Human Impact on the Earth*, New Society Publishers, Gabriola Island, B.C., 1996.

6. World Business Council for Sustainable Development, *Measuring Eco-efficiency: A Guide to Reporting Company Performance*, 2000. Available in pdf at <www.wbcsd.org/newscenter/media.htm>

   World Business Council for Sustainable Development, *Eco-efficiency: Creating More Value with Less Impact*, 2000. Available in pdf at <http://www.wbcsd.org/newscenter/media.htm>

7. R. Welford, *Corporate Environmental Management: Systems and Strategies*, Earthscan Publications, London, U.K., 1996.

8. V. H. Dale and M. R. English, eds., *Tools to Aid Environmental Decision Making*, Springer, NewYork, 1999.

9. <www.greenbiz.com/toolbox>

10. Canadian Standards Association, *ISO 14001-96 Environmental Management Systems — Specification with Guidance for Use*, CSA, Etobicoke, Ontario, 1996, Section 3.5.

11. Canadian Standards Association, *Environmental Management System Z750-94*, CSA, Rexdale, Ontario, 1994, p. xi.

12. Paul Hawken, *The Ecology of Commerce: A Declaration of Sustainability*, Harper Business, New York, 1993.

13. M. S. Dennison, *Pollution Prevention Strategies and Technologies*, Government Institutes Division, ABS Group, Rockville, MD, 1996;

    T. E. Higgins, ed., *Pollution Prevention Handbook*, Air and Waste Management Association, Sewickley, PA, 1995.

14. Livio DeSimone and Frank Popoff, *Eco-Efficiency: The Business Link to Sustainable Development*, MIT Press, Cambridge, MA, 1998;

    National Round Table on the Environment and the Economy, *Measuring Eco-efficiency in Business*, Renouf Publishing, Ottawa, Ontario, 1999;

    Robert De Andraca and Ken McCready, *Internalizing Environmental Costs to Promote Eco-Efficiency*, The Business Council for Sustainable Development, Geneva, 1994;

    National Round Table on the Environment and the Economy, *Calculating Eco-efficiency Indicators: A Workbook for Industry*, National Round Table on the Environment and the Economy, Ottawa, 2001. <www.nrtee-trnee.ca/eco-efficiency>;

    World Business Council for Sustainable Development, op. cit.

15. Herman Daly, *Beyond Growth*, Beacon Press, Boston, MA, 1996;

    Herman Daly and J. B. Cobb, *For the Common Good: Redirecting The Economy Toward Community, the Environment and a Sustainable Future*, Beacon Press, Boston, MA, 1989.

16. Wolfgang Sachs, *Greening the North: A Post-Industrial Blueprint for Ecology and Equity*, Zed Books, London, U.K., 1998.

17. P. Burall, *Green Design*, The Design Council, London, U.K., 1991;

    H. Lewis, J. Gertsakis, T. Grant, N. Morelli, and A. Sweatman, *Design + Environment: A Global Guide to Designing Greener Goods*, Greenleaf Publishing, Sheffield, U.K., 2001.

18. J. Fiksel, *Design for the Environment: Creating Eco-efficient Products and Processes*, McGraw-Hill, New York, 1999;

19. John Elkington, op. cit.

20. E. Von Weizsacker, Amory Lovins, and Hunter Lovins, *Factor Four: Doubling Wealth and Halving Resource Use*, Earthscan, London U.K., 1998.

21. Paul Hawken, Amory Lovins, and Hunter Lovins, "A Road Map For Natural Capitalism," *Harvard Business Review* (May-June 1999): pp. 145-158;

    Paul Hawken, Amory Lovins, and Hunter Lovins, *Natural Capital: Creating the Next Industrial Revolution*, Little, Brown and Company, New York, 1999b.

22. <www.zpg.org>

23. <www.clubofrome.org>

D. H. Meadows, D. L. Meadows, J. Randers, and W. W. Behrens, *The Limits to Growth: A Report for the Club of Rome's Project on the Predicament of Mankind*, Universe Books, New York, 1972;

D. H. Meadows, D. L. Meadows, and J. Randers, *Beyond the Limits: Controlling Global Collapse, Envisioning a Sustainable Future*, Chelsea Green Publishing, Post Mills, VT, 1992.

24. C. S. Holling, ed., *Adaptive Environmental Assessment and Management*, John Wiley and Sons, Toronto, Ontario, 1978.

25. L.-H. Kirkland, D. Thompson, L. Stoughton, and K. Bondy, "The Role of Organization and Contextural Culture in Designing and Implementing Effective Environmental Management Systems," forthcoming.

26. Carl Frankel, *In Earth's Company*, New Society Publishers, Gabriola Island, B.C., 1998.

Chapter 2. Environmental Management Systems

1. Canadian Standards Association, *ISO 14001 – 96 Environmental Management Systems – Specification with Guidance for Use*, CSA, Etobicoke, Ontario, 1996, p. 2.

2. Canadian Standards Association, *Environmental Management Systems Z750-94*, CSA, Etobicoke, Ontario, 1994, p.xi.

3. <www.gemi.org>

4. CSA, 1996, op. cit.

5. <www.europa.eu.int/comm/environment/emas/index.htm>

6. Standards Council of Canada, "ISO 9000 and 14000: Align, but Don't Combine," *Consensus* (March/April 1998): p. 7.

7. <www.europa.eu.int/comm/environment/emas/index.htm>

8. <www.bsi-global.com>

9. <www.projectsigma.com>

10. L. J. Midgelow, "ISO 14001: A Status Review," *EM* (December 2001): pp.16-23.

11. "German Companies Favor 14001 Revisions That Accent Performance," *ISO 14000 Update* VII, no. 6 (2001): pp. 1-2. Cutter Information Corp., Washington DC. <www.14001news.de>

12. <www.fedgovcontracts.com/fedregs/65f24593.htm>

13. "Environmental Management Systems Drive Agencies to Meet EPP Goals," *EPP Update* 10 (January 2002): pp. 1-2.

14. <www.ec.gc.ca/eog-oeg/ems/EMS.htm>

15. <www.oag-bvg.gc.ca/domino/other.nsf.html>

16. S. L. McAleer, "Recommendations for the Integration of an Occupational Health and Safety System and an Environmental Management System," master's thesis, Faculty of Environmental Design, University of Calgary, Alberta, 2001.

Chapter 3. Analysis of Driving Forces

1. R. Grandon, "Convincing the Boss Is Job One: GEMI Is Here to Help," *EM* (February 1999): pp. 5-6.

2. GEMI (Global Environmental Management Initiative), *Environment: Value to Business*, GEMI, Washington DC, 1998;

B. Willard, *The Sustainability Advantage: Seven Business Cases, Benefits of a Triple Bottom Line*, New Society Publishers, Gabriola Island, B.C., 2002;

M. A. Berry and D. A. Rondinelli, "Proactive Corporate Environmental Management: A New Industrial Revolution," *Academy of Management Executive*, 12, no. 2 (1998): pp. 38-50;

P. Hawken, A. Lovins, and H. L. Lovins, *Natural Capitalism: Creating the Next Industrial Revolution*, Little, Brown and Company, New York, 1999;

Reinhardt, F. L., "Bringing the Environment Down to Earth," *Harvard Business Review* 77, no. 4 (1999): pp. 149-157.

3. KPMG, *Canadian Environmental Management Survey*, Toronto, Ontario, 1994;

KPMG, *Canadian Environmental Management Survey*, Toronto, Ontario, 1996.

4. A. J. Hoffman, *Competitive Environmental Strategy: A Guide to the Changing Business Landscape*, Island Press, Washington DC, 2000.

5. J. Andriof and M. McIntosh, *Perspectives on Corporate Citizenship*, Greenleaf Publishing, Sheffield, U.K., 2001.

6. <www.gemi.org>

7. M. A. Berry and D. A. Rondinelli, "Proactive Corporate Environmental Management: A New Industrial Revolution," *Academy of Management Executive* 12, no. 2 (1998): pp. 38-50.

8. Organization for Economic Cooperation and Development, *The OECD Guidelines for Multinational Enterprises*, 2000. Available in pdf at <www.oecd.org>;

"Interest Widens in International Ethical Business Standard," *BATE* (November 2001): pp. 2-3. Cutter Information Corp., Washington DC.

9. L.-H. Kirkland and D. Thompson, "Challenges in Designing, Implementing and Operating an Environmental Management System," *Bus Strat Env* 8 (1999): pp. 128-143.

10. P. Garcia, J. Gonzalez, and D. Thompson, "Driving Forces and Barriers to Implementing

Sound Environmental Management in the Andean Region of Latin America," in W. Wehrmeyer and Y. Mulugetta, eds., *Growing Pains: Environmental Management in Developing Countries*, Greenleaf Publishing, Sheffield, U.K., 1999, pp. 132-147.

11. J. Parvin, "Mr. Dithers Goes to Jail," *Resources* (October 1999): pp. 11-12;
S. Berger, "The Varnicolour Prosecution," *Hazardous Materials Management*, (December 1992): pp. 30-32.

12. L. Griffiths and P. Granda, "Environmental Enforcement Statistics," *Hazardous Materials Management* (February/March 1999): pp. 43-45.

13. B. Pritchard, "Washington Report," *EM* (April 2000): p. 6.

14. Alberta Environmental Protection, "Announcement: Administrative Penalties," September 1994 media release, Edmonton, Alberta;
Standing Committee on Environment and Sustainable Development, *Enforcing Canada's Pollution Laws: The Public Interest Must Come First!* Third Report, Public Works and Government Services Canada, Ottawa, 1998.

15. D. Saxe, "New CEPA Tool," *Hazardous Materials Management* (December/January 2002): p. 70.

16. J. J. Bouma, M. Jeucken, and L. Klinkers, *Sustainable Banking: The Greening of Finance*, Greenleaf Publishing, Sheffield, U.K., 2001.

17. H. Brill, J. A. Brill, and C. Feigenbaum, *Investing With Your Values*, New Society Publishers, Gabriola Island, B.C., 2000;
David Skinner, *The Ethical Investor*, Stoddart, Toronto, Ontario, 2001;
D. Abbey and M. Jantzi, *The 50 Best Ethical Stocks for Canadians*, McMillan Canada, Toronto, Ontario, 2000.

18. "Australia Publishes Guides on Investment and Sustainable Development," *BATE* (September 2001): pp. 10-11.

19. G. Vaz-Oxlade, "The Greening of Canadian Investors," *Globe and Mail*, 26 May 2001, p. B8.

20. "Third Annual Vale Investing Guide," *Report on Business Magazine, Globe and Mail*, Oct 2001;
R. G. Eccles, R. H. Hertz, E. M. Keegan, and D. M. H. Phillips, *The Value Reporting Revolution: Moving Beyond the Earnings Game*, John Wiley, New York, 2001.

21. Tellus Institute, "Greening Capital Markets: What Motivates Wall Street?" *Environmental Perspectives* 14 (February 1999): pp. 1-4.

22. B. W. Feltmate, B. A. Schonfield, and R. W. Yachnin, *Sustainable Development, Value*

Creation and the Capital Markets, Conference Board of Canada, Ottawa, 2001. Available in pdf at <www.conferenceboard.ca>

23. J. Prestbo, "Explaining the Dow Jones Sustainability Group Index," World Business Council for Sustainable Development, 2000. <www.wbcsd.org/newscenter/speeches/ebc/EBC DowJones.pdf >

24. "Sustainability Screen Compares Companies, Builds Mutual Fund," *BATE* (March 2001): pp. 8-9;
"Sustainability Fund Beats Benchmark Indexes," *BATE* (December 2001): p. 8.

25. "Goodies Are Named, Baddies Exposed by 'Footsie' Investment Lists," *BATE* (August 2001): pp. 7-8.

26. "Corporate Environmental Ratings Available to Investors," *BATE* (March 2001): p. 7.

27. "As Green Investment Indexes Grow, So Does the Grumbling," *BATE* (July 2000): pp. 4-5.

28. See for example: M. E. Porter and C. van der Linde, "Green and Competitive: Ending the Stalemate," *Harvard Business Review* (September-October 1995): pp. 120-143;
W. C. Zegel, "Message from the President: Worldwide Marketplace Demands Environmental Performance Improvements," *EM* (September 1997): p. 4;
T. O'Brian, "The Green Machine," *EM* (January 2000): pp. 22-23.

29. Standards Council of Canada, "ISO 14000 in Japan," *Consensus* (September/October 1999): pp. 14-15.

30. Commission for Environmental Cooperation, *Voluntary Measures to Ensure Environmental Compliance: A Review and Analysis of North American Initiatives*, Montreal, 1998.

31. <www.vcr.mvr.ca>

32. <www.vcr-mvr.ca>

33. *Corporate Action on Climate Change - 1997: An Independent Review*, Pembina Institute, Pembina, Alberta, 1998.
<www.pembina.org/pubs/vcr97.htm>
Environment and Trade: A Handbook, UNEP and IISD, Winnipeg, Manitoba, 2000. Available at
<www.iisd.org/pdf/envirotrade_handbook.pdf>

34. <www.ec.gc.ca/aret>

35. See for example: J. Elkington, *Cannibals with Forks: The Triple Bottom Line of 21st Century Business*, New Society Publishers, Gabriola Island, B.C., 1998;
J. Andriof and M. McIntosh, eds., *Perspectives on Corporate Citizenship*, Greenleaf Publishing, Sheffield, U.K., 2001;
D. A. Rondinelli and M. A. Berry,

"Environmental Citizenship in Multinational Corporations: Social Responsibility and Sustainable Development," *European Management Journal* 18, no. 1 (2000): pp. 70-84.

Chapter 4. Analysis of Barriers

1. W.M. Cohen and D.A. Levinthal, "Absorptive Capacity: A New Perspective on Learning and Innovation," *Administrative Science Quarterly* 35 (1990): pp. 128-152.

2. E. M Rogers, *Diffusion of Innovations*, 4th ed., Free Press, New York, 1995.

3. M. Kubr, ed., *Management Consulting: A Guide to the Profession*, 2nd rev. ed., International Labour Office, Geneva, 1986, pp. 57-59.

4. J. Pfeffer, "When It Comes to 'Best Practices' – Why Do Smart Organizations Occasionally Do Dumb Things?" *Organizational Dynamics* (summer 1996): pp. 33-43.

5. <http://calvin.arentfox.com/enviro/state-selfaudit.html>

6. M. Kubr, 1986, op. cit.

7. Stafford Beer, *Brain of the Firm*, Allen Lane The Penguin Press, London, U.K., 1972, p. 53.

8. C. J. Gersick and J. R. Hackman, "Habitual Routines in Task-Performing Groups," *Organisational Behavior and Human Decision Processes* 47 (1990): pp. 65-97.

9. R. K. Reger, L. T. Gustafson, S. M. Demarie, and J. V. Mullane, "Reframing the Organization: Why Implementing Total Quality is Easier Said Than Done," *Academy of Management Review* 19, no. 3 (1994): pp. 565-584.

10. K. J. Klein and J. S. Sorra, "The Challenge of Innovation Implementation," *Academy of Management Review* 21, no. 4 (1996): pp. 1055-1080.

11. S. B. Bacharach, P. Bamberger, and W. J. Sonnenstuhl, "The Organizational Transformation Process: The Micropolitics of Dissonance Reduction and the Alignment of Logics of Action," *Administrative Science Quarterly* 41 (1996): pp. 477-506.

12. J. P. Kotter, *Leading Change*, Harvard Business School Press, Boston, MA, 1996, p. 13.

13. <www.beyondgreypinstripes.org/environmental.html>

Chapter 5. Strategic Environmental Management

1. J. A. Pearce II and R. B. Robinson, Jr., *Strategic Management: Formulation, Implementation, and Control*, 6th ed., Irwin, Toronto, Ontario, 1997.

2. Charles Handy, *Understanding Organizations*, 4th ed., Penguin, London, U.K., 1993, p. 18.

3. Ibid., p. 327.

4. P. Schwartz, *The Art of the Long View: Planning for the Future in an Uncertain World: Paths to Strategic Insight for Yourself and Your Company*, Currency Doubleday, Toronto, Ontario, 1996, pp. 219-220.

5. Institute of Environmental Management, "Being Strategic: Building Skills to Manage for the Future," *Journal of the Institute of Environmental Management* 4, no.1 (1996).

6. T. W. Mason, A. T. Roper, and A. Porter, "Integrating Environmental Consequences and Impact Assessment into Design Processes and Corporate Strategy," *Impact Assessment and Project Appraisal* (June 1999): pp.141-145.

7. H. Mintzberg, J. B. Quinn, and J. Voyer, *The Strategy Process*, collegiate ed., Prentice Hall, New Jersey, 1995.

8. H. Mintzberg, B. Ahlstrand, J. Lampel, *Strategy Safari: A Guided Tour Through the Wilds of Strategic Management*, The Free Press, Toronto, Ontario, 1998.

9. S. Beer, *Brain of the Firm: The Managerial Cybernetics of Organization*, Allen Lane The Penguin Press, London, U.K., 1972, p. 54.

10. Institute of Environmental Management, op. cit., p. 9.

11. H. Mintzberg, "The Fall and Rise of Strategic Planning," *Harvard Business Review* (January-February 1994): pp. 107-114.

12. D. C. Hambrick and J. W. Fredrickson, "Are You Sure You Have a Strategy?" *Academy of Management Executive* 15, no. 4 (2001): pp. 48-59.

13. Schwartz, op. cit., pp. 237-239.

14. Beer, op cit.

15. Global Environmental Management Initiative, *Benchmarking: The Primer: Benchmarking for Continuous Environmental Improvement*, GEMI, Washington DC, 1994. Available in pdf at <www.gemi.org>

16. G. Crognale, ed., *Environmental Management Strategies: The 21st Century Perspective*, Prentice Hall PTR, Upper Saddle River, New Jersey, 1999, p. 156.

17. Global Environmental Management Initiative, GEMI Benchmarking Surveys, GEMI, Washington DC, 2000. Available at <www.gemi.org>

18. Benchmark Environmental Consulting, *The State of Global Environmental Reporting: The 1999 Benchmark Survey*, Cutter Information Corp., Washington DC, 1999. <www.cutter.com>

19. World Business Council for Sustainable Development, *Measuring Eco-efficiency: A Guide to Reporting Company Performance*, 2000.

Available in pdf at
<http://www.wbcsd.org/newscenter/media.htm>
World Business Council for Sustainable
Development, 2000, *Eco-efficiency: Creating
More Value with Less Impact.* Available in pdf at
<http://www.wbcsd.org/newscenter/media.htm>

20. GEMI, 2000, op. cit.

21. Schwartz, op. cit.

22. Conference Board of Canada, 2002 Great
    Expectations, *Report On Business Magazine,
    Globe and Mail,* February 2002, advertising sup-
    plement. See also <www.conferenceboard.ca>

Chapter 6. Environmental Policy

1. Canadian Standards Association, *ISO 14001 –
   96 Environmental Management Systems –
   Specification with Guidance for Use,* CSA,
   Etobicoke, Ontario, 1996.

2. J. A. Pearce and R. B. Robinson, *Strategic
   Management: Formulation, Implementation and
   Control,* 6th ed., Irwin, Toronto, Ontario, 1997,
   p. 322.

3. J. Cascio, G. Woodside, and P. Mitchell, *ISO
   14000 Guide: The New International
   Environmental Management Standards,* McGraw-
   Hill, New York, 1996, Chapter 5,
   Environmental Policy;
   R. Welford, *Corporate Environmental
   Management: Systems and Strategies,* Earthscan
   Publications, London, U.K., 1996;
   Global Environmental Management Initiative,
   *ISO 14001 Environmental Management System
   Self-Assessment Checklist,* GEMI, Washington
   DC, 1996, rev. ed. November 2000. Available in
   pdf at <www.gemi.org>;
   Canadian Standards Association, *ISO 14000
   Essentials: A Practical Guide to Implementing the
   ISO Standards Plus 14000,* CSA, Etobicoke,
   Ontario, 1996, pp. 22-26.

4. Canadian Standards Association, *ISO 14004
   Environmental Management Systems – General
   Guidelines on Principles, Systems and Supporting
   Techniques,* CSA, Etobicoke, Ontario, 1996, pp.
   6-7;
   Canadian Standards Association, *Plus 1113 First
   Steps to Environmentally Responsible Management:
   A Comprehensive Workbook for Environmental
   Policy Development (Based on ISO 14001),* CSA,
   Etobicoke, Ontario, 1996.

5. Council of European Communities, "Council
   Regulation (EEC) No 1836/93, allowing voluntary participation by companies in the industrial
   sector in a community eco-management and
   audit scheme," Annex I, Section A., Council of
   European Communities, 1993.

6. D. A. Rondinelli and G. Vastag, "International
   Environmental Standards and Corporate

Policies: an Integrative Framework," *California
Management Review* 39, no. 1 (1996): pp. 106-
122.

7. Global Environmental Management Initiative,
   *ISO 14001 Environmental Management System
   Self-Assessment Checklist,* Washington DC, 1996,
   rev. November 2000. Available in pdf at
   <www.gemi.org>

8. Chris Ryley, "Corporate Environmental Policy
   Statements," master's degree project, Faculty of
   Environmental Design, University of Calgary,
   Alberta, 1995.

9. G. B. Doern, *Green Diplomacy: How
   Environmental Decisions Are Made,* Policy Study
   16, C. D. Howe Institute, Toronto, Ontario,
   1993.

10. Z. A. Smith, *The Environmental Policy Paradox,*
    Prentice Hall, New Jersey, 1992.

Chapter 7. Environmental Management Structures

1. H. Mintzberg, J. B. Quinn, and J. Voyer, "The
   Strategy Process," in *Structure and Process,*
   Prentice Hall, Englewood Cliffs, NJ, 1995, pp.
   133-167.

2. J. A. Pearce and R. B. Robinson, *Strategic
   Management: Formulation, Implementation and
   Control,* 6th ed., Irwin, Chicago, IL, 1997, pp.
   339-352.

3. S. Beer, *Brain of the Firm: The Managerial
   Cybernetics of Organization,* Allen Lane The
   Penguin Press, London, U.K., 1972, chapter
   11, "Corporate Structure and its
   Quantification," and chapter 14, "Multinode –
   System Five."

4. J. Child and R. G. McGrath, eds., "Special
   Research Forum on New and Evolving
   Organizations Forms," *The Academy of
   Management Journal* 44, no. 6 (December
   2001): pp. 1135-1322.

5. H. Mintzberg and L. Van der Heyden,
   "Organigraphs: Drawing How Companies
   Really Work," *Harvard Business Review*
   (September/October 1999): pp. 87-94.

6. S. Beer, 1972, op. cit., chapter 14, "The
   Multinode – System Five."

7. Charles Handy, *Understanding Organizations,*
   4th ed., Penguin, London, U.K., 1993.

8. J. Champy, *Reengineering Management: The
   Mandate for New Leadership,* Harper Business,
   New York, 1995;
   W. Bennis and M. Mische, *The 21st Century
   Organization: Reinventing through Reengineering,*
   Pfeiffer, San Diego, Calif., 1995.

9. KPMG, *Canadian Environmental Management
   Survey,* KPMG Environmental Management
   Services, Toronto, Ontario, 1994;

KPMG, *Canadian Environmental Management Survey*, KPMG Environmental Risk Management Practice, Toronto, Ontario, 1996.

10. L.-H. Kirkland and D. Thompson, "Challenges in Designing, Implementing and Operating an Environmental Management System," *Bus Strat Env* 8 (1999): pp.128-143.

11. W. G. Ouchi, *Theory Z: How American Business Can Meet the Japanese Challenge*, Avon, New York, 1981.

12. Business and the Environment (BATE) 9, no. 7 (July 1998): p. 7.

13. J. Casio, G. Woodside, and P. Mitchell, *ISO 14000 Guide: The New International Environmental Management Standards*, McGraw-Hill, New York, 1996.

14. See for example H. Mintzberg, J. B. Quinn, and J. Voyer, op. cit., pp. 139-144.

15. Handy, op. cit.

16. Beer, op. cit.

Chapter 8. Environmental Auditing

1. Canadian Standards Association, *ISO 14012, Guidelines for Environmental Auditing: Qualification Criteria for Environmental Auditors*, CSA, Etobicoke, Ontario, 1996.

2. Ibid.

3. J. L. Greeno, G. Hedstrom, and M. A. DiBerto, *Environmental Auditing: Fundamentals and Techniques*, 2nd ed., Arthur D. Little, Inc., Cambridge, MA, 1987.

4. J. Reed, "Environmental Auditing: A Review of Current Practice," master's thesis, York University, Toronto, Ontario, 1984.

5. L. B. Cahill and R. Kane, *Environmental Audits*, 6th ed., Government Institutes Inc., Rockville, MD, 1989.

6. Environmental Protection Agency, "Environmental Auditing Policy Notice," July 9, 1986, p. 25004.

7. J. Reed, op. cit.

8. Environment Canada, *Canadian Environmental Protection Act: Enforcement and Compliance Policy*, report published under authority of the Minister of Environment, Minister of Supply and Services, Ottawa, 1988.

9. Canadian Standards Association, *ISO 14010, Guidelines for Environmental Auditing – General Principles*, CSA, Etobicoke, Ontario, 1996.

10. Canadian Standards Association, *ISO 14011, Guidelines for Environmental Auditing – Audit Procedures – Auditing of Environmental Management Systems*, CSA, Etobicoke, Ontario, 1996.

11. Canadian Standards Association, *ISO 14012, Guidelines for Environmental Auditing:*

Qualification Criteria for Environmental Auditors, CSA, Etobicoke, Ontario, 1996.

12. D. Stevenson, "Back to the Drawing Board," *Hazardous Materials Management* (April/May 2001): pp. 16-17.

13. CEAA/ACVE website, 1999.

14. R. G. Eccles, R. H. Hertz, E. M. Keegan, and D. M. H. Phillips, *The Value Reporting Revolution: Moving Beyond the Earnings Game*, John Wiley, New York, 2001, p. 117.

Chapter 9. Education and Training

1. Air and Waste Management Association, *Resource Book and Membership Directory*, Pittsburgh, 2001, p. RB20-RB21.

2. W. Wehrmeyer, ed., *Greening People: Human Resources and Environmental Management*, "Part 3: Training and Skills towards Environmental Improvement," Greenleaf Publishing, Sheffield, U.K., 1996.

3. J. Millimanand and J. Clair, "Best Environmental HRM Practice in the US," in W. Wehrmeyer, ed., *Greening People: Human Resources and Environmental Management*, The Durrell Institute, University of Kent, U.K., 1996, pp. 49-73.

4. G. Crognale, "Training: Preparations for Maintaining Effective Environmental Management Systems," in C. Sheldon, ed., *ISO 14000 and Beyond: Environmental Management Systems in the Real World*, Greenleaf Publishing, Sheffield, U.K., 1997, pp. 293-307.

5. A. Wells, "Training and Environmental Management Systems," in C. Sheldon, ed., *ISO 14000 and Beyond: Environmental Management Systems in the Real World*, Greenleaf Publishing, Sheffield, U.K., 1997, pp. 183-205.

6. R. MacLean, "Building the Case for EH&S Training," *EM* (September 1999): pp. 9-11.

7. K. Garbesi and T. D. Patane, "Education Improves Regulatory Compliance for Hazardous Materials Handling: A Silicon Valley Case Study," *EM* (September 1999): pp. 13-18.

8. P. Senge, *The Fifth Discipline: The Art and Practice of the Learning Organization*, Currency Doubleday, New York, 1994;
P. M. Senge, A. Kleiner, C. Roberts, R. B. Ross and B. J. Smith, *The Fifth Discipline Fieldbook: Strategies and Tools For Building a Learning Organization*, Currency Doubleday, New York, 1994.

9. Canadian Standards Association, *ISO 14001-96 Environmental Management Systems – Specification with Guidance for Use*, CSA, Etobicoke, Ontario, 1996.

10. Canadian Standards Association, *ISO 14004 – 96 Environmental Management Systems – General*

Guidelines on Principles, Systems and Supporting Techniques, CSA, Etobicoke, Ontario, 1996.

11. Council of European Communities, "Council Regulation (EEC) No 1836/93, allowing voluntary participation by companies in the industrial sector in a community eco-management and audit scheme," Annex I, Section A., Council of European Communities, 1993.

12. Canadian Standards Association, *The ISO 14000 Essentials: A Practical Guide to Implementing the ISO 14000 Standards*, CSA, Etobicoke, Ontario, 1996, pp. 50-54.

13. Global Environmental Management Initiative, *ISO Environmental Management System Self-Assessment Checklist*, 1996, rev. November 2000, pp. 23-25.

14. P. E. J. Green, "A New Due Diligence Precedent for EMS," *Hazardous Materials Management* (October/November 1998): p. 20.

15. A. Gordon, "35 Best Companies to Work For," *Report on Business Magazine Globe and Mail*, February 2000, pp. 24-32.

16. Center for the New American Dream, <www.newdream.org/procure>

17. O. Sacks, *The Man Who Mistook His Wife for a Hat and Other Clinical Tales*, Simon and Schuster, New York, 1985.

18. Senge, op. cit.

19. E. M. Rogers, *Diffusion of Innovation*, 4th ed., Free Press, New York, 1995.

20. ISO website <www.iso.org> or see J. Cascio, G. Woodside, and P. Mitchell, *ISO 14000 Guide*, McGraw-Hill, New York, 1996, "Appendix B, ISO Member Bodies and Designated Representative Organizations," pp. 163-166.

21. <www.iema.org.uk>

22. <www.eia.asn.au>

23. <www.cchrei.ca>

24. <www.iatca.org>

25. <www.iaf.nu>

26. <www.iasc.org.uk>

27. <www.cmnet.org>

28. Stephen D. Hill, "Mental Models for the Management of Environmental Risks by Organizations," unpublished Ph.D. dissertation, Faculty of Environmental Design, University of Calgary, 2002.

29. T. F. Hartig, G. Kaiser, and P. A. Bower, "Psychological Restoration in Nature as a Positive Motivation for Ecological Behavior," *Environment and Behavior* 33, no. 4 (2001): pp. 590-607;
P. Bansal and K. Roth, "Why Companies Go Green: A Model of Ecological Responsiveness," *Academy of Management Journal* 43, no.4 (2000): pp. 717-736.

Chapter 10. Risk Management

1. P. L. Berstein, *Against the Gods: The Remarkable Story of Risk*, John Wiley, New York, 1996.

2. Canadian Standards Association, *Risk Management: Guidelines for Decision Makers*, Q850-97, Canadian Standards Association, Etobicoke, Ontario, 1997, p. 3.

3. Ibid.

4. The Presidential/Congressional Commission on Risk Assessment and Risk Management, *Framework for Environmental Health Management*, Washington DC, 1997.

5. Ibid.

6. CSA, 1997, op. cit.

7. Presidential/Congressional Commission, op. cit., p.1.

8. S. Kaplan and B. J. Garrick, "On the Quantitative Definition of Risk," *Risk Analysis* 1, no. 1 (1981): pp. 11-27.

9. CSA, op. cit.

10. American Chemical Society, *Understanding Risk Analysis: A Short Guide for Health, Safety and Environmental Policy Making*, Internet ed., ACS, 1998, p. 9.
<http://pubs.acs.org/>

11. Ibid., p. 10.

12. CSA, op. cit., section 8.2.

13. ACS, 1998, op. cit., p. 11.

14. A. Hopkins, *Lessons from Longford: The Esso Gas Plant Explosion*, CCH Australia Limited, Arcadia, NSW, Australia, 2000.

Chapter 11. Environmental Site Assessment

1. Crittenden, G., ed., *Hazardous Waste Management*, personal communication.

2. Building Operators and Managers Institute (BOMI), *Environmental Site Assessments*, BOMI, Arnold, MD, 1994.

3. Canadian Standards Association, *Phase I Environmental Site Assessment, Z768-94*, CSA, Etobicoke, Ontario, 1994.

4. Servicios SA v. Northern Badger Oil & Gas Ltd., 1991.

5. CERCLA (Comprehensive Environmental Response Compensation and Liability Act) 601, (35)(b);

6. American Society for Testing and Materials (ASTM), *1996 Standard Practice for Environmental Site Assessment Transactional Screen Process*, ASTM, Conshohooken, PA, 1996.

7. Canadian Standards Association, 1994, op. cit.

8. Ibid.

9. Ibid.

10. U.S. Environmental Protection Agency (EPA)

website on brownfields:
<www.epa.gov/swerosps/bf/index >

11. Canada Mortgage and Housing Corporation
(CMHC), *Phase I Environmental Site Assessment
Interpretation Guidelines*, CMHC, Ottawa,
Ontario, 1994.

Chapter 12. Environmental Indicators

1. P. Senge, *The Fifth Discipline: The Art and
Practice of the Learning Organization*, Currency
Doubleday, New York, 1994.

2. Global Reporting Initiative, 2000, *Sustainability
Reporting Guidelines on Economic, Environmental
and Social Performance*, June 2000. Available at
<www.globalreporting.org>;
Global Reporting Initiative, 2002, *Sustainability
Reporting Guidelines on Economic, Environmental
and Social Performance*, April 2002. Available at
<www.globalreporting.org>

3. World Business Council for Sustainable
Development, *Measuring Eco-efficiency: A Guide
to Reporting Company Performance*, 2000.
Available in pdf at
<http://www.wbcsd.org/newscenter/media.htm>
World Business Council for Sustainable
Development, 2000, *Eco-efficiency: Creating
More Value with Less Impact*. Available in pdf at
<http://www.wbcsd.org/newscenter/media.htm>

4. National Round Table on the Environment and
the Economy, *Calculating Eco-efficiency
Indicators: A Workbook for Industry*, National
Round Table on the Environment and the
Economy, Ottawa, 2001, <www.nrtee-
trnee.ca/eco-efficiency>

5. Ibid., p.1.

6. Ibid.

7. <www.globalreporting.org>

8. W. L. Neuman, *Social Research Methods:
Qualitative and Quantitative Approaches*, Allyn
and Bacon, Toronto, 1997.

9. W.-A. Thomas, ed., *Indicators of Environmental
Quality*, Plenum Press, New York, 1972.

10. V. W. Maclaren, "Urban Sustainability
Reporting," *Journal of the American Planning
Association* (1996): pp. 184-205.

11. A. Willis, "For Good Measure." *CA Magazine*
(1994): pp. 16-25.

12. J. E. Innes, *Knowledge and Public Policy: The
Search for Meaningful Indicators*, Transaction
Publishers, New Brunswick, NJ, 1990.

13. Maclaren, 1996, op. cit.

14. Ibid.;
T. Hodges, "Toward a Conceptual Framework
for Assessing Progress Toward Sustainability,"
Social Indicators Research (1997): pp. 5-98.

15. <www.globalreporting.org>

16. Maclaren, 1996, op. cit.

17. V. M. H. Borden and T. W. Banta, *Using
Performance Indicators to Guide Strategic Decision
Making*, vol. 82, Jossey-Bass Inc., San Francisco,
California, 1994.

18. R. A. Howell, *Management Accounting Guideline
31: Developing Performance Indicators*, The
Society of Management Accountants of Canada,
Hamilton, Ontario, 1994.

19. The Canadian Institute of Chartered
Accountants, *Reporting on Environmental
Performance*, The Canadian Institute of
Chartered Accountants, Toronto, Ontario,
1994;
International Organization for Standardization,
*ISO 14031 Environmental Management -
Environmental Performance Evaluation -
Guidelines*, ISO, New York, 1998.

20. Organisation for Economic Co-operation and
Development, *OECD Core Set of Indicators for
Environmental Performance Reviews*,
Environment Monographs no. 83 OCDE/GD
(93)179, OECD, Paris, 1993.

21. C. Schuh, "Performance Indicators for Indoor
Air Quality," unpublished Ph.D. dissertation,
Faculty of Environmental Design, University of
Calgary, Alberta, 2000.

22. ISO, 1998, op. cit.

Chapter 13. Environmental Reporting

1. J. Elkington and F. van Dijk, "Socially
Challenged: Trends in Social Reporting," in
Sustainable Measures, M. Bennett and P. James,
eds., Greenleaf Publishing: Sheffield, U.K.,
1999.

2. D. Wheeler and J. Elkington, "The End of the
Corporate Environmental Report? Or, the
Advent of Cybernetic Sustainability
Reporting," *Business Strategy and the
Environment* 10 (2001): pp. 1-14.

3. KPMG, *Canadian Environmental Management
Survey*, Toronto, 1996.

4. G. Greene, S. Meyer, J. Moffet, and J. Pezzack,
*Stepping Forward: Corporate Sustainability
Reporting in Canada*, Stratos, Ottawa, 2001.
Available at <http://www.stratos-
sts.com/pages/publica010.htm>

5. United Nations Environmental Programme,
*Company Environmental Reporting: A Measure of
the Progress of Business and Industry Towards
Sustainable Development*, Industry and the
Environment, Paris, 1994.

6. Global Environmental Management Initiative,
*Environmental Reporting and Third Party
Statements*, GEMI, Washington DC, 1996.

7. M. Bennett and P. James, eds., *Sustainable
Measures: Evaluation and Reporting of*

Environmental and Social Performance, Greenleaf Publishing, Sheffield, U.K., 1999.

8. Elkington, John, *Cannibals with Forks: The Triple Bottom Line of 21st Century Business*, New Society Publishers, Gabriola Island, B.C., 1998.

9. Bennett and James, op. cit.

10. <www.keidanren.or.jp>

11. N. Luscombe, "When Clean Means Green," *CA Magazine*, 1993, p. 3;

International Institute for Sustainable Development, *Coming Clean: Corporate Environmental Reporting*, IISD, Winnipeg, Manitoba, 1993.

12. IISD, op. cit.

13. D. Wheeler and M. Sillanpaa, *The Stakeholder Corporation*, Pitman Publishing, London, U.K., 1997.

14. <www.talisman-energy.com>

15. Stephen D. Hill, "Mental Models for the Management of Environmental Risks by Organizations," unpublished Ph.D. dissertation, Faculty of Environmental Design, University of Calgary, Alberta, 2002.

16. J. J. Bouma, M. Jeucken, and L. Klinkers, *Sustainable Banking: The Greening of Finance*, Greenleaf Publishing, Sheffield, U.K., 2001.

H. Brill, J. A. Brill, and C. Feigenbaum, *Investing With Your Values: Making Money and Making a Difference*, New Society Publishers, Gabriola Island, B.C., 2000;

David Skinner, *The Ethical Investor: A Guide to Socially Responsible Investing in Canada*, Stoddart, Toronto, Ontario, 2001;

D. Abbey and M. Jantzi, *The 50 Best Ethical Stocks for Canadians*, McMillan Canada, Toronto, Ontario, 2000;

"Australia Publishes Guides on Investment and Sustainable Development," *BATE* (September 2001): pp. 10-11;

G. Vaz-Oxlade, "The Greening of Canadian Investors," *Globe and Mail*, 26 May 2001, p. B8.

17. Global Reporting Initiative (GRI) 2000, *Sustainability Reporting Guidelines on Economic, Environmental and Social Performance*, June 2000. Available at <www.globalreporting.org>; Global Reporting Initiative (GRI) 2002, *Sustainability Reporting Guidelines on Economic, Environmental and Social Performance*, April 2002. Available at <www.globalreporting.org>

18. R. M. Skinner, *Accounting Standards in Evolution*, Holt, Rinehart, and Winston of Canada Limited, Toronto, Ontario, 1987, p. 422.

19. GRI, 2000, op. cit.

20. Ibid.; GRI, 2002, op. cit.;

G. Greene, S. Meyer, J. Moffet, and J. Pezzack, *Stepping Forward: Corporate Sustainability Reporting in Canada*, Stratos, Ottawa, Ontario, 2001. Available at <http://www.stratos-sts.com/pages/publica010.htm.>

21. United Nations Environment Programmme, 1994, op. cit.

22. GRI, 2000, op. cit.; GRI, 2002, op. cit.

23. <www2.shell.com>

24. <www.suncor.com>

25. <www.tallisman-energy.com/pdfs/csr_2001_report.pdf>

26. <www.bp.com/environ-social/review_2001/index.asp>

27. Global Reporting Initiative Verification Working Group, *Overarching Principles for Providing Independent Assurance on Sustainability Reports*, Global Reporting Initiative, 2001.

28. Ibid.

29. Federation des experts comptables european, *Providing Assurance on Environmental Reports*, discussion paper, Brussels, Belgium, no date. <http://www.fee.be/publications/main.htm>

30. M. Wilson and C. K. Schuh, "Auditing Corporate Sustainability Reports," in Canadian Environmental Auditing Association Annual Technical Conference, Vancouver, 2001. Available at <http://www.ceaa-acve/WilsonP.pdf>

Chapter 14. Environmental Impact Assessment

1. United Nations Environment Programme, "Environmental Impact Assessment," Decision 14/25 of the Governing Council of the United Nations Environment Programme, Nairobi, 1987.

2. Canadian Environmental Assessment Research Council (CEARC), *Evaluation Environmental Impact Assessment: An Action Prospectus*, CEARC, Hull, Quebec, 1988.

3. B. Sadler, *International Study of the Effectiveness of Environmental Impact Assessment: Final Report: Environmental Assessment in a Changing World: Evaluating Practice to Improve Performance*, Canadian Environmental Assessment Agency, Hull, Quebec, 1996, p. 1.

4. R. B. Beattie, "Everything You Already Know About EIA (But Don't Often Admit)," *Environmental Impact Assessment Review* 15, no. 2 (1995): pp. 109-114, Elsevier, Boston, MA.

5. R. Carson, *Silent Spring*, Fawcett Publications, Greenwich, CT, 1962.

6. B. Commoner, *The Closing Circle: Nature, Man and Technology*, Bantam Books, New York, 1973.

7. G. Hardin, "The Tragedy of the Commons," *Science* 162 (1968): pp. 1243-1248. Available at <www.ranchwest.com/hardin.html>

8. International Association for Impact Assessment: <http://www.IAIA.org>

9. United Nations Environment Programme, 1987, op. cit.

10. Ibid.

11. B. Sadler, 1996, op. cit.

12. P. Morris and R. Therivel, *Methods of Environmental Impact Assessment*, UBC Press, Vancouver, B.C., 1995.

13. UNEP, 1987, op. cit.

14. B. Sadler, 1996, op. cit., p. 109.

15. United Nations Task Force on Environmental Impact Assessment Auditing, *Post-project Analysis in Environmental Impact Assessment: Analysis of European and North American Case Studies*, United Nations, Geneva, 1990.

16. United Nations Environment Programme, 1987, op. cit.

17. W. A. Ross, "Cumulative Effects Assessment: Learning from Canadian Case Studies," in *Impact Assessment and Project Appraisal*, Beech Tree Publishing, Guildford, U.K., 1998, pp. 267-276.

18. G. Hegman, C. Cocklin, R. Creasey, S. Dupuis, A. Kennedy, L. Kingsley, W. Ross and D. Stalker, *Cumulative Effects Assessment Practitioners Guide*, Canadian Environmental Assessment Agency, Hull, Quebec, 1999.

19. B. Sadler, 1996, op. cit., p. 151.

20. Thomas W. Mason, A. Thomas Roper, and Alan Porter, "Integrating Environmental Consequences and Impact Assessment into Design Processes and Corporate Strategy," in *Impact Assessment and Project Appraisal* 177, no. 2 (1999): pp. 141-146, Beech Tree Publishing, Guildford, U.K.

21. Jules Scholten, "Recent Progress in EIA and SIA," Plenary Presentation to Annual Conference, International Association for Impact Assessment, Glasgow, Scotland, 1999.

22. <www.pembina.org>

Chapter 15. Environmental Accounting

1. M. Bennett and P. James, *The Green Bottom Line: Environmental Accounting for Management: Current Practice and Future Trends*, Greenleaf Publishing, Sheffield, U.K., 1998.

2. S. Schaltegger and R. Burrit, *Contemporary Environmental Accounting: Issues, Concepts and Practice*, Greenleaf Publishing, Sheffield, U.K., 2001.

3. The three workbooks will be available at <www.un.org/esa/sustdev/estema.htm>

Business and the Environment (March 2001): pp. 2-3.

4. The report is available at <www.epa.gov/oppt/acctg/eacasestudies.pdf>

5. T. D. Wilmhurst and G. R. Frost, "The Role of Accounting and the Accountant in the Environmental Management System," *Bus Strat Env* 10 (2001): pp. 135-147.

6. A. J. Buonicore and D. P. Crocker, "Environmental Accounting Stumbles," *EM*, (May 2001): pp. 8-9.

7. Schaltegger and Burritt, op. cit.

8. CICA, Environmental Stewardship: Management Accountability and the Role of Chartered Accountants, CICA, Toronto, Ontario, 1993.

9. CMA (Certified Management Accountants), *Tools and Techniques of Environmental Accounting for Business Decisions*, M. J. Epstein, lead author, Society of Management Accountants of Canada, Hamilton, Ontario, 1997.

10. M. J. Epstein, *Measuring Corporate Environmental Performance*, Irwin Professional Publishing, Burr Ridge, IL, 1995; CMA, 1997, op. cit.

11. GEMI (Global Environmental Management Institute), *Total Quality Environmental Management: The Primer, TQE-101*, GEMI, Washington DC, 1993.

12. S. Schmidheiny, *Changing Course: A Global Business Perspective on Development and the Environment*, World Business Council for Sustainable Development, Geneva, 1992; R. DeAndraca and K. F. McCready, *Internalizing Environmental Costs to Promote Eco-efficiency*, World Business Council for Sustainable Development, Geneva, Switzerland, 1994; F. Cairncross, *Costing the Earth: The Challenge for Governments, the Opportunities for Business*, Harvard Business, Boston, MA, 1994.

13. D. B. Rubenstein, *Environmental Accounting for the Sustainable Corporation: Strategies and Techniques*, Quorum Books, Westport, CT, 1994; EPA (Environmental Protection Agency), *Environmental Accounting Case Studies: Full Cost Accounting for Decision Making at Ontario Hydro*, EPA 742-R-95-004, Office of Pollution Prevention, Washington DC, 1996b.

14. L. Greer and C. Van Loben Sels, "When Pollution Prevention Meets the Bottom Line: Cost Savings Are Not Always Enough to Convince Industry to Adopt Prevention Actions," *Environmental Science and Technology* (September 1997) 31, no. 9: pp. A148-422.

15. A. L. White, M. Becker, and D. E. Savage,

"Environmentally Smart Accounting: Using Total Cost Assessment to Advance Pollution Prevention," *Pollution Prevention Review* 3, no. 3 (summer 1993): pp. 23-35; D. E. Savage and A. L. White, "New Applications of Total Cost Assessment," *Pollution Prevention Review* 5, no. 1 (winter 1995): pp. 7-15.

16. CMA, 1997, op. cit.

17. EPA, 1996b, op. cit.

18. De Andraca and McCready, 1994, op. cit.

19. White et al., 1993, op. cit.

20. White et al., 1993, op. cit.;
D. Ditz, J. Ranganathan, and R. D. Banks, *Green Ledgers: Case Studies in Corporate Environmental Accounting*, World Resources Institute, Washington DC, 1995.

21. Ditz et al., 1995, op. cit.

22. EPA (Environmental Protection Agency), *Valuing Potential Environmental Liabilities for Managerial Decision-making: A Review of Available Techniques*, EPA 742-R-96-003, P. E. Bailey, lead author, Washington DC, 1996.

23. EPA, 1996b, op. cit.

24. W. Nordhaus and J. Tobin, *Is Growth Obsolete?* 1972, cited in C. W. Cobb and J. B. Cobb, *The Green National Product: A Proposed Index of Sustainable Economic Welfare*, University Press of America, New York, 1994.

25. H. E. Daly and J. B. Cobb, *For the Common Good: Redirecting the Economy Toward Community, the Environment, and a Sustainable Future*, 2nd ed., Beacon Press, Boston, MA, 1994.

26. C. W. Cobb and J. B. Cobb, *The Green National Product: A Proposed Index of Sustainable Economic Welfare*, University Press of America, New York, 1994, p. 8.

27. S. L. Harris, "Economics of the Environment: A Survey," *The Economic Record* 72, no. 217 (1996): pp. 154-171.

28. C. S. Holling, "What Barriers? What Bridges?" in *Barriers and Bridges to the Renewal of Ecosystems and Institutions*, L. H. Gunderson, C. S. Holling, and S. S. Light, eds., Columbia University Press, New York, 1995.

29. W. F. Barron, R. D. Perlack, and J. J. Boland, *Fundamentals of Economics for Environmental Managers*, Quorum Books, Westport, CT, 1998.

30. C. Folke, M. Hammer, R. Costanza, and A. Jansson, "Investing in Natural Capital – Why, What, and How?" in *Investing in Natural Capital: The Ecological Approach to Sustainability*, C. Folke, M. Hammer, R. Costanza, and A. Jansson, eds., Island Press, Washington DC, 1994.

31. R. Costanza et al., "The Value of the World's Ecosystem Services and Natural Capital," *Nature* 387, no. 6630 (1997): pp. 253-260.

32. Holling, 1995, op. cit.

33. Costanza et al., 1997, op. cit.

34. Harris, 1996, op. cit.

35. Ibid.

36. Barron et al., 1998, op. cit.

37. J. Boyd, *Searching for Profit in Pollution Prevention: Case Studies in the Corporate Evaluation of Environmental Opportunities*, discussion paper 98-30, Resources for the Future, Washington DC, May 1998.

Chapter 16. Economic Instruments for Environmental Management

1. Organization for Economic Cooperation and Development, *Managing the Environment: The Role of Economic Instruments*, OECD, Paris, 1994.

2. S. Schmidheiny, *Changing Course: A Global Business Perspective on Development and the Environment*, MIT Press, Cambridge MA, 1992; R. De Andraca and K. F. McCready, *Internalizing Environmental Costs to Promote Eco-efficiency*, The Business Council for Sustainable Development, Geneva, 1994.

3. International Institute for Sustainable Development (IISD) has reports on economic instruments produced in 1996 that can be downloaded from their website: <www.iisd.org>

4. Chapter 8 of Agenda 21 is titled: "Integrating Environment And Development in Decision-making" and includes making effective use of economic instruments and market and other incentives as a key part of the program. Also chapter 3 of "Global Environmental Outlook 2000" <http://www.unep.org/geo2000/>

5. *Enviro Magazine* of Transboundary Pollution special issue: "Putting a Price on the Environment: Economic Instruments in Environmental Policy," no. 12 (November 1991), Swedish Environmental Protection Agency, Solna, Sweden.

6. Government of Canada, *Economic Instruments for Environmental Protection*, discussion paper, Ministry of Supply and Services, Ottawa, 1992.

7. D. Saxe, "A Look at The Gibbons Report," *Hazardous Materials Management* (April/May 2001): p. 38.

8. A. Taylor, M. Jaccard, and N. Olewiler, *Environmental Tax Shift: A Discussion Paper for British Columbians*, School of Resource and Environmental Management and Department of Economics, Simon Fraser University, October 1999.

9. <www.pembina.org>

10. <www.sustainbleusa.org>

11. The case study can be downloaded as a pdf document from the EPA website: <www.epa.gov>

12. S. Schaltegger and R. Burritt, *Contemporary Environmental Accounting: Issues, Concepts and Practice*, Greenleaf Publishing, Sheffield, U.K., 2000, pp, 97-99.

13. J. Stackhouse, "Robert's Show," *Report on Business Magazine, Globe and Mail*, December 2001, pp. 46-52.

14. <www.bp.com>

15. Costanza et al., 1997, op. cit.

16. Sweden's Second National Communication on Climate Change, submitted in accordance with Article 12 of the United Nations Framework Convention on Climate Change to the Third Conference of the Parties, Kyoto, April 1997.

17. R.W. Hahn, "Economic Prescriptions for Environmental Problems: How the Patient Followed the Doctor's Orders," *Journal of Economic Perspectives* 3, no. 2 (1989): pp. 95-114.

18. R. W. Hahn and G. Hester, "'Where Did All the Markets Go?' An analysis of EPA's emissions trading program," *Yale Journal of Regulation* 6, no. 1 (winter 1989): pp. 109-53.

19. M. Porter and C. van der Linde, "Green and Competitive: Ending the Stalemate," *Harvard Business Review* 1 (October-November 1995), pp. 120-134.

20. J. A. Cassils, *Exploring Incentives: An Introduction to Incentives and Economic Instruments for Sustainable Development*, unedited working paper for the National Round Table on the Environment and the Economy (NRTEE), Ottawa, 1991.

21. N. Myers and J. Kent, *Perverse Subsidies: Tax Money Undercutting Our Economies and Environments Alike*, International Institute for Sustainable Development, Winnipeg, Manitoba, 1998.

22. <www.oag-bvg.gc.ca>

Chapter 17. Product and Technology Assessment

1. <www.ota.nap.edu>

2. W. B. Thompson, ed., *Controlling Technology*, Prometheus Books, Buffalo, NY, 1991.

3. Ernest Braun, *Futile Progress: Technology's Empty Promise*, Earthscan Publications Ltd., London, U.K., 1995.

4. Ibid., p. 125.

5. Ibid.

6. A. L. Porter, "Technology Assessment," *Impact Assessment* 13 (1995): pp. 135-151.

7. D. Day, *The Eco Wars: True Tales of Environmental Madness*, Key Porter Books, Toronto, Ontario, 1989.

8. R. Coenen and M. Rader. "Technology Assessment in Europe," *Industry and Environment* 18, no. 2-3 (1995): pp. 61-63.

9. J. R. Bright, *Practical Technology Forecasting: Concepts and Exercises*, 1st ed., The Industrial Management Center, Austin, Texas, 1972.

10. J. F. Coates, "Technology Assessment: A Tool Kit," *Chemtech* (June 1976), in Porter, 1995, op. cit., p. 136.

11. Braun, 1995, op. cit., p. 129.

12. J. Schell, "The Fate of the Earth," in *Controlling Technology*, W. B. Thompson, ed., Prometheus Books, Buffalo, NY, 1991, pp. 19-33;
W. Leiss, *Under Technology's Thumb*, McGill-Queen's University Press, Montreal, Quebec, 1990;
Braun, 1995, op. cit.;
A. Forty, *Objects of Desire*, Pantheon Books, New York, 1986;
L. Winner, "Reverse Adaptation and Control," in *Controlling Technology*, W. B. Thompson, ed., Prometheus Books, Buffalo, NY, 1991, pp. 120-130;
J. Cramer and W. C. L. Zegveld, "The Future Role of Technology in Environmental Management," *Futures* (June 1991): pp. 451-468;
Thompson, 1991, op. cit.

13. Marshall McLuhan, *The Gutenberg Galaxy*, Mentor, New York, 1969, p. 43;
Marshall McLuhan and Quentin Fiore, *War and Peace in the Global Village*, Bantam, New York, 1968.

14. Grete S. Bridgewater, "The Environmental Impact Assessment of Policy in Canada," a master's degree project, Faculty of Environmental Design, University of Calgary, Alberta, 1991.

15. T. La Porte, "Technologies, Decision Making Processes, and Technology Assessment," *Technology: Whose Costs? Whose Benefits?* The International Symposium on Technology and Society 1993, George Washington University, Washington DC, pp. 21-22.

16. J. F. Coates and A. Jain, "Anticipating the Environmental Effects of Technology: the Preparation of a Primer and Workbook," *Industry and Environment* 18, no. 2-3 (1995): p. 54;
Porter et al., 1980, op. cit.

17. La Porte, 1993, op. cit.;
Porter, 1995, op. cit.

18. Braun, 1995, op. cit.

19. See section on backcasting in chapter 5, Strategic Environmental Management.

20. Porter, 1995, op. cit.

21. Coenen and Rader, 1995, op. cit.;
Braun, 1995, op. cit.

22. B. Kneen, *Farmageddon: Food and the Culture of Biotechnology*, New Society Publishers, Gabriola Island, B.C., 1999.

23. B. Weston, "Buy Any Other Name," *Report on Business Magazine, Globe and Mail*, October 1999, p. 13.

Chapter 18. Life Cycle Asseessment

1. CSA, *ISO 14040-97 Environmental Management — Life Cycle Assessment — Principles and Framework*, Canadian Standards Association, Rexdale, Ontario, 1997.

2. J. A. Fava, R. Denison, B. Jones, M. A. Curran, B. Vigon, S. Selke, and J. Barnum, *A Technical Framework for Life-Cycle Assessments*, SETAC, Washington DC, 1991.

3. J. R. Stewart, M. W. Collins, R. Anderson, and W. R. Murphy, "Life Cycle Assessment as a Tool for Environmental Management," *Clean Products and Processes* 1 (1999), Springer Verlag, pp. 73-81.

4. "Life Cycle Assessment," *SETAC Globe* 2, no. 5 (Sept-Oct 2001): pp. 35-38.

5. Ibid.

6. R. G. Hunt, J. D. Sellers, and W. E. Franklin, "Resource and Environmental Profile Analysis: A Life Cycle Environmental Assessment for Products and Procedures," *Environmental Impact Assessment Review* 12 (1992): pp. 245-269.

7. M. A. Curran, "Broad-based Environmental Life Cycle Assessment," *Environmental Science and Technology* 27, no. 3 (1993): pp. 430-436.

8. Hunt et al., 1992, op. cit.

9. Fava et al., 1991, op. cit.

10. C. Bast, C. Johnson, T. Korpalski, and J. C. Vanderstraeten, "Globalization of and 'Guiding Principles' for Environmental Legislation and Public Policy Development," Proceedings of the 1995 IEEE International Symposium on Electronics and the Environment, The Institute of Electrical and Electronics Engineers Inc., Piscataway, NJ, 1995, pp. 220-224.

11. J. A. Fava, "Life Cycle Thinking: Application to Product Design," Proceedings of the 1993 IEEE International Symposium on Electronics and the Environment, The Institute of Electrical and Electronics Engineers Inc., Piscataway, NJ, 1993, pp. 69-73; S. Bisson and M. Bérubé, *Life-Cycle Studies: A Literature Review and Critical Analysis*, Ministère de l'Environnement du Quebec, Quebec City, 1993.

12. Fava et al., 1991, op. cit.; and 1993, op. cit.

13. CSA, 1994, op. cit.; B. W. Vigon, D. A. Tolle, B. W. Cornaby, H. C. Latham, C. L. Harrison, T. L. Bogusk, R. G.

Hunt, and J. D. Sellers, *Life-Cycle Assessment: Inventory Guidelines and Principles*, U.S. EPA, Document EPA/600/R-92/245, Cincinnati, OH, 1993; ISO, *ISO 14040 Environmental Management — Life Cycle Assessment — Principles and Framework*, Geneva, Switzerland, 1997; ISO, *ISO 14041 Environmental Management — Life Cycle Assessment — Goal and Scope Definition and Inventory Analysis*, Geneva, Switzerland, 1998.

14. Maria Adragna, ed., *Life Cycle Impact Assessment Methodology for the Production Phase of the Pulp and Paper Life Cycle: Environmental Technology*, CSA, Etobicoke, Ontario, 1996.

15. Bast, 1994, op. cit., p. 33.

16. K. Christiansen et al, eds., "LCA in Government Policies and Regulations," *Application of Life Cycle Assessments*, Oestfold Research Foundations, Norway, 1995, pp. 90-112.

17. "Life ever after," *The Economist*, 9 October 1993, p. 77.

18. M. Bradley, Director, Technology, Canfor Pulp and Paper Marketing, personal communication, 1996.

19. B. Vigon, "Norway Drafts Electronics Takeback Legislation." *LCA News* 17, no. 6 (1997a): p. 6.

20. MHSPE (Ministry of Housing, Spatial Planning and the Environment of the Netherlands), "Policy Document on Products and the Environment," Government of the Netherlands, The Hague, 1994.

21. Bast, 1994, op. cit.

22. U.S. EPA, "The Use of Life Cycle Assessment in Environmental Labeling Programs," U.S. EPA Document 742/R 93/003, Washington DC, 1993.

23. F. Consoli, D. Allen, I. Boustead, J. Fava, W. Franklin, A. A. Jensen, N. de Oude, R. Parrish, R. Perriman, D. Postlethwaite, B. Quay, J. Seguin, and B. Vigon, *Guidelines for Life-Cycle Assessment: A "Code of Practice,"* SETAC, Pensacola, FL, 1993.

24. SPOLD (Society for the Promotion of LCA Development), *The LCA Sourcebook: A European Business Guide to Life-Cycle Assessment*, SustainAbility, SPOLD, and Business in the Environment, London, U.K., 1993.

25. E. Maxie, "Supplier Performance and the Environment," Proceedings of the 1994 IEEE International Symposium on Electronics and the Environment, The Institute of Electrical and Electronics Engineers Inc., Piscataway, NJ, 1994, pp. 323 - 327.

26. J. Besnainou and S. Goybet, "Life Cycle

Assessment and End-of-Life Management," Proceedings of the 1995 IEEE International Symposium on Electronics and the Environment, The Institute of Electrical and Electronics Engineers Inc., Piscataway, NJ, 1995, pp. 310-313.

27. M. Finkbeiner, M. Wiedemann, and K. Saur, "A Comprehensive Approach Towards Product and Organization Related Environmental Management Tools: Life Cycle Assessment (ISO 14040) and Environmental Management Systems (ISO 14001)," *International Journal of Life Cycle Assessment*, 3, no. 3 (1998): pp. 169-178.

28. MIT Technology, Business and Environment Program, *Life Cycle Assessment: From Inventory to Action: Report from the Conference*, conference held November 4-5, 1993, Cambridge, MA.

29. J. B. Guinée, H.A. Udo de Haes, and G. Huppes, "Quantitative Life Cycle Assessment of Products 1: Goal Definition and Inventory," *Journal of Cleaner Production* 1 (1993): pp. 3-13.

30. Curran, 1993, op. cit.

31. E. Huang and D. Hunkeler, "Life-Cycle Concepts for Minimizing Environmental Impacts: A Corporate Survey," International Conference of Industrial Waste Minimization, Taipei, Taiwan, 1995, pp. 733-746.

32. MHSPE, 1994, op. cit.

33. P. White and B. DeSmet, "LCA Back on Track, Is It One Track or Two?" *SETAC News* 15, no.4 (1995): pp. 29-30.

34. L. Barnthouse, J. Fava, K. Humphreys, R. Hunt, L. Laibson, S. Noesen, J. Owens, J. Todd, B. Vigon, K. Weitz, and J. Young, *Life-Cycle Impact Assessment: The State-of-the-Art*, 2nd edition, SETAC, Pensacola, FL, 1997;

35. B. Vigon, "LC Impact Assessment — Combined Work Group Report Summary," *LCA News* 18, no. 3 (1998): pp. 1-9;
B. Vigon, "Impact Assessment Workgroups Complete Reports," *LCA News* 17, no. 3 (1997): pp. 1-2.

36. Huang and Hunkeler, 1995, op. cit.

37. BATE, "Instant Lifecycle Assessment," available online, November 1999, p. 9.

Chapter 19. Environmental Purchasing Guidelines

1. E. E. Scheuing, *Purchasing Management*, Prentice Hall, Edgewood Cliffs, NJ, 1989.

2. S. Schmidheiny, *Changing Course: A Global Business Perspective on Development and the Environment*, The MIT Press, Cambridge, MA, 1992;
P. Hawken, *Ecology of Commerce*, Harper Business, New York, 1993;

M. J. Epstein, *Management Accounting Guideline 37: Implementing Corporate Environmental Strategies*, The Society of Management Accountants of Canada, Hamilton, Ontario, 1995.

3. Business in the Environment, *Buying into the Environment: Guidelines for Integrating the Environment into Purchasing and Supply*, Business in the Environment, London, U.K., 1993.

4. T. Russel, ed., *Greener Purchasing: Opportunities and Innovations*, Greenleaf Publishing, Sheffield, U.K., 1998.

5. *EPP Update*, no. 10 (January 2002): p. 4.

6. Business and the Environment, "Danish Public Sector Makes Progress on Green Purchasing," *BATE* (March 1999): p. 15.

7. TerraChoice Environmental Services, *Going for Green: Meeting Foreign Demand for Environmentally Preferable Products and Services through Federal Procurement*, National Round Table on the Environment and the Economy, Ottawa, 1997.

8. A. Husseini and B. Kelly, eds., "Environmentally Responsible Procurement ('Green Procurement')," *Environmental Technology*, Z766-95, Canadian Standards Association, Toronto, Ontario, 1995.

9. The second edition of GIPPER was issued in March 1995. <http:www.buygreen.com/gipper/>

10. D. Grant, ed., *Transport Canada Choose Green Procurement Guide*, Material Management, Corporate Administration Services, Transport Canada, Ottawa, 1993.

11. A. Husseini and B. Kelly, eds., op. cit.

12. The Delphi Group, *Summary Report: Development of Criteria for Green Procurement*, National Round Table on the Environment and the Economy, Ottawa, 1996.

13. Department of Foreign Affairs and International Trade Sustainable Development "Environmental Procurement," website, 1997: <www.dfaitmaeci>

14. Energy Pathways Inc., "Greening Government Operations, The New Imperative: Green Procurement," Environment Canada Workshop Participant Notes, Ottawa, 1996/97.

Chapter 20. Environmental Communications

1. H. Mintzberg, B. Ahlstrand, and J. Lampel, *Strategy Safari: A Guided Tour Through the Wilds of Strategic Management*, The Free Press, Toronto, Ontario. 1998.

2. J. E. Grunig, *Excellence in Public Relations and Communication Management*, Lawrence Erlbaum Associates, Hillsdale, NJ, 1992, p. 118.

3. J. A. Pearce and R. B. Robinson, *Strategic*

Management: Strategy Formulation and Implementation, Irwin, Homewood, IL, 1982.

4. Adapted from S. Smith and J. Yates, CommPlan Canada, Strategic Communication Planning Workshop, 1999.

5. Taken from Creative Media Relations Workbook, Jim Stanton and Associates, Ottawa: <www.jim-stanton-associates.com>

6. A. Mackey and R. Kendall Craden, material produced for Issue Management Workshop, 2000.

7. S. L. Vibbert, "Corporate Communication and the Management of Issues," paper presented at the meeting of International Communication Association, Montreal, Quebec, May 1987.

8. Sun Tzu, The Art of War, trans. S. B. Griffith, Oxford University Press, London, U.K., 1963, p. 87.

9. Managing Surprise, An Issue-Management Process, pamphlet produced by the Public Affairs Bureau, Government of British Columbia, Victoria, B.C., 1990.

10. D. Dougherty, Crisis Communications: What Every Executive Needs to Know, Walker, New York, 1992, pp. 93-94.

11. G. Crognale, ed., Environmental Management Strategies: The 21st Century Perspective, Prentice Hall, NJ, 1999, p. 301.

12. J. Mulligan, "Toward Proactive Risk Communication: A Look at Alberta's Petroleum Industry," unpublished master's degree project, EVDS, University of Calgary, Alberta, 1997.

13. National Research Council, Improving Risk Communication, National Academy Press, Washington DC, 1989, p. 21.

14. V. T. Covello, D. B. McCallum, and M. T. Pavlova, eds., "Principles and Guidelines for Improving Risk Communication," in Effective Risk Communication: The Role and Responsibility of Government and Non-government Organizations, Plenum Press, New York, 1989, pp. 3-16.

15. Ibid.
B. J. Hance, C. Chess, and P. M. Sandman, Improving Dialogue with Communities: A Risk Communication Manual for Government, Department of Environmental Protection, Trenton, NJ, 1988.

16. V. T. Covello, P. M. Sandman, and P. Slovic, "Guidelines for Communicating Information about Chemical Risks Effectively and Responsibly," in D. G. Mayo and R. D. Hollander, eds., Acceptable Evidence: Science and Values in Risk Management, Oxford University Press, Oxford, 1991, p. 73.

17. Canadian Standards Association, CSA Z764-96

A Guide to Public Involvement: Environmental Technology, CSA, 1996.

18. C. Chess, "Encouraging Effective Risk Communication in Government: Suggestions for Agency Management," in V. T. Covello, D. B. McCallum and M. T. Pavlova, eds., Effective Risk Communication: The Role and Responsibility of Government and Non-government Organizations, Plenum, New York, 1989, pp. 359-365;
Hance et al., op. cit.

19. W. Cannell and H. Otway, "Audience Perspectives in the Communication of Technological Risks," Futures 20, no. 5 (1988): pp. 519-531;
B. Fischhoff, "Risk Perception and Communication Unplugged: Twenty Years of Process," Risk Analysis 15, no. 2 (1995): pp. 137-145.

20. P. Slovic, "Perception of Risk," in S. Krimsky and D. Golding, eds., Social Theories of Risk, Praeger, Westport, CT, 1992, pp. 117-152.

21. P. M. Sandman, Responding to Community Outrage: Strategies for Effective Risk Communication, American Industrial Hygiene Association, Fairfax, VA, 1993.

22. Ibid.

23. A. C. Howatson, Toward Proactive Environmental Management: Lessons from Canadian Corporate Experience, a Conference Board of Canada report from the Business and the Environment Research Program, Ottawa, 1990.

24. Crognale, op cit., p. 294.

Chapter 21. Human Factors as an Environmental Management Tool

1. M. S. Sanders and E. J. McCormick, Human Factors in Engineering and Design, 7th ed., McGraw-Hill, New York, 1993.

2. National Research Council of Canada, Ergonomics at Work, Ottawa, undated brochure.

3. Center for Chemical Process Safety, Guidelines for Technical Management of Chemical Process Safety, American Institute of Chemical Engineers, New York, 1989.

4. A. Chapanis, "Introduction to Human Factors Considerations in Systems Design," in C. M. Mitchell, P. Van Balen, and K. Moe, eds., Human Factors Considerations in Systems Design, NASA Conference, Pub. 2246, National Aeronautic and Space Administration, Washington DC, 1983.

5. Sanders and McCormick, 1993, op. cit.

6. N. Meshkati, "An Etiological Investigation of Micro- and Macroergonomics Factors in the

Bhopal Disaster, Lesson for Industries of Both Industrialized and Developing Countries," *International Journal of Industrial Ergonomics* 4 (1989): pp. 161-175;

N. Meshkati, "Human Factors in Large-scale Technological Systems' Accidents: Three Mile Island, Bhopal, Chernobyl," *Industrial Crisis Quarterly* 5, no. 2 (1991): pp. 131-154.

7. T. A. Kletz, *What Went Wrong: Case Histories of Process Plant Disasters,* 2nd ed., Gulf Publishing, Houston, TX, 1988;

N. Schlager, ed., *When Technology Fails: Significant Technological Disasters, Accidents and Failures of the Twentieth Century,* Gale Research, Washington DC, 1994.

8. R. W. Bailey, *Human Performance Engineering: A Guide for System Designers,* Prentice-Hall, New York, 1982.

9. Ibid., p. 192.

10. Sanders and McCormick, 1993, op. cit.

11. M. Ashley, "Measuring Design Quality," *Interface,* Microsoft Technical Education, Microsoft Corporation, Redmond, WA, 1999.

12. Ibid.

13. <www.bcpe.org>

Chapter 22. Clean Development Mechanism and Joint Implementation

1. M. C. Trexler and L. Kosloff, "The 1997 Kyoto Protocol: What Does it Mean for Project-based Climate Change Mitigation?" *Mitigation and Adaptation Strategies for Global Change* 3 (1998): pp. 1-58.

2. R. Sedjo, B. Sohngen, and P. Jagger, "Carbon Sinks in the Post-Kyoto World," 1998: <www.weathervane.rff.org/features/feature051.html>;

Josef Janssen, "Joint Implementation, Multiple Benefits of Tropical Rainforest Protection and International Policy Coordination," paper presented at the XI World Congress of the United Nations Food and Agriculture Organization, Antalya, October 13-22, 1997.

3. Trexler and Kosloff, 1998, op. cit.;

Paige Brown, *Climate, Biodiversity and Forests: Issues and Opportunities Emerging from the Kyoto Protocol,* World Resources Institute in collaboration with The World Conservation Union, 1998;

J. Janssen, 1997, op. cit.;

Eveline Trines, "Project Certification under the CDM," paper presented at COP4 in Buenos Aires, November 6, SGS International Certification Service Ltd., Oxford Centre for Innovation, 1998.

4. Intergovernmental Panel on Climate Change,

The Social Costs of Climate Change: Greenhouse Damage and the Benefits of Control, World Meteorological Organization/United Nations Environment Programme, Geneva, 1995.

5. Ibid.

6. <www.unfccc.int>

7. P. H. Raven, R. Evert, and S. Eichhorn, *Biology of Plants,* 4th ed., Worth Publishers, New York, 1986;

N. A. Campbell, *Biology,* 2nd ed., The Benjamin/Cummings Publishing Company Inc., Redwood City, CA, 1990.

8. J. Bainbridge, "Climate Change Has the Potential to Create the Largest Regulatory Framework Ever, Says CIPEC Head," *Canadian Environmental Regulation and Compliance News* (December 1998): pp. 1523-1533.

9. J. Bernstein and P. Chasek, "Whither the Spirit of Rio?" prepared for the Earth Council, 1997: <www.ecouncil.ac.cr/about/contrib/spiritrio/whither.htm>

10. United Nations, "Report of the United Nations Conference on Environment and Development, Annex 1," Rio Declaration on Environment and Development, 1992.

11. Aline Cornford, "Afforestation Could Eliminate 10% of Canada's Emissions," *Enviroline* 9, no. 4 (1998): p. 6.

12. <www.suncor.com>

13. N. J. Cutright, "Joint Implementation: Biodiversity and Greenhouse Gas Offsets," *Environmental Management* 20, no. 6 (1996): pp. 913-918.

14. Campbell, 1990, op. cit.;

R. E. Ricklefs, *Ecology,* 3rd ed., W. H. Freedmand and Company, New York, 1990.

15. International Institute for Sustainable Development (IISD), 1998: <www.iisd.ca> Trexler and Kosloff, 1998, op. cit.; Trines, 1998, op. cit.

16. Trines, 1998, op. cit.

17. Ibid.

18. P. Frumhoff, D. Goetz, and J. Hardner, "Linking Solutions to Climate Change and Biodiversity Loss Through the Kyoto Protocol's Clean Development Mechanism," briefing paper from the Union of Concerned Scientists, 1998; Trexler and Kosloff, 1998, op. cit.;

E. Watt and J. Sathaye, *The Institutional Needs of Joint Implementation Projects,* U.S. Environmental Protection Agency, Berkeley, CA, 1995;

Paige Brown, op. cit.

19. Trines, 1998, op. cit.

20. Ibid.

21. Cutright, 1996, op. cit.;
Trexler and Kosloff, 1998, op. cit.

22. United Nations, "Press Kit for the Fourth Session of the Conference of the Parties, United Nations Framework Convention on Climate Change," November 2-13, 1998: <www.unfccc.int>

23. H. Jacoby, R. Prinn, and R. Schmalensee, "Taking the Long View on Global Warming," *Foreign Affairs* (July/August 1998): p. 4.

24. Brown, 1998, op. cit.;
Greenpeace International, "No Time to Waste," Greenpeace briefing paper, sixth session ad hoc group on the Berlin mandate, March 1997, pp. 3-7;
Jacoby et al., 1998, op. cit.;
Chris Rolfe, "An Environmental Perspective on International Greenhouse Gas Emissions Trading," speaking notes for a presentation at After Kyoto – Allocating Responsibility for Reducing Canada's Greenhouse Gas Emissions, Toronto, Ontario, April 16-17, 1998.

25. Bernstein and Chasek, 1997, op. cit.;
Greenpeace, 1997, op. cit.;
Tata Energy Research Institute (TERI), *Clean Development Mechanism: Issues and Modalities*, prepared for the Center for Global Environment Research, Tata Energy Research Institute, New Delhi, 1998.

26. Trexler and Kosloff, 1998, op. cit.;
Brown, 1998, op. cit.

27. IISD, 1998, op. cit., p. 2.

Chapter 23. Ecosystem-Based Management

1. Kakabadse as quoted in J.-Y. Pirot, P. J. Meynell, and D. Elder, eds., *Ecosystem Management: Lessons from Around the World*, International Union for Conservation of Nature and Natural Resources, Gland, Switzerland, 2000, p. viii.

2. M. S. Boyce and A. Haney, *Ecosystem Management: Applications for Sustainable Forest and Wildlife Resources*, Yale University Press, New Haven, CT, 1997;
N. L. Christensen, A. M. Bartuska, J. H. Brown, S. Carpenter, C. D'Antonio, R. Francis, J. F. Franklin, J. A. MacMahon, R. F. Noss, D. J. Parsons, C. H. Peterson, M. G. Turner, and R. G. Woodmansee, "The Report of the Ecological Society of America Committee on the Scientific Basis for Ecosystem Management," *Ecological Applications* 6, no. 3 (1996): pp. 665-691;
J.-Y. Pirot, P. J. Meynell, and D. Elder., eds., 2000, op.cit.;
S. L. Yaffee, A. F. Phillips, I. C. Frentz, P. W. Hardy, S. M. Maleki, and B. E. Thorpe,
Ecosystem Management in the United States: An Assessment of Current Experience, Island Press, Washington DC, 1996.

3. Aldo Leopold, *A Sand County Almanac*, Oxford University Press, New York, 1949.

4. Ibid., p. 240.

5. Ibid., p. 190.

6. L. K. Caldwell, ed., *Perspectives on Ecosystem Management for the Great Lakes*, State University of New York Press, Albany, NY, 1988;
S. H. Mackenzie, "Toward Integrated Resource Management: Lessons about the Ecosystem Approach from the Laurentian Great Lakes," *Environmental Management* 21, no. 2 (1997): pp. 173-183.

7. IUCN/UNEP/WWF, *World Conservation Strategy: Living Resource Conservation for Sustainable Development*, IUCN, Gland, Switzerland, 1980.

8. United Nations Conference on Environment and Development, *Agenda 21*, United Nations, New York, 1992.

9. G. K. Meffe and C. R. Carroll, *Principles of Conservation Biology*, Sinaur Associates, Inc., Sunderland, MA, 1994.

10. F. B. Golley, "Development of Landscape Ecology and Its Relation to Environmental Management," in M. E. Jensen and P. S. Bourgeron, eds., *Volume II: Ecosystem Management: Principles and Applications*, Gen. Tech. Rep., PNW-GTR-318, USDA Forest Service, Pacific Northwest Research Station, Portland, OR, 1994, pp. 34-41.

11. J. K. Agee and D. R. Johnson, eds., *Ecosystem Management for Parks and Wilderness*, University of Washington Press, Seattle, WA, 1988.

12. Pirot et al., 2000, op. cit.;
Yaffee et al., 1996, op. cit.

13. R. E. Grumbine, "Reflections on 'What is Ecosystem Management?'" *Conservation Biology* 11, no. 1 (1997): pp. 41-47.

14. Agee and Johnson, 1988, op. cit.

15. Grumbine, 1994, op. cit.

16. Christensen et al., 1996, op. cit.

17. Pirot et al., 2000, op. cit.

18. J. C. Overbay, "Ecosystem Management," in proceedings of a national workshop on taking an ecological approach to management, April 27-30 1992, Salt Lake City, Utah, WO-WSA-3, USDA, Forest Service, Watershed and Air Management Washington DC, 1992, pp. 3-15.

19. F. H. Wagner, "What Have We Learned?" in proceedings of the symposium Ecosystem Management of Natural Resources in the Intermountain West, April 20-22 1994, Logan, edited by F. H. Wagner, College of Natural

Resources, Utah State University, Logan, UT, 1995, vol. 5, pp. 121-125.

20. Daniel Botkin, Patrick Megonigal, and R. Neil Sampson, *Considerations of the State of Ecosystem Science and the Art of Ecosystem Management*, The Center for the Study of the Environment, Santa Barbara, CA, 1997.

21. R. E. Grumbine, "What is Ecosystem Management?" *Conservation Biology* 8 (1994): pp. 27-38.

22. Grumbine, 1997, op. cit.

23. Christensen et al., 1996, op. cit.

24. M. E. Jensen, P. Bourgeron, R. Everett, and I. Goodman, "Ecosystem Management: A Landscape Ecology Perspective," *Water Resources Bulletin* 32, no. 2 (1996): pp. 203-216.

25. Golley, 1994, op. cit.

26. G. E. Likens, *The Ecosystem Approach: Its Use and Abuse*, Ecology Institute, Oldendorf/Luhe, Germany, 1992.

27. D. Botkin, *Discordant Harmonies: A New Ecology for the Twenty-first Century*, Oxford University Press, Oxford, U.K., 1990;

P. L. Fiedler, P. S. White, and R. A. Leidy, "The Paradigm Shift in Ecology and Its Implications for Conservation," in *The Ecological Basis of Conservation: Heterogeneity, Ecosystems and Biodiversity*, eds. S. T. A. Pickett, R. S. Ostfeld, M. Shachak, and G. E. Likens, Chapman Hall, New York, 1997, pp. 83-92;

S. T. A. Pickett, V. T. Parker and P. L. Feidler, "The New Paradigm in Ecology: Implications for Conservation Above the Species Level," in *Conservation Biology: The Theory and Practice of Nature Conservation, Preservation and Management*, eds. P. L. Fiedler and S. K. Jain, Chapman Hall, New York, 1992, pp. 66-88.

28. J. W. Crossly, "Managing Ecosystems for Integrity: Theoretical Considerations for Resource and Environmental Managers," *Society and Natural Resources* 9 (1996): pp. 465-481;

J. Kay, "A Non Equilibrium Thermodynamic Framework for Discussing Ecosystem Integrity," *Environmental Management* 15, no. 4 (1991): pp. 483-495;

S. Woodley, "Monitoring and Measuring Ecosystem Integrity in Canadian National Parks," in *Ecological Integrity and the Management of Ecosystems*, eds., S. Woodley, J. Kay, and G. Francis, St. Lucie Press, St. Lucie, FL, 1993, pp. 155-176.

29. J. Lubchenco, P. G. Risser, A. C. Janetos, J. R. Gosz, B. D. Gold and M. M. Holland, "Priorities for an Environmental Science Agenda for the Clinton-Gore Administration: Recommendations for Transition Planning,"

Bulletin of the Ecological Society of America 74 (1993): pp. 4-8.

30. J. A. Livingston, "Nature for the Sake of Nature," in *Endangered Spaces*, ed. Monte Hummel, Key Porter Books, Toronto, Ontario, 1989.

31. F. Egler, *The Nature of Vegetation: Its Management and Mismanagement*, Aton Forest, Norfolk, CT, 1977.

32. C. S. Holling, ed., *Adaptive Environmental Assessment and Management*, John Wiley and Sons, London, U.K., 1978;

Kai Lee, *Compass and Gyroscope: Integrating Science and Politics for the Environment*, Island Press, Washington DC, 1993;

C. J. Walters and C. S. Holling, "Large-Scale Experiments and Learning by Doing," *Ecology* 71 (1990): pp. 2060-2068.

33. B. Taylor, L. Kremaster, and R. Ellis, *Adaptive Management of Forests in British Columbia*, B.C. Ministry of Forests, Forest Practices Branch, Victoria, B.C., 1997.

34. R. T. Lackey, "Seven Pillars of Ecosystem Management," *Landscape and Urban Planning*, 40 (1998): pp. 21-30.

35. D. Williams, "Mapping Place Meanings for Ecosystem Management," unpublished technical report, USDA Forest Service, Walla Walla, WA, 1995.

36. D. W. Orr, *Ecological Literacy: Education and the Transition to a Postmodern World*, State University of New York Press, Albany, NY, 1992.

37. Grumbine, 1994, op. cit.; Grumbine, 1997, op cit.

38. Christensen et al., 1996, op. cit.

39. D. Ludwig, "Environmental Sustainability: Magic, Science and Religion in Natural Resource Management," *Ecological Applications* 2 (1993): pp. 221-225.

40. T. R. Stanley, "Ecosystem Management and the Arrogance of Humanism," *Conservation Biology* 9, no. 2 (1995): pp. 255-262.

41. S. L. Yaffee, 1996, op. cit.

42. S. L. Yaffee, "Three Faces of Ecosystem Management," *Conservation Biology* 13, no. 4 (1999): pp. 724-727.

43. Lackey, R. T., 1998, op. cit., pp 21-30.

44. G. Machlis, J.-E. Force, W. R. Burch, Jr., "The Human Ecosystem, Part 1: The Human Ecosystem as an Organizing Concept in Ecosystem Management," *Society and Natural Resources* 10, no. 4 (1997): pp. 347-367.

45. Pirot et al., op. cit.;

D. S. Slocolmbe, "Environmental Planning, Ecosystem Science, and Ecosystem Approaches for Integrating Environment and Development,"

Environmental Management 17 (1993): pp. 289-303;

Yaffee et. al., 1996, op cit.

46. M. T. Brush, A. S. Hance, K. S. Judd, and E. A. Rettenmaier, "Recent Trends in Ecosystem Management," unpublished master's project, The University of Michigan School of Natural Resources and Environment, Ann Arbor, MI, 2000.

47. Pirot et al., 2000, op. cit.

48. M. S. Quinn and J.C. Theberge, in prep., "Ecosystem Management in Canada," results of a national survey.

49. SNEP Science Team, University of California, *Sierra Nevada Ecosystem Project: Final Report to Congress*, Vol. 1., University of California, Berkeley, CA, 1996.

50. Yaffee et. al., 1996, op. cit.

Chapter 24. The Natural Step

1. B. Nattrass and M. Altomare, *The Natural Step for Business: Wealth, Ecology and the Evolutionary Corporation*, New Society Publishers, Gabriola Island, B.C., 1999.

2. B. Nattrass and M Altomare, *Dancing with the Tiger: Learning Sustainability Step by Step*, New Society Publishers, Gabriola Island, B.C., 2002; K.-H. Robert, *The Natural Step Story: Seeding the Quiet Revolution*, New Society Publishers: Gabriola Island, B.C., 2002.

3. Nattrass and Altomare, 1999, op. cit., p. 18.

4. Ibid.

5. M. Scott, "The Natural Step: Sweden's Commonsense Green Scheme Comes to America," *Utne Reader* (January/February 1996): p. 2.

6. Nattrass and Altomare, 1999, op. cit.

7. H. Bradbury, *Learning with The Natural Step: A Jointly Told Tale of the Early Stages, 1988-94*, Carroll School of Management, Boston College, Boston, MA, 1998, p. 12.

8. "Electrolux and the Environment: Vision, Policy and Steps Taken," Electrolux Corporation Information and Public Affairs, Stockholm, Sweden, 1994.

9. Electrolux, 1998, <www.electrolux.se/corporate/environment>

10. E. S. Woolard, speech made at the National Academy of Engineering International Conference on Environmental Performance Metrics, Irvine, California, November 3, 1998. See <www.dupont.com/corp/whatsnew/speeches/woolard/eswnae.html>

11. Du Pont, 1998, <www.dupont.com/sitemap.html>

12. S. Schley and J. Laur, "Creating Sustainable Organizations: Meeting the Economic, Ecological, and Social Challenges of the 21st Century," Pegasus Communications, Cambridge, MA, 1998, p. 15.

13. <http://www.cga.state.ct.us/ps99/Act/pa/1999 PA-00226-R00HB-06830-PA.htm>

14. L. Holme, "Corporate Social Responsibility," speech at a conference organized by Norsk Hydro on April 28, 1999. Available at <www.wbcsd.ch/Speech/s55.htm>

15. P. Senge, "Rethinking Leadership in the Learning Organization," *The Systems Thinker* (1996): p. 4.

16. P. Senge, *The Fifth Discipline: The Art and Practice of the Learning Organization*, Currency Doubleday, New York, 1990.

17. S. Schley and J. Laur, 1998, op. cit., p. 2.

18. Senge, 1990, op. cit.

19. Nattrass and Altomare, 1999, op. cit, p. 42.

20. M. Eitel, speech to shareholders at the annual meeting on September 23, 1998 in Memphis, TN. Available at: <www.nikebiz.com/media/n_mariaspeech.shtml>

21. S. Schley and J. Laur, 1998, op. cit.

22. K.-H. Robèrt, J. Holmberg, and G. Broman, "Simplicity Without Reduction: Thinking Upstream Towards a Sustainable Society," *The Natural Step*, 1996, p. 1.

23. K.-H. Robèrt, *The Natural Step: A Framework for Achieving Sustainability in Our Organizations*, Pegasus Communications, Cambridge, MA, 1997, p. 10.

24. Paul Hawken, "Taking the Natural Step," in *Context*, 41(1995): pp. 36-38.

25. P. McKeague, "Big Companies Attracted to New Environmental Organization," *Vancouver Sun*, 18 March 1997, p. D11.

26. *The Natural Step International Newsletter* 1 (1996): p. 8.

27. World Business Council for Sustainable Development, *Eco-efficient Leadership for Improved Economic and Environmental Performance*, 1996, p. 7. Available at <www.wbcsd>

28. H. Bradbury, *Learning with The Natural Step: A Jointly Told Tale of the Early Stages, 1988-94*, Carroll School of Management, Boston College, Boston, MA, 1998, p. 56.

29. Ibid., p. 62.

30. Nattrass and Altomare, 1999, op. cit.; K.-H. Robert, 1997, op. cit.

Chapter 25. Where Do We Go from Here?

1. E. Von Weizsacker, A. B. Lovins, and L. H. Lovins, *Factor Four: Doubling Wealth — Halving*

Resource Use: the New Report to the Club of Rome, Earthscan Publications, London, U.K., 1998.

2. W. Sachs, R. Loske, and M. Linz, Greening the North: A Post-Industrial Blueprint for Ecology and Equity, Zed Books, London, U.K., 1998.

3. <www.projectsigma.com>

4. <www.beyondgreypinstripes.org/environmental.html>

5. BATE, "Canada Has Best Environmental Reports Among Five Governments," Cutter Information Corp, November 2001, pp. 7-8.

6. <www.oag-bvg.gc.ca/domino/oag-bvg.nsf/html/environment.html>

7. P. M. King, "An International Focus on POPs: The Stockholm Convention on Persistant Organic Pollutants," EM (April 2001): pp. 14-15; <www.irpte.unep.ch/pops/>

8. BATE, "Report on Body Burdens Could Harden Opinions on Chemical Use," BATE (April 2001): pp. 15-16; <www.cdc.gov/nceh/dls/report>

9. <www.cec.org>

10. See for example B. Laghi, "Pharmaceuticals Found in Canada's Water System," Globe and Mail, 5 September 2001, pp. A1 and A6; J. Armstrong, "Toxic Whale Confounds Scientists" Globe and Mail, 9 May 2002, pp. A1 and A6.

11. T. Peters and R. Waterman, In Search of Excellence: Lessons from America's Best-run Companies, Harper, New York, 1982; "Retrospective: In Search of Excellence," The Academy of Management Executive 16, no. 1 (February 2002): pp. 38-56.

12. "Fallen Idols," The Economist, 4 May 2002, p. 11.

13. R. Prescott-Allen, The Wellbeing of Nations: A Country-by-Country Index of Quality of Life and the Environment, Island Press, Washington DC, 2001.

14. H. E. Daly and J. B. Cobb, For the Common Good: Redirecting the Economy Toward Community, the Environment, and a Sustainable Future, 2nd ed., Beacon Press, Boston, MA, 1994; C. W. Cobb and J. B. Cobb, The Green National Product: A Proposed Index of Sustainable Economic Welfare, University Press of America, New York, 1994.

15. Science Council of Canada, Natural Resource Policy Issues in Canada, Report No. 19, Ottawa, 1973;

Science Council of Canada, Canada as a Conserver Society: Resource Uncertainties and the Need for New Technologies, Report No. 27, Ottawa, 1977; D. Thompson, "On the Way to the Stable State: The Conserver Society," Thoughts (June 1973).

16. M. Strong, Where on Earth are We Going? Knopf Canada, Toronto, Ontario, 2000.

17. ICSID, "International Centre for Settlement of Investment Disputes," 1999 web page. Available at <http://www.worldbank.org/icsid/index.html>; IISD, "Investment - Avoiding a Dangerous Minefield for the WTO," no. 3. International Institute for Sustainable Development, 2001. Available online at: <http://www.iisd.org/trade/qatar.htm>; John Wickham, "Toward a Green Multilateral Investment Framework: NAFTA and the Search for Models," The Georgetown International Environmental Law Review 12 (2000): pp. 617-46; IISD, "Trade and Investment in Sustainable Development," 2002, website: <http://www.iisd.ca/process/trade_invest_in_sd.htm>

18. Rachel McCormick, Ph.D. candidate, Faculty of Environmental Design, University of Calgary, Alberta, work in progress.

19. Weizsacker et al., 1998, op. cit.

20. Sachs et al., 1998, op. cit.

21. T. F. Homer-Dixon, The Ingenuity Gap: How Will We Solve the Problems of the Future? Knopf, New York, 2000. T. F. Homer-Dixon, The Ingenuity Gap: Facing the Economic, Environmental and Other Challenges of an Increasingly Complex and Unpredictable World, Vintage, New York, 2002.

22. G. Suter, review of State of the World 2002, by C. Flavin, H. French, and G. Gardner, SETAC Globe 3, no. 2 (March-April 2002): pp. 14-15.

23. M. Cernetig, "Poverty Threatens World Order, Anan Says," Globe and Mail, 5 February 2002, p. A10.

24. T. F. Homer-Dixon, "We Ignore Misery at Our Peril," Globe and Mail, 26 September 2002, p. A11. T. F. Homer-Dixon, Environment, Scarcity and Violence, Princeton University Press, Princeton, NJ, 1999.

25. J. Steele, "J. K. the Lionheart," Globe and Mail, 15 April 2002, pp. R1 and R5.

ABOUT THE AUTHORS

Edie Adams

Edie Adams is the Manager for Hardware User Research at Microsoft, leading a team in the research of physical, cognitive, and emotional interactions of people and products and its application to Microsoft Hardware and Strategic Business products. Prior to joining Microsoft in 1994, she was senior ergonomist at The Joyce Institute, an industry-leading ergonomics consulting firm. She has juried several design competitions, including ID Magazine Design Award for Equipment in 1998. She was a technical advisor to the Input Device Subcommittee of the ANSI-HFES VDT 100 Revision Committee and a member of Washington State's Voluntary Ergonomics Guidelines Committee. She is president of The Office Ergonomics Research Committee and a member of the Human Factors and Ergonomics Society and the Industrial Designers Society of America. Her work is included in the Permanent Collection of the Museum of Modern Art in New York, The Chicago Antheneum, and the Tacoma Art Museum. She is a CPE (Certified Professional Ergonomist) and holds an M.E.Des. in Industrial Design and a B.Sc. in Psychology from the University of Calgary.

Karla Berg

Karla Berg is a Professional Engineer with a Civil Engineering degree from the University of Saskatchewan. She completed her Master of Environmental Design (Environmental Science) at the University of Calgary in 1997. She then spent four years working domestically in Canada's upstream oil and gas industry as an Environmental Specialist with Anderson Exploration Ltd. (now Devon Canada). During this time, her primary responsibilities centred on environmental compliance monitoring and air quality management. She is currently working as an Environment, Health and Safety Coordinator (EHS) with the International Divisions of EnCana Corporation in Calgary, Alberta, where she has been focused on the development and implementation of an Integrated Environment, Health and Safety Management System and providing EHS support to new venture projects.

Andrew Higgins

Andrew Higgins is currently an Environmental Advisor with VECO Canada Ltd., an engineering firm that provides consulting services to the oil and gas industry. He has a B.Sc. in Biochemistry from the University of British Columbia, and a Masterof Environmental Design from the University of Calgary, where he did graduate work on life cycle assessment. He has worked in the oil and gas industry for the past seven years, the bulk of which has been on the management and remediation of contaminated sites. This work has included coordinating site assessment activities, evaluating remediation options, and implementing the chosen remediation option. This work has also included communications with regulators, landowners, and other stakeholders and emission inventories and air quality assessments.

Maureen Hill

Maureen Hill graduated from the University of Calgary with a B.Sc. in Ecology and a Master of Environmental Design (Environmental Science). She completed her master's thesis on the Clean Development Mechanism, focusing on the role of forest ecosystems in carbon sequestration in developing countries, and a case study in the Sierra Gorda Biosphere Reserve, Mexico. She was awarded a research fellowship from the Government of Japan where she studied the cross-cutting issues between forestry sinks and the Clean Development Mechanism at the National Institute for Environmental Studies. She is currently an environmental scientist with Highwood Environmental Management Limited in Calgary and is registered with the Alberta Society of Professional Biologists.

Stephen Hill

Stephen Hill is a post-doctoral fellow with the Research Chair Program in Risk Communication and Public Policy in the Haskayne School of Business at the University of Calgary where the focus of his research is climate change policy. He holds bachelor's degrees in Chemical Engineering and Biology from Queen's University in Kingston and a doctorate from the Faculty of Environmental Design at the University of Calgary. He is a registered professional engineer and has worked as an environmental specialist in industry and consulted with the federal government on risk management and public policy.

Lynne Kailan

Lynne Kailan has more than 25 years experience providing communications advice and services to private and public sector organizations. She has worked with some of the major Canadian professional services firms, accounting firms, management consultants, and law firms including Coopers & Lybrand, Clarkson Gordon/Woods Gordon, and McCarthy & McCarthy. For the past 10 years, she has worked with various ministries and agencies of the Government of British Columbia and has been involved in major projects such as the XV Commonwealth Games and provincial budget announcements. Most recently, she has specialized in the field of environmental communications with the Ministry of Environment, Land and Parks including stakeholder consultation on the Drinking Water Protection legislation, beverage container deposit and return regulations, and the annual non-compliance reports on organizations that have failed to meet their environmental obligations.

Lisa-Henri Kirkland

Lisa-Henri Kirkland is an environmental management systems specialist with nineteen years experience in the oil and gas industry and environmental management. Her work includes the development and implementation of environmental management systems, auditing, the development of internal assessment and auditing protocol, assessment of over 100 commercial and industrial properties, design and implementation of soil and groundwater sampling and remediation programs on a wide variety of industrial, commercial, and oil and gas sites, and supervision of underground storage tank removal programs. She has also instructed courses in site assessment, auditing, and EMS in North America and overseas. She is a professional geologist with a Master of Environmental Design and is a principal in Wolfwillow Environmental, an environmental consulting firm.

Linda Miller

Linda Miller established Ergo Works Inc. in 1991 to provide ergonomics consulting, design reviews, user testing at both industrial and office environments, training, and educational courses. Using a team approach, she customizes each training program to coincide with an organization's goals. Prior to forming Ergo Works Inc., she was employed as an ergonomist by the Alberta Worker's Compensation Board (WCB) and provided recommendations for a variety of industries. She has experience working at the Calgary General Hospital where she assessed and treated people with physical dysfunctions and assisted with the development of devices that aid the physically challenged. She received a bachelor's degree in Rehabilitation Medicine (Occupational Therapy) from the University of Alberta and a Master of Environmental Design from the University of Calgary. She is a member of the Alberta Association of Registered Occupational Therapists, the Canadian Association of Occupational Therapists, and the Human Factors Association of Canada (HFAC).

Michael S. Quinn

Mike Quinn holds a B.Sc. in Forest Science from the University of Alberta, an M.Sc. in Forest Wildlife from the University of Alberta, and a Ph.D. in Environmental Studies from York University. After teaching at the University of New Brunswick, Ryerson Polytechnical University, Lakehead University, and Boston University (School for Field Studies), he joined the Faculty of Environmental Design at the University of Calgary in 1997. In 2001, he accepted the additional responsibilities of Director of the Miistakis Institute for the Rockies, a research support organization specializing in spatial data and analysis. His teaching and research interests are in the areas of ecosystem management, protected areas management, community-based natural resource management and urban ecology. He also enjoys studying the history of natural history. Current research projects include landscape-scale cumulative effects assessment in the Central Rockies, green infrastructure demonstration research in the city of Calgary, and integrated landscape planning in southern Alberta. He co-manages the Transboundary Environmental Policy, Planning and Management initiative between the University of Calgary and University of Montana. Before accepting his present position at the University of Calgary, Faculty of Environmental Design, he was the Center Director for a post-secondary, interdisciplinary environmental field school on the west coast of Vancouver Island.

William A. Ross

William Ross is involved in developing and improving the professional practice of cumulative effects assessment. This has included professional instruction at the Banff Centre for Management and OLADE in Quito and Ecuador. He has also provided professional instruction for the Thai Office of Environmental Policy and Planning in Bangkok, Thailand, as well as Environment Canada and the Canadian Environmental Assessment Agency in Ottawa. He teaches his environmental impact assessment course at the University of Calgary, in Quito and Bangkok. His involvement extends to urban environmental management in Southeast Asia, especially through the Asian Institute of Technology in Bangkok. He is involved with another CIDA funded project: the offering of an interdisciplinary master's program in Quito on energy and the environment primarily for Latin Americans. He serves on the independent Environmental Monitoring Agency for the Ekati Diamond Mine in Yellowknife, Northwest Territories. The Agency is a watchdog for both the Ekati Mine and the regulators of the mine. In this capacity he works closely with other Agency members, the governments regulating the Mine, BHP, the Mine operator and the four aboriginal groups affected by the Mine. He is a professor of Environmental Science in the Faculty of Environmental Design at the University of Calgary and the President of the Western and Northern Canada Affiliate of the International Association for Impact Assessment.

Christine Schuh

Christine Schuh is a Manager in the Sustainability practice of PricewaterhouseCoopers' Global Risk Management Solutions group. She specializes in environmental management systems, environmental due diligence and management system auditing, corporate social responsibility management systems, attestation of triple bottom line reports, and the development of non-financial performance indicators. She has worked with many industries including the oil and gas, chemical processing, pulp and paper, mining, and manufacturing. She has been a professional engineer since 1991 and holds a Ph.D. in Environmental Design from the University of Calgary.

Sherry Sian

Sherry Sian is a Project Manager for Inuvialuit Environmental & Geotechnical, Inc. where she specializes in capacity building and governance for integrated resource management and sustainable development. For the past six years, she has been working with communities, businesses, non-governmental organizations, Aboriginal groups, and government agencies to improve environmental decision making based on an integrated view of human communities and ecosystems. An advocate of Canadian involvement in international environmental and science programs, she recently presented a report on the status of, and potential for, ecotourism certification in Canada at the World Ecotourism Summit. She also participated in the North American World Preparatory Meeting for the World Conference on Science and the Young Scientists Forum on Science Education. She is an Honorary Director for the Canadian Biosphere Reserves Association, a member of the Canadian Commission for UNESCO, and a co-founder of the Sustainable Tourism Association of Canada. She holds an M.E.Des. from the University of Calgary and a B.Sc. in Biology from McMaster University.

Dixon Thompson

Dixon Thompson is a Professor of Environmental Science in the Faculty of Environmental Design, the University of Calgary. Since 1973 he has developed and taught graduate level courses in environmental science and environmental management, including product and technology assessment and life cycle assessment, environmental management systems and ISO 14000, environmental impact assessment, environmental auditing, water management, environmental chemistry, and toxicology. He was a pioneer in the development of graduate courses in environmental management that complement courses in environmental science. He has supervised more than 80 graduate students including more than 30 who have done research on various aspects of environmental management.

He has extensive international experience, developing and teaching graduate level programs and professional development courses in Latin America and assisting with curriculum development for a major university in Russia. He was a member of the Canadian Standards Association committee that developed Life Cycle Impact Assessment Guidelines for the Pulp and Paper Production Processes and has worked as a Science Advisor for the Science Council of Canada. As a consultant, he has applied environmental management tools for resource based industries such as Nova, PetroCanada, Alberta Energy Company, IntraWest, and BC Gas International. He continues to be an active writer, speaker, and panelist on environmental management topics as well as on the environmental impacts of outdoor recreation. He is a principal in Wolfwillow Environmental, an environmental consulting firm. He has a Ph.D. in Organic Chemistry and Biochemistry (Illinois 1970).

Ron Wardell

Ron Wardell's background is a blend of social sciences and design. He has worked in electrical engineering, computer hardware design, and product design. He has also worked in ergonomics, environmental psychology, and organizational development. He enjoys the contrasts between hard and soft sciences, analytical and synthetic ways of thinking, the systematic and the intuitive. The ends that he seeks are thoughtful, sensitive, and careful considerations of the humans for whom we design and build. These considerations range from the pragmatics of human physical characteristics to the ephemeral questions of social context and product meaning. He teaches courses in empirical methods, the interaction of people with products, and courses and studios in ergonomics and human factors.. His research is dominated by an interest in how ergonomics is applied in industry. Although occupational ergonomics is based largely on hard sciences like biomechanics and physiology, in his opinion the success of its implementation depends on soft issues of culture and behavior. The processes of ergonomics are much more critical than its substance. From this point of view, improving the health and safety of an industrial worker has much in common with designing a successful consumer product. He is an Associate Professor of Industrial Design in the Faculty of Environmental Design at the University of Calgary.

Mel Wilson

Mel Wilson is a Senior Manager within PricewaterhouseCoopers' Sustainability Practice in Calgary, Alberta. Mel specializes in environmental, health and safety, and social responsibility assurance services, ranging from compliance and management system auditing to verification of corporate sustainability reports. He has worked with national and multinational companies in many sectors, including petroleum, transportation, agriculture, high tech, and utilities. He is a professional biologist, a Certified Environmental Auditor, and a Certified Management Consultant, a graduate-level instructor at the University of Calgary, and is formerly a Director and Vice President of the Canadian Environmental Auditing Association. He holds a B.Sc. in Biology, a Master of Environmental Design, and is currently pursuing his Ph.D. in Environmental Design at the University of Calgary.

INDEX

Chapter subjects are in bold.